Mindset Befo

For Your Network Marketing Journey

David Ross

imageplus publishing

imageplus publishing

Published by: Imageplus Publishing
PO Box458, Macclesfield, Cheshire SK10 2WY, England
Telephone: +44(0)845 607 6724
info@imageplus.org.uk
www.imageplus.org.uk

First Edition: 2016 David Ross

Printed in Great Britain by Imageplus, Macclesfield

A CIP catalogue record for this book is available from the British Library

ISBN 978-0-9570506-2-4

This book is dedicated to

Diana Ross (AkA Mum), Clive Leach

and the

Network Marketing Professionals

of the world

ABOUT THE AUTHOR

David was first introduced to network marketing aged 11 when his mother stumbled upon an old VHS opportunity video that her neighbour was about to throw out. It was shortly after this point that David's mother and her new partner Clive, her upline in the business, would begin an amazing journey that would see them build three massive global organisations, travel the world and build an incredible future for their family.

Growing up in a network marketing household exposed David to experiences and a lifestyle that would imprint on him a huge desire for success. However network marketing would not be David's first stop.

With a huge passion for the arts and theatre, David worked his way up the educational ladder teaching expressive and performing arts at college level in one of the leading visual arts schools in the UK.

In 2004 his entrepreneurial flare gave birth when he opened his own acting school for children, which would go on to become one of the largest acting schools in the North West of England and win Business of the Year North West 2008.

After nearly purchasing a franchise business, David took this idea and licensed his own school out as a franchise opportunity, opening up a number of schools.

Finally in 2009 he joined the world of network marketing in his parents organisation. David has focused his efforts on developing a strong and positive team and family culture, mentoring and coaching, mindset and team building as well as speaking and training on the world stage. He has interviewed dozens of top leaders worldwide in the profession and believes in providing value to the network marketing community.

Although I have earned a fortune in network marketing, I decided to read this book with "fresh eyes" as if I were new to the profession. As a newer distributor, reading "Mindset Before Matter" would seriously excite me about my future in network marketing. This book will help you to see things in a way you have never seen before and will open up a whole new world of opportunity for you. Everything that could ever prevent you from succeeding is now addressed in this fantastic book, which is both humorous and moving, clever and real. I can honesty tell you that reading this book got me excited about my business all over again!

Jordan Adler, Beach Money (Author), #1 Earner, Network Marketing Millionaire

David Ross packs a powerful punch with this new book on creating success in network marketing. His unique perspective of growing up in a network marketing family provides an incredible amount of depth to what he is teaching you. Devour this book NOW. Your business will love you for it!

Todd Falcone, Network Marketing Trainer and Author

We first got to know David after seeing him speak at a convention as a rising star in Las Vegas. We were instantly drawn to his passion and his straight talking manner. David makes an outstanding contribution to the network marketing profession, truly showing what success looks like at a young age. We have had the chance to work with him personally and have spent time sharing ideas and thoughts on how we can create a stronger profession. It is clear that he has a deep empathy for people, prospects and distributors and an incredible understanding of how people think.

Joseph & Amani McDermott, (Diamonds), Ontario, Canada

From the moment I met David I was impressed with his clear, concise, effective communication style with a twist of humor. His professional, honest, and caring approach gives him an amazing ability to connect with others, helping them realise their potential, while making everything relatable. The ideas you are about to discover in this book will be essential to keeping you on the right path to building a massive network marketing business as mindset is the #1 factor when seeking success. For anyone serious about success, this is a must-read! Read it and tell your entire organisation.

Babette Gilbert-Teno, (Ambassador), California, USA

A MESSAGE FROM THE AUTHOR

There is no other profession on earth where you can earn a rock star lifestyle by investing a small nominal amount of money and by working consistently and persistently over a period of time.

The fundamental laws of network marketing simply ask and require that you keep people's eyes on your presentation, that you promote and attend events, and that you have a 'noble why' to attract people to you, and a 'powerful why' to keep you attracted to your business.

Simply by reading this book you have made a choice that puts you on the success curve, (the upward progression towards your goals by making the correct choices and decisions), but remember, 'knowledge is king' however a king is nothing without an army, and an army is what we are creating with our network marketing business.

Many of you reading this will be looking for the secret, or you will simply be addicted to education but maybe a little scared of implementing it, and that's OK, but that can stop here!

The information this industry makes available to you will help to prepare your mind for success in your network marketing business. Secrets and fears are just a manifestation in your own mind. They are not the reality of the physical world in which you live.

"The one attribute that I would want every network marketing distributor to have is the ability and desire to join in and participate"

ACKNOWLEDGEMENTS

Being surrounded by great leaders in the network marketing profession all my life has undoubtedly been the catalyst that has made this book possible.

A lifelong thank you to Clive Leach and Diana Ross, my life coaches who have tirelessly dedicated their lives to the profession worldwide, their team, their company, and their children. Thank you for keeping us all on the success curve.

A special thank you to Eric Worre and his wife Marina who gave me the breakthrough I needed at a critical point in my career. I thank you with all my heart for giving me the opportunity to contribute to and become part of your network marketing family.

To Stephan Longworth, one of the most passionate and inspirational leaders I know and somebody who has supported my journey, along with all the amazing leaders and incredible team members in our organisation. This book is for you.

To Steve Critchley, Wes Linden, Jimmy Chapman and Robin Brooks, thank you for your support. To The Hon.Charles Wigoder, Andrew Lindsay MBE, Wayne Coupland and Paul Goundry and the rest of the amazing team who do a wonderful job and pave the way for us all.

To so many other phenomenal industry leaders who have inspired me. Jordan Adler, a true gentleman and friend of the profession, your story is phenomenal. To Lisa Grossmann, one of the finest trainers I know. Thank you for the council you have provided me, your knowledge is unrivalled. To Todd (The Fearless Recruiter) Falcone. Thank you for bringing the cool to network marketing, and to Kat Zeweniuk, Babette Gilbert-Teno, Joseph & Amani McDermott and John Holowaty for the hours of sharing ideas!

A big thank you to Helen Parker and Jemma James for reviewing the ideas in this book and to Lynne Round for proofing and copy editing.

Finally to Alan Hamilton at Imageplus for bringing this book to life.

CONTENTS

CHAPTER 1

INTRODUCTION

Before you get started, it is important to understand how to use this book, who it is for, and its purpose.

This book is 'not' a blueprint for how to build a network marketing business. For that I highly recommend many other great books that serve as blueprints for building your network marketing business. You can find the details of these at the back of this book under 'Recommended Reading'.

This book has been produced to help prepare you for some of the personal obstacles you may encounter within your network marketing business, and to keep you pushing through so that you don't quit. 'Mindset Before Matter' is ideal for people who are new to network marketing and are in the early stages of building their business. Maybe you have some hurdles that you need to jump. This book is your springboard! It is also a useful tool for seasoned leaders who may be looking for training ideas on mindset and overcoming obstacles. You may also wish to use this book as a recruitment tool to give to your prospects to raise some awareness of what you do.

'Mindset Before Matter' contains information to help you come to terms with some of the ideas, thoughts and concepts that you need to understand if you are going to ramp up your business and gain the momentum in the early days or help your team members do the same. The content contained within should help your mental filters deal with whatever comes your way.

If you are just stepping into the world of being an entrepreneur and becoming the CEO of your own life, you will be faced with some ideas that until now have never been shared with you, not in your job nor in your formal education. These ideas are not likely to come up in conversation with friends and family and may well go against what you have previously been taught. Ideas that will truly test whether you are open to a totally different thought process
Spend the next 2 hours digesting the information in this book and refer back to it when you feel yourself having a bad day so that you can change your mindset to give yourself your best day ever.

CHAPTER 2

DEAR PROSPECT

So, your friend or somebody you know gave you this book to read. I would like to start by saying congratulations on being open-minded enough to take a look. You should feel proud and special that somebody thought highly enough of you to give you this book. Please make sure you give it back to them when you have finished with it because they will need it!

In this chapter I am talking directly to you, the prospect, because you are not involved in this business, yet somebody sees something in you and believes that there may just be an opportunity or something in it for you! Whoever gave you this book may have already explained a little bit about what it is that they do, or they may have shared lots of information with you. Perhaps you have seen some videos with happy smiley people, some business tools or maybe you took the time to attend a presentation. We call those exposures, a little bit like this book. They are simply designed to educate and show you more about what we do so that you can make a decision as to whether or not you want to join in and get involved.

I appreciate that making a decision to do something that's potentially life changing can often be difficult, much more difficult than deciding what's for dinner or what to watch on TV, or whether or not to go out. What I would say is that while a good decision is great, a bad decision is also great because it can be fixed and you can learn from it. It's the 'I can't or won't make a decision' that often leaves you wondering, what if? So either way, once you have finished reading this chapter or indeed the entire book, and if you are feeling intrigued, let your friend know if you would like to get involved or simply take another look! Don't flip your phone to voicemail and avoid giving them this book back, there is nothing noble about avoidance. They are only interested in a decision, not the decision. Your feedback is greatly appreciated.

Please understand that it makes no difference to your friend or the network marketing profession whether or not you choose to get involved. We hope you decide to give it a go, but it's not essential! There will be others who are always ready to get started. You join this business to make a difference, not to be the difference.

We appreciate that the opportunity to have your own business is not for everybody. Maybe the timing is not quite right for you and that's OK. The fact that you are reading this book shows that you are supporting somebody you know. That's what this business is about. It's a support network; the fact that you can make friends and earn some money at the same time is a bonus.

"Whoever gave you this book is working hard to build a better future for themselves and is simply sharing their gift, so thank you for being supportive of their journey."

If at this time this opportunity isn't for you, and if you are not ready, perhaps you could try the great services or product they are offering. If you know anybody who you believe would benefit, then perhaps refer them back to the person who gave you this book. Thank you for taking the time to read and to share.

CHAPTER 3

A BUSINESS IN A BOX

How many people have ever considered or talked about starting their own business? Especially in more recent times as people are becoming more open to opportunity. There is also the growing realisation that having multiple streams of income is the path to greater wealth and long-term security. How many of those people fail to spot that right under their feet is a much simpler solution to starting a business? A business solution that would take care of most of the typical obstacles you would face when launching a traditional business, getting a product to market or even setting up a franchise. A business model that could provide you with a good profit quickly, with an equal and fair chance to grow and at far less of a financial risk.

What they don't teach you in school, or on any business course that I am aware of, are the benefits of a network marketing business. Sadly, it is an easy opportunity to miss unless you stumble across it, or you are invited to take a look by somebody you know or meet someone who is already involved. Lack of education and information is often the reason why there is so much ignorance surrounding this profession. Yet this amazing industry has been around since the 1920s.

There will be some people you meet who claim that they know all about it, most likely because they have already been 'prospected poorly' by somebody involved with network marketing.

> **"A network marketing business is a business in a box. The idea is that for a small nominal fee, you can partner with a company that takes care of everything you don't want to take care of."**

You already have a great product or service in place and a company with a proven track record. There is a demand or need for the service or product you are marketing. The manufacturing and logistics of that service or product is taken care of for you by the company. Staffing issues and legal and licence formalities are all taken care of, and your company generally invoices your customers directly. That's a major headache gone! Your job is to simply show people and help share that idea and help other people to get started in the same way that you did.

You are not buying a 'business'; you are buying a 'solution'. Too many people get involved with this industry expecting a quick return. A business in a box still needs to be built and put together by you! It is your responsibility to build your business, along with the support of whoever introduced you. Don't over complicate this notion. Your job is to 'show and educate' not 'convince and sell'. This mindset can be the difference between success and failure.

For years people, including you, have unknowingly demonstrated network marketing skills. Ironically this includes many of the people you know who choose not to join the profession and even those people you know who believe they can't do it. The simple act of sharing an idea or concept with people we know and meet and that same message being passed on. This is a concept as old as time. Imagine how many people are sharing information you originally introduced some time ago, but are you getting paid for it? No!

All of a sudden we can now transfer those skills and use them to help people, and get paid for it by investing a small amount of money to receive the initial training, support and materials we need to get started. This is usually where, for many, the problem starts. This is because when money becomes involved, expectation becomes present, and when expectation isn't met, failure can often occur.

Many people do fail to recognise an opportunity, especially when it is all wrapped up in a small amount of money such as a network marketing business. There may be questions over how you can invest so little money by comparison to traditional means, and have the potential to replace your salary, buy back your time freedom and live the lifestyle you deserve by committing a few hours a week to begin with.

You may even encounter the 'it seems too good to be true' syndrome. This is why your network marketing business will not be for most people, and it won't be, and that's OK. There will be people out there in the world who get it, and who want it! You do have to go and find those people. This is the part of your business that isn't provided in the box. This is the part your joining fee doesn't cover.

This is why this business is not too good to be true. It's just true that it's good!

CHAPTER 4

MANAGING YOUR EXPECTATIONS

Before you get started, you need to embrace the mindset that you are a 'messenger' not a 'sales person', there is a difference. Your business in the early stages will be built on 20% knowledge and 80% excitement and urgency or mindset. How excited do we get when we see a fabulous film, or eat in a great restaurant? We tell the world, devoid of fear or objection and irrespective of what people think of us. I can assure you, for most of us our knowledge of how a film is put together, or how a restaurant operates, is far less than 20%. All you do know is that you are excited by it. Most people may not be, including some people who are closest to you, and that's normal and to be expected, but you already know this.

Don't expect it to be any different with your network marketing opportunity, service or product.

> **"Just consider how much money you have made for other individuals and companies in the past because of the power of your voice."**

Use the power of your voice to build your own wealth and time freedom and not somebody else's, but be prepared to mess up and have some rejection from friends, family and people you know.

When you join a network marketing business, it will usually be for a small nominal fee, certainly by comparison to traditional businesses, franchises and investments and with much lower hassle and risk. This doesn't mean you should treat it with any less respect!

The chances are that you haven't spent a huge amount of time thinking about joining this business and years planning its launch. For many of you, it may have just seemed like a good idea at the time, or even a bit of a punt. Hopefully not, and your reasons for joining are far more noble and powerful.

For many, there is a low financial investment but also a low emotional investment. This means that it will be easy for you to 'put the business down' when things don't go your way.

Time and consistency are the only things that can reward you, and unfortunately they are the greatest two things that most people are simply not prepared to give. You can be different! If your expectations are correct, and you are prepared to handle the emotion that comes with those expectations, you can have anything you want.

CHAPTER 5

THE TRUTH ABOUT FAILURE

I believe to this day that a formal education is crucial to early social development. I was a student until my early twenties; some of the best days of my life were spent at school and university. I dare say that without it, my life may have turned out quite differently. That being said, educational institutions have a lot to answer for when it comes to the teaching of real principles and the philosophies needed to survive in this new economy, this new world we now live in.

One of the biggest misconceptions that plagues our education system is the notion of success and failure. Failure to my friends and I was always highlighted as a single negative event, which took place in a single moment.

Failure in school was like the end of the world. Something you feared, something you would be chastised or mocked for, the consequences of which meant that your future was bleak. We also see this attitude spill over into our society, so much so that instinctively we do everything we can to avoid failure, as our first instincts are survival and self-preservation. It is here that the problem lies.

Another misconception that 'most' people have is that those people with wealth and success have acquired this as a result of 'not failing' as opposed to the reality that they have failed their way to success and failed hundreds of times in the process.

> **"The cruel twist of irony is that the average person is doing everything they can to avoid failure and as a result we continue to have fewer successful people."**

Real failure is not a single act, which is what we are taught and which imprints on our children. If this was the case, Thomas Edison, Steve Jobs, Richard Branson and many of the world's leading entertainers and entrepreneurs would be deemed failures. In the real world, failure is the result of giving up, stopping and packing it in, usually because of a single or collection of negative outcomes. Success is failing over and over again until you are successful. Two completely different philosophies, wouldn't you agree?

What is your philosophy?

A short story for you that illustrates my point ...

There was a girl in my school, a quiet girl with a nervous disposition. I remember her being mocked repeatedly because she failed her driving test eight times. It was a standing joke in our final year of college. I remember that by the time the school dance came around she had passed her test, she even had a small runaround car which was more than most of the kids mocking her had.

Did she fail? Absolutely! Could she have given up after the seventh attempt? Sure! But was she successful? You bet!

Failure is a stepping stone. One of many on the path to your success!

CHAPTER 6

YOUR DEGREE IN PERSONAL DEVELOPMENT

If you were to approach any large company and conduct an interview with all of the 6 and 7 figure earners within the organisation, you would most likely find that many of them would hold degrees in business, finance, economics or similar qualifications. If you were to conduct that same interview with the 6 and 7 figure earners from any network marketing organisation, you may be surprised by what you find; most hold no degree of any kind, nor do they have business related qualifications. Many don't even have a formal education. So, how is it that they earn the same as, if not more than, those with a formal degree and they have a lot more fun doing it?

Well, fortunately for us, becoming a great leader and top earner in network marketing isn't governed by a certificate with your name on it, nor is it determined by any of your past achievements. Rather, it is a collaboration of skills, qualities and attributes that you develop over time by working consistently and persistently on yourself and your business. It is not quitting when your expectation of early reward is not met, or when you are just having a really bad day! This persistency and consistency to work on your vision of how you want your life to be is best defined as grit; sticking with your future day in, day out and not just for a week, not just for a month, but for years.

> **"Generally, only a small percentage of people who embark on a degree course will become a high achiever in their chosen subject area."**

If an actual degree in network marketing were available, you could expect to see a similar pattern. If you have been an achiever in formal education you can be proud of that and hold on to it forever.

So, how can you get to the top in the network marketing industry? Start by being prepared to leave your belief systems, learned behaviours and conditioned comfort zones at the door! Many people who join the network marketing profession believe that what they already know will serve them moving forward. They hold on to past achievements, believing that 'I've got this'! That is not to say that we should discount the skills and experiences that have been learned before an individual's network marketing journey begins, but instead have faith that each person who commits to becoming a professional network marketer has the ability to develop the new skill set and mindset needed to succeed. This industry doesn't care what you know or don't know, just as long as you are willing to learn and develop. If you believe otherwise, your expectations will not be met and you will position yourself for failure.

We unquestioningly pay a high price to obtain a formal education and gain qualifications, because we have been conditioned to believe that this is the key to having a fruitful and happy life. Most people give many years to earning their qualifications and then have to add to that the tangible costs incurred too. Don't misunderstand me, there is a huge sense of pride and achievement in becoming a qualified individual; I know, I was one of them! However, I believe that for most people, it isn't the knowledge that you acquired in your three year degree which drives you. Rather, it is the time and money, married with the emotional investment made into developing yourself personally. This drive is what will keep you on the success curve!

So, what happens when the investment stakes are low? When the monetary input into a network marketing venture is tiny by comparison and little time or emotion has been invested in thinking about joining a company? It's a lot easier to put down and walk away from, right? This is often the experience for a prospect transitioning towards becoming a distributor. You may have felt this at some point. If we were to pinpoint the origin of most failures in network marketing, you could most likely put it down to the low financial and emotional investment.

Imagine if a college degree in network marketing was made available and a class of 30 regular people took a three year course to study it. The chances are that only 5% would acquire great success, with some doing OK and most never pursuing it. This pattern is true of the team building process in network marketing. It's actually a general pattern for most things in life. What is interesting is that the large financial and emotional investment you would put into doing a network marketing degree would most likely keep you on the course for much longer, possibly the full three years. In reality, keeping a new team member in the game for three years would be a dream come true for any recruiter. As it stands right now, most new distributors don't see their first three years, simply because they have not invested enough time, money or emotion in preparing themselves personally for their limitless career opportunity.

Here is how you can take it to the next level! This is why you should go 'all in' with your network marketing business. What most people fail to see is that the incredible thing about this profession is that it is a personal development course disguised as a business. These are not my words, I am sure most of the world leaders in network marketing will tell you the same. I hear it time and time again. I like to think of it as a Phd in 'personal development'.

If I were to put my commission cheque to one side and look at what I have achieved in terms of personal development, the knowledge and understanding, the high emotional intelligence, coaching skills, communication skills and confidence ... I could go on. It would most likely represent this level of qualification. No matter at what scale or rate you decide to build your business, after three years you would have the equivalent of a degree in personal development, within four years a masters degree and seven years a Phd. Let that sink in a minute ... YOU can qualify yourself to be the best that you can be and all you need is vision and grit.

If you can't treat it like a business or you can't treat it like a job, then please treat your network marketing business like a course. A 'personal development' course or a 'self-help' course to becoming the best version of you possible. Think about how this will benefit all the other areas of your life. Your current job, your other interests and hobbies, your personal relationships, your self-awareness and all round well-being, not to mention the incredible positive associations you will make because of it.

It's worth staying with your network marketing business and absorbing its information for that reason alone, even if you don't intend to go all the way to the top. Going to the top isn't necessary, personal development really is!

Here at the university of 'being a network marketing distributor', you have the world's greatest lecturers, trainers, mentors and coaches on tap. Inspirational people who have carved the tracks for you to run on, because they want you to succeed.

Consider for one moment the cost of obtaining a Phd with global world leaders such as Eric Worre as your mentors. Anywhere up to £100,000 is a reported cost of obtaining this type of qualification. You can obtain the equivalent right here in the subject of 'personal development' just for getting involved and sticking with your network marketing business! It's not the certificate that defines you, it's what you can do with the knowledge you obtain. Most people will tell you that they have learned more in a few weeks or months in this industry than they have during their entire time spent in formal education. I can tell you that, after 16 years in education and 8 years working as a teaching professional, the same is true for me.

If monetary wealth doesn't motivate you or it eludes you, then consider the value of what you will learn by being part of this industry. An industry where to succeed you have to help others. An industry where your efforts and activity translate into income. An industry where everybody shares their knowledge and experience for your benefit. Imagine a life where everybody shares, works hard, has fun and helps. It does exist right here, and imagine how you can apply this to other areas of your life.

CHAPTER 7

ADVISE CAUTION!

At some point in our lives we have all made decisions based on what other people have told us or suggested to us. Your current situation and circumstances will be partly due to the things that other people have suggested or told you. This can be to our detriment and sometimes it can be a positive thing. The truth about 'social proof' is that it can either be a powerful form of advertising and endorsement or a destructive force that will pull you away from any opportunity to grow.

People often feel secure with social proof and making the same choices that large, and sometimes smaller, groups of other people make and moving with the masses. Would you take advice from those people if they were not qualified to give that advice? Hopefully not, though many people do and it's one of the saddest things I see.

The key word is 'proof'. If lots of customers are happy with a product or service, such as the one that you promote in your network marketing business, there is a level of social proof that it is indeed a good product and this group of people are all qualified to tell us this.

However, if that same group of people are telling you not to get involved with a network marketing opportunity, what proof do they have that you shouldn't pursue it?

Some of them may know somebody who joined a network marketing business and didn't make any money. In a few cases, they may have joined one themselves and didn't make any money. On this basis, you would probably think twice and not pursue the opportunity. In turn, you then reduce your wealth-building options by taking advice from somebody who has been unsuccessful in this area. In so many negative instances, people take social proof advice from just one or two unsuccessful people. How tragic is that?

May I suggest this?

"Find a successful, impartial person in the opportunity or idea you wish to pursue, whatever it is, and follow their council."

People who are not qualified to give us success driven advice, usually give us the easy advice. After all, if you go and see the doctor, the dietitian, the successful businessman or somebody who has been successful in network marketing, the advice they give will generally guide you towards the correct but more uncomfortable action requiring more effort and, most likely, self-sacrifice.

If all this seems too much, then consider this. Try to adopt the habit of taking advice from people you would want to trade places with, this will then hopefully steer you onto the right path to happiness and fulfilment.

When considering your wealth plan, consider that 97% of the world's wealth is owned by just 3% of the people, so doing what most people do and making similar choices may not be in your best interest.

If you want to be successful at something, do not take social proof advice from somebody who has been unsuccessful or has no knowledge in that same venture. It makes no sense!

CHAPTER 8

HOW VALUABLE ARE YOU?

If you asked most people if they believed that they were getting paid what they are worth, what do you think the responses would be? No, would be the common answer.

In many circumstances, our employers will value us far less than we value ourselves and in most employment/employee scenarios, you will be paid on the basis of how another individual, or group of individuals values you and your role. This will often be less than the value you actually bring to the company or organisation that you work for.

> **"If you want to make a lot of money in your chosen field, become a consultant at what you do."**

As an employee in your chosen field, your compensation/wage or salary is often stipulated by what another person thinks you are worth and because of this, your room for growth is usually out of your control. As a self-employed consultant in your chosen field, your time and value is much greater as you can often determine it. Therefore you have much greater control over your success & wealth plan.

Here is an example:

As a teacher in my final year working 40 hours per week, employed under the government and local education authority, I was paid around £25K per year. When I left teaching to set up my own school in the same subject field, theatre studies and the performing arts, I was working 10 hours per week earning £50K per year.

It took me three years to build this up, as it takes time to bring value to the marketplace as opposed to receiving an instant wage. As a result, my time and value had become greater.

The interesting thing is that in both instances I was probably bringing the same amount of value to the marketplace. I was teaching the same amount of children in the government school as I was in my own school, but as a consultant in my chosen field I was worth a lot more money as I determined my own value.

There is a catch, you do have to work hard, and you cannot coast, so it is a trade-off. The relaxed attitude that you can receive a pay cheque for simply turning up and giving your time doesn't apply in this instance and you will be taken out of your comfort zone.

The rewards however are far greater and you will be compensated for what you do and the contribution you bring to the marketplace.

> **"As a professional network marketer, you are a consultant in helping people meet a need and solving financial problems and this brings lots of value to the marketplace. You control how much value you bring in the form of how many people you help and you will be paid accordingly."**

The icing on the cake is that, unlike employed and traditional business and consulting work, the income/commission that you earn with your network marketing business is residual or passive. This means that once you have helped an individual to a certain point, you will continue to be paid forever on that activity.

Most of us have come from a time for money background at some point and having a steady job is important as it builds character and provides for you and your family.

When working on your network marketing business you need to figure out a way to switch your working mindset. Forget about the money and focus on the needs of other people. This can be a difficult transition. This shift however takes you from the coin-operated mindset to an entrepreneurial mindset.

You are far more valuable than people realise, but very few people will tell you this and mean it with sincerity. You can do anything you put your mind to. Your mind is just a programme but you have to be the decision maker. We humans do not have the luxury of increasing our value while remaining static. You can keep a car in the garage or hang a painting on the wall and keep it there for forty years and its value will go up. Our value will usually go down unless we get to work on ourselves and not for somebody else.

CHAPTER 9

ARE YOU A 'TRIAL PERIOD' PERSON?

We have all quit something at some point in our lives. Understanding why people quit things will help to keep you in the game when it comes to your network marketing business. Quitting your business, amongst other things, occurs when the feelings you had when you started are different to the feelings you have in the moment of quitting. This usually happens on a bad day. We see this time and time again.

> **"Distributors have the feeling of excitement when positive things happen in their business, and then they hit a low point when nothing or something negative happens. Team members can be your friend when things are going right and don't want to know you when things are not going their way."**

This is the potential 'quit zone'.

The decision to quit is usually triggered by one or more factors that may or may not have anything to do with their business. This may be external distractions, illness, stress, negative opinion, insecurities or frustration, lack of results or activity, or possibly a disagreement with your upline or sponsor.

In the early stages of your business, be aware that it's very easy to quit. The long-term positive effect of pushing through with your business can be superseded by the need for immediate short-term relief. The low emotional and financial investment makes your business very easy to put down early on.

Most people have little awareness that the things that are bad for you, and have a long-term negative effect, are much harder to quit and give up. People who are trying to quit drinking, smoking, eating junk food, giving up entertainment and partying and spending too much money, and other addictions, will tell you this. This is the reason why so many people live tough lives and can't figure out why they ended up where they are.

Poor short-term choices are the easy choices are usually the hardest things to quit.

> **"Quitting something that has a long-term POSITIVE effect is easy, especially if it does not provide you with a result or meet your expectations early on."**

The answer is that you need to turn your business into a healthy addiction, this makes it much harder to quit. It's just the way the human brain, for so many of us, has been programmed. What is your programming? Are you a quitter? You have to learn to love what you are doing and accept that it doesn't always go your way every day.

Quitting for self-preservation and short-term relief will usually take priority for most people. This is why very few people enjoy true wealth and indeed good health and other forms of happiness and abundance.

The same rules apply to your health as well as to your business. Don't be surprised if many of the people you introduce to your business quit. This is actually quite normal, as any successful network marketing professional will tell you. The key is to become 'permanent' at your network marketing business. How do you become 'permanent' at something? How do you push through the wall so you don't quit?

Generally, when the pain of quitting outweighs the 'pain of continuing' with your business! When does it become impractical to quit? When is your business so beneficial, it is too great to put down? This is a difficult point to get to in any venture.

You will from time to time experience a lack of interest or lack of passion. No more so than in your first 90 days. You will have bad days where nothing seems to happen. Rest assured that great things always follow if you stay around long enough! It is often said that people quit just before their breakthrough.

I can tell you that you are not going to quit your business on the day you introduce a new distributor or sign up a new customer. Your excitement of progression will prevent this, so you need to be doing the activity as often as possible. You have an opportunity and product that can help change the lives of so many people. That is the 'passion' you need if you are going to be successful. Make your business about 'others' and not 'yourself'. If you experience loss of interest and passion, the problem is with you, not the business. Your company is already helping to change the lives of so many people, whether you throw your toys out of the pram or not!

We don't join something to quit unless we are a 'trial period' person. You can't dip your toes in and out and learn to swim. Trial period people don't make money because only consistency and persistence pays!

Be here one year from now and you will be in a better place. Quit and there is a high probability you will be in exactly the same place as you are now, maybe even worse off.

One of the hardest things to witness in this business is the success and growth of the people who stuck with it when you decided to leave. Don't wait an entire lifetime to regret the things you didn't do today!

CHAPTER 10

'HIRED, FIRED OR PROMOTED'

A part-time worker is someone who works fewer hours than a full-time worker. There is no specific number of hours that makes someone full or part-time, but a full-time worker will usually work 35 hours or more per week. Part-time workers should get the same treatment with regards to pay rates, maternity, paternity and adoption leave and pay, opportunities and benefits, holidays, training and career development and selection for promotion.

When you get involved as a part-time worker of any kind, these entitlements and benefits can often be forgotten or ignored. Except for your network marketing business, which is the fairest business in the world! Your entitlement and treatment is equal and relative to all other individuals in your organisation, irrespective of rank and number of hours worked, race, religion, gender or sexual orientation. So why would you treat it with any less respect than it deserves.

If you joined your business on a part-time basis, it's easy to forget that 'professional' and 'professionalism' can be two separate things. Can you look at your own productivity and honestly ask yourself:

"If this were my real day job or part-time job, or my chosen profession, would I be 'hired', 'fired' or 'promoted'?"

This is a real question you should ask yourself, as it can help to put things into perspective when assessing your productivity and results. Can you honestly justify the idea of leaving, quitting or abandoning your business because it's not moving forward, when your current levels of activity, work ethic and participation would in fact result in you possibly being fired and certainly not promoted.

In your network marketing business, the opportunity for promotion, bonuses and incentives is equal amongst everybody, but you have to behave in a professional manner if you want to achieve them!

The network marketing world is different because anybody can be hired and nobody can be fired. This is ultimately why you may see lots of people doing nothing, some doing something and a few doing a lot!

The truth is you can be a part-time drifter or a part-time professional. Here is the crunch, both still take up the same time, whether you are dedicating 2, 5 or 10 hours per week to this business. If you committed 5 hours part-time to your business when you initially joined, and you do nothing, you are doing 5 hours of nothing, and that will not make you feel good.

> **"Activity and progression are the only things that can bring you happiness."**

Here is an interesting thought. Most new distributors enrolling in a network marketing business choose to commit around 5 hours per week, which is very part-time. Are you really doing that?

Just to give you an idea: a call centre operative works around 8 hours in one day, makes an average of 40 calls in that time and most likely earns an average of £8 per hour, or £70 per day. This may vary.

Now I am not suggesting that you have to speak to 40 people a day, or even in a week, but if you can't show a minimum of 3 people per week your presentation, business opportunity, service or product, then you are not working part-time, it's no-time and you are just playing small.

If we reversed that idea, and a call centre operative had the same amount of productivity as a network marketer on 'a good day', then they would most likely get fired. Can you imagine a call centre operative speaking to 3 people in a week? What do you think the outcome of that would be?

Your network marketing business asks very little of you, so you should respect it, and what it can do for you long-term. If you can't treat it like a business, then treat like a job and that's OK, in fact I highly recommend it.

It does take time to become a professional at anything, but professionalism is an attitude anybody can possess for FREE and immediately. Having a professional attitude also helps to build your relationships and will earn you respect from others. If you dedicate the time you said you would to your team and prospects, and avoid the temptation of avoidance, you will do well in your business. If you can become a 'can' person rather than a 'can't' person, you will do well in your business. If you are able to take the call rather than hide behind voicemail, you will do well in this business. If you are able to bring conversation and contribution to your team, you will do well in your business.

You are capable of so much but if you don't show professionalism, then you can expect to get paid like an amateur. It's simple social economics. With a small change in mindset the rewards long-term can be huge.

CHAPTER 11

HOW DO YOU FIND THE PRODUCT OR SERVICE?

If you are recommending services or products, it all starts with being a true ambassador for your company by using the products or services yourself.

After spending many years in this business, I have come to learn that all successful distributors not only love their product but they are loyal customers to the company they represent. I have also come to learn that all distributors who do not use the products or services of their company do not last very long in the business, or do very little at best.

Belief in the product you are recommending is essential. That's why finding the right company for you is important! You need to have the belief that your product or service is truly the best above all other competitors. More importantly, the belief you carry will be something that potential customers will see and feel when you speak to them. It will make the whole process of signing a new customer a much more pleasurable experience. You will be positioned to truly educate a potential customer as opposed to simply trying to convince them. You will be able to show them your results in a professional manner.

> **"The chances are that you are partnered with a company which has a fantastic and beneficial service or product that makes a real difference to people's lives. There should be a huge sense of pride you carry with that belief."**

If you are trying to build a team of distributors who are not using the product, it is unlikely that they are talking to their friends, family and people they know and meet. At least not about their business.

By not being a 'product of the product' you are promoting, it is unlikely that you will ever acquire the level of belief you need to build an army of distributors in your organisation. It is also likely that any team members you do introduce will duplicate this behaviour. This will create a weak business! If you are not able to become a customer right away that's

OK, but it is something you should aim to address if you expect to get results. People make decisions based on emotion, not data. Knowing the facts and numbers about a product is not enough. People will see through you if you don't use or believe in the product or service, and you can expect your results to reflect this. Furthermore, how will you ever deal with the killer question that potential customers ask?

"So how do you find the product or service?"

FAN

CHAPTER 12

A FAMILY BUSINESS

Each distributor joining a network marketing business should be given an equal and fair chance to join in and participate. Despite this, it does not always happen. You can often find that some distributors take to the business like a 'fish to water', while others prefer to keep themselves to themselves. To 'go it alone' at 'their own pace'. If they are the latter, you will generally find coaching and supporting them a difficult task with little result.

The ability to build relationships and create rapport with the people in your network, your upline and cross-line team, will play a large part in your overall success. You will often hear the word 'orphan' being thrown around in this business and it's important not to confuse this term. We tend to associate distributors who are either at a distance from their team or have no real active upline as 'orphans' and this can be very damaging.

Distributors should never be made to feel like they are alone, otherwise it can become a self-fulfilling prophecy leading to insecurity and doubt in one's own ability.

> **"Many distributors don't choose to distance themselves from the team and it's important to help distributors in this situation to see that they are the CEO of their own business and that it is up to them to go the extra mile to participate."**

Distributors who **choose** not to become part of their network marketing family are a different matter altogether!

Some distributors joining the business may prefer to keep the company of their current and existing social circle and refrain from joining in with their team members and organisations events. This is OK, but they have to accept that this will not provide them with the correct association, inspiration and motivation they need for self-improvement or growth in their network marketing business.

Distributors have to be able to make the connection between being part of an inspirational and motivational network marketing family and being successful at creating time freedom. This requires education. Just like all students, some want to learn and join in and some want to mess about. Some want to be first in line and some want to sit at the back of the class.

We should be educating and encouraging our team members to abandon the feeling of 'a victim of circumstance'. This can be difficult, especially when they are not getting the results they had hoped for. I refer to the term 'independent distributor'. Just like a real family, we teach our 'dependants' to be 'independent'.

Even if you deserve and want support, you may sometimes not receive it at the level you expect. It may also be less than the next person gets, depending on your distance and relationship with your upline recruiter. You can invest your time in being bitter and full of blame about this, or you can get to work on building your own business as many other successful people have done.

Support and attention are nice but it does not guarantee you success. Similarly, lack of it does not mean you are doomed to failure. Take responsibility for travelling a distance to see your team and to join in and work on forming those relationships yourself. Waiting for somebody to pick up the phone to tell you what to do is not an entrepreneurial trait. Don't allow yourself to fall into the trap of feeling disadvantaged.

Failure is not bestowed upon you because of your circumstances; it's a result of the choices and decisions you make. You have to work at joining in with your network marketing family, just like you would your own family!

CHAPTER 13

A GREAT NETWORK MARKETING DAY

There is no such thing as a perfect network marketer, but what if you could have a perfect (network marketing) day, irrespective of how much time on a daily basis you choose to dedicate to your business? Certainly for a new distributor starting out on a part-time basis, managing time spent on the correct activity during the day can be difficult.

Firstly, we need to understand that time cannot be managed; take a look at your watch and have a go, it can't be done! Secondly, there is no clearly defined job description of what activities need to be done, which can leave you confused about what you need to be doing to make money each day. This is why treating your part-time business like it is a 'part-time job' can be useful when starting out. It's a mindset that may seem more familiar.

A part-time job is generally not performance or target driven. It requires you to turn up on the specific days agreed and that you complete the activities that are required of you during the time you agreed to work. The advantage of the part-time job is that you are mostly being paid for your time and not necessarily for the results you produce.

If you work a 5-hour day, it's the 5 hours of your time that you are being paid for, not what you do during that 5 hours. Although lack of activity or productivity may result in you losing that job.

> **"With your part-time network marketing business, the rules are flipped. You are being paid for your activity, not your time! Although the more time you choose to spend on the required business activities, the greater the result and the more money you will earn."**

It is easier to plan in days rather than in hours. When you are getting started with your network marketing business, may I suggest that instead of dedicating 5 hours per week, you dedicate 2 days per week minimum and ensure that, no matter what happens, the required activities get completed on that day. How much time you dedicate to your business on that day will very much depend on your lifestyle and circumstances.

You should realise that everybody in your team will make different contributions at different times. Not everybody clocks in and out at the same time. The great news is that activities can be duplicated. So rather than trying to manage how much time you and your team will spend on the business, manage the activities that you are doing irrespective of the time it takes to do them.

A great way to do this is to use the 4 P's principle. Some may call this a DMO (Daily method of operation), which should include:

- **Prospecting**
- **People**
- **Personal Development**
- **Promotion**

Managing these activities on a daily basis gives you far more control over how you get paid and the result you want. You can spend as long or as little as you like on each one. The more time you choose to dedicate to these activities during the day, the faster and bigger the business you will build.

All 4 activities need to get done at some point, substitutions don't work. You may only do 1 or 2 of the activities in a day, but it will need to be compensated for further on.

Call it performance related pay without somebody else dictating the hours you work! Ultimately you are accountable to yourself.

You may find it difficult to set specific times to do these activities each day because you cannot manage how time will treat you on a daily basis. Life can get in the way and other distractions will arise. You can however manage these activities and how much time you spend on each on a daily basis because they are controlled by you. You get to choose how much time you spend per day on these activities in accordance with your daily routine, which will be different each day. How you prioritise the events of your day will directly affect the level of financial success you achieve. If you choose to prioritise your business activities, your business will reward you in equal measure.

So what exactly do you need to do, what is your job description?

Prospecting: The number one money making activity. The one you will be most tempted to avoid. This is simply the art of inviting people to look at your business and services or product and correctly following up to see if they wish to get involved or take a second look. You also need to be following up!

People: Communicating with your team, your mentor and the team members you are working with. Conversations build business and speaking with your team members on a daily basis will keep you in the game and keep everybody motivated.

Personal Development: Self-education is very important, e.g. books, audio CD's and videos.

Promotion: Professional network marketers are promoters. Promote your business, your industry, your mentor and your services. Promote and attend events, trainings, and meetings that are taking place.

CHAPTER 14

YOUR 'SAT NAV' TO SUCCESS!

People are generally not used to planning their life in the correct way, many don't plan at all. Often, what they want, and NOT how they intend to get what they want, is the focus. This is because they are running on 'autopilot' with a mental sat nav and NO planned route.

The first step to putting any plan in place, is to know the destination or the goal. Secondly, you need the directions (the plan or route) to get to that destination.

Another problem for many people is that they do not know their destination. This is why goal setting is so important! Have your goals and destinations written down or posted where you can see them every day!

It is crucial that you confirm your destination (or set your goals) before you plan a route to success. These can range from small short-term goals to larger more ambitious goals. Keep in mind that success is a continued journey of progression with a worthy ideal and not an end point.

Any road leading to a destination or goal can sometimes be filled with road blocks and traffic jams, slowing you down with distractions and causing you to stop temporarily. We all know this. You may arrive much later than you had intended but you will get there. Goals are only set in sand and not in stone. That is an important thing to remember for your own sanity. Over fixation on deadlines can sometimes knock you back a step.

Without a planned route and without that mental sat nav correctly programmed, you are leaving your destination to fate and chance. You are simply running on autopilot, which is a problem for the human brain. This is because our brain is guided by emotion, which will not take you to the destination you ultimately wish to reach. It will take you the 'quickest' and 'easiest' route to avoid coming out of your 'comfort zone'.

This will prevent you from making that prospecting call or messaging that person on your 'chicken list' (the people you are scared to talk to).
Avoiding these key money making activities in the short-term will undoubtedly lead to disappointment and mediocrity in the long-term. This is the inconvenient truth.

So what route should you follow and what maps should guide you if you want true success and wealth?

Your mental sat nav programming should have a 'success map' installed. The good news is that a success map has already been created for you by somebody else, and it's FREE. It has been created by somebody who is already successful in your network marketing business. You simply need to follow their map. These people are very accessible, but it will require initiative and willingness on your part to join in and participate. You can't expect them to chase you!

Here is the problem. There is a good chance that the maps you are currently following are the same maps used by your peers, friends, and family. This is OK as they are an easy and convenient reference point for you and this is how most people operate.

However, if the people you spend the most time with are NOT at the places you wish to be, you will need to install some new maps or you will most likely end up at their destination, not yours.

Many people you know will not have arrived at the destination they set out to, or that they wanted to reach. This is why you may sometimes feel surrounded by a vacuum of negativity with people often complaining about their job or lack of money situation.

They have got to this point because the autopilot on their mental sat nav has taken them to their current destination. They had no planned route to success or the correct guidance needed to get there.

> **"Seek out the successful people in your business. By listening to them and spending more time with them, you can load these new maps into your mental sat nav."**

Unless you are prepared to do this and be proactive, your maps will default to that of those around you and before you know it, you will arrive at the same destinations as those closest to you. This is OK if that's what you want, but it is a problem if you aspire to greater things.

CHAPTER 15

'TIC TOC' YOUR MENTAL CLOCK

We all have two clocks, our 'mental clock' and the 'world clock', both moving at different speeds. The world clock is the 'real passing of time', equal and relative to every human on earth. Your mental clock is the clock in your head. Most people are governed by their mental clock. Time will always appear to move either quicker or slower for different people while the world clock remains constant. The illusion is that time often appears to move much quicker if you are a 'busy' person with lots going on or you have an active lifestyle and a busy mind. Time will generally appear to move slower if you don't have a lot going on and are less of an over thinker.

"The problem with the mental clock is that it often tricks you into believing that a task or activity will take longer than it actually does."

Why would an individual believe that they didn't have the time to make a 5 minute call in a 12 hour day, when we know that 20% of that day would have been available to make that call?

Something that may only take 15 minutes may appear to take 2 hours, furthermore it continues to rob you of the ability so see when you have time available. That means that many people can't distinguish between 2 hours and 5 minutes respectively.

This can be a huge barrier to overcome. However, with the correct education and raised awareness, and 'awareness' being the operative word, distributors can become more conscious of the 30 hours in a week that are often available to them.

This available time is more than enough to do the money making activity required to build their network marketing business.

What prevents the awareness of 'real time' to do money making activity is your mental time clock being used up with concern, worry, insecurities, misery, despair, tax bills, daily annoyances, low-level anxiety, physical decay, hair loss, trodden-in dog mess and global economic meltdown. This negative mental activity speeds up your mental clock so that you may spend one hour thinking about something and the moment to act is lost.

After a seminar some time ago on this particular subject matter, one of the ladies in our organisation wrote to me. She was a busy mum who had 2 children with special needs.

Along with the rest of the audience, she was tasked with raising awareness of her own time availability.

She said: *"David, I just wanted to thank you for the training and making me see that I have 30 hours a week free."*

I would like you to imagine that all the free time YOU have available in one week was spent staring at a wall. Figure out how much time that is. Would that not seem like all the time in the world, even if it were only an hour? Would time not start to slow down for you? Of course it would, and faced with that situation, the chances are that you would be itching to do some business activity and start making some calls. You would also be insisting that this time could be used more productively.

You have 70,000 conversations with yourself everyday. You may speak to yourself more in one day than you do to your closest friend in an entire lifetime. Be careful what stories you are telling yourself.

Just imagine what you could do with all the FREE time that you don't believe is available!

CHAPTER 16

THE EXCITEMENT OF URGENCY

How many people do you know who get paid for waiting? If they do, would you exchange your place for theirs? Isn't it ironic, that for a race that 'dislikes' waiting so much, we sure love to wait?

Wait until Monday, wait until the end of the month, wait until the New Year. It is difficult to get excited when you are moving slowly and difficult to have 'urgency' in your business without getting excited.

Ask yourself this question: is your upline, sponsor or maybe even your team more excited than YOU are about your business? Are you able to prioritise your business?

If you were having 30 friends over for a birthday or celebration party, how much time and effort would you put into the planning? How much effort would you go to? What reason would you have to cancel or call it off? If it were a launch party for your business and you wanted to invite 30 people over to your house to celebrate and get their support, would you give it the same level of priority?

The point here is that YOU NEED to be more excited and more urgent than anybody else in the world when it comes to your own business. This is how success is built. It's how jobs get done and how money is made. Examine your current attitude towards your business. Do you wake up happy because of it? You need to love it more than the football match or the golf tournament. You need to love it more than a spa day or lunch with the girls.

Money can be earned standing around all day, but it can't be made! You are your business, and you control 100% of the excitement and urgency you carry. Even when your team has slowed down and potential customers and distributors are saying 'NO', your ability to keep going will drive you towards the positive result you are seeking.

Don't let the result control your emotions and actions, let your emotions and actions control the result! This is an easy mindset to change; all you have to do is put value on the negative. All negatives have value when you keep going, they are nothing more than a statistical inevitability paved on the road to success, as we have discussed previously. You can always be excited and urgent about your activity, irrespective of the outcome or result.

Be excited about an upcoming event and be urgent about booking it. You can be excited and urgent about sharing things with your team and about getting engrossed in some good personal development. Stop being the last to know and don't be that team member who needs to be told ten times. Just do it!

> **"There are very few things that should take higher priority than the business you have invested in. This business, which can give you time freedom and future security."**

What is there not to get excited and urgent about? The waiting game does not pay! 'Now' pays you much quicker than 'later' in business. Why wait until Monday, or the end of the month or next year? Money and opportunity are LOST in that time.

People are generally not excited by their current situation or their future no matter what they say, but you can be. For many, the next pay day or next break or next Friday will be the only thing they look forward to. So people will feed off YOUR excitement. Excitement is the most cost-effective fuel to power your team, and drive your prospective clients and the people around you into making a decision.

They will, at the very least, remember the way you make them feel. Help drive people to be excited by something again!

In the end, your leaders are looking for motivated people, not people to motivate. Which one are you?

CHAPTER 17

THE MIRACLE OF TIME FREEDOM

Depending on which network marketing company you join, it will no doubt have a wealth of incentives, promotions and pin/rank and status levels available. These are all put in place to recognise your hard work and progress.

> **"Time freedom is the real milestone that every network marketer should be aiming for and the only one that matters for true long-term wealth & happiness."**

Time freedom is created when you no longer need to swap or sell your time 'wholesale' to an employer in exchange for a wage/salary. If you are reading this article, there is a good chance that you are being paid, or have at some point been paid a 'linear income' and that's OK. It does mean however that if you stop giving your time, you stop receiving money. This is not determined by your level of salary, and is irrespective of whether you are paid a low, medium or high salary or if you are employed or self-employed. Many self-employed people still need to give their time in order to 'get paid'.

True wealth is having the ability to make the choices you want to make when you want to make them and spend time with those you love without being a slave to the alarm clock or a boss. Traditional education and values have taught us to 'earn more money'. The problem with this is that if you want to earn more money you have to give more time. It's also worth knowing that when times are hard our governments teach us to 'cut back' rather than 'strive for more'.

People tend to do neither of these things and will often find the answer in living beyond their means and getting into debt. We all know people who have fallen foul of this.

Network marketing is one of the very few vehicles that can allow you to build up a 'passive income'. This means that you continue to be paid but are no longer required to sell your time for money as you would in conventional employment or time for money situations.

Time is the most precious commodity. You can make more money but you cannot make more time. You can however buy back your time by growing a business that pays you passively, allowing you to grow an income without cutting back and, if need be, get out of debt.

So how much money do we need for time freedom? Well, it's not a million pounds, as some would have you believe! Plenty of millionaires have no time freedom.

Imagine if the salary you were paid now in your conventional employment was paid to you each month without you having to do the work or 'sell your time'. That is time freedom. All the top earners and leaders you see in this business first gain 'time freedom' and continue to build their business. Six and seven-figure passive income is eventually created through continued hard work. You do not necessarily need to be a six or seven-figure earner to have true time freedom. This is achieved once your network marketing residual income matches your salary.

The beauty is that your passive or residual income continues to grow from here on, which means money is being made without your intervention. This is why building a team is so important. Leveraged income is only created when you are paid on the time and activity of others. You become non-essential to your income. To achieve this you will need to create **'duplication'** in your business.

> **"Duplication is the art of getting everybody in your business to follow the system. This will not happen automatically. It will require you to support and lead your team members. To teach them the system and teach them to teach the system."**

This will usually require you to work 3 or 4 levels in your business to create a duplicating team. Not everybody will duplicate, most won't, some will duplicate to a degree and a few will grow into leaders. Some of those leaders could go on to be rock stars in your business.

> **"People cannot be duplicated, only the system can be duplicated. So stop trying to be like other networkers & stop comparing yourself."**

There is the catch for those of you who think it all sounds 'too good to be true'. If you are one of those (TGTBT) thinkers, please understand that you will need to set aside 3-5 years of hard work in order to achieve leveraged income. You do not buy time freedom with the purchase of your business or starter pack. This is a misconception many people have, often leading to instant failure.

Your time freedom has to be earned. A price has to be paid, but it's a small price in comparison to the only other real option. Forty years into somebody else's dreams, or four into your own. Most, if not all of your friends, family and people you know will be living by the former. What if you could show them the latter?

CHAPTER 18

HELP, I NEED SOMEBODY!

I still find it fascinating that some people do not always respond well to our help, or our offer of help, especially if it wasn't asked for in the first place. Regardless of your relationship with an individual, whether it is a family member, friend or stranger, uninvited help can sometimes arouse 'suspicion' and thoughts of 'motive'.

People are generally programmed to see the worst in people, especially in today's society where we have created this vacuum of negativity, which in turn has become malignant and contagious.

Why do we slow down when we see a car wreck? Why do we crowd round when we see a fight? Why are we entertained by violence and macabre subject matter and why do other people's failures often make us feel better about ourselves, whilst their success makes us envious, resentful, and suspicious and insecure?

There is something not quite right with this picture, would you not agree? We somehow seem to gravitate towards the negative, which in turn affects how we view things and respond to the people around us, even those closest to us.

So when you are launching your network marketing business and setting appointments to show somebody your product or opportunity, don't be surprised if you are occasionally met with some resistance. It's nothing personal against you; it's social conditioning in the individual you are trying to help. We all get it, I did and many times over!

> **"The good news is that you can absolutely alleviate any resentment and have people looking at your opportunity and product all day long with little resistance."**

They are not always going to buy and most won't join your business, and that's OK because it is 'eyes on the presentation' that matters, to as many people as possible, as quickly as possible because that's what you get paid for! We have highlighted this on several occasions in this book!

You only need a few good people to join you, a few, not a thousand, because the few you find are going to do the same. This is called duplication and this is why it is important to develop this team culture and share this material with your team.

To change your strategy, to get as many eyes on the presentation as possible, don't try to **help people**, get them to **help you**.......... sounds crazy. People are less mean than you think. When you **ask for help** and tell somebody 'WHY' you are 'starting a business', a few things happen.

Firstly, people connect with you emotionally and people make decisions based on emotion. Secondly, you give them an important role to play and feed their ego by putting them in control. Finally, you will never be a perfect network marketer, if there is such a thing, and if you are not perfect, then you are practising, constantly. So practise your presentation on everybody you meet. Practising is a noble and respected action. If you asked to practise a 5-minute presentation on somebody, I would safely bet that you would rarely hear no, nor would you be met with much resistance. You would also get fewer cancelled appointments because there is a noble purpose to the meeting.

Just for a second imagine that you and I both have ten people stood in a line. You say to your group, "I can help you" and I say to my group, "I need your help", who do you think will get the warmest most positive response? What would your response be in both instances?

Be mindful, we are in the business of helping other people but you need the support and help of other people if you are going to launch and, indeed, create momentum in your business.

CHAPTER 19

WORK THAT HOT LIST BABY!

Who do you know who would want to make more money this year than they did last year? 'Everybody' may be the answer you are thinking of.

If you were putting a wedding list together or organising a major birthday party, who would be on that list? What if you needed a small favour from as many people as possible, who would you go to, who would you ask? How would you pick and choose who goes on this list?

If you stumbled upon something great, a fantastic idea that could help everybody, who would you share this with and who would you miss out? The truth is that all of those lists would be different sizes but, interestingly enough, the amount of friends, family and people you know remains the same. With each list you create, there is a tendency to prejudice people based on how you feel about that individual. There is emotion attached to each list.

So when you are asked to create your initial 'list' of potential prospects and customers for your business, you may find yourself creating a list of the people who you believe would be interested and excluding those you believe wouldn't be or, simply put, you would include those who you are comfortable going to speak to.

This will be a thin list and will not give you the ramp up you need!

"Have fun with your list. There is no rule that says you have to speak to everybody."

Start with the 'hot list'. These are 'friends', 'family' and 'people you know' who you would be happy to go to and ask for a small favour. Work down from your 'nearest and dearest' to 'social contacts' and 'friends of friends'.

A good list will have 200 names and contacts, 30 of these can usually be described as 'hot list prospects', hopefully more. Have it written down in a journal with contact numbers. Your list needs to be seen and written down. It will not suffice to simply store your contacts in your phone. Out of sight, out of mind.

"Your list will stay with you forever and will grow and expand as you meet people and develop relationships."

Your list will initially consist of 'hot' and 'warm' prospects. People you know well and see or speak to often, and those who you know but may have lost touch with. A good skill to have is moving people from 'warm' to 'hot' by reconnecting with those people. The key is to understand how to approach people on your list. The 'less hot' they are, the more curious and genuinely interested you will need to be 'in them' when reconnecting. It is important you are sincere in reconnecting. People will know if you have an agenda!

It won't be long before they ask you what you are doing. You are then positioned comfortably to offer to show them.

With the initial 30 people on your hot list, you can simply ask for a favour or for some help. You could even ask them outright if they will try your product or service to help you get started. We call this 'inviting'. The first point of contact with people from your list is the invitation for them to take a look. Like with all invitations, how they are put across to an individual will normally determine the response.

People who have less familiarity with you or are further removed because of a time span or association may be less obliging. You will need to make the effort to reconnect and have a conversation if they are to become a 'hot' prospect.

There are enough people on your hot list to ramp up your business. Where many new distributors fail is that they only show the business to 3 people from their list.

Some may get in front of 10 but few make it to 30 people and beyond. If 1 in 3 people you see becomes a customer, and 1 in 10 will join as a distributor, then showing 3 to 10 people will not 'cut it'. It will also not provide you with the belief or the desire you need to carry on and push through.

If you focused on the 'activity' rather than the 'rejection', then you would gain enough momentum to ramp up your business.

In showing 30 or more people from your hot list, you may encounter some of the following hurdles:

- **Prospect 1:** May cancel an appointment.
- **Prospect 2:** You thought would say 'yes' but they said 'no'.
- **Prospect 3:** May respond negatively or in a way you didn't expect.

If this happens with the first 3 people you go to see, don't let it prevent you from getting to see 4, 5, and 6 and so on up to 30 people and beyond. Focus on the 'activity' not the 'negativity'.

> **"You should approach your hot list with 'excitement and urgency' just as you would if you were passing out party invites. The exciting thing is, you can do this with all your new team members. For each new team member you introduce, there are at least 30 hot prospects on their list."**

If you talk to any established network marketers with a big business they will tell you that only a tiny percentage of their team is made up of friends and family or people on their initial hot list, so do not get disheartened if you seem to get a lot of rejection. Sometimes the people closest to you can be the most difficult because they are either trying to protect you or you are simply reminding them of what they are not doing and they are having a hard time dealing with it. Some are just plain awkward.

This is not the case with every distributor you introduce. It will very much depend on each distributor's family culture and values and their social environment that will determine how supportive their friends and families are. You just don't know. Above all be human when you speak to people you know. Don't become something you are not. Think about how you invite people out to the movies or out to dinner or out for a drink. If all of a sudden you stop being you that's when they think something is wrong or they are being sold to. You shouldn't care if some of your friends and family don't join, as they are here simply to practise your craft on and provide you with a ramp up! You can't control how they will respond but you can control how you react.

If you are struggling to add people to your list, then 'Network Marketing Pro' offers a fantastic free resource to help jog your memory. You can obtain it here:

http://networkmarketingpro.com/unlimited/memoryjogger.pdf

CHAPTER 20

PRESENTING FOR FREE!

Imagine if you were paid £100 or the value of your joining fee for every short opportunity/business presentation you made during the week. Imagine how that would drive you to make as many presentations as possible, irrespective of the outcome or how much knowledge you had. That's because 'money for time' eliminates the emotional outcome of the presentation.

You wouldn't care if they said no, questioned you, or laughed at you (which nobody really does) as you are compensated by instant 'money for time'. This is actually a poor mindset as it is in direct conflict with what is required to be an entrepreneur.

> **"For true long-term wealth and to release that entrepreneurial mindset, you have to make the activity of presenting your opportunity both fun and free."**

After all, we are willing to not get paid for things that are fun, in fact we will even pay for the privilege of having fun. If you can't have fun with your business, it is unlikely you will achieve the level of success you want!

So what if you could make your presentations fun, knowing that one day all this fun could pay you more money and give you more time freedom than your previous 'time for money' attitude ever could?

Practise on the people you know and love. It doesn't have to be perfect, it just has to give them the information they need to make up their mind.

A presentation is fun when there is no 'perceived' motive, when you can easily arrange it and when you don't need to know it all and you have the knowledge that what you have to offer is a gift to both yourself and the person you are showing.

Your organisation will provide you with plenty of tools to help you present. The key is to say the least amount to as many people as possible. We spoke earlier about getting in front of a minimum of thirty people quickly. This will take some hard work and effort on your part so use the tools you have. You may have to use all your tools and resources as different exposures, depending on how many exposures it takes for a prospect to make a decision.

- **DVD's & Company Videos**: Great when meeting people face to face or you need to send information out. Also great for one-to-one meetings.

- **Home Meetings**: Invite 30 people to your house or to a venue and either present yourself using the tools or have your upline support come along and present.

- **Opportunity Presentations**: Invite your prospects to your local company presentation evenings.

- **Event or Seminar**: Invite your prospects to a company event, convention or seminar.

- **3-way Call**: Invite your prospect to speak with your mentor.

- **A Magazine or Published Article**: A book or other network marketing publication. Generic or company specific.

- **Business Cards**: Very useful for on the fly daily exchanging of information.

- **Generic Tools**: Rise of the Entrepreneur DVD: Eric Worre (networkmarketingpro.com) or non-company specific videos and webinars.

- **Social Media Profile:** A business page or profile you host.

CHAPTER 21

DONT FEAR THE FOLLOW UP!

I enjoy a little retail therapy from time to time just like the next person. While I have always been a good decision maker in business, like so many of us, when it comes to shopping and purchases, I can be indecisive. Choosing not to make a purchase does not mean I don't want something. Just because I walk away it doesn't mean I am not interested. In many cases, there has been nobody around to help me get to the next stage. Nobody to ask me if I would like to try on the jacket or perhaps take a look at some others. Nobody to help me to get to the next exposure. Further assistance could have easily swayed me.

I am not a fan of shop staff pouncing on me the second I walk through the magnetic security barriers. I do however realise that after a few minutes of browsing, I may need some help to make that all important decision. If I am choosing to look at somebody's product, I have to be open to a 'follow up'. This is a professional part of the process, something that we should expect as potential customers and something we should also expect to do as distributors offering a business opportunity, service or product. Poor or no follow up can ultimately be the make or break for any business! A store whose staff approach and follow up on potential customers will make more money than those who leave it to fate and to the indecisive nature of people.

> **"They say the fortune is in the follow up! When following up with a potential customer or a prospective distributor who has seen what you have to offer, your aim is to ask a series of questions to find out if they want to buy, join or need to take a second look."**

It shouldn't be over complicated. What they often don't teach you as a sales adviser is how to follow up with a question that leads to a positive response. The network marketing profession teaches you to follow up with the simple question:

What did you like best?

With this approach you can then ascertain the level of interest from the potential customer or distributor. You can find out if they are ready to get started, make a purchase, or if they need another exposure. Maybe they would like to try the jacket on, or maybe they just need to see a few more options. It's the same with your network marketing business. Do they want to try the product or services or take a second look at your business?

One of the greatest blueprints for building a network marketing business is Eric Worre's GO PRO - 7 STEPS TO BECOMING A NETWORK MARKETING PROFESSIONAL. In his book we get to explore the 7 key skills that you need to acquire to become a network marketing professional. The book goes into detail on the process of how you can use 'follow up' correctly on your prospects.

Notice where the follow up is in the process. It is the central skill which gets you to the other side. The seven skills are:

- The ability to find prospects
- To invite them to look at your product & opportunity
- To present your product & opportunity
- **To follow up with your prospects**
- Help them become customers or distributors
- Help them get started properly
- Grow your team by promoting events

Everything after the 'follow up' is when the money starts to appear. So why do so many people fear follow up instead of getting excited by it? When a friend, family member or somebody you know or have met agrees to take a look, they may even be excited about looking at your new venture, then we create in our mind a 'fantasy' customer or distributor.

The mind treats it as a success, which to a degree it is because we get paid long-term for helping people 'make the decision to look', so good on you for that! It also validates our ability to get somebody to subscribe to what we are doing. Even if they haven't joined yet or made a purchase. After all, progression is happiness, and people agreeing to look is progression.

What happens next is that we can become fearful of whether we should attempt to get a decision or ascertain a further level of interest from somebody. They may decide that they don't want your product or are not interested in your business, perhaps the timing isn't right! We like to cling to the hope that they will join. 'Following up' can diminish that hope. This is actually backward thinking.

A prospect who is looking or who has agreed to look, and a prospect who then says 'no', equates to exactly the same thing! No sign up. It's the feeling of your small temporary success being stripped away that you fear. So you forget to follow up.

People are 'not going to beg' for your business, opportunity or services. Some may approach you from time to time but not enough for you to light up the sky! You are not an open shop. You need to go and find people to speak to, show them what you have and then 'follow up'. The 'follow up' is the key central mechanism to acquiring a purchase or successful sign up!

When you offer people what you have, they become your 'number one priority'. It becomes your priority to successfully convert them. They will not return the gesture. They may be interested, but they will prioritise many other things on their list before they call you up to get started. After all, life gets in the way for many people! So much so that they may never call you up because to them what is urgent in the short-term comes before what is important in the long-term. That's how many of your prospects are operating! It is also how you will operate from time to time.

The truth is that following up is easy, you have done the hard part which is inviting people to look, and presenting what your business offers. There is no excuse to miss out this most basic of skills! There is no excuse to play small. Always have a few people in your pipeline. Having a number of people to follow up with will improve your posture and make you less desperate in the 'follow up' process. Fear of losing 'the one' will diminish and you will be more confident in the approach. Following up is the bridge that takes you to the other side.

You can't move forwards if you can't get across.

CHAPTER 22

GIFT OR GUILT?

You must realise that what you have with your network marketing business is a gift. Even if you are just getting started it is so powerful, so powerful you may not even be aware of it.

It is your responsibility to share your gift with the world. Know that many people are hurting, and many, even if they are not fully aware, are looking for opportunities to break away from the bondage of their day jobs and the pressures and strains placed on them by their conventional jobs and traditional businesses.

This fear we hear about in network marketing is irrational, it is a self-fulfilling prophecy and it is manifested because people are choosing to preserve their self-image, not wanting to look stupid or embarrassed in front of those people they know and love, being a secret agent and not sharing their opportunity.

> **"If you truly believed that what you had was a gift, if you were truly excited by it, then you would tell the world regardless of how you appeared."**

Stop feeling guilty about what you have, and if you do, why are you here?

People will join in with your excitement regardless of your knowledge. After all, we are the biggest promoters of the things we love and find exiting, despite the fact we really know very little about them.

Think of the last film you were excited about and rushed out and told everybody to go and see, when really your knowledge of how that film was put together, pre/post production, distribution and marketing was miniscule.

Knowledge is important and fills your head. Excitement and sharing fills your bank.

CHAPTER 23

A HIGHLY PAID SKILL

When it comes to promoting a company event to team members, so many distributors often rely on fate to promote it and live in hope that people will simply turn up and attend. You should never underestimate the power of team and company events. Being a great promoter of events is one of the most highly paid skills you can acquire in this business. I have been fortunate to learn from the best. My mother, who has been described as one of best promoters of network marketing events in the world.

If you want to build a significant network marketing business, you need to treat each event like it was your own. We know that there will be people who will not turn up and those who will cancel at the last minute or simply not want to join in.

Consider that if you can get 50 people to a party which can cost you hundreds of pounds, then why can't you get 50 people to a company event which can make you thousands of pounds. Inviting and promoting both require the same core skill.

After years in this business, you will see some distributors with greater and greater numbers of team members attending the conferences, team meetings and jumping on the webinars and generally joining in and participating. Then you will see some distributors who seem to remain lonely or stagnant at each event, that is if they turn up at all. I believe there is not one, but a number of reasons why this happens. The question remains, why do many distributors not promote events, share resources or encourage participation correctly within their teams?

It's only through education and personal development that we learn that this 'thinking' will not serve us and that the only way to create 'long-term wealth' and 'success' is to help and serve everybody else. To share and to care and to have a noble and powerful why for doing it. Most people don't want to share. Sharing is something that we generally see as taking away from us. This is dangerous! Not communicating and sharing information with your team will harm you more than you know.

Never rely on your sponsor or your company to promote and share everything for you. They may do a sterling job, however your team will mostly listen to you and pay the most attention to you.

If the extent of your promotional skill is simply to share a post on Facebook or throw out an unpersonalised message or simply mention something in passing, you may as well leave it to fate to get your team to join in!

If it was your big day, how many people would you have there? What lengths would you go to in order to get people to attend or join in? You are not without the skill to do this. It is mindset, getting people to join in and participate and attend events pays you!

I read that the meaning of the word ego is your idea or opinion of yourself, especially your feeling of your own importance and ability. We are all human and most of us are guilty of having an ego at some point in our lives, however it's important to understand that 'ego' can prevent us from realising what is best for the many, including our own team members. Don't let your ego be dented by promoting somebody else's events, ideas or resources. It will cost you dearly.

What about fear, fear of failure, fear that you are putting your team under unnecessary pressure, worried that they will drop out of your business if you ask them for participation, time or money. All I will say is that key people will follow you and those who drop out because you have asked them to participate were never meant to be.

Finally, and probably the cruellest of all, is assumption. We just assume our team members won't want to be included and this is a major error in judgement.

Promoting an event, though it is a skill, is more of a mindset that you have to get right. You need to be aware that losing and spending money is far easier than making money, so expect that promoting a company event will be more difficult than promoting a celebratory or social occasion because of its positive financial outcome. There are no shortcuts here.

Imagine that you get paid for every company meeting, training and event that you promote on the basis of how many people you get to attend.

Finally, trust in the process that payment will be received further down the line. Abandon the idea of time for money when it comes to attending and promoting events, though it's worth noting that what follows an event for most distributors is money making activity. This means that effectively you can get paid for each event you and your team attend.

Attending and promoting events is one of the key wealth-building activities in our network marketing profession. It sadly gets missed or undervalued as a skill and mindset. You will often hear that you become a product of your associations and the people you spend the most time with. Association is key and the relationships and friendships you create as a result of participation and joining in with events will put you on the right path to wealth and success.

Tell your team members why they need to be there, who will be speaking and how to book! Understand that taking notes and bringing back at least one key concept and applying it consistently to your business will put the most value on an event. Don't fall into the trap of simply being a knowledge gatherer. Apply what you learn and have your breakthrough moment! Take it to your team. It only takes one nugget of information gathered at an event to take your business to the next level.

Many of the company events you promote in your career will be run by other people and some will be your own. Let go of ego, vanity, fear and laziness, because these are the things that prevent you and your team from joining in and participating. If you care, you need to share! If you don't care, network marketing will not work for you.

CHAPTER 24

----

007 - LICENCE TO SUCCEED!

There are far too many secret agents involved in network marketing. They enrol in the programme, do the training, subscribe to the services, buy the products, yet the rest of the world and the people around them still don't know what they do.

> **"It is important for a secret agent to protect their identity and what they do so as not to put their lives at risk. This is the mindset of some people in this amazing business we call network marketing. Rarely do secrets pay out!"**

Many of the comforts you enjoy today are built on not speaking up, keeping quiet and remaining anonymous. This is OK, and in society it is necessary some of the time. However the truth is that you simply cannot have what you want, nor can you progress past where you currently are, if you are not prepared to speak up, take action and let people know what you are doing. Being a secret network marketing agent may protect your self-image for a time if that is what truly matters to you.

There will however be a price to pay in the long-term as your enemy closes in. He's called failure, he is relentless and he doesn't care about your reasons, circumstances, excuses or what you think you know or don't know. He comes for us all and can only be prevented if you are prepared to speak up and take action.

Network marketing is 'the great revealer' of people. It will shine a torch so brightly on you and let you know if you are truly ready for success. It will let you know whether you simply 'want more' or truly 'deserve more'.

If a secret business is what you have, or intend to have, and you choose to keep it from your friends, family and people you know and love, this may help you to avoid the 'I told you so' or the indecisive, negative nature of people or to avoid people telling you 'no' and the good old-fashioned dream stealers. It will however reveal you to 'yourself'. It will highlight your true desire for a better life and let you know if you are ready to take control.

SO ... are you ready for success? Or do you just want people to think you are?

Either way, right here, right now we will find out! If like so many people you are seeking damage limitation, it is simply not going to work for you in this business, or any business. After all, James Bond didn't win without kicking some butt and everybody, including his enemies, knew his name. He was the (non) secret agent, and he always won!

Like the greatest secret agent of all time, you are an anti-hero. You are here to do good things, you are here to help and protect people. However, like all anti-heroes, you must accept that some people will misunderstand you, run away from you, disagree with you, some may even try to stop you. This does not change your most important mission; it's called 'success'.

All missions in life are designed to challenge us; nature doesn't pave the way for success. You have to clear your own path. It starts with the first step of announcing to the world what you are doing and why you are doing it.

You have a licence to succeed. Use it!

CHAPTER 25

THOSE WHO CAN!

You will develop a profound awareness of the different personality types on your network marketing journey. This can be a useful attribute when learning how to deal with certain prospects and distributors and people in general. In business, I like to keep things simple. I have always worked on 2 personality types:

The 'can' and the 'can't' people.

There are very few spontaneous people left in the world. Nothing reveals this more than network marketing. One's ability to think freely and make a decision that can be of benefit long-term, and then following through with it, is becoming a lost attribute for so many. 'Can' seems to be a word of the past, while 'can't' appears to be the order of the day. 'Can' is a great word, it fixes things, while 'can't' generally keeps things as they are. This is why we see so many broken people who are stuck in a rut. You will know some of these people, some may even be your friends! 'Can't' is much easier, it requires zero effort, commitment or contribution, while 'can' requires some sort of sacrifice. The exciting thing about 'can' is that it opens up a world of possibilities, sometimes beyond your wildest imagination. It can lead you to places you never could have expected! Many of the choices you make over the course of a lifetime will boil down to a 'can' or 'can't' decision.

> **"Choose caution though, because as long as you only do the things that you want, it is unlikely that you will ever get what you want!"**

We are all guilty of not wanting to do the things we should be doing from time to time, and we are all guilty of backing out on occasion when we should have been there. We want to deal with the urgent over the important, the easy over the hard, the exciting over the not so exciting. We obsess over what needs to be done today and not what will benefit us three years down the line. It's how you treat your decision making that affects your future. There is a difference between not doing something because it's logistically impossible, or simply because it's not important enough to you.

For the 'can' people amongst us, it means more risk and more sacrifice. Occasionally it means doing things we don't really want to do. It means recognising that we can gain and profit from a 'can' decision, while possessing some fear of what we may lose from a 'can't' decision.

Here is the punchline. It's unlikely that you will lose anything immediately or suffer in the short-term from a 'can't' decision. That's why it's so easy! You are more likely to lose out long-term with 'can't' decisions, but then that is the nature of people. Many people don't see past the end of the month, this puts awareness of long-term benefit way off the radar. Many people would rather not risk losing or would prefer not to exert too much effort, failing to see that the chance of success is far better than the chance of failure. Some people are crippled by uncertainty and doubt. If we knew 100% that a 'can' decision would benefit us, then we would do it, every day of the week! Consider the 'can' and 'can't' stories you are telling yourself each day! Which way do you sway?

You will often hear distributors in this industry saying that they can't attend an event or that they can't speak to people and that they can't recruit. This is less to do with their circumstances, fear, or the logistics of it, and more about not understanding its value. Turning 'can't' into 'can' is largely about educating people. That's why it is important for you to be coachable and to find people who are coachable.

People are more likely to make a 'can' decision when it's fun or entertaining or something they enjoy. Something they are familiar with and that is well within their comfort zone or something they see a value in. 'Can' decisions are much easier when they involve losing or spending money as opposed to making it. That's why we have fewer wealthy people. The easy choices are way more popular for far too many people, and it's the easy choices which keep people from living the life of their dreams. It is important to recognise that most people will make 'can't' decisions most of the time. The people who are making the 'can' decisions most of the time are called your future leadership. The same goes for you, watch your words because people are listening.

The 'can't' people who you encounter will remain this way unless they plug into personal development and develop a profound sense of self-awareness. If they don't, there is not a lot you can do to help them.

Give the 'can' people most of your time, they are the ones who will keep you uplifted, the ones who may surprise you. These are the people you need to spend the most time with. 'Can't' people will rarely surprise you, they will remain predictable in the things they say and the choices they make. They will continue to use their circumstances as a reason for their decisions, trying to convince you of:

- **The time they don't think they have.**
- **The projects and other stuff they think they have going on.**
- **Their head which isn't in the right place.**

People can be so sold into their own stories that they begin to believe it themselves. Take a look on social media and observe the activities of the people who say they can't. Most of the time you will see that there are no circumstances that would prevent them from working the business they originally decided to join. Please understand that this is a trend and does not apply to everybody. We all have things going on in our lives. You wouldn't believe the adversity that I have seen overcome by people walking across the stage in this industry. I once had the pleasure of recognising a lady in our business who, despite nursing 2 parents with dementia, raising 2 teenage daughters and running a traditional business, hit the first rank in our compensation plan in just a few months.

Achievement in all forms is a result of what can be done, not what can't. Think about all the things you have achieved since you were a child. Certificates, awards, grades acquired and other accolades. You didn't achieve them because of a 'can't' decision! You achieved them because you are a 'can' person. I know this because you are reading this book.

A 'can't' decision is often a 'defence mechanism' that kicks in when we are required or asked to do something that has no emotional value at the time. It is not a priority or may take us out of our comfort zone. Maybe we are not getting paid for it at the time. To us, it holds no value. They are the things that we put to the bottom of the pile. These things we ignore are cruelly disguised as 'inconvenient', yet they are often the things that can bring us long-term happiness and success.

Our role as network marketers is to help people believe that they can achieve more, that they can step outside of their comfort zone. 'Can't' is not an absolute, it's not real. It translates to 'I won't because I don't believe it' or 'it's just not that important to me'. You must become a 'can' person and find like-minded 'can' people to work with, if you are going to succeed in this business!

CHAPTER 26

A HALLMARK OF SUCCESSFUL PEOPLE

Have you ever noticed how successful people in network marketing are generally very good at acknowledging and edifying other's greatness and achievements. This is not a coincidence; it is actually a skill and a mindset that can pay you lots of money. It is also a 'noble and respected' act that has more impact than you may realise.

How often do you hear people 'bigging up' their boss, singing their praises, listing their achievements or telling their story to their friends? You don't. So when you introduce a new distributor into your business, or if you are new to the business, it may seem strange promoting your upline sponsor or mentor to people that you know.

> **"Edification is a hugely important skill in the network marketing industry and often goes ignored."**

You need to know how to correctly edify your upline or the 'expert' within your business. It may seem like a simple task, but many people struggle with this. Knowing how to edify somebody properly is key because if you don't, connecting your prospect or potential new distributor to an expert or your support line may be difficult. You may have a prospect only wanting to work with you, which may not give your prospect the best start if you are not experienced enough to get a new distributor started!

Edification is simply the art of saying something good or praising someone else. You should get to know their stories, because stories sell! The process of saying something positive about your upline, down line, cross-line, network marketing company, or our industry is fundamental. This is a hallmark of successful people in the network marketing profession.

Get to know the experts in your business and their stories before choosing the attributes you want to use. Talk to them first, if they are a close personal friend this may be easier.

Here are some attributes that you may wish to include in your edification, the highlighted ones are those that I like to use regularly:

- **Committed**
- Knowledgeable
- Top Performer
- **Has Vision**
- Top Earner
- Leader
- **Passionate**

You are more than likely working with your upline, sponsor, mentor or an expert in your business, if you are not then you should be. Simply get better at telling your prospects a few good things about this person. This usually works best after you have presented your business to them and they have shown a level of interest.

Obviously, you want to be honest and not make things up. You want to say nice things that position your mentor as the authority, or as a successful distributor. Respect between your prospective new distributor and your support line is important.

If you are working with your down line distributors, you want to do the same thing. That means that if you are the expert doing a three-way call with your down line and their prospect, you tell the prospect something nice about their potential sponsor or friend.

Edification works very well as a bridging exposure. For example, if you have shown your third party tools or a presentation video to a prospect, and they are interested in taking a second look, they may want to go to a meeting that could be a week away.

Getting them to speak to an expert first is a fantastic exposure to the business, which you have more control over as interest by your prospect can soon be lost.

For many people, the thought of saying something good about another individual might be unusual. We are often surrounded by a vacuum of negativity where people generally don't have anything nice to say about the other person.

Many people have never edified someone before and it can seem foreign to them. It is not a skill that people generally get paid for.
Edification is something you have done all your life without realising and it should not be seen as a new skill relating solely to network marketing. It's nothing more than telling somebody's story to somebody you know, which can lead to a connection.

As an example, I was telling my friend all about my new gardener, his story, how skillful he was and how he took pride in my garden. As a result my friend is now using his services, but I am not getting paid. So I am recommending somebody's services while edifying them by telling their story.

In your network marketing business, edification pays!

CHAPTER 27

RECOGNITION IS A POWERFUL SOCIAL CURRENCY

If I had to say "congratulations & well done" 50,000 times, it would be worth it!

In a world where you are loyal to a company for 40 years and then recognised at the end with a pat on the back and a pen, with little recognition or notice for your efforts in between, one of the things people crave most, besides wealth and time, is 'recognition'.

One of the other hallmarks of our industry is recognising achievement, not just on the world stage with cheques, holidays and cars but on a social level, recognising the smaller steps that distributors take. Their first customer, or qualifying their position, getting their initial investment back or introducing a new team member.

Recognising team members who have brought guests and team members to an event in larger numbers is a great way to promote the importance of events. You can recognise almost anything, it's so easy and so powerful. I even show my appreciation for team members who show up and are visible at an event or meeting despite adversity and odds, where many people would fall into witness protection and vanish.

Here is a thought for you:

> **"When you sponsor a new team member, make sure everybody knows who they are. Getting them to an event and plugged into social media can be very effective in doing this."**

In my experience, people who are known within an organisation seem to be doing ok! One of the best pieces of advice for keeping a distributor in your business is to elevate them quickly so that they become a recognisable face, recognised by the team.

Recognition is a powerful social currency, which if used correctly can form a positive culture in your team, leading to long-term wealth and success for everybody.

CHAPTER 28

HOW IS YOUR NETWORK MARKETING DIET GOING?

I often laugh when I listen to my personal trainer, friends and colleagues. The vast wealth of dietary and workout advice they give me can often be overwhelming and sometimes conflicting, however they are all still united with one piece of advice, move more and eat better. So even when we are faced with a vast amount of information and content given to us through meetings, trainings, events, books, audio and speakers, we can all agree on one thing, our network marketing diet needs to change.

> **"Do more presentations each week, call them workouts (at least 3 a week) and have a better social diet in the form of the associations and people you surround yourself with."**

One thing we can all agree on is that a simple change in your network marketing diet can create a healthier-looking business. Garbage in, garbage out as they say, and without those 3 workouts a week and a better diet, your health will suffer, as will the health of your business.

Your mind is like a sponge and in a business which is 20% skill and 80% mindset, certainly in the early stages of your network marketing career, you need to 'err on the side of caution' when it comes to what you let inside your head. The books you read, the company you keep, the media you view and the advice you choose to take. All these play a key part in keeping you either on the success curve or the failure curve. Your mind is no different to your body. You need to respect it and what you feed it if you wish it to remain healthy.

I like a pizza and a stupid movie every so often. I will even admit to the vice of video games. This form of pleasure and entertainment however only plays a small part in my life and is vastly superseded by the personal development I engage in, the company I keep and the conversations I choose to have.

Awareness of your social input is critical and something you can fix quickly. Do this and you will start to see a noticeable result.

They say that being healthy starts in the kitchen. If that is true, and I believe it is, then your network marketing diet should be prepared in the meeting room or the convention centre with all the other students in your organisation who are willing to learn.

CHAPTER 29

BE A PLAYER NOT A SPECTATOR

A spectator sport is a sport that can be watched by spectators for a fee. In this life you will always get the most, 'the spectators', watching the few, 'the players', out there doing the work, getting the recognition and making the money.

So why do so many people who join our amazing profession, pay their entrance fee, turn up and watch other people playing the game, while they sit there often in admiration or envy for a while, before eventually fizzling out or leaving the arena, so to speak?

With network marketing, unlike all spectator sports, it's so easy to come down from the stands and join in with the players. Imagine paying your entrance fee to a football game and just being allowed to come right onto the pitch and start playing, well you can do that in this business, you just have to make the decision. The choice doesn't rest with a talent agent or a manager, the choice is yours.

Yes you might be on the bench for a while and not be making as much as the others, you may even get sent off from time to time when you have a bad moment. The important thing to remember is that you are a player and not a spectator.

> **"Make sure people know who you are, make sure they know your name, because people who are known are usually doing OK."**

Finally, never feel guilty, because in being a player you can bring joy and happiness to thousands of people while increasing your value in the market place and actually get paid what you are worth and not what somebody else thinks you are worth.

CHAPTER 30

DO YOU HAVE THE X-FACTOR?

I have never been a fan of reality TV shows, due to the fact that they don't truly depict reality or the real world, a place where I am truly happy to be and you can be too once you learn to master your environment. If you are one of the few people who are not familiar with the 'X – Factor', it's a show that runs for several months in the year where thousands of hopefuls compete in a musical talent show to win a £1 million recording contract.

As you would expect with a show of this nature, most of the competitors don't make the grade, drop out, fail in their quest and fade into the distance never to be seen again. A few do a little bit better, get some recognition, and even make some money as a result. A handful go on and do something special, make a record or fall into some other celebrity role, with one winner receiving a £1 million contract.

The mentors on this show, despite working with thousands of individuals, only end up with one superstar and a handful of talent each year. The same can usually be said for any network marketing business. So when it comes to your network marketing business, the objective is to show and give the opportunity to lots of people with the objective of finding a few who will be responsible for most of the commission you earn.

You may be thinking one of two things at this point. Either, I need to find some superstars, in which case congratulations you understand this business, or you will be thinking, the chances are that you will fail or have mediocre success at this business. If this is the case, then this will most likely be the outcome for you unless you work on your mindset. As you are taking the time to read this book, let's assume you are working on that right now.

People who don't understand our business don't realise that most drama students never make money in acting, most music students don't make money in music, most people who study business are not successful in business, most people who start piano lessons quit and don't make a successful career as a pianist, most people who train as a personal trainer are not successful. In fact, the money that these groups invest in their chosen venture is rarely recouped nor is any profit made as a result of that same venture.

"The good news for you is that you don't need the X-factor to get into profit or make money in this business."

You don't need to have the X-factor to quit your job and retire before your friends. You don't need a million pounds to retire. If you simply worked half as hard on your network marketing business as you do in your job, you could have more success than you imagined.

CHAPTER 31

DON'T PLAY THE LOTTERY WITH YOUR BUSINESS!

The lottery is a voluntary tax for the mathematically challenged and most of us are guilty of subscribing to this at some point. For the vast majority who participate, the purchasing of a lottery ticket will at least buy hope for another week. The hope of a large instant payout which will solve all their problems, because acquiring wealth by any other means seems impossible or off the radar.

Why would you rest your future happiness and security on the hope of a big payout, when statistically you stand more chance of acquiring wealth and success through your network marketing business? The very best lottery ticket you can purchase is the ticket to your next company convention. The likelihood is that at a single event during your network marketing career, you will receive the breakthrough moment that allows you to take your business to the next level. That's much more likely than your lottery numbers coming up.

> **"Every successful person in network marketing has had a single defining moment in their career. That moment has usually taken place at a key company event that had they otherwise missed, they may not have acquired the level of success that they have now."**

Missing an event is like an actor missing an audition, the budding entrepreneur missing the meeting to demonstrate their idea or not taking the call that could change your life. Perhaps deciding not to go to the party where you would meet your future wife or husband. In essence, another missed opportunity. When it comes to attending events in the network marketing profession, we often see the mindset that it doesn't matter, or it doesn't apply to me, or for many, it is having the coin-operated mindset that you are giving up your time for free for something that isn't going to pay you.

In fact, in most instances, company events will cost you, so you adopt the thinking that you are paying out money not to get paid. If you don't invest in yourself you massively limit your earning potential. How much of the money you currently earn actually goes on improving yourself physically and mentally? Add that figure up, what percentage of your salary is it?

Failure in your network marketing business is largely down to the simple things you don't do. Those things that are keeping you on the failure curve, a silent but deadly pathway.

Things will change for you at an event. It may not be at your first, or even after your fiftieth but it will happen at an event and many of the 6 and 7 figure millionaire earners I know in this business would agree with me.

If you don't buy the ticket, you can't be in with a chance when it comes to your business.

CHAPTER 32

THE TRIO OF EXCUSES

We have all done it, we are all guilty. We reach for excuses like a soldier reaches for the sword. The second we are challenged it is there in our armoury. We are so good at it that we don't even need to think about it. Making excuses becomes the instinctive habit that keeps us on the failure curve. It is important to understand that excuses are not always lies. Often they are reasons. However, if the reason is not greater than the requirement, what you have, ladies and gentlemen, is an excuse.

Excuses usually fall into three categories and are often used to seek or lessen the blame attaching to a fault or offence, or used simply to try to justify an action or lack of action. The trio of excuses are:

- **Health**
- **Time**
- **Family**

The interesting thing about these excuses is that your network marketing business provides you with a vehicle to pay you during ill health, and to free up your time as discussed previously. It can also provide a legacy for your family and extra long-term security. What is more important than these things?

> **"The trio of excuses should be the reasons that you are doing this business, NOT to provide you with 'go to' excuses when you decide you don't want to play."**

We are human. We will all get sick at some point and time will never be our friend and family issues will always arise. These are natural milestones of life. You have to weigh up whether you are going to be driven by the need to improve and support these things, or use them as a destructive force and contribute to their deterioration.

Simply being aware of this idea will keep you on the success curve more often and keep you conscious of when excuses are unacceptable, and of course justified.

Ultimately your reasons and your why power for doing this business will determine the parameters for your excuses, and in the end, your success! Your belief in this business can work for you and will carry you through the need to make any excuses.

Whatever you are trying to avoid will often pay you in the long-term if you stick with it!

CHAPTER 33

YOU ALWAYS HAVE THE TIME!

I just don't have the time!" How many times have we all heard that excuse? I like to call it the 'go to' excuse. A means to quickly removing ourselves from any form of commitment or decision making.

When it comes to time, the thing to remember is that we are all allocated 24 hours in a day. It's how we choose to use that time and prioritise the activities contained within it with respect to their importance. It is also worth understanding that the very things we choose to prioritise may well be the very things that are causing us to tread further into worrying financial times. While the things we choose to abandon and avoid, the money making activities, could be the very things that can protect us from what we fear most.

> **"We have 168 hours in a week, we generally work for 50 hours, sleep for 40 hours and spend 30 hours socialising with friends and family, this will naturally vary from person to person. That's 120 hours allocated, leaving 48 hours a week to do something productive."**

Here lies the problem. For most people this non-allocated time is spent either losing or spending money or making somebody else money, with zero time dedicated to the activities which build our own wealth.

So why do we have this mentality? Activities involving spending and losing money are easy, as we have previously discussed. Making other people money is easy. Money making activities for ourselves are perceived as hard because they will generally take us out of our comfort zone. This highlights the point that people generally choose comfort over freedom. It is that simple!

This wonderful gift we have, our network marketing business, actually asks very little of your time compared to your job, a traditional business or franchise, especially considering how we can be rewarded with time and financial freedom.

If you were making a minimum of 3 presentations each week, showing your opportunity and service or product, which is the main money making activity, how much of your weekly 48 free hours would that eat into? If you had to do a weekly conference call or webinar for 30 minutes each week, how much of your 48 free hours would that eat into? If you had to attend three big company events each year, how much of your 48 hours a week would that eat into?

Let's get to grips with where your time goes and how it's being used. We have a gift; let's stop killing it with time excuses!

CHAPTER 34

USE DEAD TIME EFFICIENTLY

"My father always said that boredom was a sign of a lack of inner resourcefulness." I always get excited when I watch a TV show that throws out a great quote that resonates with me and yes, I am a fan of 'Game of Thrones', which is where I found this little nugget.

Another great quote I found in the TV show 'Sons of Anarchy' was, "People don't really want freedom, they want to be comfortable." Brilliant and true.

So how can we acquire this inner resourcefulness?

As I lay incapacitated one day from a sickness bug I had acquired, I realised that I was in what's called 'dead time', time where otherwise you can't do anything productive, or can you?

> **"The one thing you can do when all other actions seem impossible is feed the mind. The mind is a powerful thing."**

If you call in sick when you are not, your mind will start believing that it's true and nothing productive will get done and your mind becomes consumed by guilt.

As I lay sick I couldn't feed my stomach, I needed some positive input. So I flipped up the laptop, fired up YouTube and for 3 hours I listened to Zig Ziglar and his power of motivation collection and no word of a lie, that evening I felt well. The next morning I was up and bouncing around. The key message here is to use dead time, time when you are likely to be bored or you can't do anything else. Use this time to feed the mind.

Personal development, self-help and the power of motivation, call it what you will, is just so foreign to 97% of people and that's OK. The power of self-improvement and motivation may seem strange to people who have been raised in a household or worked in an environment where you just don't see or hear the term 'personal development'.

Consider this when you introduce a new team member and you are throwing all the books, resources and events at them in the first 24 hours of them joining. Don't worry, they will grow into it once they are plugged in. A little personal development, a good book and a meeting/convention yes, but don't get too carried away as they may become overwhelmed.

CHAPTER 35

COFFEE & CAKE

I remember many years ago complaining to a mentor of mine that too many distributors were attending all the meetings, trainings and events, however their businesses were remaining stagnant and they were doing nothing. They were all 'talking the talk' but had introduced no new customers and no new team members.

He told me, in his wisdom, that many of these distributors had turned their businesses into a club. A 'social club', or more eloquently, a 'coffee and cake club'.

This may appear humorous and somewhat absurd, however it can be damaging.

This happens when distributors have fallen out of love with their businesses but they are still in love with the people. The problem is, time will eventually expose you and you will get left behind by those distributors who are progressing with their businesses.

It's important for you to make a choice! Either you are a part of the business or you are not. There is much more respect and fulfilment in choosing another path where you can progress and be truly happy.

As an active and, more importantly, new distributor it is essential to protect yourself from the people within this group. Association is everything, as you will inherit the habits of those you spend the most time with.

This problem is not exclusive to the professional world of network marketing.

> **"Pockets of negativity and distraction exist in all social, business and educational institutions and they will distract you from your objective and place you swiftly on the failure curve."**

Getting in with the 'wrong crowd' at school is a primary example of how detrimental this can be. Your philosophy needs to be correct. You are here to build a business, to help people and to strengthen relationships. Strike the balance between money making and non-money making activity and know what the difference is.

This is a culture that you want to drive into your team. Understand 'the fundamental laws' of network marketing and apply them. Find people who are 'walking the walk'. Seek out a mentor and allow these people to influence your decisions and steer you towards success. Attend the same meetings, join in and participate.

Find five key people in your organisation and introduce yourself to them, making sure they know your name, what your goals are and your success plan.

CHAPTER 36

WHILE THE CAT IS AWAY THE MOUSE WILL PAY!

There is an expression that I have heard a number of top network marketing professionals use. 'When you go on holiday, your team goes on holiday'. One way I can spot a potential leader is by observing the distributors who continue to work while I rest. The team members who continue to take action, even when I have gone on holiday.

> **"In the early stages of building your business, it is key that you dissolve the 'employee mindset'. You are NOT being paid for your time you are paid on your ACTIVITY."**

'Taking a break' because your upline leader has will be a costly affair for you and will simply expose you as the team member less deserving of support.

It is your responsibility to earn continued support and 'one-to-one' attention from your upline. You do this by demonstrating consistent and persistent activity and the willingness to join in and participate, irrespective of your upline leader's presence.

Your leader will always be working with multiple people. Be active in letting them know you are doing the work. Stand out rather than blend in! Earn the attention, rather than feel it is your right to have it.

The term 'independent distributor' is the clue to your role. Resting when your team rests makes you a follower, not a leader, and certainly not somebody who is assuming the title of an 'independent distributor'.

Your ability to become independent and help others to become independent is key to having a duplicating business. Continuing to work when your upline is away demonstrates your ability to be independent, while at the same time shows your potential as a future leader.

CHAPTER 37

QUALITY & QUANTITY

A number of years ago I had the great fortune of being on our company cruise. It was an incentive prize for recognition of hard work. I remember one evening being in the 'cigar lounge' drinking some cognac with some of my colleagues, sharing stories and ideas regarding our profession.

When the serious conversation had concluded, we somehow began playing a new kind of game. It was called 'your ideal team'. The idea was that you could pick five, and only five, key figures from history, politics and entertainment, including fictional characters, to be on your team. These would be your first five front line distributors. The individuals who you would go out and recruit quickly, before somebody else did. The idea from there was to debate on who would build the biggest team.

What started out as fun, soon turned into a serious yet friendly debate. Despite our different choices in our team members, we were all united and agreed on the types of characteristics we were looking for. Let me share with you my five:

- **Ghandi**
- **Mark Zuckerberg**
- **Mother Teresa**
- **Martin Luther King**
- **Bono**

With honourable mentions going to:

- **Oprah Winfrey**
- **Walt Disney**

It is important to mention at this stage that we should leave aside all personal and political views on these people and explore the attributes that would make them great network marketers.

What attributes do they all have?

Influence over many, a powerful voice and they are all incredibly passionate about something. Ordinarily, you will meet very few people with all these attributes, certainly not on this scale. However, if this exercise has taught us anything, it is that we should be looking for quality prospects who have the attributes to be successful in this business.

Here is the catch. You are going to have to recruit lots of people to find five team members who have all these attributes. Many of the top network marketing professionals in the world were not born great, they were not rock stars or leaders when they got involved. They became great, they just had it within them and they worked tirelessly and recruited lots of people.

> **"You can try to predict who will be great, who will be average and who will fail and often you will be wrong. You can only be conscious of what you are looking for in your team members, and teach people the attributes they need to be successful in this business."**

This business is about getting lots of people to do a little bit and bringing as many of them as possible through as leaders. Not everybody has leadership quality. Some people prefer to follow and that's OK. They are no less deserving of our support, but consider how your time is spent.

CHAPTER 38

IT SHOULD ALWAYS BE BETTER!

We don't like to be challenged by others regarding our efforts and results. Yet internally, we know that we are capable of so much more.

There is the story that we all tell ourselves and the story we tell others. Why is it OK for us to have the inner knowledge that we played small and maybe didn't do our best? Yet we scoff at other people when they tell us what we already know. That, indeed, we could have done better!

> **"Do you really feel better when you perform poorly and others tell you, 'it could have been worse'? No, of course not. The comforting words of those who know you can do more damage long-term than you may realise."**

Here is where association is key. The natural tendency is to seek friendship and comfort from those who are lesser or equal to ourselves, because we are less likely to be challenged by this audience. Whilst those we look up to, who really want to see us succeed, are more likely to 'hit us with the truth'.

The truth only stings for a moment but it will put you on the right path. Lies and words of comfort may lessen the blow in the short-term but will keep you forever lost and on a road to nowhere.

Aim high, be your own biggest critic. Know that no matter how badly you have done or how fantastic you have been in achieving something, you can always improve. Don't justify your result by comparing it to worse or lesser outcomes. Compare it to the greatest outcome possible and allow others to share in this belief. Be humble with the compliments you get but welcome positive and constructive criticism by those people who know you are capable of more.

This is NOT easy and it takes time to adapt to this mindset. Especially when you believe in your own mind that you have done the best you can.

Avoid 'trying' and 'hoping'. These are non-committal words. It's announcing that failure is an option. Remember earlier chapters. Failure is a mistaught concept and only occurs when you give up and not when you receive a negative outcome. This is 'loser language'. Commit to success and being the best. It's a much more fun journey, even if you don't get the outcome you had been expecting. Goals are only set in sand and not in stone!

When you announce to the world that you will 'try', what you are really saying is, I hear YOU, but expect me to fail. When you say you 'hope', what you are really saying is that I have no control of the outcome and I will leave it to fate and chance to deliver me a positive outcome.

Fate and chance don't often swing in our favour and we are far more likely to achieve success if we stay in control of our own actions and commit to success.

Commit to the best possible outcome!

CHAPTER 39

EMBRACE THE PYRAMID

The single biggest misconception of our business is the confusion between a 'network marketing opportunity' and a 'pyramid scheme' or 'pyramid selling'.

I have learned to enjoy helping people to understand this misconception. You should too!

It is important to understand that what you know and what you tell your prospects are two different things. It is also crucial to understand that it is NOT the stupidity of our prospects or the people we speak to that has created this misconception. This can all usually be avoided if you present your opportunity correctly, ethically and with the correct training.

Many industries damage themselves by the way they behave from time to time. The unprofessional methods that a few network marketers have used to recruit and 'hunt' people have, over time, confused the minority about what our opportunity really is.

You may have experienced this yourself. I know I have, and still do! Fortunately, we have the power to change public perception by being a generation of professional network marketers who present our opportunity correctly. We also need to train the next generation of network marketers to do the same.

You should firstly know that a network marketing business in many ways least resembles a 'pyramid scheme' compared to a traditional business and organisation model, and the same goes for most government and corporate entities. A pyramid has always been considered a strong shape and society by its very nature will always have fewer people at the top of any organisation earning more money, with more people earning less money the further down that organisation you go. Each person is usually placed where they are in the organisation because of the life choices, decisions and, in many cases, the sacrifices they made to get them there. You should immediately ignore the perceived belief that people have been placed where they are because of their circumstances. I know this can be a tough pill to swallow!

> **"You should never disrespect or belittle your prospect if challenged on this matter. To defend your position by undermining them is distasteful and unprofessional."**

So what do we tell our prospects should they challenge us on the Pyramid question. Do try to see it as a question rather than an objection.

On the rare occasion that somebody challenges you regarding 'The Pyramid', you should not get defensive. Promote and compliment their inquisitive mind and find out what they know! Never defend your position.

Never alienate a prospect or try to make them feel stupid because they are misinformed. We are in the business of educating people. If they challenge you, or ask you if it is a 'pyramid thing', the likelihood of them signing on the spot first time is low.

So you can either leave feeling great that you have educated somebody, planted a seed and kept them in your pipeline. Or you can shoot them down where they stand, be defensive and lose them forever. When challenged, simply say:

"Tell me what you know about pyramid schemes?"

Let them educate you! It will usually be a misguided, poorly constructed explanation proclaiming that:

"It's one of those things where all the people 'at the top' make all the money."

Then ask for permission:

"Would it be OK if I explained the difference between a network marketing opportunity and a pyramid scheme?"

Ask them:

*"**Would you agree that we have a great product or service?**"*

It is important to remember that a pyramid scheme, unlike network marketing, has:

- **No product or service or customer base.**
- **It is illegal.**
- **No possibility of overtaking your sponsor.**

An interesting fact for you. Most, if not all, people will not realise that a pyramid scheme is actually illegal, so by confirming this for them, it will reinforce your authenticity.

It is also important to realise what '*at the top*' means, when a prospect says this.

To most people, the individual at the top of their organisation, workplace or corporation makes the most money. So with our business, if 'at the top' means those with the biggest businesses, then of course they make the most money, but not 'all the money'. This is all learned behaviour and it's not the prospect being 'mean' or 'awkward'.

> **"The people 'at the top' do make the most money because they have worked harder for a longer period of time. They have been to more events and have had more rejection. It's that simple!"**

If a prospect is suggesting that '*at the top*' means that the people who '*got in first*' make all the money, then this is very misguided. This is another huge misconception.

> **"People who joined the business first are not necessarily at the top of the compensation plan."**

There are many people who joined network marketing businesses 20 years ago making less money than someone who joined a year ago. Why? Simply because we work on a 'performance related pay' model which, in this new economy, is the way that the rest of the world is going.

We are just waiting for them to catch up with us.

CHAPTER 40

TOOLS & WEAPONS

As social media has gripped the world in the last decade, and with the increase in smart phones and apps, there are even more tools at our disposal to help us grow our business.

As wonderful as they are, they can be somewhat overwhelming, particularly if you are from a generation of 'old school' network marketing, where you had to call somebody's landline and have a conversation to connect with them.

I use social media as a daily tool for personal development, giving me access to content and information to help me grow personally. You do need to be careful, as misuse of social media can soon turn it into a weapon, which can be detrimental to you and your business, your organisation and the profession as a whole if used incorrectly. Remember how we discussed misconceptions being created in earlier chapters. Poor use of social media has been a contributing factor to this.

Facebook, the leading social media tool, is an excellent platform to connect with new people, build relationships and grow your list. Primarily, it should be used to tell the 'story of your life', to create curiosity in a positive and indirect way. It is important to be indirect and brand yourself rather than decorating your online profile with information about your company and the services and products it has to offer. This is a common mistake made by many. The key is to create curiosity, not eliminate it altogether. Why? To get people asking you questions and taking an interest. Call it 'lead generation'. People are obsessed with other people's lives on social media. One of the first things they do when they wake up in the morning is log on to see what you are up to. The first thing they do when the plane lands is log on to see what you are up to. This is not a healthy habit, but one you can capitalise on.

Social media is a platform that enables you to be watched 24 hours a day. We have spoken many times on the significance of 'events'. Your social media profile is a daily event hosted by you! Everybody you know will be in attendance each day at some point. Social media is your stage, yet some people behave like nobody is watching. Does what you are putting out there match what you would be prepared to share with a live audience?

How useful it would be if people came to you! You have to be thoughtful and anticipatory with your social media. It takes work and planning. It's about having good, informative information on your profile. Something that may resonate with people. What you think people want to see and what they actually want to see can be two different things. We are all guilty of this! Passive marketing in this way is OK. It takes a while to build up, however it should not be a substitute for active prospecting in the field, which is the main money producing activity. This is required to build and grow your business.

Facebook is a great tool for connecting and growing your list on a daily basis but you are going to need to build and grow your relationships outside of cyberspace at some point. While there are some network marketers, and some good friends of mine, who have built large organisations off the back of social media, they are in the minority and they are highly skillful. This should not be relied upon and you shouldn't wait around for social media to make you your fortune. The problem is that most people think they are great on social media, blind to the fact that they are alienating people and crippling their ability to build an income.

Look at your own and your team members Facebook profiles and ask yourself, 'would I join this person or am I even interested or curious about what this person is doing'? For most distributors, 90% or more of their 'hot and warm market' will be on Facebook, so look at your team members who are not recruiting and look at their Facebook profiles, there will almost certainly be a connection.

> **"Misuse of social media will dilute your own company's opportunity in time and make it harder and harder for newer distributors to introduce new team members."**

One thing you have to be aware of is poor social media prospecting skills. If you are lazy you will have people running from your business opportunity. Spamming people with links to your opportunity privately or publically, without inviting them personally or without establishing a rapport, is one sure way to do this. It will also give you, and more importantly the profession of network marketing, a bad name. It will also dilute your own company's opportunity, as this poor culture will spread quickly. Do you really want everybody knowing about your business before you get a chance to speak with them? Intrigue and curiosity in your opportunity can soon be lost and this can saturate some businesses.

There are distributors using social media ethically and to positive effect and passing this down through the culture of their business. Make sure you are part of this culture.

There is a good chance you have been prospected poorly by individuals on social media before. As your business grows it will happen more and more as people take an interest in you. Our first gut instinct is either to lose our temper, block or delete people. Remember that these are people who have simply not been taught the correct way; they are hurting, so try reverse prospecting. Simply ask them:

"How is that method of prospecting working out for you? Would you be interested in some coaching and mentoring? If so I have something I would love you to take a look at. Would you be open to this?"

Turning this negative into a positive will be uplifting for you even if it doesn't result in a successful sign up.

CHAPTER 41

READY, STEADY...NO!!!!

Did you realise that nobody really says no? It's more like 'Yes' or something else. A set of pre-defined excuses we have designed over the years to avoid making a decision. It's true. People make decisions based on emotion, so if they are not connected emotionally to the idea of your opportunity or product, it will be 'something else'.

Do you want to know the cool part? Firstly, to do this, you have to let go of the conventional teachings that failure is instant, as we have discussed previously.

Imagine you show 100 people your business opportunity over a period of time, and as a result you successfully recruit 10. That means that 90 of those people haven't joined your business immediately, either because they are currently not emotionally connected to it or because there is another reason.

Furthermore, out of those 90 people, how many over the next few years are going to find themselves looking for work, needing extra income or will experience some sort of major life or emotional shift? Most likely, all of them. That is 90 seeds that have been planted. The untrained mind sees that as 90 failures. In fact, the individual with that traditional mindset would most likely not make it to the point of showing 100 people, they would have quit way earlier.

Which are you? Would you make it to 100?

The entrepreneurial mindset would have fun with it, safe in the knowledge that their future pipeline is filling nicely because they have simply shown 100 people their opportunity. They are aware that 90 seeds are still planted. Some will grow and blossom, even though many may never surface.

Interestingly, a presentation usually takes about 10 minutes, which equates to about 16 hours of presentation time. That's not actually a week's worth of work if you use solid working hours. Simply by showing your third party tool, video or presentation to your family, friends and people you meet and build a rapport with.

Take those same 90 people. How many of those people are going to put on weight, age, deteriorate in health, require some form of insurance or legal protection, travel or have a dispute with their utility provider? Most likely, all of them. So while at the present time they may not emotionally connect with, need, require or in fact want your service or product, there will come a time when they need you!

In this business, that's a great position to be in.

> **"Don't be so quick to accept failure as an instant 'NO' experience."**

Consider five years down the line, not the end of the presentation. The pre-defined answers given by people who do not currently want your product, service or opportunity are a result of programming and should not be taken personally. That programming will change as time moves forward.

In the meantime, you just carry on telling the world about what you have to offer!

CHAPTER 42

HOW DO YOU LOOK?

For the last few years I have regularly visited a chiropractor, just to keep my body in check and ensure that everything is working fine mechanically. When I first started to experience neck and back problems, I was told by a professional that one of the reasons I was experiencing pain and discomfort was that I had poor posture. I did not like the sound of that! I was never aware of it and for a long time I hadn't felt any pain or discomfort. Apparently this was caused by remaining in the same position 'incorrectly' for too long. This was a bad habit of mine and it needed fixing. I was told that with regular movement, corrections and raised self-awareness, my posture would soon correct itself and reduce the risk of long-term issues.

Good posture to me had always been a physical concern. However being involved in network marketing over the years has taught me that good posture and how you carry yourself is vitally important to creating long-term success. Your physical body language and posture can tell a story that reveals your confidence, your belief in what you are doing and many other character traits that can either promote you or not! It can almost always affect how other people judge you and interact with you.

> **"To an extent, the posture you carry in your business will determine to what extent people trust you, believe in you and ultimately, in the case of your network marketing business, join you."**

Correcting your posture is not difficult but it does mean regular movement. You can't wait for it to correct itself. Following the advice of the experts is usually a good start. In this case that means your mentors in the business. Seek out those successful distributors and see how they carry themselves, observe their posture.

Regular movement in the form of speaking to people and 'inviting them to take a look' means that your skills will improve quicker and greatly reduce weak posture. It will, perhaps most importantly, eliminate the desperation that distributors sometimes carry when trying to get people enrolled in their business.

Desperation kills your posture and your result. We can help you overcome this!

The greater the choice, the greater your posture. Imagine 2 new distributors join a business. The first distributor invites 1 prospect to look at their business and then spends 2 weeks presenting, following up and trying to get them to join their business, while waiting for them to make their decision before making another move. This is how many people operate. They are dipping their toes in. The other distributor in that same 2 week period invites 10 people from their list to take a look at their business, putting each one through a number of exposures. Which distributor is likely to develop the best posture? Who is going to improve at a quicker rate and more importantly, who will appear less desperate and carry more excitement and urgency? Finally, who do you think will introduce the most distributors and have fun doing it?

"Trying to work 'one prospect at a time' until they either join or don't is poor use of your time. It will naturally make you appear more desperate, the killer flaw in this business. This will be a huge turn-off for any prospect you are putting through the exposures."

Desperation is often caused by lack of choice and while poor posture can give you the appearance of ill or weak health, in business it can translate into desperation, lack of confidence and lack of belief. Nobody will want to join that kind of individual.

Always position yourself to 'have choice'. This greatly improves your posture and gives you the power and not the prospect. This is most important. Having power is a subtle thing, it is an internal feeling you have that should barely be noticeable to your prospects. A prospect should sense that they are not your only choice and should not be made to feel like they are a single target being hunted. I have seen this being done too many times and the result is always the same, you alienate people. They will sense if they are being hunted. They need to realise that they have been offered an opportunity, it's not vital that they join because there are other people in your pipeline who will want to join in.

"The people you invite to take a look at your business do not need to be skilled observers to detect such discrepancies in your behaviour and they will not fail to spot poor posture. They will know if something isn't right. They will know if you are desperate."

One of the most powerful positions you can be in as a network marketer is to have choice. This posture will make you more attractive to the multiple prospects you are speaking to. The ability to show people and simply follow up irrespective of the outcome makes you a powerful network marketer. Your posture will become attractive to others when desperation leaves the body and excitement, urgency and your role as the educator becomes established. This is the posture that you need to acquire. It takes a bit of practise and it's just a case of getting on with it and not waiting for people to join you.

Be aware of the two basic forms of posture, 'open' and 'closed', which may reflect your degree of confidence, status or receptivity to another person. This is something your prospects will pick up on. Someone seated in a closed position might have his/her arms folded, legs crossed or be positioned at a slight angle from the person with whom they are interacting. If you only have one prospect to speak to and nothing else in your pipeline you may behave this way. You will be more nervous about the outcome and be focused on the result of them either joining or not joining. This will affect the confidence and posture in your presentation. Your prospect will pick up on this and it will generally not have a positive outcome! If you have closed posture it might imply discomfort or disinterest in what you are doing. In an open posture, you might expect to see someone directly facing you with hands apart on the arms of the chair. An open posture can be used to communicate openness or interest in someone and a readiness to listen. I would suggest this approach in speaking with your prospects. After all, the presentation is about them not you!

'Excitement and urgency' not 'fear and desperation' should be the dynamic. Allow your body to come from the angle that you are 'showing and educating' and not 'convincing and trying to get'. You have third party tools to do the work for you! Just keep getting eyes on the presentation and simply sort those who are showing a level of interest from those who are not. You plant the seeds and keep coming back to water them in the form of more exposures to your business. Remember amateurs convince, professionals sort!

> **"You don't have to be the person who looks down at the pavement when you walk down the street. Nor do you need to be the person who gets on the train and looks for where there are no people ... be on purpose."**

It's the things you don't see in yourself, that lack of self-awareness that everybody else notices. That's why the correction of your posture is vitally important. Your long-term wealth will be governed by how many people trust, join and follow you! Poor posture will prevent this! As you grow and develop as a leader in your business, your posture and your spatial awareness will develop and drastically improve. There are three types of spatial awareness that you need to get to grips with to compliment your posture in your growing business.

Personal Distance: Personal distance is considered to be the most appropriate for people holding a conversation and 'face to face' meetings to show your product, service and opportunity. I like to call it an 'over the kitchen table' meeting. Pay attention to this, as it should be happening more frequently in the early stages of your business.

Social Distance: This is the normal distance for impersonal business meetings. For example working together in the same room or during social gatherings. Team trainings, home meetings and business launches or working in a small group. You should be involved as a participant in these as often as you can and then start to run your own as a leader/ facilitator as your business starts to grow.

Public Distance: At such distances exaggerated non-verbal communication is necessary for communication to be effective. Opportunity presentations, seminars or speaking on the main stage at your company convention. This is where you want to be! Do enough personal and social meetings, and you will see yourself on the stage at public events.

Becoming a professional network marketer is about having character, passion, and posture and having fun. It's about being somebody who another person would want to join and follow. It's about being open and honest and educating people on the gift that you have. It's about waking up in the morning and being excited about your business and your future. This should be reflected in how you carry yourself every day.

CHAPTER 43

IMPROVE YOUR RECOVERY TIME!

A final short story I would like to share with you. When I was little, I was famous in our neighbourhood for always getting into scrapes and spending lots of time in casualty. My injuries were so minor that my mother would often be more concerned about what the doctors would think of the frequency of my visits, rather than the injuries themselves. As a child, you heal quickly. Bumps and grazes start to heal in a matter of minutes. A child falls off the bike, cries for 2 minutes, and jumps right back in the saddle and off they go without a care in the world.

> **"The human body has an incredible capacity to start healing itself quickly. So why is the 'mind' so very different when it comes to recovery time?"**

A mental graze or bump in our business can irritate and bother us for weeks, sometimes months, affecting our productivity, and in some cases affecting it so much that it can change the course of an entire lifetime. Yet a physical bump can be forgotten in minutes and the pain is gone! With our network marketing business, we do have a tendency to treat small bumps and grazes in our business like the loss of a limb. This is a mindset that has to be conditioned!

A customer cancelled an appointment, an order went wrong, a distributor didn't sign up or a distributor drops out of your business. We can sometimes give these small mental bumps far more attention and credit than they deserve. They are the inconvenient reality of what happens within your network marketing business. The reality is they have very little impact on what is important in the long-term.

Don't mistake battered pride or loss of self-esteem for something that is truly life impacting. Bring your mental recovery time into balance as you would a physical bump. Allow yourself to forget about it quickly so that you can move on. I could hit my head hard and you could lose a team member. Just make sure that you recover before I do!

Treat small mental injuries in this business quickly. You want to reduce your recovery time to 2 minutes, like a scratch or a bump. Anything longer than that and time and money is being wasted. I speak to distributors who are still recovering from a team member who dropped out 2 months ago, and in that time they did nothing. In a flash 10% of the year has vanished on something minor.

Have the right support and treatment from the experts who know how to help. Develop your knowledge so that you can remedy it yourself. Lie down with an ice pack for a few minutes! Mental pain is something that, as humans, we seem far more willing to put up with. We can sometimes put up with it for years or for an entire lifetime.

You only have to listen to the vacuum of negativity and the conversations taking place in society to see that many people need serious help. The problem lies in the fact that mental bumps are less intense than physical pain. It can take an entire lifetime until you realise how much the bumps and grazes have affected you, both economically and socially. Become an observer of people and you will see this.

It's important to be aware of potential minor injury. After all, who seriously launches a business and expects everything to go right all of the time? Who seriously raises a child and expects them not to hurt themselves occasionally? For a customer not to purchase, or for something to be sent back, or for a staff member to leave, or for somebody to find a service or product they prefer elsewhere.

When you join network marketing, you buy a business solution, not a cure for all the things that don't go your way! Should you choose to walk about with a 'closed sign' on your mouth through fear of getting grazed, then you can't expect to generate any income. The only variable is you. Take the right medicine, in the right doses and you will see this. If you don't, it will spread into everything you ever try to accomplish.

Whatever you choose to do with your life outside of your network marketing business, the resources this business provides can help with the correct medicine and treatment in the form of your personal development. You have experts you can speak to, they are called your support network and mentors, call them! You have places you can go to, they are called meetings, training and events. You have treatments that can make you feel better such as personal development books.

> **"I believe that many of the mental injuries we sustain can be treated by our 'environment'; I call it the 'mental medicine'."**

The things that you often want to avoid are the things that will ultimately help you. This applies to your health and your wealth. You only have to look around, observe and listen to people speak to know they are not taking the correct medicine. Listen to some of the people who you get drawn to. Poisoning the mind with gossip, news, poor association, poor environment, negativity, and the perceived reality that someone or something else is to blame and that success is meant for other people who are lucky enough never to fail!

The only difference between somebody who is on the success curve and somebody who is having no result is that they have taken more mental blows and taken more medicine in the form of personal development to improve their recovery time.

Let's not be so blissfully unaware that the best treatment for mental bumps and grazes may be our 'environment'. Use your company environment; it's a positive one! It's the best place you can be if you hit a low! If you can't be there then read a good book, watch an inspirational video. Have a conversation with a happy and successful person in your business to treat the mental bumps and grazes caused by small setbacks.

Don't seek consolation with the words of people who are feeling low and burnt out. Seek recovery from the words of people who are where you want to be. One of the biggest flaws of the human character is seeking out the negative experiences of other people to make ourselves feel better. It doesn't!

Get to work on improving your recovery time. Go the full 12 rounds in this business and you can be a winner. Take some bumps and grazes, they don't hurt that much. After each round go to your corner and listen to some wise words.

CHAPTER 44

FOLLOW THE LEADER

There is a saying that you may have heard, 'if you want to be successful, then you have to do what successful people do'. Furthermore, if your way isn't working, perhaps it is time to try somebody elses. In earlier chapters we highlighted the importance of having a mentor and seeking out leaders or somebody who is demonstrating success in your business. You will know by now if this is something you need to seek out, or whether you have indeed found a leader you are happy to follow and work with.

> **"Know that you cannot duplicate a good leader. Good leaders are unique, so be the greatest version of yourself. This mindset is very important."**

Leaders in network marketing come in all shapes and sizes and they have all built businesses at different speeds using different character attributes. They do however all have one thing in common, they follow the system. A system that remains constant throughout network marketing and which needs to be duplicated by you and the team members you introduce. This is the system of: gathering customers, recruiting distributors and attending events. Neither one can survive without the other. Meaning that you have to consistently engage in all 3 if you eventually want to become a leader.

Good habits and correct activity are vitally important because your team will copy you. People copy people, it has always been this way, sometimes for good, sometimes not so good. Not all of your team will follow the system and copy you, and they will copy you to varying degrees. Achieving duplication in your team requires a distributor to stay in the business long enough and to acquire the correct mindset and develop the necessary skills. It will rarely happen immediately, but it will happen if you are consistent in finding the right people.

Finding a few good people who want to join in and participate is important. That's why it is important for you to join in and participate and lead from the front. If you can do this, then you can create the foundations of a great leader. Avoid the common mistake of turning your business into a game of 'Chinese Whispers'. This means that you don't allow the message you send throughout your team to become diluted the further down into your business you go. Work with all your team members void of prejudice, as long as they are showing a willingness to join in. Work down on at least 4 levels, this way you will allow your more seasoned team members to learn how to work with the newer distributors and eventually take over and grow into leaders themselves.

It is unlikely that you will achieve a duplicating business unless you are working deep into your business. It is hard to recruit a lot of people and then simply sit back and hope that one of them makes you rich. This is a poor attitude, but one we see all too often. I call this LLS (lazy leader syndrome). By working with all your team members in depth and breadth, you can move your business from a small retail business selling products or services, to a larger organisation that pays you a leveraged passive income, and in the long-term earns you time freedom.

No leader wants to lead forever, therefore you want to aim to bring people through as leaders so that you can eventually relax down. For the first 3 to 5 years you need to be seriously working hard, reinforcing again that there are no 'zombie ideas' in this business, such as 'get rich quick' or 'too good to be true'. If we really want people to do what we do, we have to 'show and not tell' them. People will do as we do! Parents often have the misguided notion of 'do as I say, not as I do'. It doesn't work that way. That's why different generations within families often repeat themselves down. This is OK if good habits and teachings are in place. Unfortunately we have seen what happens when poor leadership within families gets passed down the generations. Things can fall apart. The generations (or levels) in your business are no exception. Good habits and bad habits get passed down. A 'do as I say' attitude makes you nothing more than a poor manager of people, as opposed to a leader in a network marketing business.

Assuming the mantle of a good leader is about 'leading by example'. We don't ask our team to do anything that we are not prepared to do or have 'not' done previously. Leadership is about sharing information, promoting and recognising. It's about helping people achieve their goals and not being self-serving and leaving everything to others.

The route of leadership is not for everybody. Most of the people that join a network marketing business will want to follow and will naturally fall into that category. Following is what we have been taught to do from day 1. That is the learned behaviour that most people joining this business will bring. Whether or not you grow into a leader will very much depend on how open you are to personal growth and your ability to be coached. It's not an attribute that you can be bullied into. You have to want it.

> **"Leadership is not often on somebody's radar when they first join a network marketing business. They don't join this business to be a leader, they often join to get away from poor leadership."**

It's a path that we do encourage all distributors to take, but ultimately it's your decision which direction you want to go. You may have already decided by the end of this book that leadership is the path you want to take. If it's not, that's OK, and nobody will think any less of you.

It is important though to understand that you cannot have time freedom without establishing some level of leadership. Responsibility and reward need to be balanced. Your organisation will have a stairway to success, different levels of leadership, pins or ranks, each one requiring more sacrifice but offering greater reward. As you grow as a leader you will need to balance your personal life and your business life. As your team grows and you start to become a noticeable figure in your organisation, a truly wonderful thing starts to happen. Your positive associations grow and you will start to notice that much of the negativity you have encountered begins to filter out and the scales will begin to tip in your favour. This is inevitable when growing as a leader and something you can look forward to.

Have parameters that your team understand. Leaders in your business have a life too. This is an emotional business where the expectation of leaders can be great. A leader you are working with could be dealing with 100 different team members. There is a line you don't cross between what is expected and what is inappropriate, so it is important not to make yourself the issue. Preserving relationships is important, this is paramount if one day you are going to lead. Learn how to drive people yet still have the ability to empathise with less experienced team members. A good leader understands this as they have usually been faced with similar challenges. Appreciate that, as you grow, this gesture may sometimes not be returned. Do not expect the same level of empathy from all of your team members. It's nice to have team members who understand your position as a leader, but remember not to make yourself the issue. This can be hard if you are an emotional person. Lead with passion and void of ego. This will challenge you from time to time, but it is so important to remain grounded. This needs to be kept in check if you want to keep a positive culture in your business. A positive culture can be the driving force of your business and send a ripple effect through your team that can work in your favour but it all starts with you.

Leading from the front means that you will need a heightened sense of self-awareness of what is going on in your business. This is hard to do if you are too wrapped up in yourself and your own motives. The leaders' first mistake is not putting their team first!

Whatever you want to achieve with your network marketing business, whether it is simply personal growth, or just to ease the financial burden, or maybe now you really do want to go all the way to the top, it really doesn't matter. What I can tell you is that there is no feeling on earth like helping another individual to realise that there is more to life than what they have been shown previously. It is not about how much you are earning, it is about helping others to realise their earning potential. Do this and you have the makings of a truly great leader.

CHAPTER 45

LET'S RAMP IT UP!

By now you have hopefully come to understand that skills are something you can and will acquire over time, but mindset is something you have to get right quickly. You are the most incredible creation with the power to achieve great things. You are capable of so much more. The only obstacles you will ever face are those obstacles in your mind. Be aware of what is real and your perceived reality. Consider the choices and decisions you make every day. Think about the reactions you give and the stories you tell yourself. This book has introduced you to the idea of getting your mindset right for this incredible network marketing business you have chosen to embark on. It is important now that you act on the information you have taken in. You don't need to remember everything you read in this book; it only takes one piece of information to take your business to the next level. I am still learning every day and I am loving the journey. I do hope that we get to meet in the future and I compliment you for taking the time to grow.

SUMMARY

Make your next job after you have read this book to connect with 5 successful leaders in your business. Make sure they know who you are and what your plan is.

Remove your emotion from the art of sharing and promotion and you will prevail.

You can't be successful at anything if you are running it for a trial period.

Own the morning, you can get the most work done during this time. Imagine the compound effect if you did simple activity each morning for a year.

'Commitment' is doing the thing you said you would do long after the mood to do it has passed.

Keep the lines of communication open. Problems are only solved and money is only made when people are talking.

Everybody has an equal amount of time, it is the activities you choose to engage in within that time which will determine your future outcome.

Make sure your mental sat nav has the success maps installed and you know your destination. Have those goals and destinations written down where you can see them every day.

No such thing as fear of no, only preservation of self-image.

Be excited, tell people why you are doing what you are doing and ask for help!

Get your mental recovery time to 2 minutes.

Fortune is in the follow up.

Be a can person, not a can't person, and check your posture

RECOMMENDED READING

Go Pro 7 Steps to Becoming a Network Marketing Professional, by Eric Worre

Building an Empire, by Brian Carruthers

Think & Grow Rich, by Napoleon Hill

Beach Money, by Jordan Adler

The Unemployed Millionaire, by Matt Morris

How to Win Friends and Influence People, by Dale Carnegie

The Four Year Career, by Richard Brooke

No Excuses! by Brian Tracy

What to Say When You Talk to Your Self, by Shad Helmsetter

79 Network Marketing Tips, by Wes Linden

The Magic of Thinking Big, by David J. Shwartz

How full is your bucket? by Tom Rath & Donald O Clifton

The Impact System, by Stephan Longworth

Go for No! by Andrea Waltz, Richard Fenton

The Compound Effect, by Darren Hardy

The Slight Edge, by Jeff Olson

Building Your Network Marketing Business, by Jim Rohn

NOTES

A GARDEN
OF
SOLITUDE

A GARDEN
OF
SOLITUDE

Edited by Rowland Croucher

AN ALBATROSS BOOK

© Rowland Croucher 1998

Published in Australia and New Zealand by
Albatross Books Pty Ltd
PO Box 320, Sutherland
NSW 2232, Australia
and in the United Kingdom by
Lion Publishing plc
Peter's Way, Sandy Lane West
Oxford OX4 5HG, England

This paperback edition 1998

National Library of Australia
Cataloguing-in-Publication data

A garden of solitude.

Bibliography.
Includes index.
ISBN 0 7324 1074 6

1. Meditations. I. Croucher, Rowland.

242

Cover photograph: John Waterhouse
Printed by Kyodo Printing Co. Pte Ltd, Singapore

Contents

Preface

HERE IS THE FIFTH and final volume in the *Still Waters, Deep Waters* series of devotional anthologies.

Many have helped in practical and editorial ways: to them all, my thanks!

W. Somerset Maugham wrote this about his reading habits:

> I keep on hand a volume of poetry in case I feel in the mood for that and, by my bedside, I have one of those books, too rarely to be found, alas, which you can dip into at any place and stop reading with equanimity at the end of any paragraph.[1]

This is one of the purposes of the *Still Waters* series. Other purposes include quotes for church bulletins, material for sermons (the index at the back of this book should be of help to preachers or small group leaders), and for morning or bedtime private or couples' devotions.

Many Christian organisations have walked through these books with their staff — and Christian touring parties have done the same. They have been used as gifts to relatives and friends with a wide range of Christian experience (or none).

As noted in previous volumes, we have chosen not to reveal who wrote the homilies for two reasons: many men are not reading what women write (and occasionally vice versa); and guessing an author's theological stance sometimes inhibits our hearing from God through his or her words.

As we read and reflect — and change and grow — let us heed this exhortation from Thomas Merton: 'We are called to create a better world. But we are first of all called to a more immediate and exalted task: that of creating our own lives.'[2]

Shalom!

Rowland

Rowland Croucher
John Mark Ministries
7 Bangor Court
Heathmont
Victoria   3135
Australia

Endnotes

1.   W Somerset Maugham, *Books and You*, London, William-Heinemann, 1940, p.8

2.   *The Shining Wilderness: Daily Readings with Thomas Meton*, Aileen Taylor (ed.), Darton, Longman & Todd, 1988, p.7

Theme: Harmony. . .

to enjoy God's beauty

'I am the true vine, and my Father is the vinegrower. He removes every branch in me that bears no fruit. Every branch that bears fruit he prunes to make it bear more fruit. You have already been cleansed by the word that I have spoken to you. Abide in me as I abide in you. Just as the branch cannot bear fruit by itself unless it abides in the vine, neither can you unless you abide in me.

'I am the vine, you are the branches. Those who abide in me and I in them bear much fruit, because apart from me you can do nothing. Whoever does not abide in me is thrown away like a branch and withers; such branches are gathered, thrown into the fire and burned. If you abide in me and my words abide in you, ask for whatever you wish and it will be done for you. My Father is glorified by this, that you bear much fruit and become my disciples.

'As the Father has loved me, so I have loved you; abide in my love. If you keep my commandments, you will abide in my love, just as I have kept my Father's commandments and abide in his love. I have said these things to you so that my joy may be in you, and that your joy may be complete.

'This is my commandment, that you love one another as I have loved you. No-one has greater love than this, to lay down one's life for one's friends. You are my friends if you do what I command you. I do not call you servants any longer, because the servant does not know what the master is doing; but I have called you friends, because I have made known to you everything that I have heard from my Father.'

John 15: 1-15, NRSV

1

The garden of God

Now the Lord God had planted a garden in the east, in Eden; . . .The Lord God took the man and put him in the Garden of Eden to work it and take care of it. . . Then the man and his wife heard the sound of the Lord God as he was walking in the garden in the cool of the day.

Awake, north wind, and come, south wind! Blow on my garden, that its fragrance may spread abroad. Let my lover come into his garden and taste its choice fruits.

The Lord will guide you always; he will satisfy your needs in a sun-scorched land and will strengthen your frame. You will be like a well-watered garden, like a spring whose waters never fail.

You were in Eden, the garden of God; every precious stone adorned you: ruby, topaz and emerald, chrysolite, onyx and jasper, sapphire, turquoise and beryl. Your settings and mountings were made of gold; on the day you were created they were prepared.

A man planted a vineyard, rented it to some farmers and went away for a long time. At harvest time he sent a servant to the tenants so they would give him some of the fruit of the vineyard. But the tenants beat him and sent him away empty-handed. . . Then the owner of the vineyard said, 'What shall I do? I will send my son, whom I love; perhaps they will respect him.'

Then Jesus went with his disciples to a place called Gethsemane, and he said to them, 'Sit here while I go over there and pray'. . . Going a little farther, he fell with his face to the ground and prayed, 'My Father, if it is possible, may this cup be taken from me. Yet not as I will, but as you will.'

'Woman,' he said, 'Why are you crying? Who is it you are looking for?' Thinking he was the gardener she said, 'Sir, if you have carried him away, tell me where you have put him and I will get him.'

(Genesis 2: 8, 15; 3: 8; Song of Songs 4: 16; Isaiah 58: 11; Ezekiel 28: 13; Luke 20: 9, 10 and 13; Matthew 26: 36 and 39; John 20: 15 — all NIV)

One of the most moving incidents in the life of Jesus Christ occurred when he and Peter, James and John went into the Garden of Gethsemane to be at peace and pray to God the Father. Those who visit Gethsemane today and walk among the ancient gnarled olive trees can easily imagine Jesus there praying for direction and inspiration and also agonising in prayer as he sought a way forward in his mission. The garden setting is appropriate because, since the beginning of time, God's presence in gardens has been known to his people.

While living in Japan some years ago, I thoroughly enjoyed the experience of visiting well-known Japanese gardens near Osaka. They were beautifully laid out, carefully tended and greatly enjoyed by Japanese people and many tourists. The tourists tended to look at the gardens rather as a spectacle that could be admired and enjoyed, while the Japanese seemed to visit the gardens simply to be at peace in them. It was quite moving to see people, even children, sitting quietly in gardens contemplating the trees and grass and shrubs and obviously finding inspiration from this delightful environment. Although we plant gardens, they have a life and a spirit of their own and are an expression of the wonder of God-created order.

The Bible narrative begins with Adam and Eve in the Garden of Eden. The story not only places humans in their true context within the created order but, under the hand of God, they are given responsibilities for its well-being. The tragedy of the Adam and Eve story is that they did not accept this responsibility, but used the created order for their own purposes. Destruction followed, and still follows, this course of action.

The Adam and Eve saga reminds us that it is in the setting of a garden that we can become aware of the personal presence of God himself. This came to them as a surprise, because they soon found there was a conflict between their ways and the intentions and ways of God.

As the Bible narrative unfolds, this becomes a recurring theme. There are incidents like the story of Naboth's vineyard where an honourable man saw his vineyard or garden as his inheritance and refused to be deprived of it by a very avaricious king, Ahab. In the end, Naboth was killed because of his insistence on maintaining and caring for his inheritance.

Gardens are not merely part of the decor of creation, but are an essential part of the life and well-being of every person who lives on God's earth. For this reason, droughts and natural disasters can be so devastating and destructive.

We have a number of responsibilities and we are familiar with them. One, of course, is to develop and extend the vision of the Garden of Eden in the environment in which we live in our homes, our properties and our comunities.

In Townsville, Queensland, a well-known citizen inspired the city and its residents to plant one hundred thousand trees to celebrate Australia's Bicentenary. Townsville was dry and, in many places, barren. Everybody rose to the challenge and the result was not only pleasing, but had a dramatic effect on the whole life and outlook of the citizens. It changed the spirit of the city.

Apart from planting and tending our garden, we should also remember that it is in this environment that we become aware of the presence and the purposes of God. We perceive the vigour of creation and are somewhat overawed by the splendour of it as we look on great trees, and we perceive the beauty of it as we gaze on flowers and shrubs.

It is also a wonderful environment in which to pray, as Jesus did in Gethsemane and, while he prayed in agony amongst the peaceful old olive trees, something of the spirit of the garden would have upheld him in that critical hour. In the garden, he found a way forward by dedicating himself to the will of God the Father.

There is a bold contrast between Jesus and his dedication, and the confusion that arose in the minds of Adam and Eve as they walked away from the will of God. We should always thank God for the joys of his creation and pray that we can live and walk in it aware of him, aware of the beauty of the life he has given us — and be eternally grateful.

❧❀❧

So was I speaking and weeping in the most bitter contrition of my heart, when, lo! I heard from a neighbouring house a voice, as of boy or girl, I know not, chanting and oft repeating, 'Take up and read; Take up and read.' Instantly my countenance altered. I began to think most intently whether children were wont in any kind of play to sing such words, nor could I remember ever to have heard the like.

So, checking the torrent of my tears, I arose, interpreting it to be no other than a command from God to open the book and read the first chapter I should find. For I had heard of Antony, that coming in during the reading of the Gospel, he received the admonition, as if what was being read was spoken to him: 'Go, sell all that thou hast and give to the poor, and thou shalt have treasure in heaven, and come and follow me.' And by such oracle he was forthwith converted unto Thee.

Eagerly then I returned to the place where Alypius was sitting, for there had I laid the volume of the Apostle, when I arose thence. I seized, opened and in silence read that section on which my eyes first fell: Not in rioting and drunkenness, not in chambering and wantonness, not in strife and envying: but put ye on the Lord Jesus Christ, and make not provision for the flesh.

St Augustine of Hippo

Those who have been walking in a beautiful garden do not leave it willingly without taking away with them four or five flowers, in order to inhale their perfume and carry them about during the day: even so, when we have considered some mystery in meditation, we should choose one or two or three points in which we have found most relish and which are specially proper to our advancement, in order to remember them throughout the day and to inhale their perfume spiritually. Now we should do this in the place where we have made our meditation, either staying where we are, or walking about alone for a little while afterwards.

St Francis de Sales

The place to which the King of Love now brought them was a most beautiful valley among the peaks of the High Places. The whole of this sheltered spot was laid out in quiet gardens and orchards and vineyards.

Here grew flowers of rarest beauty and lilies of every description. Here, too, were trees, almonds and walnuts and many other varieties which Grace and Glory had never seen before. Here the King's gardeners were always busy, pruning the trees, tending the plants and the vines, and preparing beds for new seedlings and tender shoots.

These the King himself transplanted from uncongenial soil and conditions in the valleys below so that they might grow to perfection and bloom in that valley high above, ready to be planted in other parts of the Kingdom of Love, to beautify and adorn it wherever the King saw fit. They spent several delightful days watching the gardeners as they worked under the gracious supervision of the King himself and accompanying him as he walked in the vineyards, teaching and advising those who tended the vines.

Hannah Hurnard

For as the rain cometh down, and the snow from heaven, and returneth not thither, but watereth the earth, and maketh it bring forth and bud, that it may give seed to the sower, and bread to the eater:

So shall my word be that goeth forth out of my mouth: it shall not return unto me void, but it shall accomplish that which I please, and it shall prosper in the thing whereto I sent it.

Isaiah 55: 10–11, KJV

Most High Almighty Good Lord,
Yours are the praises, the glory, the honour,
   and all blessings!
To you alone, Most High, do they belong,
   And no-one is worthy to mention you.
Be praised, my Lord, with all your creatures,
   Especially Sir Brother Sun,
   By whom you give us the light of day!
And he is beautiful and radiant with great splendour.
   Of you, Most High, he is a symbol!
Be praised, my Lord, for Sister Moon and the Stars!
   In the sky you formed them bright and lovely
   and fair.
Be praised, my Lord, for Brother Wind
   And for the Air and cloudy and clear and all Weather,
   By which you give sustenance to your creatures!
Be praised, my Lord, for Sister Water,
   Who is very useful and humble and lovely and chaste!
Be praised, my Lord, for Brother Fire,
   By whom you give us light at night,
   And he is beautiful and merry and mighty and strong!
Be praised, my Lord, for our Sister Mother Earth,
   Who sustains and governs us,
      And produced fruits with colourful flowers and
leaves!
Be praised, my Lord, for those who forgive for
   love of you
   and endure infirmities and tribulations.
Blessed are those who shall endure them in peace,
   For by you, Most High, they will be crowned!

St Francis of Assisi

Sometimes when faith is running low
And I cannot fathom why things are so. . .
I walk alone among the flowers I grow
And learn the 'answers' to all I would know!
For among my flowers I have come to see
Life's miracle and its mystery. . .
And standing in silence and reverie
My faith comes flooding back to me!

Field Flower
I hold it in my hands, and see
Frail marvel of divinity.

For this: fresh winds of morning blew,
And meadows fed night-long on dew.

Or some June songbird pleaded rain
To ease the brown earth's fevered pain.

Came dawn, and under summer skies
A wonder feast to hold my eyes.

For fairest heaven wooed earth, to place
Its seal of beauty on her face.

So delicately rare, so fine —
This perfect thought of God is mine!

I hold it in my hands, and see
Frail marvel of divinity.

Michael J. Douglas

Father, let all become aware that they are your willing
  collaborators in the work of creation.
Lord, today I ask your forgiveness
  for the places that will remain empty in your vineyard,
  for needs that are created artificially,
  for talents that will never be developed. . .
  for the countless workers, your [children] who will be
  deprived of the development that you want them to have,
  for my own lack of fervour in trying to find out what you
  want of me, and for my lack of generosity in neglecting to
  try as hard as I can to be what you want me to be.
Lord, I thank you
  for the talents you've given me,
  for the physical and intellectual gifts I've received,
  for the education I've received,
  for the opportunities I have to choose the profession that
  I want.

Lord, let me be like putty in your hands.
Let me accept your guidance through events so that,
  conscious of the real needs of others,
I may discover:
  where you are waiting for me,
  and the part that you want me to play,
  through my work,
  in the completion of your creation.

Michel Quoist

A Benediction

Go forth into the world in peace; be of good courage; hold fast
that which is good; render to no one evil for evil; strengthen
the fainthearted; support the weak; help the afflicted; honour
everyone; love and serve the Lord, rejoicing in the power of the
Holy Spirit; and the blessing of God Almighty, the Father, the
Son, and the Holy Spirit, be with you and remain with you
always.   Amen.

2

Be still and know God

Before he chose the twelve, he spent the entire night alone in the desert hills. . . After sending the people away, he went up a hill by himself to pray. . . And he said to them, 'Come. . . apart into a desert place.'

Jesus went with them to a place called Gethsemane; and he said to his disciples, 'Sit here while I go yonder and pray.'

[There is] a time to be silent and a time to speak.

But whenever you pray, go into your room and shut the door and pray to your Father who is in secret; and your Father who sees in secret will reward you.

Be still and know that I am God.

(Luke 6: 12, RSV; Matthew 14: 23, GNB; Mark 6: 31, KJV; Matthew 26: 36, RSV; Ecclesiastes 3: 7, NIV; Matthew 6: 6, NRSV; Psalm 46: 10, KJV)

We live in a hectic world. It is difficult to find time for contemplation, to be still with God. Moreover, Christians are 'Rushins'! Life is too fast for our emotional, physical and spiritual health. Yet, in the midst of his busyness, Jesus called his friends to come apart and rest a while.

He calls us to do the same. This is a call to be alone, not in order to be away from people, but to hear the Lord's voice better. Jesus always lived in inward solitude, a discipline of mind, body and soul. Jesus frequently experienced outward solitude. In company with the twelve, who were with him much of the time, the Lord still found some time to be with his Father alone.

To be alone with God is to listen to him, to be attentive

to what God has to tell us. We cannot listen well while we are moving or talking!

To be alone with God is to relax in him. Six days God worked and on the seventh day he rested. We are not called to work harder than our Creator! It is an important discipline to take time off each day and each week to give oneself refreshment of body, mind and soul. The Letter to the Hebrews calls it entering 'into God's rest'.

To be alone with God is to 'wait upon' him. Waiting is all about prayerful service, trustful faithfulness and patient endurance. Patience is a fruit of the Spirit. Jesus told his disciples to wait — for the gift of the Holy Spirit which will come upon them and empower them for the ministry. Waiting is the precious time God allows us to reflect upon ourselves and him, and his will for us in this world.

The sabbath-keeping Creator of all things invites us to come apart in stillness and rest. This is our only source of strength and hope.

❧

In his poem 'Canciones del Alna', St John of the Cross uses the phrase, 'my house being now all stilled'. Here he indicates the importance of allowing all the physical, emotional, psychological and spiritual senses to be silenced. Every distraction of the body, mind and spirit must be put into a kind of suspended animation before this deep work of God upon the soul can occur.

Richard Foster, *Celebration of Discipline*

'Let [the one] who cannot be alone beware of community . . .Let [the one] who is not in community beware of being alone. . . Each by itself has profound pitfalls and perils. One who wants fellowship without solitude plunges into the void of words and feelings, and one who seeks solitude without fellowship perishes in the abyss of unity, self-infatuation and despair.

Dietrich Bonhoeffer, *Life Together*

The spirit of bondage is identified with the spirit of sub-servience to other human beings. George Fox speaks of 'bringing people off of men', away from that spirit of bondage to law through other human beings. And silence is one way of bringing us into this liberation.

Richard Foster, *Celebration of Discipline*

Be still and know that I am God. 'Relax' . . .Psychology has something to say about the relationship of relaxation to sanity, and the familiar exhortation is rendered in the Vulgate, *Vacate, et videte*. Indeed, the treatment of minds broken by the cataclysms of earth and the inhumanity, fancied or real, of one's fellows demands relaxation as the first step in therapy. 'Give place and see!'

Edwin McNeill Poteat, *The Interpreter's Bible*

When you are able to create a lonely place in the middle of your actions and concerns, your successes and failures slowly can lose some of their power over you. For then your love for this world can merge with a compassionate understanding of its illusions. Then your serious enjoyment can merge with an unmasking smile. Then your concern for others can be motivated more by their needs than your own. In short: then you can care.

Let us therefore live our lives to the fullest, but let us not forget once in a while to get up long before dawn to leave the house and go to a lonely place.

Henri Nouwen, *Out of Solitude*

Jesus calls us from loneliness to solitude. . . Loneliness is inner emptiness. Solitude is inner fulfilment. Solitude is not first a place, but a state of mind and heart. . . There is an old proverb to the effect that. . . 'who opens his mouth, closes his eyes!' The purpose of silence and solitude is to be able to see and hear.

Richard Foster, *Celebration of Discipline*

Teach me thy patience; still with thee
In closer, dearer company,
In work that keeps faith sweet and strong,
In trust that triumphs over wrong.

Washington Gladden

Settle yourself in solitude and you will come upon him in yourself.

Teresa of Avila

Come ye yourselves apart and rest a while,
Weary, I know it, of the press and throng;
Wipe from your brow the sweat and dust of toil,
And in my quiet strength again be strong.

Edward Henry Bickersteth

Sweet hour of prayer, sweet hour of prayer,
That calls me from a world of care,
And bids me at my Father's throne
Make all my wants and wishes known.
In seasons of distress and grief
My soul has often found relief,
And oft escaped the tempter's snare
By thy return, sweet hour of prayer.

W.W. Walford

Lord,
If in quietness and confidence is my strength;
If I know you best by being still;
If I rest by 'coming apart' from life's busyness;
And if I get more and better work done in six days
*   than in seven. . .*
Help me to understand that my life's quality is not to be
*   measured by its speed or my self-worth by multiple*
*   attainments. . .*
Most of nature praises you in silence. . .
The best of music is enhanced by its pauses. . .;
life's most beautiful things are often still and quiet:
*   Sunsets,*
*   Flowers,*
*   The night sky,*
*   A tree at dusk,*
*   A sleeping baby.*
You are waiting in the silence

'Midst the rush and roar of life. . .,
Waiting someone's heart to enter,
Someone quiet in the strife.
Here I am, Lord, ready and waiting.
Come and fill my life with your peace.
Amen.

A Benediction
Now, may the God of peace grant you serenity to know what's
best for you this day. May he guide you with his spirit and
may you be obedient to his leading. May you know Jesus close
to you this day, this night, and forevermore. Amen.

3

Grace before judgment

Simon answered, 'Master, we have worked all night long, but have caught nothing. Yet if you say so, I will let down the nets.' When they had done this, they caught so many fish that their nets were beginning to break. So they signalled their partners in the other boat to come and help them. And they came and filled both boats, so that they began to sink. But when Simon Peter saw it, he fell down at Jesus' feet, saying, 'Go away from me, Lord, for I am a sinful man!'

And as he [Jesus] sat at dinner in Levi's house, many tax collectors and sinners were also sitting with Jesus and his disciples — for there were many who followed him. When the scribes of the Pharisees saw that he was eating with sinners and tax collectors, they said to his disciples, 'Why does he eat with tax collectors and sinners?' When Jesus heard this, he said to them, 'Those who are well have no need of a physician, but those who are sick; I have come to call not the righteous, but sinners.'

Do not judge, so that you may not be judged. For with the judgment you make you will be judged, and the measure you give will be the measure you get. Why do you see the speck in your neighbour's eye, but do not notice the log in your own eye? Or how can you say to your neighbour, 'Let me take the speck out of your eye,' while the log is in your own eye? You hypocrite, first take the log out of your own eye, then you will see clearly to take the speck out of your neighbour's eye.

He went up the mountain and called to him those whom he wanted and they came to him. And he appointed twelve, whom he also named apostles, to be with him, and to be sent out to proclaim the message, and to have authority to cast out demons.

Three times I appealed to the Lord about this, that it would leave me, but he said to me, 'My grace is sufficient for you, for power is made perfect in weakness.' So, I will boast all the more gladly of my weaknesses, so that the power of Christ may dwell in me. Therefore I am content with weaknesses, insults, hardships, persecutions and calamities for the sake of Christ; for whenever I am weak, then I am strong.

(Luke 5: 5–8; Mark 2: 15–17; Matthew 7: 1–5; Mark 3: 13–15; 2 Corinthians 12: 8–10 — all NRSV)

I took the lift to the seventh floor of the high-rise flats. I was full of apprehension. As part-time chaplain at the local high school, I had been asked to visit the family of a new student. It was eight o'clock at night as I knocked on the security door of their flat. Eventually, the door opened and several heads appeared in the gap; the faces suggested that all had been waiting with bated breath to finally see this ministerial manifestation.

Mum, Dad, the three kids, a neighbour and I sat around the kitchen table. (On my rounds, neighbours often materialised — I always felt they were there to check out a minister close-up!) The family extended an unpretentious but genuine hospitality to which I had become accustomed in this predominantly working-class part of inner-city Melbourne.

Inevitably, they raised the topic of the church. They used to go. . . a long time ago. They do believe in God, said Mum defensively, as she drew long and hard on her cigarette. Mum said she never feels good enough to go to church. Anyway, she declared, they aren't married and Dad swears too much (some laughter). In fact, said the daughter, Dad does everything too much. They gave each other a severe look. Dad reclined further back into his chair. Tattoos peeked out everywhere from behind his dark blue tank top. Toward the end of our time together, as the others were distracted, Dad confided in me that he has never liked church people. 'They judge you,' he said.

No wonder the church has often fared so badly within our culture. Many Christians have intentionally or unconsciously proclaimed a gospel of judgment. Those outside the formal church have recoiled accordingly. Thus, Christians have deservedly earned for themselves the title 'wowsers'. Many people perceive the Christian sub-culture as a culture of 'give-ups'. People have been told overtly or covertly that to be 'in' they must 'give things up'.

These 'things', so-called sins, have mainly been in the sphere of personal morality and behaviour — for example, smoking, drinking, language codes, gambling, divorce, birth control, sexual orientation, sexuality, gender codes, dress norms and so on. A sincere searcher once lamented to me, 'Why is it that all the things I like doing most have to be sinful?'

In peddling a gospel of judgment, the church has not only alienated potential believers; it has also distorted the gospel. The process of judging people and in effect manipulating them to repent of certain aspects of their lifestyles before they are allowed past the door is *not* good news. Demanding repentance in order to receive grace is antithetical to the gospel.

Such a process is no different from that of most human institutions, societal systems and cultural norms. For instance, we expect to earn our way through school, develop our education and modify our behaviour to get a job or gain promotion, or change certain attitudes and patterns of living to be accepted by friends or clubs and associations.

Not so with the good news concerning Jesus of Nazareth. In a story about the religious authorities' abuse of a woman (John 8: 1–11), Jesus accepts the woman as she is though, according to the Law of Moses, she should be killed for her sexual misdemeanour. Surprisingly, in the context of this culturally accepted 'mortal sin', Jesus does not back down. Unlike the scribes and Pharisees in the story, Jesus makes no moral judgments — not initially.

Jesus saved her from certain death. Jesus' acceptance of her as an important human being did not hang on her religious and social respectability.

The gospel, first and foremost, is about God's grace: grace, love and understanding before judgment. When and if we invert this process in our proclamation and mission, we side with the scribes and Pharisees against Jesus. If we are truly biblical Christians, we no longer lay down the law; rather, we 'lay down the Christ'.

Certainly, judgment and repentance are important ingredients in the process of our salvation. However, they are not prerequisites. It is only after Jesus has saved the woman's life that he invites her to repent: 'Neither do I condemn you. Go your way, and from now on do not sin again.' Grace first, then judgment and repentance.

◑◐

We might also say that he [Jesus] was more revolutionary than the revolutionaries. . . Jesus did not proclaim a judgment of vengeance on the children of the world and of darkness; nor did he promise a kingdom of unlimited goodness and unconditional grace, particularly for the abandoned and distressed. . . What is it really that stands here between God and humans?

Paradoxically, it is our own morality and piety: our ingeniously devised moralism and our selective technique of piety. It is not — as people of the time thought — the tax swindlers who find it most difficult to repent, not being able to remember all those whom they have cheated or how much they would have to restore. No: it is the devout who find it most difficult, being so sure of themselves that they have no need of conversion. They became Jesus' worst enemies. Most of the sayings on judgment in the Gospels apply to these, not to the great sinners. Those who finally sealed his fate were not murderers, cheats, swindlers and adulterers, but highly moral people.

Hans Kung, On Being a Christian

One of the greatest surprises in the early church must have been the fact that it was Peter, of all people, who became the first of the great apostolic preachers (Acts 2: 24–36). Only a short while earlier, despite his outspoken profession of allegiance (Luke 22: 31–34), he had denied Jesus three times in the courtyard of the high priest. Yet this broken and defeated leader became the successful spokesman for the church on the day of Pentecost.

Athol Gill, Life on the Road

The quickest way to kill an Aussie party is to be introduced by your hosts as the pastor.

Kim Thoday

The people . . . were immediately struck by the differences between John [the Baptist] and Jesus. A pericope in the New Testament reminds us of this. Whereas John impressed his contemporaries as being a strictly ascetic man, Jesus was felt to be 'an eater and drinker', eating and drinking especially with tax-collectors and sinners (Mark 2: 16). Some played the one prophet off against the other to avoid having to listen to either.

Matthew 11: 16–19 and Luke 7: 31–35 in their parable of the children playing in the marketplace give pregnant expression to the obvious difference: ' . . .this generation . . .is like children sitting in the marketplaces and calling to their playmates: We piped to you and you did not dance; we wailed and you did not mourn. For John came neither eating nor drinking, and they say: he has a demon! The Son of Man came eating and drinking, and they say: behold, a glutton and a drunkard, a friend of tax-collectors and sinners!'

If John came across to the people as a grim ascetic, in complete harmony with his message of God's approaching and inexorable judgment, as a sort of dirge; therefore, Jesus came across as a song! This parable. . . serves to illustrate the basic difference between the prophet of woe and Jesus, the prophet of salvation.

Edward Schillebeeckx, Jesus

If God's act of grace is really the decisive factor, if it is he who 'is at work in us, both to will and to work his good pleasure' (Philippians 2: 13), even when we answer him in faith, if it is the vine itself that creates the fruit of the branches (John 15: 4), if the seed does sprout and grow, its sower not knowing how (Mark 4: 27), would it not be right to say that God looks with mercy on all our activities and that he blesses them and makes them fruitful by his grace whenever and wherever it pleases him? Then all our lives of searching for God, longing after him, even of answering his revelation in gratitude, in piety and in good works are certainly important, but on a secondary level. They are good only when permeated by his grace.

Eduard Schweizer, *Jesus Christ*

I asked a number of intimate friends recently where they would begin with a man who was penitent about the past, who really wanted to have done with it, who really wanted to find the new life about which the New Testament writers know so much and we so little.

One said he would have to know the circumstances of the man's case first. That seemed to me an evasion. Another said he would instruct the man to go home, and pray and read the Bible. That doesn't sound very exciting. Another said it was quite simply stated — 'Believe on the Lord Jesus Christ and thou shalt be saved.' That doesn't sound very explicit. One said that it was a matter of imitating Christ. It sounds a hopeless business. Another, who has been preaching for forty years, said that he had found that the first thing to do was to straighten out intellectual difficulties.

I am quite sure they were all right as far as secondary things went. At least there was a bit of truth in it all. I think they were all wrong about the beginning of the matter. Then I asked a layman, white-haired and, as I once thought, narrow-minded. He took up his Bible. I can hear his quiet voice now. . . 'How much more shall your heavenly Father give the Holy Spirit to them that ask him.' He said that the new life was a gift from God. 'You simply had to kneel down and ask for it, go out and live as if you had received it, only to find that it was yours indeed.'

That layman helped me enormously because, from all the tangle of thought, he took me right back to the beginning. I found about fifty passages scattered all over the New Testament in which the new life is spoken of as a gift. I think that is the beginning of the good news: God gives me a gift.

Leslie Weatherhead, *The Transforming Friendship*

He [Jesus] followed the tradition of the Jewish rabbis by gathering a group of disciples around him but, unlike them, went travelling throughout the country. In fact, although he was part of this tradition, he broke many of its rules.

He did not shun the company of women. He had high regard for children. He proposed an unusually egalitarian concept of authority. It was a people's religious style. His teaching reverberated with the sounds of ordinary life and he repeatedly made adjustments in traditional religious practices to accommodate to the needs of ordinary folk.

It appears to be this aspect of his behaviour that infuriated the church authorities. They followed a style of religion which called for separation from the world. Their pursuit of holiness led them to deny the worldly pleasures of common people.

David Millikan, *The Sunburnt Soul*

Sin and grace are bound to each other. We do not even have a knowledge of sin unless we have already experienced the unity of life, which is grace. And conversely, we could not grasp the meaning of grace without having experienced the separation of life, which is sin. . . And in light of this grace, we perceive the power of grace in relation to ourselves. We experience moments in which we accept ourselves, because we feel that we have been accepted by that which is greater than we. If only more such moments were given to us! For it is such moments that make us love our life, that make us accept ourselves — not in our goodness and self-complacency, but in our certainty of the eternal meaning of our life.

Paul Tillich, *The Shaking of the Foundations*

When other people look at us with friendly eyes, we come alive. When other people recognise us for the individuals we are, we become free. And when we feel accepted and affirmed, we are happy.

For human beings depend on acceptance as birds depend on air and fish on water. Acceptance is humanity's element. If acceptance is lacking, the air becomes thin, we cannot breathe properly and shrivel up. That is why we shrink back under an indifferent glance, are wounded by disregard and perish as human beings if we are rejected. It is easy for us to accept one another when other people are like ourselves. But if they are different from us, we find it difficult.

Jurgen Moltmann, *The Power of the Powerless*

The Jews knew that God is a gracious God as well as a God who is angry with the sinner, so far as it can be known through the possession of an intellectual concept of God. And no-one has spoken more forcibly of the wrath of God (although without using the word) than Jesus, precisely because he proclaims God's grace.

Because he conceives radically the idea of the grace of God, he makes it plain that God's forgiveness must be an event in time, that the relation of 'I' and 'Thou' exists between God and us, that God stands opposite to us as another Person over whom we can have no sort of control, who meets us with his claim and with his grace, whose forgiveness is pure gift.

This is the reason that the preaching of Jesus is addressed first of all to the poor and sinful and that he allowed himself to be blamed as the friend of tax-collectors and sinners.

The gospel of deliverance is proclaimed to the poor (Matthew 11: 5). For such perceive God's claim more clearly than the respectable people, and also know better how to accept a free gift.

Rudolph Bultmann, *Jesus and the Word*

Loving, Creator God, we are awed by your grace. It is often hard to accept. How can such imperfect beings as we are possibly accept your unconditional love? Yet in your unfathomable wisdom, you offer us an unending stream of grace.

Despite our faults, our imperfections and our inhumanity, you continually offer us the opportunity to relax into the refreshingly cool and purifying waters of your love and nurture. Through the active, initiating force of your grace, there is hope for us and our world. Your grace gives us the chance to refocus our lives, to begin anew, to explore again the potentiality within us, to transcend our human limitations and ultimately our separation from your divine goodness and grace.

We give you thanks for the wisdom of your grace. In Jesus' name, we praise you. Amen.

A Benediction
The grace of our Lord Jesus Christ, the love of God and the fellowship of the Holy Spirit is with us always. Amen.

WEEK

4

Theme and variations

I am my beloved's and his desire is for me. Come, my beloved, let us go forth into the fields and lodge in the villages; let us go out early to the vineyards and see whether the vines have budded, whether the grape blossoms have opened and the pomegranates are in bloom. There, I will give you my love. The mandrakes give forth fragrance and over our doors are all choice fruits, new as well as old, which I have laid up for you, O my beloved.

Everyone then who hears these words of mine and acts on them will be like a wise man who built his house on rock. The rain fell, the floods came and the winds blew on that house, but it did not fall, because it had been founded on rock. And everyone who hears these words of mine and does not act on them will be like a foolish man who built his house on sand. The rain fell, and the floods came, and the winds blew and beat upon that house, and it fell — and great was its fall!

Then Jesus said to the Jews who had believed in him, 'If you continue in my word, you are truly my disciples; and you will know the truth, and the truth will make you free. So if the Son makes you free, you will be free indeed.'

The hour is coming, and is now here, when the true worshippers will worship the Father in spirit and truth, for the Father seeks such as these to worship him.

(Song of Songs 7: 10–13; Matthew 7: 24–27; John 8: 31–32 and 36; John 4: 23–24 — all NRSV)

A movie which has created continuing interest has been *Dead Poets' Society*. A new English teacher, John Keating, came to Helton Academy for Boys. Helton was a very traditional and legalistic school, whose four pillars were 'Tradition, Honour, Discipline and Excellence'.

Keating asked one boy to read this verse from a poem written by Robert Herrick:

> Gather ye rosebuds while ye may,
> Old time is still a'flying,
> And this same flower that smiles today
> Tomorrow will be dying.

He gave them another motto, 'Seize the Day' — in Latin, *'Carpe diem'*. He went on to explain that there are two essential but different dimensions to life — dependent on each other, but each capable of destroying the other.

The first includes the world of ideas and intellectual endeavour — those objective realities like law, science and engineering necessary to sustain and shape life; the basics, the principles, the foundational. This is where 'Tradition, Honour, Discipline and Excellence' fit. But second, there was the affective and the poetic — those subjective experiences and personal pursuits that give life meaning; 'beauty, romance and love are what we stay alive for'.

The Bible recognises both dimensions. Dietrich Bonhoeffer said that there is a 'polyphony' in life and in scripture. While the Law is the foundation, there is also room for the Song of Solomon 'as a protest against those who believe that Christianity stands for the restraint of passion'.

Jesus said that the gospel embraced both the rock on which we must build our lives and the freedom which belongs as a right to the children of God. He said that even God is worshipped in both truth and spirit. But each is capable of destroying the other.

Within us are two apparently conflicting needs, each crying out for fulfilment. One is the need for security, safety, certainty, tradition, authority and objective truth. The other is the quest for freedom and creativity — to 'mount up on wings like eagles'; to recognise what we are, uniquely and inwardly; to discover with surprise and wonder our gifts and dreams; to break out of our inner prison and be set free. Studdert Kennedy writes of:

> . . .those bright wings
> on which my spirit flies —
> To talk with angels on the heights
> in solemn, sweet surprise.

The church and the individual Christian have both suffered over the centuries by their inability to achieve a creative balance and tension between these two dimensions. There are those who want their faith to be set in concrete. Others spurn the past and reject tradition, foundation and structure and fly off at whatever tangent their fancy takes them.

The reality is that while each can destroy the other, we need both! They exist in creative tension — like that between the wind that lifts the kite and the cord which ties it to the earth; without either, there can be no flight or movement. Or take the tension between the power and speed of the 'Bullet' train in Japan and the restricting rails which make it impossible for it to go in any other direction. The speed is only possible because of the restraints.

As a German and a Lutheran, Bonhoeffer saw it clearly in the music of Bach. Bach's music has an eternal quality about it. Of all music, Bach's is the least likely to exhaust us because it is both deep and variable. His music has two characteristics. First, the foundational structure or theme is so predictable that it can actually be drawn in a mathematical graph! It is firm and solid — like the foundation Jesus said was underneath the house built on rock. But there is also an endless series of variations — now soaring above the central pattern, now plunging beneath it — notes running in cadenzas, with almost no two bars exactly the same. He rings the changes and often reverses them.

On its own, the foundation would be precise, but boring. And on its own, the counterpoint — the variations — would be light, even trivial. But together!

Jesus said, 'It is only when you know the truth, that

you can be liberated!' 'If the Son sets you free, then you are really free.'

❦

God requires that we should love him eternally with our whole hearts, yet not so as to compromise or diminish our earthly affections, but as a kind of *cantus firmus* to which the other melodies of life provide the counterpoint.

Earthly affection is one of these contrapuntal themes, a theme which enjoys an autonomy of its own. Even the Bible can find room for the Song of Songs — and one could hardly have a more passionate and sensual love than is there portrayed. It is a good thing that the book is included in the Bible as a protest against those who believe that Christianity stands for the restraint of passion. (Is there any example of such restraint anywhere in the Old Testament?)

Where the ground bass is firm and clear, there is nothing to stop the counterpoint from being developed to the utmost of its limits. Both ground bass and counterpoint are 'without confusion and yet distinct', in the words of the Chalcedonian formula, like Christ in his divine and human natures.

Perhaps the importance of polyphony in music lies in the fact that it is a musical reflection of this Christological truth, and that it is therefore an essential element in the Christian life. . . We must have good, clear *cantus firmus*. Without it, there can be no full or perfect sound. But with it, the counterpoint has a firm support and cannot get out of tune or fade out, yet is always a perfect whole in its own right. Only a polyphony of this kind can give life a wholeness.

Dietrich Bonhoeffer, *Letters and Papers from Prison*

Love, and do what you will.

St Augustine of Hippo

It has been said that there are only two things in life that we parents and teachers can give our children — roots and wings. So simple a message and yet so challenging a task!

To give our young people strong roots for their lives is to provide them with a set of values which will help them to weather the inevitable storms of life, to separate substance from image and distinguish the enduring from the fashionable. Not that we want to arm our children against life. Far from it! We want them to be people living generously and happily in their world with strong values and firm roots — like the sensible person in the Gospels who built his house on rock to withstand all that the elements could hurl at it.

For some time now, I have kept a poster on my study wall depicting two seagulls in full flight. A quotation from Virgil is inscribed below them: 'They *can* because they *think* they can.' It is a marvellous picture of wings, of freedom, the other great gift we can offer our young people. . .

Values and freedom are inseparable companions. . . Parents and teachers, as significant and trusted adults, share the task of helping our young people to balance values and freedom, responsibilities and rights, and to understand the capacity to do what they want they must be governed by the strength to do what they ought.

Freedom without limits is not freedom at all. It is licence. Freedom without values — wings without a proper launching pad, without strong roots — is a recipe for self-destruction.

Christopher Gleeson, Striking a Balance

There is a life of the spirit higher still than that of the mind, and that is the only life that can satisfy a person.

Antoine de Saint-Exupery

If you try to think where we went wrong, it was in de-linking rights and responsibilities.

Roger Conner, 'American Alliance for
Rights and Responsibilities'

We walk a narrow line between law and grace, between morality and gospel, structure and creativity. These are the two poles around which the whole of life revolves.

They are the Right and Left of politics. They are the twin centres of gravity which determine how all societies are ordered and controlled. They are the traditional and institutional foundations of Christianity, on the one hand, and the liberal or charismatic expressions of Christianity on the other. The success of life depends upon embracing them both, realising the creative tension between them and the potential of each to destroy the other.

Neil Adcock, unpublished sermon

Make me a captive, Lord,
   and then I shall be free;
Force me to render up my sword,
   and I shall conquerer be.
My heart is weak and poor
   until it master find;
It has no spring of action sure;
   it varies with the wind.
It cannot freely move
   till thou hast wrought its chain;
Enslave it with thy matchless love,
   and deathless it shall reign.

George Matheson

God, you are both almighty and all-pervasive. I fill my mind with you now, within my limited intellectual and spiritual capacity.

I worship you as creator, sustainer and provider for all life.

I worship you as saviour, companion and life-giver.

I worship you as inner strengthener and inspirer of all that is good.

We have all been made in your image and likeness. You are both lawgiver and imaginative creator. Within us also is the need for law as well as expression.

As a society, teach us to live securely and creatively by the laws and ultimate values you have given, and manifested so perfectly and clearly in Jesus Christ.

Deliver us from both legalistic oppression and moral anarchy; from carrying unnecessary burdens, grievous to be borne; and also from doing that which is right only in our own eyes, because it feels good.

Give us both roots and wings. May life be music, with a firm and satisfying bass, and with cadenzas and thrilling variations. Let us ring all the possible changes with all the gifts, interests and aspirations your creative power has placed within us.

May we accept the life Jesus came to give us — life in all its fullness. Life abundant, in all directions.

So, today, help me to be firm on the rock and strong in you. May I reach out with eagerness and excitement to all you offer me, and all you call me to do. May your saving gospel always be good news for me, for others and for the whole world.

Keep me loyal to the truth and therefore to find its freedom. And what I find, may I share with everybody. To the glory of your holy name. Through Jesus Christ. Amen.

A Benediction

Now to him who by the power at work within us is able to accomplish abundantly far more than all we can ask or imagine, to him be glory in the church and in Christ Jesus to all generations, forever and ever. Amen.

5

A garden of solitude

The heavens are telling the glory of God; and the firmament proclaims his handiwork. . . O come, let us worship and bow down, let us kneel before the Lord, our Maker! For he is our God, and we are the people of his pasture and the sheep of his hand.

Blessed be the God and Father of our Lord Jesus Christ, who has blessed us in Christ with every spiritual blessing in the heavenly places. . . I pray that you may have the power to comprehend, with all the saints, what is the breadth and length and height and depth, and to know the love of Christ that surpasses knowledge, so that you may be filled with all that fullness of God.

May my meditation be pleasing to him, for I rejoice in the Lord. . . Surely goodness and mercy shall follow me all the days of my life, and I shall dwell in the house of the Lord my whole life long. . . The Lord is my shepherd, I shall not want. He makes me lie down in green pastures; he restores my soul. He leads me in right paths for his name's sake.

Blessed are the pure in heart, for they will see God. . . When the Lord saw that he had turned aside to see, God called to him out of the bush, 'Moses, Moses!' And he said, 'Here I am.' Then he said, 'Come no closer! Remove the sandals from your feet, for the place on which you are standing is holy ground.'

Let the words of my mouth and the meditation of my heart be acceptable to you, O Lord, my rock and my redeemer.

(Psalm 19: 1; 95: 6–7; Ephesians 1: 3; 3: 18 and 19; Psalm 104: 34; 23: 6, 1–3; Matthew 5: 8; Exodus 3: 4–5; Psalm 19: 14 — all NRSV)

One day, a friend and I were spending a leisurely day together. We saw a sign 'Fragrant Gardens'. We had both seen the sign many times before, but we were always too busy to go and investigate. The red dirt road was uninviting and yet, as we travelled it, there was a sense of tranquillity.

Finally, a sign welcomed us, invited us to park the car and to come on into the garden. We sat there mulling over whether it was worth getting out of the car — or was this another dead end like the one earlier in the day?

But the garden beckoned us. We felt welcome and yet there was a sense of invading someone's privacy. The feel of the garden was one of intimacy — a place of tranquillity, a place of solitude. For while there was evidence of the work of a loving gardener, there was no-one to disturb us. It was as if we were walking on holy ground.

We walked and the garden's peace seeped into our being. This was God's place. Finally, we wandered back to the car, but were hesitant to get in and drive away. We climbed the old wooden fence. We looked again and breathed in the beauty and peace of this place, enjoying the sense of God's presence. Here was a garden of solitude. A garden rich with the presence of God. A place of quiet retreat, a place of exquisite beauty — and here we were refreshed.

My friend and I hardly spoke. This time was too precious to be lost in chatter. For here we were experiencing a oneness with the Lord, with each other and with the beauty of his creation.

Later over a cup of tea, we shared our experiences in the garden. Our sense of the Lord's presence and our response to him had been remarkably similar. As we reflected together, the hand of the creative gardener, though unseen, was surely evident. The garden embodied humility and beauty; it invited us and others to come and enjoy freely, to drink in its beauty and its peace. We wanted to share this place with others — but would they experience the solitude and the powerful presence of the Lord as we had?

The memory of that brief time in the garden is indelibly written upon my heart and mind. We can experience the powerful presence of God in a garden, in the wilderness or in a church or chapel. It's in these 'secret' places where we meet with our Lord in worship and prayer in a special way.

The location doesn't matter. What does matter is that we recognise that we are on 'holy ground' and that we linger and delight in this time with our Lord. These are moments of solitude when we experience the awesomeness of the one who is our God. More often, as Richard Foster notes of the experiences of solitude, 'we are sifted in the stillness'. The Lord challenges our 'vain images of ourselves in charge of everything and everybody'. God may confirm to us his will and his purpose, and we affirm our allegiance to him.

We can't always create the experience of solitude, but we can surely set aside time to be available, to 'waste' time with God, to ask the Holy Spirit to open our ears that we might hear what he would say to us. As we are faithful in taking the time to be silent in the presence of our Lord, then there will surely be times when he draws very near.

❦

Solitude is not simply a quiet time and place. It is not only a matter of stilling the many inner voices so that we can come to a point of quietness and inner peace. It is much more than that. . . Solitude is thus not only a place of aloneness. It is also the place of companionship and fellowship. It is not only the place of stillness. It is also the place of conversation.

Solitude is not withdrawal in order to get away. It is withdrawal in order to be with someone who normally gets crowded out of our lives. . . Solitude allows us to practise the presence of God as attentive listeners and as companions who are at peace in each other's company.

Charles Ringma, *Dare to Journey*

Without solitude, it is virtually impossible to live a spiritual life. Solitude begins with a time and place for God and for him alone. If we really believe not only that God exists, but also that he is actively present in our lives — healing, teaching and guiding — we need to set aside a time and space to give him our undivided attention. Jesus says, 'Go to your private room and, when you have shut your door, pray to your Father who is in that secret place' (Matthew 6: 6).

Henri Nouwen, *Making All Things New*

In solitude, however, we die not only to others, but also to ourselves. To be sure, at first we thought solitude was a way to recharge our batteries in order to enter life's many competitions with new vigour and strength. In time, however, we find that solitude gives us power not to win the rat race, but to ignore the rat race altogether. Slowly, we find ourselves letting go of our inner compulsions to acquire more wealth than we need, look more youthful than we are, attain more status than is wise. In the stillness, our false, busy selves are unmasked and seen for the imposters they truly are.

Richard Foster, *Prayer: Finding the Heart's True Home*

I had never delighted in God in this way before. And it had never occurred to me that God wanted me to linger in his presence so that he could show me that he delighted in me. Until now, my prayer had been vocal, busy, sometimes manipulative, always achievement-orientated. To kneel at the foot of a cross, allow music to wash over me so that I could 'just be' with God in stillness which convinced me that 'he is', that 'he is God', was a new experience. But to 'waste time' for God in this way was changing my life, changing my view of God, changing my perception of prayer, changing my understanding of listening to God.

Joyce Huggett, *Listening to God*

Deserts, silence, solitudes are not necessarily places, but states of mind and heart. These deserts can be found in the midst of the city and the everyday of our lives. We need only to look for them and realise our tremendous need for them. They will be small solitudes, little deserts, tiny pools of silence, but the experience they will bring, if we are disposed to enter them, may be as exultant and as holy as all the deserts of the world, even the one God himself entered. For it is God who makes solitude, deserts and silences holy.

Catherine de Hueck Doherty, *Poustinia*

Christian ministry is born in solitude, expressed through an active caring for the world and the people in it and sustained by an openness to the presence of God in every aspect of human life. It is a way of life that allows us to find solitude even when we are surrounded by people: solitude involves being alone with God.

There are times when this will mean withdrawal and a significant change of pace. There are other times when solitude is found in walking on a city street, in quietly praying for a stranger, or in simply being still in the midst of activity. Underlying all this is a sense of expectation — the sense that, in the most mundane experience, there is always the possibility of meeting God in a new way.

James C. Fenhagen, *Ministry & Solitude*

Perhaps true communication does not consist in the skilful use of words or in their abundance. Rather, it is an exchange of hearts. The speaker opens his or her heart to the other and speaks words that transmit the deepest self. . . The first step towards achieving this true communication is to sweep away all the useless words, the endless chattering, and to begin to listen.

Stephen Rossetti, 'The Pure Gold of Silence'

My friends, prayer is like that. If you fall in love, then it's impossible to separate life and breath from prayer. Prayer is simply union with God. Prayer does not need words. When people are in love, they look at each other, look into each other's eyes, or a wife simply lies in the arms of her husband. Neither of them talks. When love reaches its apex, it cannot be expressed anymore. It reaches that immense realm of silence where it pulsates and reaches proportions unknown to those who haven't entered into it. Such is the life of prayer with God. You enter into God and God enters into you, and the union is constant.

Catherine de Hueck Doherty, *Poustinia*

Solitude in prayer is not privacy. The difference between privacy and solitude is profound. Privacy is our attempt to insulate the self from interference; solitude leaves the company of others for a time in order to listen to them more deeply, be aware of them, serve them.

Privacy is getting away from others so that I don't have to be bothered with them; solitude is getting away from the crowd so that I can be instructed by the still, small voice of God who is enthroned on the praises of the multitudes. Private prayers are selfish and thin; prayer in solitude enrolls in a multivoiced, century-layered community: with angels and archangels in all the company of heaven we sing, 'Holy, Holy, Holy, Lord God Almighty.'

Eugene H. Peterson, *Earth & Altar*

Gracious God, thankyou for times of solitude, when I know your presence with me in a special way. Thankyou for your grace that reaches out to love, to affirm, to challenge and to meet me at my points of deepest need.

Lord, I know that I cannot create the special times with you: always, they are your gift. But Lord, I also know that there are many times when I avoid you, when I don't want you to come too close, I don't want to be challenged to live for you alone, for you to examine my motives and to serve you through loving and caring for others about me.

Forgive me for being too busy, too preoccupied to linger with you, to affirm my love for you, my dependence on you and to listen for your will and guidance for my life.

Recreate in me a desire for you alone. Help me to so want intimacy with you that I desire it above all else. Lord, I offer myself, my time and my worship to you again, that I might be transformed into the person you desire for me to be. Amen.

A Benediction
Now unto him who by the power at work within us is able to accomplish abundantly far more than all we can ask or imagine, to him be glory in the church and in Christ Jesus to all generations, forever and ever. Amen.

Ephesians 3: 20–21, NRSV

6

Rooted in Christ

As you therefore have received Christ Jesus the Lord, continue to live your lives in him, rooted and built up in him and established in the faith, just as you were taught, abounding in thanksgiving.

Happy are those who do not follow the advice of the wicked, or take the path that sinners tread, or sit in the seat of scoffers; but their delight is in the law of the Lord, and on his law they meditate day and night. They are like trees planted by streams of water, which yield their fruit in its season, and their leaves do not wither. In all that they do, they prosper.

Blessed are those who trust in the Lord, whose trust is the Lord. They shall be like a tree planted by water, sending out its roots by the stream. It shall not fear when heat comes, and its leaves shall stay green; in the year of drought it is not anxious, and it does not cease to bear fruit.

I pray that, according to the riches of his glory, he may grant that you may be strengthened in your inner being with power through his Spirit and that Christ may dwell in your hearts through faith, as you are being rooted and grounded in love.

Abide in me as I abide in you. Just as the branch cannot bear fruit by itself unless it abides in the vine, neither can you unless you abide in me. I am the vine, you are the branches. Those who abide in me and I in them bear much fruit, because apart from me you can do nothing.

Everyone then who hears these words of mine and acts on them will be like a wise man who built his house on rock. The rain fell, the floods came, and the winds blew and beat on that house, but it did not fall, because it had been founded on rock.

(Colossians 2: 6–7; Psalm 1: 1–3; Jeremiah 17: 7–8; Ephesians 3: 16–17; John 15: 4–5; Matthew 7: 24–25 — all NRSV)

'Rooted in Christ': think on that image from Paul's letter to the Colossians. Roots — the source of our life and nourishment, deep in Christ. Roots — the very basis of who we are, grounded firmly in Christ Jesus our Lord. Roots — the source of our security and sense of belonging, penetrating deeply into Jesus and giving to our lives stability and fulfilment. It is a powerful image expressing the foundation of our lives as Christians.

Earlier this year, there was a cyclone in our part of the world. A gum tree in my front garden was uprooted. The roots were big and strong, but the combination of the rain and the wind was even stronger. Our roots need to so penetrate into Christ Jesus our Lord that no matter what happens to us, we can never be destroyed. No matter how painful the experiences of life, no matter how disillusioned we may sometimes feel, or how much we have been let down by those we have trusted, we can have our lives so firmly rooted in Christ that nothing can shake us or cause harm to our relationship with the Lord.

Our circumstances are often not of our own choosing. There are many happenings over which we have little or no control. There are times when we are touched by the stabbing pain of the loss of a loved one. There are times when God allows us to go through a period when it's as if the hot sun is parching our souls and we appear to be in the midst of a spiritual drought. There are times when our Lord asks us to take a step of obedience which makes our future precarious. There are times when we live with ambiguity, pressures not of our own making, and when there seems to be nothing we can do to change what is happening to us.

In those times, our faith can be sorely tested. In those times when we feel the strength of the forces against us, a life rooted in Christ will enable us to weather the circumstances and even to penetrate more deeply into him as we trust him in the midst of the turmoil.

Sometimes, we try to kid ourselves that our roots are in Christ, when in reality they are in Christ *and* in something else. It's often in the midst of storms and pressure that Christ invites us to uproot all the other things in which we attempt to find security, prestige or nourishment and to deepen our rootedness in himself.

When our roots are firmly in Christ alone, we will be like a growing plant, with vitality and fruit in abundance, even through the times of testing. May we seek to have the roots of our life so unmeshed in Christ our Lord that we cannot separate ourselves from him — for, when we do, we are secure for time and eternity.

❧

When we are one with God's love, we own all things in him. They are ours to offer him in Christ his Son. For all things belong to the children of God and we are Christ's and Christ is God's. Resting in his glory above all pleasure and pain, joy or sorrow and every other good or evil, we love in all things his will rather than the things themselves, and that is the way we make creation a sacrifice in praise of God. This is the end for which all things were made by God.

Thomas Merton, New Seeds of Contemplation

Yet total, all-out trust on our part is not as easy as it first seems. There are periods when God's face is shrouded, when his dealings with us will appear as if he does not care, when he seems not to be acting like a true father. Can we then hang onto the fact of his love and his faithfulness and that he is a prayer-answering God?

Catherine Marshall, A Closer Walk

In my praying I find that I do with God what I do with other people in forming and nurturing intimate relationships. I disclose myself in the hearing of Another with whom I feel safe and related. I come to know I am known by God, not just because God is all-knowing, but because I have freely made myself known. In prayer, God reveals himself to me, not just because I think about what I have come to know about him, but through a contemplative understanding of what those things mean to me and for me.

My self-disclosure in the presence of the one who already knows me through and through, leads me to a self-awareness which is deeper still, and which I can disclose with increasing confidence. The cumulative effect of this kind of praying is an abiding and increasing realisation that I belong uniquely to God.

Keith Clark, *Being Sexual . . . and Celibate*

When the journey becomes long and wearisome,
the path steep and rough,
the troubles more than we can handle,
and the forces of evil appear to have the upper hand,
it is time to revert to our roots,
to assure ourselves of our vocation,
our relationship and responsibility to God,
and our commitment to his purposes for our lives.

Leslie F. Brandt, *Meditations along the Journey of Faith*

But we never can prove
the delights of his love
until all on the altar we lay,
for the favour he shows
and the joy he bestows
are for those who will trust and obey.

John Henry Sammis

We can be very good, and many people are very good, but this is not the same thing as belonging wholly to God and, if we want to belong wholly to God, then we have to be very generous. If we want to belong wholly to God, we must make sacrifices which in no way conflict with our loving duties to others, to give time to prayer.

Ruth Burrows, *To Believe in Jesus*

Lord Jesus, you alone are Lord.
Forgive me for the times I seek my security
in 'things' or in others, rather than in you.
Help me to keep my eyes on you and to rejoice
in your love for me, so that I may trust you
for all things in every situation.
May my roots be deeply in you, so that I express
your life through every part of my being. Amen.

A Benediction
The Lord bless you and keep you;
The Lord make his face to shine upon you,
and be gracious unto you;
The Lord lift up his countenance upon you,
and give you peace. Amen.

7

Do yourself a favour — forgive others!

Blessed are the merciful, for they will receive mercy.

So when you are offering your gift at the altar, if you remember that your brother or sister has something against you, leave your gift there before the altar and go; first, be reconciled to your brother or sister, and then come and offer your gift.

I say to you, love your enemies and pray for those who persecute you, so that you may be children of your Father in heaven; for he makes his sun rise on the evil and on the good, and sends rain on the righteous and on the unrighteous.

And forgive us our debts, as we also have forgiven our debtors.

For if you forgive others their trespasses, your heavenly Father will also forgive you; but if you do not forgive others, neither will your Father forgive your trespasses.

Jesus said, 'Father, forgive them; for they do not know what they are doing.'

Be kind to one another, tenderhearted, forgiving one another, as God in Christ has forgiven you.

For judgment will be without mercy to anyone who has shown no mercy; mercy triumphs over judgment.

(Matthew 5: 7, 23–24 and 44–45; 6: 12, 14–15; Luke 23: 34; Ephesians 4: 32; James 2: 13 — all NRSV)

A young man had a sharp disagreement with another member in a church. Knowing that the young man had been a Christian for a longer period than the other person, the pastor proposed to him that he initiate the process of reconciliation. The young man said to the pastor: 'He is the one who has started all these troubles. I have done nothing wrong. Why should I go to him? He should be the one to make the first move, not me.'

When a maid was standing on a stool and cleaning the clock that was hanging on the wall, one of the legs of the stool came loose. Trying to grab hold of something to prevent a bad fall, she pulled the expensive clock down with her and it crashed on the floor. Being from a poor family, she was not able to repay her master for the damage she caused. As she pleaded for forgiveness, he replied, 'Forgive you? Who is going to pay for the damage?'

Forgiving others isn't easy, mainly for two old-fashioned reasons — pride and selfishness.

Why should we forgive the one who has wronged us? Try these good reasons:

* *God commands us to forgive others.* In Luke 6: 37, we read: 'Forgive and you will be forgiven!' If we acknowledge God's sovereignty over our lives, we have no choice but to forgive.
* *Forgiving makes us more like our heavenly Father.* We are most like the animals when we kill; most like fellow-humans when we judge; most like God when we forgive.
* *Refusal to forgive may result in our suffering beyond death,* as Jesus warned when he told the story of the unforgiving servant in Matthew 18: 23–35. Jesus often talked about God using the same standard against us that we use against others.
* *Forgiving others brings peace and joy to oneself.* George Herbert wrote: 'If you cannot forgive others, you break the bridge over which you must pass if you would ever reach heaven; for everyone needs to be forgiven.'

It is actually easier to pardon than to resent. Forgiveness saves you from getting sick from anger. Hatred carries a high price-tag. And if you have not forgiven an enemy, you have never tasted one of life's most sublime enjoyments.

* *Forgiveness is needed by others for their wholeness.* Jesus' Golden Rule is the bedrock of a functioning community: 'In everything, do to others as you would have them do to you; for this is the law and the prophets' (Matthew 7: 12). When another knows they're forgiven, their sense of self-worth is emphasised, their dignity is underlined, their personhood is enhanced.

* *Forgiving others will turn enemies into friends.* A Malaysian pastor was accused by a church member of having done many wrong things. Therefore, a meeting was called with all the church leaders present to resolve this problem. During the meeting, that member was first given the chance to mention his case against the pastor. Then the pastor was allowed to give an explanation for each of the accusations brought against him.

Upon hearing the explanations, the leaders realised that the case could not stand. However, the member was not willing to admit that he was wrong and kept repeating his accusation. The pastor, not wishing to lose this member and gain an enemy, said to him: 'I am very thankful for your concern regarding my pastoral reputation. Shall we forgive one another and forget what had happened? Let us join hands and serve God in order to build up one another rather than tearing one another down.' With tears in his eyes, he hugged the pastor and asked him to pray for him.

The story did not stop there. The following day after the incident, two leaders went and said to the pastor: 'We want to express our appreciation for what you did yesterday. We are amazed and yet very happy to see how you forgave that brother. We really still have a lot to learn from you.'

So do yourself a favour — forgive others. Those who forgive most readily will be most readily forgiven — by God, by others and, not least, by oneself!

❧❧❧

[Jesus] loved others as himself. He was prepared personally to pay the price for our forgiveness. When he died on the cross for our sins, it was not because he undervalued human life, not because he was sick of living, not because he was caught up in the political circumstances of the time, not because everything was too much for him; but because he loved himself as our representative and he came to fulfil God's plan of salvation for us by reconciling us to God.

The order of God's commandments are right: love God with all your heart and you will love your neighbour as you love yourself.

Lance Shilton

The forgiveness of sins has a fundamental significance in the teaching of Jesus Christ. History reveals no prophet or founder of religion who came forward, as he did, with the claim to have power under God to forgive sin. . .

The certainty of forgiveness in Christ is, if not the sum, at least the secret of Christian religion. . .

The real truth is that our forgiveness, at its noblest, is no more than a faint echo or imitation of that eternal and transcendent divine pardon made ours in Jesus, with which everything began.

H.R. Mackintosh

The major teaching of the parable [of the prodigal son] is that God's forgiveness is completely unearned. The son did nothing to merit it — rather the reverse. . . Forgiveness is an act of grace as far as humans are concerned. At the same time, it shows a link between forgiveness and penitence, which is essential if the moral aspect of forgiveness is to be maintained. In the parable, the son had to be willing to accept forgiveness if the father was to bestow it. . .

The main point of the [Lord's] prayer [is that] those who ask for forgiveness and yet harbour an unforgiving attitude to others are asking the impossible. . .

[Then there] is the obligation of the offended person to take the initiative in setting the processes of reconciliation in motion. Anyone about to offer an offering to God must first be reconciled with the offender (Matthew 5: 23–24). . . one must take the initiative, which requires. . . a forgiving attitude. . . In the story of the prodigal son, the father takes no steps to urge the prodigal to repent, but he certainly takes the initiative in the actual reconciliation.

Donald Guthrie

[In my prayer of] confession I use the categories of the 'seven deadly sins' of Catholic piety: anger, lust, envy, greed, gluttony, sloth and pride. . . As I offer each category to God, I ask the Holy Spirit to reveal to me what my sin has been. For example, as I sit quietly with anger, sometimes the Spirit will lead me into little nooks and crannies of my being and I'll discover resentments, irritations or bitterness I hadn't been conscious of.

When I feel the Spirit has plumbed an area of sin, I'll ask the Lord to forgive me, to let me experience forgiveness and to give me the power to forgive those who have hurt me. There are times when I realise that God wants me to make some sort of intervention or restitution with certain individuals, and then I must ask for the courage to follow through.

Kenneth Swanson

Only saints and the bovine can say that there is no-one they dislike — and it was not always true of the saints.

Some people have given us great cause to dislike them. They may have injured us, by deed or word, deeply and irreparably. It is hard not to hate them.

God has a special concern that we pray for them, wanting to rid us of the mild dislike, or burning hate, and this is one way to do it. God uses prayer as a filter. The very effort to pray for them will help us. The prayer will help us even more. You cannot hate people you pray for. The two things cannot live together in the same heart. . .

If you are disliking them without a cause (and we often do dislike people without a cause), prayer brings you to that realisation. If you are disliking them for a trifling cause (their manner or some petty annoyance they gave

you), the whole thing looks trifling in the light of God.
You feel ashamed of your own pettiness. . .

Pray to love them. God's gifts include a supernatural
love by which the Christian can even love people he or
she does not like.

Once this is given, prayer is not impossible. It is not
even hard.

W.E. Sangster

If you are not getting answers to your prayers, check
yourself very thoroughly and honestly as to whether you
have resentments on your mind.

Spiritual power cannot pass through a personality where
resentment exists. Hate is a non-conductor of spiritual
energy.

I suggest that every time you pray you add this phrase,
'Lord, take from my thought all ill will, grudges, hates,
jealousies.' Then practise casting these things from your
thoughts.

Norman Vincent Peale

It is a testimony to their strength of character, forged in
the greatest adversity, that many of the ex-hostages [held
in Beirut] speak of the need to forgive their former captors.
'I'm a Christian and a Catholic,' Terry Anderson said last
week. 'It's required of me that I forgive, no matter how
hard it may be.'

Jill Smolowe

Of the Seven Deadly Sins, anger is possibly the most fun.
To lick your wounds, to smack your lips over grievances
long past, to roll over your tongue the prospect of bitter
confrontations still to come, to savour to the last toothsome
morsel both the pain you are given and the pain you are
giving back — in many ways it is a feast fit for a king.

The chief drawback is that what you are wolfing down
is yourself. The skeleton at the feast is you.

Frederick Buechner

The past is, perhaps, not totally lost, but it is no longer

ours; it is in the hands of God and is God's business. It will be retrieved in the *tota simul possessio* of eternity, but should not be stored away on earth. As far as we are concerned, we must realise that we are like children at the beginning, not the end, of a road. Whatever past achievements might bring us honour, whatever past disgraces might make us blush, all of these have been crucified with Christ; they exist no more except in the deep recesses of God's eternity, where good is enhanced into glory and evil miraculously established as part of the greater good. . .

Abba Theodotus said, 'Do not judge a fornicator if you are chaste, otherwise you will be transgressing the law, too. For he who said, "Do not fornicate", also said, "Do not judge".'

We are all equally privileged, not unentitled beggars before the door of God's mercy.

Simon Tugwell

When we forgive we adore, invoke, surrender to God as universal mercy: 'Our father, forgive us. . . as we forgive others.' All the idols of our self-serving, even if they wear the sacred names of justice, loyalty, peace, tradition or humanity — all have to go. . . Faith is never merely a reaction to evil. It is an encounter with the only kind of love that can redeem us. It is not the problem of evil that is first (and last), but the mystery of love and goodness.

Tony Kelly

Forgiveness breaks the chain of causality because people who 'forgive' you — out of love — take upon themselves the consequences of what you have done. Forgiveness, therefore, always entails sacrifice.

The price you must pay for your own liberation through another's sacrifice is that you in turn must be willing to liberate in the same way, irrespective of the consequences to yourself.

Dag Hammarskjöld

I have nothing whereof I may glory in my works: I will therefore glory in Christ. I will not glory because I am righteous, but because I am redeemed; not because I am clear of sin, but because my sins are forgiven.

St Ambrose

A clergyman I know was a prisoner-of-war in a Japanese camp. He showed me his hand. He has no fingernails. They had been drawn out one by one as punishment for an alleged offence, of which he was quite unaware.

I asked him how he felt about this sadistic, inhuman, brutal behaviour and the people who could perpetrate such dastardly crimes. He said simply: 'Every week I lead my congregation in the Lord's Prayer. We say together: "Forgive us our trespasses as we forgive those who trespass against us." I couldn't be a Christian if my heart remained unforgiving.'

John N. Gladstone

Corrie ten Boom was struck in a concentration camp, humiliated and degraded, especially in the delousing shower where the women were ogled by the leering guards. But she made it through that hell. And eventually, she had forgiven even those fiends who guarded the shower stalls.

So she preached forgiveness. . .[in] Europe, in the US, and, one Sunday, in Munich. After the sermon, greeting people, she saw a man coming towards her, hand outstretched: '*Ja Fraulein*, it is wonderful that Jesus forgives us all our sins, just as you say.' She remembered his face; it was the leering, lecherous, mocking face of an SS guard of the shower stall.

Her hand froze at her side. She could not forgive. She thought she had forgiven all. But she could not forgive when she met a guard, standing in solid flesh in front of her. Ashamed, horrified at herself, she prayed: 'Lord, forgive me, I cannot forgive.' And as she prayed, she felt forgiven, accepted, in spite of her shabby performance as a famous forgiver.

Her hand was suddenly unfrozen. The ice of hate melted. Her hand went out. She forgave as she felt forgiven. . .

Our only escape from history's cruel unfairness, our only passage to the future's creative possibilities, is the miracle of forgiving.

Lewis Smedes

Jesus, friend of sinners, you call us to love our enemies, to do good to those who hate us, to bless those who curse us and pray for those who treat us badly.

Jesus, reconciler, when someone slaps us on the cheek, you call us to offer the other; when someone takes our coat, you bid us give our shirt as well; when someone takes what is ours, we may not demand it back.

Jesus, Son of God, our friend and brother, when we love our enemies and do good we are children of God, who is kind to the wicked and ungrateful. Jesus, teacher without peer, you have turned the world upside down.

A New Zealand Prayer Book

Your goodness, your gentleness, your loving-kindness, your patient forgiveness, your love for your enemies — Lord, I want to be like you.

You are so kind, Lord; forgive my ingratitude. You are so strong; forgive my stubborn independence. You are my Master and Lord; forgive my disobedience. You are so pure and holy; forgive my sins. Amen.

A Benediction
May our forgiving God create in you a clean heart and renew a right spirit within you. May you know you are not cast away from God's presence and that the renewing Holy Spirit lives within you. May you experience the joy of salvation and the strength of a willing spirit cause you to delight to do God's will, always. Amen.

The anointing of grace and power

Then the Lord said to Moses: 'Take the following fine spices. . . Make these into a sacred anointing oil, a fragrant blend, the work of a perfumer. It will be the sacred anointing oil.'

'Anoint Aaron and his sons and consecrate them so they may serve me as priests. Say to the Israelites: "This is to be my sacred anointing oil for the generations to come. Do not pour it on men's bodies and do not make any oil with the same formula. It is sacred and you are to consider it sacred. Whoever makes perfume like it and whoever puts it on anyone other than a priest must be cut off from his people."'

'But the priests. . . are to come near to minister before me; they are to stand before me to offer sacrifices. . . They alone are to enter my sanctuary; they alone are to come near my table to minister before me and perform my service.'

They are to teach my people the difference between the holy and the common, and show them how to distinguish between the unclean and the clean.

How good and pleasant it is when [brothers and sisters] live together in unity! It is like precious oil poured on the head, running down on the beard, running down on Aaron's beard, down upon the collar of his robes. . . For there the Lord bestows his blessing, even life for evermore.

So Samuel took the horn of oil and anointed him in the presence of his brothers, and from that day on the Spirit of the Lord came upon David in power.

[David] said to his men, 'The Lord forbid that I should do

such a thing to my master, the Lord's anointed, or lift my hand against him; for he is the anointed of the Lord.'

The kings of the earth take their stand and the rulers gather together against the Lord and against his Anointed One.

'I have installed my King on Zion, my holy hill. I will proclaim the decree of the Lord: He said to me, "You are my Son; today, I have become your Father. Ask of me and I will make the nations your inheritance, the ends of the earth your possession. You will rule them with an iron sceptre; you will dash them to pieces like pottery."

'Therefore, you kings, be wise; be warned, you rulers of the earth. Serve the Lord with fear and rejoice with trembling. Kiss the Son, lest he be angry and you be destroyed in your way, for his wrath can flare up in a moment. Blessed are all who take refuge in him.'

You are most excellent. . . and your lips have been anointed with grace, since God has blessed you forever.

The Spirit of the Sovereign Lord is on me, because the Lord has anointed me to preach good news to the poor. He has sent me to bind up the brokenhearted, to proclaim freedom for the captives and release from darkness for the prisoners, to proclaim the year of the Lord's favour and the day of vengeance of our God, to comfort all who mourn, and provide for those who grieve in Zion — to bestow on them a crown of beauty instead of ashes, the oil of gladness instead of mourning, and a garment of praise instead of a spirit of despair. They will be called oaks of righteousness, a planting of the Lord for the display of his splendour.

When all the people were being baptised, Jesus was baptised, too. And as he was praying, heaven was opened and the Holy Spirit descended on him in bodily form like a dove. And a voice came from heaven: 'You are my son, whom I love; with you I am well pleased.'

(Exodus 30: 22, 25, 30–33; Ezekiel 44: 15–16, 23; Psalm 133: 1–3; 1 Samuel 16: 13; 24: 6; Psalm 2: 2, 6–12; Psalm 45: 2; Isaiah 61: 1–3; Luke 3: 21–22 — all NIV)

A normally quiet, unassuming pastor preached one night with unusual exuberance. He danced around, clapped his hands, slapped his thighs, gesticulated fervently, ducked and weaved with animation. After the message, one of his hearers raced to congratulate him. 'Pastor! You really had the anointing tonight!' he said enthusiastically. 'Anointing nothing,' replied the pastor. 'Those were mosquitoes!'

The term 'anointing' is hardly heard at all in some churches. In others, it is over-used. This is a pity, because it is a valuable and crucial aspect of Christian tradition.

The simplest way to understand this idea is to look at the life of Jesus. The name 'Christ' means 'Anointed One'. So *to be anointed is to be like Jesus!*

Jesus was anointed as Prince, Priest and Prophet. His was an anointing of grace, holiness and power. The same can apply to believers. 'Now it is God who makes both us and you stand firm in Christ,' writes Paul. 'He anointed us, set his seal of ownership on us and put his Spirit in our hearts. . .'

John says: 'You have an anointing from the Holy One. . . the anointing you received from him remains in you. . . that anointing is real, not counterfeit — just as it has taught you, remain in him.'

First, then, it is an anointing of grace — it is God who chooses to do it. This is clearly seen in the enthronement of Old Testament kings.

So important was it to recognise the sovereign choice of God in their enthronement that they were frequently referred to as 'the Lord's anointed'. There were three obvious qualities of his royal anointing. There was permanence. Once anointed as king, you were king for the rest of your life. In the same way, we have a permanent place in the kingdom of God. His anointing remains with us (1 John 2: 27) and we share his rule forever (Revelation 1: 6 – 5: 10). Grace is secure.

Also, there was a royal authority (Psalm 2: 9). To us also, as believers in the Lord Jesus Christ, has been given the authority to renounce sin and to defeat the devil (Ephesians 1: 17f.).

Finally, there was victory (2 Samuel 7: 9; 8: 14; and Psalm 18: 34). When God anoints us, we can live victoriously, daily experiencing the conquest of Christ over evil and despair.

Second, the anointing is one of holiness. When Old Testament priests were anointed, it was primarily to set them apart from normal activities for the service of the tabernacle or temple. They were clothed in garments that gave them a sense of dignity; their regular access to the holy place meant that their role was permanent; they knew the guidance of God; and the anointing was unique, involving a special, sacred oil (Exodus 30: 22 – 38).

When we come to Christ, we too regain a sense of dignity, having no guilt or shame (Ephesians 2: 10). We are able to come confidently before him in prayer (Hebrews 4: 14f.). We have a permanent place in God's family (Hebrews 9: 15). We enjoy the guidance of the Spirit (1 John 2: 27); and we know that the blessings we experience are unique — nothing else can compare with the good things God does in our lives (1 John 3: 1f.)!

Third, there is an anointing of power. Old Testament prophets experienced this — Samson, Saul, David, Elijah, Elisha, Isaiah, Amos and Zerrubabel are obvious examples. Whenever the Spirit came on them, they usually prophesied or performed a heroic act. When Jesus was baptised, he, too, was anointed with the Spirit and with power (Luke 4: 1f.; Acts 10: 38).

We, too, have the promise of the power of the Spirit to enable us to bear witness to our faith and to touch the community for Christ (Acts 1: 8).

The anointing oil of Exodus was a richly perfumed blend. If any ingredients were omitted or used in the wrong proportion, the fragrance would have been irrevocably affected. We need all facets of these 'anointings': grace, holiness and power. They are ours through Christ, who is himself the Anointed One.

In the book of Genesis, God created by his word and through his Spirit, so it was fitting that, at the very commencement of God's new work of re-creation in our hearts, there should be the same operation of the whole Godhead. Here, on Jordan's banks, God speaks his word again, and again the Spirit is brooding over the waters.

Alan Cole, Mark

Hail to the Lord's Anointed,
Great David's greater Son;
Hail in the time appointed,
His reign on earth begun!
He comes to break oppression,
To set the captives free;
To take away transgression,
And rule in equity.
He shall come down like showers
Upon the fruitful earth;
And love, joy, hope, like flowers,
Spring in his path to birth.
Before him on the mountains
Shall peace, the herald go;
And righteousness in fountains
From hill to valley flow.

James Montgomery

The spiritual unction is the Holy Spirit himself, of which the sacrament is the visible unction. Of this unction of Christ he says, that all who have it know the bad and the good; and they need not to be taught, because the unction itself teaches them. . . if there be not One within that shall teach, vain is the noise we make.

Augustine, Homilies on the First Epistle of John

We see. . . the blessing wherewith they are enriched from heaven. You have an unction. True Christians are anointed ones; their name intimates as much. They are anointed with the oil of grace, with gifts and spiritual endowments, by the Spirit of grace. They are anointed into a similitude of their Lord's offices, as subordinate

prophets, priests and kings unto God. The Holy Spirit
is compared to oil as well as to fire and water; and the
communication of his salvific grace is our anointing.

Matthew Henry, *Commentary*

Howell Harris lived in the realm of the Spirit. He believed
in direct leadings. He often would not act at all without
such a direct leading. Some would criticise him on those
grounds, and it may be that at times he did become what
Nuttal describes as 'an enthusiast'. . . But the point is
that he lived in close association with God and was sensitive to the Holy Spirit's influences.

Martin Lloyd-Jones, *The Puritans*

Holiness is the nature of the Spirit of God; therefore, he
is called in scripture the Holy Ghost. Holiness, which is
as it were the beauty and sweetness of the divine nature,
is as much of the proper nature of the Holy Spirit as heat
is the nature of fire, or as sweetness was the nature of
that holy anointing oil which was the principal type of
the Holy Ghost in the Mosaic dispensation; yea, I may
rather say, that holiness is as much the proper nature of
the Holy Ghost as sweetness was the nature of the sweet
odour of that ointment.

The Spirit of God so dwells in the hearts of the saints
that he there, as a seed or spring of life, exerts and
communicates himself, in this his sweet and divine
nature, making the soul a partaker of God's beauty and
Christ's joy. . .

Jonathan Edwards, *The Religious Affections*

Let us so act, dear brothers and sisters, in our work, that
there is never a smudge of a dirty thumb across the page,
and nothing of pride, self-seeking or hot-headedness, but
that all is done humbly, dependently, hopefully and always
in a holy and gracious spirit. . .

Can anything be difficult to the Holy Spirit? It is a
grand thing often to get into deep water so as to be obliged
to swim; but we like to keep our feet touching the sand.
What a mercy it is to feel that you cannot do anything,

for then you must trust in God and God alone, and feel that he is quite equal to any emergency! . . .Come, Holy Spirit, and work with all thy people now! Come and rouse us to the work; and when we are bestirred to a holy energy, then work thou with us!

Charles Spurgeon
in *The Metropolitan Tabernacle Pulpit*

It is nothing new and ought not to seem absurd that the Spirit and his gifts are designated by the word 'anointing'. For it is only in this way that we are invigorated. Especially with regard to heavenly life, there is no drop of vigour in us save what the Holy Spirit instills. For the Spirit has chosen Christ as his seat, that from him might abundantly flow the heavenly riches of which we are in such need. The believers stand unconquered through the strength of their king and his spiritual riches abound in them. Hence, they are justly called Christians.

John Calvin, *Institutes of the Christian Religion*

As to methods, we all admit that, whatever may be used, all will be in vain without the Holy Spirit. New and strange methods without the Spirit may for a while seem to succeed. . . but, like the morning cloud and the early dew, the effect will quickly pass away. . . We are always in danger of leaving the Holy Spirit out. . . Only let the ministers and members of the church be filled with the Spirit and, whatever methods may be used, the power of the Lord will be present to heal and sinners will be converted to God.

John Watsford, *Glorious Gospel Triumphs*

Breathe on me, Breath of God,
Fill me with life anew,
that I may love what thou dost love,
And do what thou wouldst do.
Breathe on me, Breath of God,
till I am wholly thine,

Till all this earthly part of me,
Glows with thy fire divine.

Edwin Hatch

A Benediction
May the Lord bless you
with the precious dew from heaven above
and with the deep waters that lie below;
with the best the sun brings forth
and the finest the moon can yield;
with the choicest gifts of the ancient mountains
and the fruitfulness of the everlasting hills;
with the best gifts of the earth and its fullness and the favour
of him who dwelt in the burning bush.
Let all these rest on your head,
as on the brow of a prince among his brothers.

Deuteronomy 33: 13–16

9

The sacred journey home

As the deer longs for the streams of cool water, so I long for you, O God. I thirst for you, the living God: when can I go and worship in your presence?. . . Why am I so sad, why am I so troubled? I will put my hope in God and once again I will praise him, my saviour and my God.

When the Lord brought us back to Jerusalem, it was like a dream! How we laughed, how we sang for joy! Then the other nations said about us, 'The Lord did great things for them.' Indeed, he did great things for us; how happy we were! Lord, take us back to our land, just as the rain brings water back to dry river-beds. Let those who wept as they sowed their seed gather the harvest with joy!

You will seek me and find me; when you seek me with all your heart, I will be found by you, says the Lord, and I will restore your fortunes and gather you from all nations and all the places where I have driven you, says the Lord, and I will bring you back to the place from which I sent you into exile.

I will arise and go to my father, and I will say to him, 'Father, I have sinned against heaven and before you; I am no longer worthy to be called your son; treat me as one of your hired servants.' And he arose and came to his father. But while he was yet at a distance, his father saw him and had compassion and ran and embraced him and kissed him.

The Lord sets the prisoners free; the Lord opens the eyes of the blind; the Lord lifts up those who are bowed down; the Lord loves the righteous. The Lord watches over the sojourners.

I know that your goodness and love will be with me all my life; and your house will be my home as long as I live.

(Psalm 42: 1, 2 and 11; Psalm 126: 1–5 — both GNB; Jeremiah 29: 13–14; Luke 15: 18–20; Psalm 146: 7–9 — all RSV; Psalm 23: 6, GNB)

Home is a place where we are known and loved: a restful place where it is safe to take off our protective armour and just be ourselves. If we have known a welcoming place like this, we will look forward to coming home after a time away; memories of home will warm our hearts like embers of a hearth fire. From such a place of refreshment and rest we will be enabled to go out into the world to engage in productive work and relationships of trust and reconciliation.

God is our soul's homeland and we are homesick for him. Our basic yearning is to be at home in him and have him make his home in us. This longing is expressed in a multitude of ways, for many do not know it is God they are seeking.

Coming home to God is like the journey of the exiled children of Israel to their longed-for homeland. Coming home to God is when prodigal sons and daughters in every culture turn from their own ways and set their faces towards their father's house. Coming home to God has been described by Thomas Merton (in *Seeds of Contemplation*) as finding 'our true selves within ourselves, in the inner sanctuary which is God's temple'.

Our true selves are our real selves; our false selves are fabricated selves, springing out of an illusion of independence. Our false selves hide from God in guilt, unable to fully trust his love. Many of us find elements of both selves in our beings. In his book, *Joy of God*, H.A. Williams suggests that we are 'half-in-halfers', partly fabricated false selves and partly people who have discovered their true identity in openness to others. He observes that 'as half-in-halfers', we are caught in the limitations between un-being and being, since we are both citizens of heaven on earth and self-excluded exiles from it.

The practice of the presence of God, through prayer and openness to his inspiration, is the way back home. Our simple desire to be one with the divine presence, to forget self and to rest in the ultimate mystery of God is the way back home. In *Open Mind, Open Heart*, Thomas Keating writes: 'This presence is healing, strengthening, refreshing. . . it is non-judgmental, self-giving, seeking no reward, boundless in compassion. It is like coming home to a place I should never have left, to an awareness that was somehow always there, but which I did not recognise.'

One way to cultivate this presence and begin the journey home is by means of centering prayer, that ancient method of Christian meditation where, in silent listening and the repetition of a sacred word, we open our beings to God. It is a simple practice that yet requires daily discipline.

God is our true home and he takes the initiative, drawing us home to him by his gentle yet powerful spirit. Of course, in our weakness, we stumble and fall at times; in our humanness we run off after attractive diversions. Yet glimpses of home encourage us to persevere on our journey.

❦

Deep within us all there is an amazing inner sanctuary of the soul, a holy place, a divine centre. . . to which we may continuously return. Eternity is at our hearts, pressing upon our time-worn lives, warming us with intimations of an astounding destiny, calling us home unto itself.

Thomas R. Kelly
A Testament of Devotion

I search for Home,
always for Home —
unaware, of course,
that I am already there.

Royce Rupp
May I Have This Dance?

He pictured coming home from boarding school, perhaps for the Christmas holidays, perhaps with the woods full of snow. It would be a winter dusk with the big blue spruce a-twinkle with tiny white lights like stars, the big car sweeping up the hill to the house. Then his mother's cries of welcome and her kiss, his father's handshake and his brother grinning in the background. And of course, as always, the cheery fire in the drawing-room, and through the French doors would be his own room just as he had left it.

Heaven itself, he thought, would be — must be — a coming home.

Sheldon Vanauken, A Severe Mercy

God says: By all means join the dance and sing the songs of a full life. At the same time, remember that you are a pilgrim. You are on your way to an eternal home which I have prepared for you. Eternal life is already begun in you, but it is not perfectly completed. There are still inevitable sufferings. But remember that the sufferings of this present stage of your life are nothing compared to the glory that you will see revealed to you some day. Eye has not ever seen, nor ear ever heard, nor has your mind ever imagined the joy prepared for you because you have opened yourself to the gift of my love.

On your way to your eternal home, enjoy the journey. Let your happiness be double, in the joyful possession of what you have and in the eager anticipation of what will be. Say a resounding 'Yes!' to life and to love at all times. Some day you will come up into my mountain and then for you all the clocks and calendars will have finished their counting. Together with all my children, you will be mine and I will be yours for ever.

John Powell, Fully Human, Fully Alive

Am I comfortable in the home that I call me? This home is of utmost importance, for it holds the key to my being comfortable in other homes. If I am not at home with myself, I won't feel at home anywhere else. It is such a delight to come home to myself, to become my own friend. . . Not only do we come home to ourselves, but we discover that the self we've come home to is a home for God. . .

What an awesome discovery. I am a home for the Most High. How often after long periods of self-rejection, standing in my own abandoned house, I cry out with new-found awareness, 'Truly God was in this place all the while and I never knew it.'

Macrina Weiderkehr, *A Tree Full of Angels*

In our old consciousness, where we identified ourselves as that false self made up of what we have, what we do and what others think of us, we were in a state of constant and complete self-alienation. We were not at home with ourselves at all. As we turn within and begin to know our true self, this split begins to be healed. We are coming home. . . This self-knowledge comes to fullness and we experience ourselves as one with God. . . There is unity and simplicity here beyond accurate description. . . This experience is usually brief in time and for most of us all too infrequent. Having personally experienced it but once. . . the whole of my being says: 'It is worth it.'

M. Basil Pennington, *Centered Living*

In fantasy and myth, homecoming is a dramatic event: bands play, the fatted calf is killed, a banquet prepared, and there is rejoicing that the prodigal has returned. In reality, exile is frequently ended gradually, with no dramatic, external events to mark its passing. The haze in the air evaporates and the world comes into focus; seeking gives way to finding, anxiety to satisfaction. Nothing is changed and everything is changed. . . Human existence ceases to be a problem to be solved and becomes a mystery to be enjoyed.

Sam Keen, *To a Dancing God*

Dove that ventured outside,
flying far from the dovecote:
housed and protected again,
one with the day, the night,
knows what serenity is,
for she has felt her wings
pass through all distance and fear
in the course of her wanderings.

Rainer Maria Rilke

When God has become our shepherd, our refuge, our fortress, then we can reach out to him in the midst of a broken world and feel at home while still on the way. When God dwells in us, we can enter into a wordless dialogue with him while still waiting on the day when he will lead us unto the house where he has prepared a place for us. Then, we can wait while we have already arrived and ask while we have already received.

Henri Nouwen, Reaching Out

Our gifts will bring us home: not to beginnings,
Nor always to the destination named
Upon our setting-forth. Our gifts compel,
Master our ways, and lead us in the end
Where we are most ourselves. . .

Adrienne Rich, 'Landscape of the Star'

Loving Father, you are calling us home. You seek us, yearn for us, believe in us, love us unconditionally. You wait for us and welcome us home when we have been away.

God of all seekers, bless our yearnings for home. Keep us on the path that leads to you. Fill us with courage to do what is best for the healing of our own hearts and the heart of the world. Accept our gratitude for the many times when you have sought us and have invited us to recognise you in the home of our true self. Amen.

Joyce Rypp

A Benediction

May our God, who is both the way and the end, create in you a longing for home and bring you into union with himself.

May our Lord Jesus grant you his grace and power, as the way leads through death into eternal life.

May the Holy Spirit, the indwelling one, be your constant companion, showing you Jesus as all you need for the journey.

Being free

Come to me, all you that are weary and are carrying heavy burdens, and I will give you rest. Take my yoke upon you, and learn from me; for I am gentle and humble in heart, and you will find rest for your souls. For my yoke is easy, and my burden is light.

For freedom Christ has set us free. Stand firm, therefore, and do not submit again to a yoke of slavery.

Then Jesus said to the Jews who had believed in him, 'If you continue in my word, you are truly my disciples; and you will know the truth and the truth will make you free.'

Am I not free? Am I not an apostle? Have I not seen Jesus our Lord? Are you not my work in the Lord?

So if the Son makes you free, you will be free indeed.

Now the Lord is the Spirit, and where the Spirit of the Lord is, there is freedom.

(Matthew 11: 28–30; Galatians 5: 1; John 8: 31–32; 1 Corinthians 9: 1; John 8: 36; 2 Corinthians 3: 17 — all NRSV)

In some Christian circles, I am told that God hates my sins so much that I must rid myself of them at every opportunity. Confess every wrongdoing. Confess every sentence I utter, if it could have been said better. Confess every thought that does not spring from 'pure motives'. Confess every trace of frustration and complaint about the need to confess so much.

I must 'confess', it wears me down! It does not bring me any closer to God, even if all my apologies apparently meet with divine approval. With such an introspective outlook, prayer becomes a necessary chore. With so much to say sorry for, there is hardly enough time to pray for anyone. This can become yet another sin to confess in subsequent prayers.

When I was first converted, I felt I had freedom-in-Christ. For many years now, this has been replaced with not-doing-anything-to-upset-God and apologise-because-you-have-upset-God.

In recent times, however, I have been learning more about the grace of God. I have been learning that, through Christ, we have been set free — set free from the fear of upsetting God. We do not have to worry about being good; we can be who we really are. We have been set free from the burden of apologising to God all the time. God is not as upset with us as much as we are.

I often wonder where so many of us in the church have gone wrong. Somewhere between responding to God's love and today, we have been shackled to a petty, cranky magistrate who is never satisfied. We have told God that the divine face cannot look upon sin. In so doing, we have made a mockery of Jesus' whole life, which was lived in the midst of humanity, with all the good, bad and ugliness.

Yet Jesus chose to spend much of his time with sinners. He didn't 'stick out like a sore thumb', either. He accepted people and so everyone was allowed to be who they really were. The only ones who 'stuck out like sore thumbs' were the religious leaders, who were concerned with not upsetting God.

It's been liberating to accept myself as God accepts me. Every day I'm learning to let go of guilt. It's an ongoing journey. My worst times are when I'm worried about upsetting God, thus stifling my natural self and feeling paralysed. My best times are when I encounter the given moment, living spontaneously. It is at these times that Jesus is most real for me, as if he is saying: 'Feel free to be yourself.'

❧

Most striking and characteristic of Jesus' living by the future as 'God's potential', crucial therefore to his understanding of God's lordship, is his utter indifference to the sinful past of another person. If it is one of the things that does come up (as with the adulterous woman), all that Jesus shows is an extreme reserve. He condemns no-one, therefore; his concern is with the potential, for the future, in the 'now' of the *metanoia*.

Edward Schillebeeckx, Jesus

On reaching the bedroom, we heard the voice of Miss Scatcherd: she was examining drawers; she had just pulled out Helen Burns'; and, when we entered, Helen was greeted with a sharp reprimand and told that tomorrow she should have half a dozen of untidily folded articles pinned to her shoulders.

'My things were indeed in shameful disorder,' murmured Helen to me, in a low voice. 'I intended to have arranged them, but I forgot.'

Next morning, Miss Scatcherd wrote in conspicuous characters on a piece of pasteboard the word 'Slattern', and bound it like a phylactery round Helen's large, mild, intelligent and benign-looking forehead. She wore it till evening, patient, unresentful, regarding it as a deserved punishment.

The moment Miss Scatcherd withdrew, after afternoon school, I ran to Helen, tore it off and thrust it into the fire. The fury of which she was incapable had been burning in my soul all day and tears, hot and large, had continually been scalding my cheek; for the spectacle of her sad resignation gave me an intolerable pain at the heart.

Charlotte Bronte, Jane Eyre

By thus overcoming the profound alienations that had encrusted humanity and its history, Jesus gave people back to themselves. In the important questions of life, nothing can substitute for the human person: neither law, nor traditions, nor religion. People must decide from within, before God and before others. Because of this, they need creativity and liberty. Security does not come from a minute observance of the laws and unreserved adherence to social and religious structures, but from the vigour of one's interior decision and from that responsible autonomy of those who know what they want and why they live.

. . .Jesus affected human beings at their very roots, activating their hope-principle and making them dream of the kingdom, which is not an entirely different world, but this world completely new and renewed.

Leonardo Boff, *Jesus Christ Liberator*

I used to think of you
as a symphony
neatly structured,
full of no surprises.
Now I see you as
a saxophone solo
blowing wildly
into the night,
a tongue of fire,
flicking in unrepeated
patterns.

Steve Turner, 'Spiritus'

By the time we are ready to leave home, we have learned to administer the protection of the inner custodian and to choose directives for ourselves — or so we think. It is this internalised protection that gives us a sense of insulation from being burned by life, from being bullied by others (and, even into mid-life, from coming face to face with our own absolute separateness). The illusion can serve us well while we are young, but it is also very tricky.

This inner custodian is a two-faced image. Like the self, it has two sides. The benevolent side of our internalised parent is felt to be the *guardian* of our safety. The *dictator*-side of our internalised parent has the menacing face of an administrator of shoulds and should-nots. Its influence is prohibitive.

Think of Janus, the ancient god of entrances and exits. His two-bearded profiles, back to back and looking in opposite directions, represent two sides of the same gate. But is inside the gate safety or entrapment? Is outside the gate freedom or danger? This is a riddle with which we struggle throughout life, for the answer is *yes, no, both* and *not entirely either.*

Particularly in the Pulling Up Roots passage, in which we are shedding an old familiar life system for the first time and feeling exposed and uncertain, we are tempted to take on the form of our phantom parent along with all its weaknesses. We fool ourselves by insisting that it is our choice alone or that we are really quite different. This can be a step backward on the way to a progressive solution, as we shall see. However, many who allow themselves to lapse into this form and accept passively the identity proffered (directly or indirectly) by the family, wind up locked in.

None of us wants to go too far, too fast beyond the value system of our inner custodian, to become too much an individual. Because then we cannot crawl back into the sanctuary when the growing gets rough. This is the conundrum of Pulling Up Roots; indeed, of all the decades well into the middle of the fifth.

Gail Sheehy, *Passages*

The fact that Jesus came from a despised town like Nazareth, worked with his hands and ministered primarily among marginalised people is the 'pre-Easter scandal' of Christianity.

In Western churches where we have long grown accustomed to the idea of a crucified Messiah, it is this scandal which is a stumbling block for us. We find it so difficult to accept that Christianity is based on grace and therefore our background, upbringing, education and social standing do not grant us special privileges with God. Because it is based on grace, the Christian life and the community of faith is open to everyone. And because it involves the justice of God, the poor and the outcasts have a special place.

We are Christians not because of who we are or what we do. We are Christians because of who Jesus is and what he does! If only we could believe this, the life and lifestyle of Western Christianity would be radically trans-formed and our churches would again become centres of grace and justice for all. Jesus would again be walking among us, converting our society to the kingdom of God, a kingdom of peace, justice and freedom for all.

Athol Gill, *Life on the Road*

Hence, with the decline of spiritual inwardness, it was the moralistic, meddlesome, guilt-evoking social concerns of Christianity that were to last most vigorously into our own time, making the churches increasingly hostage to the doings of those ruthless secular powers they had once tamed and tried to uplift.

Meanwhile, the still all-too-distant Christ stands beyond the crumbling margins of literal dogma, beckoning the faithful to that freedom of spirit he originally promised them. If the kingdom of God is not 'within', it is unlikely to be found in any earthly utopia humankind can hope to construct.

Ronald Conway, *The Rage for Utopia*

The Christian life is not to be some guilt-ridden, back-ward-looking, sloganeering, bubblegum, theological poster muck. The Christian life is to be a fuller and fuller fearful enjoyment of God himself, of those around us (saved or not), their talents, a deepening appreciation of all God has made, a growing longing to understand and enjoy what is around us, and to stand for those godly principles of life, beauty, truth, enjoyment and justice so clearly given us in the Bible.

. . .The Christian life does not call for us to deny the very God-given nature that the Lord himself has given us. The Christian life does not call us to deny the very creative nature of God himself.

It is time that we Christians who claim to have such an interest in life after death begin to show some interest in a little life before death.

Franky Schaeffer, *Addicted to Mediocrity*

Jesus our Lord is risen.
Lord, may we experience
  the power of your resurrection
  and live by it.
The call of freedom
  has been sounded.
Lord, may we respond
  as the community of the free.
It concerns every one of us personally,
  in our place,
  in our humanity,
  in this world of ours.
Lord, may the spirit and gift of your freedom
  break the spell of our fears and send
  us away
  obedient rebels,
  lovers of life's depths,
  and your disciples for ever. Amen.

Terry Falla, Be Our Freedom, Lord

A Benediction

There is therefore now no condemnation for those who are in
Christ Jesus. For the law of the Spirit of life in Christ Jesus
has set you free from the law of sin and of death.

Romans 8: 1–2, NRSV

Humour

For everything there is a season, and a time for every matter under heaven:

a time to be born, and a time to die;
a time to plant, and a time to pluck up what is planted;
a time to kill, and a time to heal;
a time to break down, and a time to build up;
a time to weep, and a time to laugh;
a time to mourn, and a time to dance.

Then the disciples of John came to him, saying, 'Why do we and the Pharisees fast often, but your disciples do not fast?'

And Jesus said to them, 'The wedding guests cannot mourn as long as the bridegroom is with them, can they? The days will come when the bridegroom is taken away from them, and then they will fast. No-one sews a piece of unshrunk cloth on an old cloak, for the patch pulls away from the cloak and a worse tear is made. Neither is new wine put into old wineskins; otherwise, the skins burst, and the wine is spilled, and the skins are destroyed; but new wine is put into fresh wineskins, and so both are preserved.

(Ecclesiastes 3:1-4; Matthew 9:14-17 — NRSV)

I believe that Jesus had a good sense of humour. We can't always see the twinkle in his eye when he said things. Nor can we pick up his puns and his more subtle jokes, because we don't hear what he said in the original language. So it is hard for us to hear Jesus' jokes. But they are there.

I am sure Jesus was laughing when he talked about the camel trying to get through the eye of the needle. And when he talked about the new wine being put into the old containers and they all burst, and the wine spills out. . . And the two house-builders: the one building a house just on the sand and it falls down so easily when the flood comes. There is just enough exaggeration in those stories to make them humorous.

We do know that Jesus and his disciples were accused of being too happy. They didn't take life seriously enough for some of the Pharisees. They didn't fast. They didn't go round with long faces. They were like the guests at a wedding party. They enjoyed life. They laughed and joked so much that they were criticised for it.

There is a time for laughter and fun, and a time for being serious. A time for eating. . . and a time for fasting.

I was reading about 'Dods', one of the lesser demons in the army of the devil. He is not one of the worst, by any means. In fact, there is quite a lot of good in him. Those who know about such matters hold that he could even become an angel of God, if only he had learned to laugh.

Dods likes to be called by his full title, because he is full of self-importance. His full title is 'Demon of the Deadly Serious'. He is most difficult to exorcise. He seems to be able to negate attempts at exorcism with a quick quote from a heavy tome of theology, or even from the Bible itself. And he is full of the woes of the world. As far as crises, conflicts, disasters, threats and failures go, his knowledge is encyclopedic. He can quote many, many facts and figures which give his gloom a respectability. Compared with him, a line-up of Russian leaders looks like a troupe of nightclub entertainers.

We Christians are prone to take ourselves too seriously at times. Pastors, in particular, seem to be very easy people to 'take off'. There is always a preacher in every comedy — from M*A*S*H to the two Ronnies — who takes life seriously, who sees a sermon in every absurd event.

There is a time for being serious. But there is also a time for humour and comedy. Humour is a God-given gift. Indeed, humour is a sign and a signal of the human situation and even hints at the solution which God offers.

Let me explain that.

A situation appears to us to be comic when there is a discrepancy, a contrast, a conflict between what should be the case, and what is the case. It is very funny if a judge from a courthouse slips on a banana skin or goes to sleep while he is listening to a case, but it is not at all funny if the beggar at the courthouse door slips or goes to sleep while he waits for someone to give him some money.

Nature is never funny or comic in itself — only human beings are. Animals become comic if we treat them as if they were like human beings. The fact that the tortoise wins the race is comic, because the hare was meant to win it. The fact that the chipmunks make Pluto the dog so mad is funny because Pluto is so much bigger and should be able to outwit the tiny chipmunks.

Comedy is all based on one ultimate discrepancy: the discrepancy between the human situation and the universe. Comedy reminds us that we are all locked into our situations, that we are not masters of our world.

The powerful dog can be outwitted by the little chipmunks. The hare which can run as fast as the wind can be beaten by the slowest of beasts, the tortoise. The judge in the courtroom can slip on a banana skin just as well as any of us — and when he does, we remember that he is not so far above the rest of us.

The jokes about pastors remind us that they, too, are human, with foibles and limitations of many kinds. Comedy likes making fun of people who think highly of themselves, because it wants us to realise that those people are really at the same level as all of us; that things can happen to that person, just as they can to the rest of us. We are all in the same boat. None of us is all-powerful. None of us is completely in charge of our world. All of us can slip — whether it be on a banana skin or choking on the tomato pip. Comedy recognises that the powerful are not all so powerful. The self-sufficient are not all so self-sufficient. The capable have their limitations.

But, in a sense, it is sad that humans lose out from time to time — that the person full of self-importance does slip on the banana skin. Indeed, there is a narrow gap between comedy and tragedy. Both are comments on the limitations of human experience — the fact that we do not govern our world and are subject to what happens in it.

But there is a difference between comedy and tragedy. Comedy does not see it as sad, though. By laughing at human limitations, humour implies that the imprisonment is not final. It will be overcome. We can laugh at the race between the tortoise and the hare because the hare can win another time. We can laugh at the serious man who slips on the banana skin because he can regain his composure.

Ultimately, we can laugh because the limitations of this world, of our human efforts, of our human weaknesses can be overcome. The slip is not final.

Comedy does not tell us where the answers lie. But it assumes that they exist. If there is no God, there can be no true humour. If there was no God, then the things which bring people down, the things which happen that people cannot control, would be sad. It is because such failures are not final that we can laugh at them.

Comedy looks forward to our final redemption. It looks forward to the time when we will find those true answers, when we find resources beyond ourselves which will set us free, which will give us true joy and pleasure. Comedy looks forward to the redemption which God offers us. It is when we accept God's redemption that our laughter is vindicated.

❧❦

Humour is a serious business. The immediate aim of the comedian may be simply to entertain. But if successful, comic achievement goes far beyond this limited purpose. As much as the scientist or the novelist, the humorist holds the mirror up to nature and reflects, often in sharpest focus, aspects of our human condition in the world which otherwise might pass unnoticed. Human beings, after all, are the only animals which laugh, just as they are the only animals which conduct experiments or tell stories. This simple and undeniable fact surely reveals something about the kind of beings we are and the kind of world we inhabit.

The world is not only a realm of physical order whose regularity the scientist may observe and chart; nor is it only a great theatre where the drama of human history unfolds in which human actors play and (modestly) direct their parts. The world is also comical, and the humorist perceives and participates in its comic structures.

Graeme Garrett, 'My brother Esau is an hairy man'

Unfortunately, laughing has never been the church's strong point. Whereas faith, hope, charity and the like have long-held esteemed places on our spiritual agenda, humour has barely rated. For many of us, it seems, Christianity is no laughing matter.

Yet this collective incapacity for spontaneity and wit is, frankly, no joke. Increasingly, we exemplify the kind of humourless religion described by Jewish scholar Lionel Blue as very lumpy with a heavy texture rather like a collapsed souffle!

Peter McKinnon, 'We interrupt this service for
a good belly laugh'

I have been puzzled that some pastors have become dispirited while others radiate a vitality and freedom.

I have made a point of asking those showing the 'fruit of living the good news' how they had maintained their vitality and have discovered three recurring factors: they maintained a very simple faith in the Lord Jesus, knowing him and believing he is who he says he is; they maintained *epieikeia* or commonsense; and they maintained a sense of humour.

They do not take themselves or life too seriously. They have the ability to laugh amidst the ambiguities, paradoxes and absurdities of it all. The grace of laughter lends perspective to life, reminding us of the fact that we do not have absolute control over reality. It returns us to ourselves and releases us from the pettiness of our ego projects.

Humour — even black humour — enables us to survive when the incomprehensibility and absurdity of a situation leaves us stranded.

Laughter can express optimism and faith, rejecting the pessimism of a world without the hope of the gospel. Laughing at evil, as we read God does in Psalm 2: 4, defies evil and puts it in its proper place on the eternal scale of things. At least some of the people who criticised me years ago for laughing at 'serious' things have found the burdens of this world so overwhelming that they have gone under. If we have confidence in God, we can laugh at the wiles of the devil.

Laughter can also keep us close to God. Reinhold Niebuhr wrote, 'Humour is the prelude to faith and laughter is the beginning of prayer.' Self-deprecating humour can not only ease stress, but it keeps us humble enough to be of some use to God and bearable in the company of others. 'A cheerful heart is a good medicine,' says Proverbs 17: 22. It could even be one of the 'gifts' of God. In Job, not the most cheerful of books in the Bible, we read in chapter 8: 21 that God will fill the mouth of the blameless person with laughter.

So please 'keep rejoicing' (1 Thessalonians 5: 16).

A good burst of laughter for at least six minutes has a great aerobic effect on blood pressure and heart rate. It has highly complex effects on hormonal levels and the central nervous system, and it relieves stress, perhaps releasing natural endorphin in the brain in the same way that jogging or aerobics do, to produce a natural high.

Laughter can even help people overcome neuroses. As people begin to laugh about their fear, they can learn to control that fear. It can also be very beneficial to laugh at oneself.

Jessica Milner Davis

When it comes to comedy in general, the Old Testament comes up a bit thin. We have Sarah rolling around at the news that she's pregnant (although at her age who could blame her). And we have poor old Haman hanging himself on the gallows he so carefully built for Mordecai (though gallows humour hardly lightens the spirit). There's even an odd chuckle in Jonah and Samson chimes in for a riddle or two. But, overall, it is obvious that the Old Testament just wasn't put together by a team of comedy writers.

The situation improves somewhat in the New Testament, thanks to the wry wit and comic insight of Jesus. Here, we are confronted with pictures of tax collectors up trees and cryptic invitations to catch men instead of fish.

Our vision of the face of God is enhanced by colourful verbal sketches of people straining mosquitoes through their teeth while swallowing camels, foolish rich men, logs in eyes, prodigal sons and short-sighted home owners that build on ill-fated, sandy plots.

It is bitter-sweet imagery, distinctively Jewish in its comic flavour.

The Bible offers little joy to the lover of slapstick and other more obvious comic forms. But to then dismiss it as humourless would be to overlook a pattern of humour woven through the biblical narratives that is subtle both in content and texture. Clergyman Jack Churchill notes that Jesus' theme is often that 'life is better than you think; God smiles'.

God is, in fact, a good-humoured God and this news is indeed good.

> Peter McKinnon, 'We interrupt this service for
> a good belly laugh'

A congregational poll on the appropriateness of laughter in the public worship service showed that one-fourth of the members had never thought of God as ever laughing. It was probably not coincidence that most of these same members also thought that a joyous resurrection hymn is out of place at a funeral service.

> Frederick W. Danker, 'Laughing with God'

When God had finished the stars and whirl of coloured suns

He turned his mind from big things to
   fashion little ones,
Beautiful tiny things (like daisies) he made, and then
He made the comical ones in case the minds of men
Should stiffen and become
Dull, humourless and glum:
And so forgetful of their Maker be
As to take themselves — *quite seriously.*
Caterpillars and cats are lively and excellent puns:
All God's jokes are good — even the practical ones!
And as for the duck, I think God must have
   smiled a bit
Seeing those bright eyes blink on the day
   he fashioned it.
And he's probably laughing still at the sound
   that came out of its bill!

F.W. Harvey, 'Ducks'

A small boy was listening to a minister preach on 'What is a Christian?' He was intrigued by the preacher's habit of banging his fist on the pulpit every time he asked the rhetorical question. 'Do you know, Mama, what the answer is?' the small boy asked.

'Yes, dear, be quiet,' said his mother. Finally, the minister demanded once more, 'What is a Christian?' and banged especially hard.

The boy, taking the question to heart, yelled, 'Tell him, Mama, tell him.'

There was also the time when another preacher was making a dramatic appeal for people to become Christians. Unfortunately, one of the elders of the church, who always sat in the front row, had gone to sleep. The preacher reached the high point of his sermon: 'If you are going to go to hell, stand up,' he shouted. The elder suddenly awoke, heard the words 'stand up' and stood up.

There was a hush throughout the congregation, as the preacher lost his place. 'Well,' said the elder, 'I am not sure what we are voting for, reverend, but it looks as if you and I are the only ones for it. . .'

Philip Hughes, 'Humour'

Did you hear about the time the disciples went out on the lake one night when a storm blew up? It was so rough, they got worried they were going to drown.

Anyway, Peter wakes up Jesus. He'd been asleep, mind you. Peter said, 'Fair go, we're gunna drown, can you do something?' Well, Jesus stood up, looked at the storm and said, 'Right, that's enough!' And it all went quiet. The disciples were amazed. They said, 'Who's this bloke? The weather does what 'e says.'

Anyway, John's mate says, 'I ought to take him home to meet my mother-in-law.'

Philip Hughes

The capacity to laugh at ourselves because we are not gods, though we sometimes forget it, is also to demonstrate that we may be more than clay. The comedian knows our human language is of earth and not of heaven, and yet — the comedy suggests — not just of earth. Laughter points the way toward a symbolic use of language where human words become transparent to a truth beyond the merely empirical horizon. And for those who do not discount the validity of a religious way of being, this pointer is an anticipation of that sacramental use of language in which words, by the grace of God, become the bearer of divine truth within the human realm.

Again, the comedian knows human-being-in-the-world is deeply at odds with itself. Discrepancy, incongruity, disjointedness mark its life. But laughter about this very situation hints at re-creation. Its levity anticipates that deep quality of happiness which transcends all particular circumstances and which religious faith knows as joy; its consolation foreshadows that state of 'new being' in which disjointedness is overcome and the split between human spirit and its source is healed.

For those who entertain the Christian truth, this points, albeit indirectly, towards that central event in the drama of relationships between humanity and God when the exalted became lowly and the lowly were exalted, when heaven and earth met and were truly one, without any confusion of being which would render the relationship merely comical, or any separation of being that would render it impossible. It points toward the final breaking of the prison walls — the incarnation.

Graeme Garrett, 'My brother Esau is an hairy man'

Lord, you are both a laughing and a wrathful God. You sit in the heavens and laugh: it must be hilarious for you as you look down at the strange creatures you have made, taking seriously some things which are really funny, but laughing at matters which are deadly serious!

Thankyou, Jesus, for sharing our joy as well as our sorrows. You enjoyed parties. You told many stories about people who rejoiced when good things happened to them. But you also invite us to rejoice when bad things happen to us, when we are persecuted. Thankyou, Jesus, that your language was spiced with humour. Help me to take the hint about the guy who strains mosquitoes out of his drink, but swallows camels!

If we can't laugh in church sometimes, good Lord forgive us! But if we are so childish that we can't be serious when that emotion is appropriate, forgive us for that, too.

And, finally, Lord, help me to laugh at myself. May I stand back sometimes from my guilt, anxieties and problems, and chuckle a bit. Just as the people in Jesus' stories found what was lost and then rejoiced, may I, too, be both one who rejoices and is the object of your rejoicing!

A Benediction
May the Lord God, who invites you to join his eternal party in heaven, give you also a good time in spite of your troubles down here! In the name of the laughing Jesus. Amen.

12

No darker rooms

God is our refuge and strength, an ever-present help in trouble. Therefore we will not fear, though the earth give way and the mountains fall into the heart of the sea, though its waters roar and foam and the mountains quake with their surging. There is a river whose streams make glad the city of God, the holy place where the Most High dwells. God is with her, she will not fall; God will help her at break of day.

Nations are in uproar, kingdoms fall; he lifts his voice, the earth melts. The Lord Almighty is with us; the God of Jacob is our fortress. Come and see the works of the Lord, the desolations he has brought on the earth. He makes wars cease to the ends of the earth; he breaks the bow and shatters the spear; he burns the shields with fire. 'Be still, and know that I am God; I will be exalted among the nations, I will be exalted in the earth.' The Lord Almighty is with us; the God of Jacob is our fortress.

Like sheep, they are destined for the grave and death will feed on them. The upright will rule over them in the morning; their forms will decay in the grave, far from their princely mansions. But God will redeem my soul from the grave; he will surely take me to himself.

Call upon me in the day of trouble; I will deliver you and you will honour me.

He brought them out of darkness and the deepest gloom and broke away their chains. Let them give thanks to the Lord for his unfailing love and his wonderful deeds.

Who shall separate us from the love of Christ? Shall

trouble or hardship or persecution or famine or naked-
ness or danger or sword? As it is written: 'For your
sake we face death all day long; we are considered as
sheep to be slaughtered.' No, in all these things we are
more than conquerors through him who loved us. For
I am convinced that neither death nor life, neither angels
nor demons, neither the present nor the future, nor any
powers, neither height nor depth, nor anything else in
all creation will be able to separate us from the love of
God that is in Christ Jesus our Lord.

When the perishable has been clothed with the imperishable and the mortal with immortality, then the
saying that is written will come true: 'Death has been
swallowed up in victory.'

'Where, O death, is your victory? Where, O death, is
your sting?' The sting of death is sin and the power of
sin is the law. But thanks be to God! He gives us the
victory through our Lord Jesus Christ. Therefore, my
dear brothers, stand firm. Let nothing move you. Always give yourselves fully to the work of the Lord,
because you know that your labour in the Lord is not
in vain.

(Psalm 46; 47: 14–15; 50: 15; 107: 14–15; Romans 8: 35–39; 1 Corinthians 15: 54–58 — all NIV)

Death is real. Death is final. Death must be faced.
M*A*S*H in its day was a popular television show. In one
episode, a pilot had to bale out of his damaged aircraft.
The bombing mission was a success; the pilot slightly
injured his foot. Limping into camp, the pilot was met
by the crazy but compassionate Hawkeye. As they talked,
the pilot told Hawkeye that his usual routine was to fly
out from base, drop bombs, return to base and have an
evening meal with his wife.

The pilot talked about how beautiful it was up above
the clouds, so calm and peaceful. The whole war was
quite unrealistic for the pilot. When asked by Hawkeye
if he'd ever seen what happened when bombs were

dropped, the pilot answered 'No'. Then Hawkeye introduced the pilot to a young woman who'd been injured in a bombing raid. The pilot was greatly upset as he realised what damage bombs could do to people.

Like that pilot, we prefer to stay above death, untouched by it. This is not, however, possible, for sooner or later everyone of us will be recruited by 'the grim reaper'.

Death is real. It happens daily. Sometimes, it comes very close to us. When death visits the aged, we accept it with a little more ease, even though we may grieve deeply. After all, we expect the aged to die. When, however, death comes to the young, it's harder, much harder to understand.

Death, of course, was not God's original plan for us. But it's a part of life and we need to recognise it. We keep our feelings about death and dying to ourselves and we hesitate to discuss them. It's called 'denial'. But death can't be denied. It is real. It cannot be swept under the carpet of the mind. When someone has died, we should talk about it.

Death is final in the sense that the body returns to the ground. But there is another side to death. Dwight L. Moody said: 'Soon you will read in the newspapers that Moody is dead. Don't you believe it, for I shall be more alive than I am now.'

Richard Baxter wrote:

Christ leads me through no darker rooms
Than he went through before;
And he that to God's kingdom comes
Must enter by this door.
My knowledge of that life is small,
The eye of faith is dim;
But it's just enough that Christ knows all,
And I will be with him.

It makes all the difference when we face death with Christ at our side. Here then is our hope, strength and courage. We need never be afraid of the dark night of death, for Christ has gone before us. He is the Way and the Light of the World. Dark cannot exist where there is light. Christ is the resurrection and the life and, because he lives, we will live also. Alleluia!

❦

The Lord might go on to show how Abraham's obedience would influence everyday decisions in people's lives all through history. In that brief moment on the mountain, God not only saw Abraham and Isaac, but Martin Luther, John Calvin, Dwight Moody, you and me. But how could God explain in detail how Abraham's actions would influence billions?

Similarly, how do we know what ultimate effects our obedience has on others? Or our sin? Only God sees the full ramifications of decisions which look to us to be isolated events. This God charges us to obey him, even when we don't understand. He's working the plan of ages, not the whim of the moment.

Mark R. Littleton, *A Place to Stand*

The value of life grows in magnitude when we stare death in the eye. Death is obscene, a grotesque contradiction to life. The contrast between the vibrancy of a child at play and the limp, rag-doll look of a corpse is revolting. The cosmetic art of the mortician cannot disguise the odious face of death. The death of a friend or loved one robs us of a cherished companion and reminds us of our own mortality.

Death is no stranger to my household. I have hosted its unwelcome visit too many times. The two visits I recall most vividly are the times the black angel came for my parents. Both died at home — both left trauma in my soul.

We chisel in stone the last words of epic heroes: 'I only regret that I have but one life to give for my country,' said Nathan Hale; 'Oh my God,' gasped John F. Kennedy as he clutched his throat in a car in Dallas; 'Et tu Brute. . .' Caesar moaned as he fell at the foot of Pompey's bust.

R. C. Sproul, *In Search of Dignity*

The bitter news of Dawson Trotman's drowning swept like a cold wind across Schroon Lake to the shoreline. Eyewitnesses tell of the profound anxiety, the tears, the helpless disbelief in the faces of those who now looked out across the deep blue water. Everyone's face except one — Lila Trotman, Dawson's widow. As she suddenly walked upon the scene, a close friend shouted, 'Oh, Lila. . . he's gone. Dawson's gone!' To that she replied in calm assurance the words of Psalm 115: 3:

But our God is in the heavens:
He does whatever he pleases.

All of the anguish, the sudden loneliness that normally consumes and cripples those who survive did not invade that woman's heart. Instead, she leaned hard upon her sovereign Lord, who had once again done what he pleased.

Chuck Swindoll, Second Wind

Corrie ten Boom, a Holocaust survivor and noted worldwide speaker, impressed this principle on us. 'Don't ever step in front of a group without an object or story that illustrates what you're saying,' she would tell us in her firm, heavily accented voice. 'Every place I speak, I use one. And even when I've been away for years, people still remember what I've said.'

In her travels, Corrie became a symbol of hope to anyone in spiritual or physical bondage. When she spoke before a group, she often held up a large piece of embroidery with the back side showing. Strings hung every which way and no clear pattern could be discerned.

'This is the way our lives often look,' she would say. 'When I was in the concentration camp, it seemed there was nothing but ugliness and chaos. But then I looked to God to make sense of my world' — at that point she would turn the tapestry around, revealing to her audience a beautifully embroidered crown — 'and at last I could see why he added a certain thread or colour, no matter how painful the stitching.'

Gary Smalley and John Trent, The Language of Love

The deepest fear to many is the fear of the unknown future. This crystallises in some minds round the fear of the destruction of the world or surviving as a maimed person in a partially destroyed world. In others, it revolves round the fear of their marriage breaking down and their home breaking up. Some dread bereavement; others unemployment, poverty and starvation. Some fear being left on the shelf, battling through life alone; others are worried stiff about the folk at home, far away. These are some of our modern fears.

Every fresh discovery, every new scientific conquest, while opening up new horizons, stirring up new hope and imparting a fresh sense of achievement, brings its own crop of new fears or fans into flame some of the old fears. . .

The Psalmist says, 'I sought the Lord, and he heard me, and delivered me from all my fears' (Psalm 34: 4). But it is such a far cry back to the simple living of the days of David that someone may say: 'His ideas were all right for that sort of civilisation, when people felt that God was near them. But look how far back we have pushed his frontiers now! Is it any use seeking the Lord today? Is he near enough? Is he big enough to stand up to our modern world? Can he handle our complex situations? Will he hear us as he heard David? Or, to be more personal, can he deliver me from my fears?'

The answer to these questions is an unhesitating 'Yes'.

Leith Samuel, *There is an Answer*

We are not much different than burdened travellers, are we? We roll in the mud of self-pity in the very shadow of the cross. We piously ask for his will and then have the audacity to pout if everything doesn't go our way. If we would just remember the heavenly body that awaits us, we'd stop complaining that he hasn't healed this earthly one.

Our problem is not so much that God doesn't give us what we hope for as it is that we don't know the right thing for which to hope. (You may want to read that sentence again).

Hope is not what you expect; it is what you would never dream. It is a wild, improbable tale with a pinch-me-I'm-dreaming ending. It's Abraham adjusting his bifocals so he cannot see his grandson, but his son! It's Moses standing in the promised land not with Aaron or Miriam at his side, but with Elijah and the transfigured Christ. It's Zechariah left speechless at the sight of his wife Elizabeth, gray-headed and pregnant. And it is the two Emmaus-bound pilgrims reaching out to take a piece of bread, only to see that the hands from which it is offered are pierced.

Max Lucado, *God Came Near*

Are we to conclude, then, that there are occasions when we will pray for the will of God to be known and yet we may 'hear' no immediate reply?

I think so, but I'm also convinced that God is as close to us and as involved in our situation during those times when we feel nothing as he is when we are spiritually exhilarated. We are not left to flounder. Rather, our faith is strengthened by these testing periods.

The only comforting attitude to hold during these stressful times is beautifully summarised in 2 Corinthians 4: 8–10: 'We are pressed on every side by troubles, but not crushed and broken. We are perplexed because we don't know why things happen as they do, but we don't give up and quit. We are hunted down, but God never abandons us. We get knocked down, but we get up again and keep going. These bodies of ours are constantly facing death just as Jesus did; so it is clear to all that it is only the living Christ within (who keeps us safe)' (TLB).

James Dobson, *Emotions: Can You Trust Them?*

Lord of life and death, thankyou that you are eternal and that you move far beyond 'this vale of tears'. Thankyou that beyond this life there is far more.

When death strikes — and it is never far away — help me to see further than the here and now to the wonders you have in store 'beyond the mind's horizon'. Help me to know that you are working out your rich purposes in a way that is not mine to see or even imagine. Grant, I pray, a richer wisdom than I have at present so that even when death pays a visit I may stand strong in the knowledge that nothing can separate me from your love which I experience in Christ Jesus my Lord. Amen.

A Benediction
Grant me, Lord, this day and this night a renewed confidence in your eternal power. Help me to find a new sense of peace and rest, knowing you are able to bring life out of death.

13

A full existence

Do not be surprised at this: the time is coming when all the dead will hear the voice of the Son of Man and come out of their graves. . .

Jesus said, 'Our friend Lazarus has fallen asleep, but I will go and wake him up.' The disciples answered, 'If he is asleep, Lord, he will get well.' Jesus meant that Lazarus had died, but they thought he meant natural sleep. So Jesus told them plainly, 'Lazarus is dead. . . Let us go to him.' Martha said to Jesus, 'If you had been here, Lord, my brother would not have died.'

'Your brother will rise to life,' Jesus told her. 'I know,' she said, 'that he will rise on the last day.' Jesus said to her, 'I am the resurrection and the life. Those who believe in me, even though they die, will live; and everyone who lives and believes in me will never die.' . . .'Lord,' Mary said, 'if you had been here, my brother would not have died!' Jesus saw her weeping and he saw how the people with her were weeping, also. . . Jesus wept. . . Jesus went to the tomb. . . 'Take the stone away!' Jesus ordered. Jesus said. . . 'Didn't I tell you that you would see God's glory if you believed?' They took the stone away.

Jesus looked up and said, 'I thank you, Father, that you listen to me. . . I say this for the sake of the people here, so that they will believe that you sent me.' After he had said this, he called out in a loud voice, 'Lazarus, come out!'

He came out, his hands and feet wrapped in grave clothes and with a cloth around his face. 'Untie him,' Jesus told them, 'and let him go.'

(John 5: 28–29; 11: 11–15, 21 and 23–24 — all GNB; 25, NRSV; 32–33, 35, 38–44 — all GNB)

The words in John 5, 'all the dead will hear his voice and come out of their graves', remind us of the story of Lazarus in John 11. The dead man, Lazarus, heard the voice of Jesus, the Son of Man, and came out of his grave.

In the story of Lazarus, four things happened. First, Lazarus died. Jesus spoke gently of his friend's death as a falling asleep. The disciples did not take the hint and so Jesus told them plainly that Lazarus had died. Second, Jesus made the reassuring statement that he was the resurrection and the life. This assertion was prompted by the exchange between Martha and Jesus. Martha was bemoaning the fact that Jesus wasn't there during Lazarus' terminal illness. Jesus was underlining the hope of life beyond the grave.

Third, Jesus wept. This action was provoked by Mary's reiterating the fact that Jesus wasn't there and by the crying of Mary and her companions. Jesus was truly human. Fourth, Lazarus was brought to life after Jesus ordered the removal of the tombstone, after Jesus prayed to his Father, God, and after Jesus commanded Lazarus to come out of the tomb. These four events summarise the story of Lazarus.

Behind the story is the plot. The plot gives us the undercurrents in four stages, too. First, there was the stage of denial. The disciples felt the need to downplay the fact of death. They spoke of Lazarus falling asleep. Jesus faced the facts and told them plainly that Lazarus was dead. Jesus spoke of Lazarus' dying. We are like the disciples when we speak of someone's 'passing away'. We can be like Jesus and face reality by speaking of death.

Second, there was the stage of idolatry. The sisters felt the need to elevate Lazarus to sainthood. Both Martha, the active sister, and Mary, the contemplative sister, were sure that their brother would not have died if Jesus had been there. Martha, indeed, saw in her mind's eye the raising of Lazarus at the last day among those who have done good. Jesus, however, acknowledged a higher loyalty. Jesus, not Lazarus, was the object of reverence. 'I am the resurrection and the life.' We, too, must learn to put our trust in the Lord of life, not in the saints who have departed this life.

Third, there was the stage of grief. Jesus showed the way out of denial. He expressed his grief in the face of death. He wept buckets of tears. We are in good company when we weep over the loss of someone near and dear to us. Jesus wept.

Fourth, there was the stage of faith. Jesus spoke of seeing the glory of God and of believing that God had sent him. Jesus raised Lazarus from death and relocated faith in God through himself. We also are in good company when we trust in God, the goal of all that is, through Jesus, the guide of all that is.

Beyond the story and the plot is what John 11 means to me. When I suffered deep loss and profound grief, my former pastor wrote: 'I have no words of explanation — only great sadness and empathy for you and your loved ones. I have found in my "valleys of the shadows" that I was mysteriously and graciously sustained. . . I have more reason than ever to believe in the resurrection. When we get to the place where we have to say: "If there is anything more, it is up to God," I have found there is more.'

Jesus continues to say to us: 'I am the resurrection and the life. Those who believe in me will live, even though they die; and whoever lives and believes in me will never die.'

❧

E.M. Forster says that a story is a narrative of events arranged chronologically as in 'the king died and then the queen died,' whereas a plot, although also a narrative of events, concentrates more on the *because* of things, as in 'the king died and then the queen died of grief'. This account is full of *becauses*.

Frederick Buechner, *Telling Secrets*

From a theological point of view, the two issues at stake in any grief experience are, first, the temptation to idolatry and, second, the shrinking back from the inner appropriation of the power of the resurrection by attempting to avoid the way of the cross.

Wayne Oates, *Anxiety on Christian Experience*

What makes you and me Christians is not only our belief that he who was without sin died for our sake on the cross and thus opened for us the way to his heavenly Father, but also that through his death our death is transformed from a totally absurd end of all that gives life its meaning into an event that liberates us and those whom we love.

Henri Nouwen, *A Letter of Consolation*

'She is in God's hand.' That gains a new energy when I think of her [his wife] as a sword. Perhaps the earthly life I shared with her was only part of the tempering. Now perhaps [God] grasps the hilt; weighs the new weapon; makes lightnings with it in the air. 'A right Jerusalem blade.'

C.S. Lewis, *A Grief Observed*

Eternal life may be enjoyed here and now by those who respond to the word of Christ. . . the same power which assures eternal life to believers during their earthly existence will, after the death of the body, raise the dead to renewed existence in a world beyond.

C.H. Dodd, *The Interpretation of the Fourth Gospel*

We had the suspense of having to wait for three weeks until last Friday when Barbara's body was found. On Tuesday, we had her funeral service. The service was a great relief. It marked the end of the chapter, but not, as we who are Christian believe, the end of the book.

William Barclay's letter to Rita Snowden
after the drowning of his daughter

The New Testament speaks of 'resurrection' rather than

'immortality' and thereby ensures that a full existence is meant. . .

John Macquarrie, *Principles of Christian Theology*

When the cold, bleak wind of sorrow blows, there is calm and comfort in the presence of Jesus Christ. When the hot blast of passion blows, there is peace and security in the presence of Jesus Christ. When the storms of doubt seek to uproot the very foundations of the faith, there is a steady safety in the presence of Jesus Christ. In every storm that shakes the human heart, there is peace with Jesus Christ.

William Barclay, *The Gospel of Matthew*

As long as one believes, he or she has eternal life in Jesus. This includes life before physical death and life after physical death.

Dale Moody, *The Word of Truth*

The sad things that happened long ago will always remain part of who we are, just as the glad and gracious things will, too, but instead of being a burden of guilt, recrimination and regret that make us constantly stumble as we go, even the saddest things can become, once we have made peace with them, a source of wisdom and strength for the journey that still lies ahead.

Frederick Buechner, *Telling Secrets*

For all that has been — Thanks!
To all that shall be — Yes!

Dag Hammarskjöld, *Markings*

Jesus of the City of Joy, you who are eternally crucified, you who are the voice of the voiceless ones, you who suffer within each one of these people, you who endure their anguish, their distress and their sadness, but you who know how to express yourself through their hearts, their tears, their laughter, and their love. . . you know that I am here simply to share. . . you and your Father, the Father of mercy, the Father who sent you, the Father who forgives. And to tell you, too, you who are the light and the salvation of the world, that here, in the City of Joy, we are living in darkness. So Jesus, our light, we need you, for without you we are lost.

A prayer of Stephan Kovalski, Polish Catholic priest

A Benediction

God brought our Lord Jesus back from the dead, and his sacrificial death made him the great shepherd of the sheep and the inaugurator of the eternal covenant. And may that God of peace equip you with every good thing you need to enable you to do what he wants you to do, and may he make us and our life such as he would wish us and it to be through Jesus Christ, to whom be glory for ever and ever! Amen.

Hebrews 13: 20–21, Barclay

Theme: Encounter. . .

to experience God's presence

But Mary stood weeping outside the tomb. As she wept, she bent over to look into the tomb; and she saw two angels in white, sitting where the body of Jesus had been lying, one at the head and the other at the feet. They said to her, 'Woman, why are you weeping?'

She said to them, 'They have taken away my Lord, and I do not know where they have laid him.' When she had said this, she turned around and saw Jesus standing there, but she did not know that it was Jesus. Jesus said to her, 'Woman, why are you weeping? Whom are you looking for?' Supposing him to be the gardener, she said to him, 'Sir, if you have carried him away, tell me where you have laid him, and I will take him away.' Jesus said to her, 'Mary!' She turned and said to him in Hebrew, 'Rabbouni!' (which means teacher).

Jesus said to her, 'Do not hold on to me, because I have not yet ascended to the Father. But go to my brothers and say to them, "I am ascending to my Father and your Father, to my God and your God."' Mary Magdalene went and announced to the disciples, 'I have seen the Lord'; and she told them that he had said these things to her.

John 20: 11-18, NRSV

God is with us

'Look, the virgin shall conceive and bear a son, and they shall name him Emmanuel, which means, God is with us.'

And as he sat at dinner in the house, many tax collectors and sinners came and were sitting with him and his disciples.

Whoever is not with me is against me, and whoever does not gather with me scatters.

Then he said to them, 'I am deeply grieved, even to death; remain here, and stay awake with me.'

Go therefore and make disciples of all nations, baptising them in the name of the Father and of the Son and of the Holy Spirit, and teaching them to obey everything that I have commanded you. And remember, I am with you always, to the end of the age.

(Matthew 1: 23; 9: 10; 12: 30; 26: 38; 28: 19–20 — all NRSV)

One of the most essential insights the Bible gives is that God is with us. The Gospel of Matthew is structured so that the beginning and the ending both highlight this basic theme. God is with us in the birth of Jesus and remains with us as we follow Jesus in his mission.

The presence of God permeates our world. God made this planet and every tree, animal and person reflects the divine source. We can see God involved with our everyday life.

Babies are born every day and so a new person, with a new life, begins. On an ordinary day in the back blocks of the Roman empire, Jesus was born. In this tiny, vulnerable baby, God entered human experience from the inside. By becoming one of us, God reveals in the most profound way what it means to be with us.

This baby grew up and, as an adult, Jesus was found in the midst of ordinary people. He was always in the company of those who were usually left alone. In this way, Jesus showed us that God's presence is seen from the bottom of society, moving upwards. No-one need miss out, although those who thought that they were holy often shunned Jesus' choice of friends and denied themselves this presence.

Although God is seen in such everyday life, the presence of pain, suffering and evil leaves many people with no place to find any trace of the divine. But God is present there, too. God is bruised and battered daily at the hands of torturers. God is sitting with families at funerals, crying over a young girl's death by cancer.

The crucifixion of Jesus brings pain, suffering and evil face-to-face with God. In Jesus' undeserved death, God identifies with our death.

But this Jesus is raised from the dead. God has the final word, given to all of us. God says: 'I am with you.'

⚭

Christ did not leave this world with the resurrection. He penetrated it in a more profound manner and is now present in all reality in the same way that God is present in all things: 'I am with you always, yes, to the end of time' (Matthew 28: 20). Christian faith lives on this presence and has developed a viewpoint that allows it to see all reality as penetrated by the reverberations of the resurrection.

Leonardo Boff, *Jesus Christ Liberator*

After being taken back to the ward following surgery, I can remember my sister being there. Every time I drifted back into consciousness, she was there. It meant everything to have someone with me who knew me and cared for me within the impersonal setting of the hospital.

Bruce Turley, *Turning Points*

Instead of standing apart, Jesus goes through the whole country, bringing glad news to all, without exception: he goes looking for the single lost sheep; he is not there to help the healthy (those who think they are 'righteous'), but the sick (Mark 2: 17) — and that they are. Thus, he eats and drinks with tax-gatherers and sinners to bring them also the evidence of God's love for them. What we have here cannot be other than a message and style of conduct that proclaim God's universal love, the true God's lordship, without reservation.

Edward Schillebeeckx, *Jesus*

'Well, Helen?' said I, putting my hand into hers. She chafed my fingers gently to warm them, and went on — 'If all the world hated you, and believed you wicked, while your own conscience approved you, and absolved you from guilt, you would not be without friends.'

'No; I know I should think well of myself; but that is not enough; if others don't love me, I would rather die than live — I cannot bear to be solitary and hated, Helen. Look here; to gain some real affection from you, or Miss Temple, or any other whom I truly love, I would willingly submit to have the bone of my arm broken, or to let a bull toss me, or stand behind a kicking horse, and let it dash its hoof at my chest. . .'

Charlotte Bronte, *Jane Eyre*

Following Jesus on the road always brings us into new relationships with sisters and brothers who are on the same journey. God knows that it would be a terrible journey to undertake on our own, for so few of us are people of vision and courage. Alone, we are easily discouraged and diverted into less demanding enterprises, but together we are able to dream dreams and plan and scheme and work towards the kingdom of God where his will is done on earth as it is in heaven.

While we remain fragmented and isolated, the powerful of the earth are able to beat us every time, but together with Jesus we may become a force that is able to defy the demonic, overthrow the physical and spiritual oppression that is rampant in so many places, and offer the liberating power of the gospel to women and men groaning under the weight of their oppressors.

Athol Gill, *Life on the Road*

I want everything you throw out
I'll do anything you want to
Please let me go with you
I'll wear the smile on your face.

Crowded House, 'As Sure As I Am'

Middle age presents many couples with the opportunity for true companionship, for by now it is clear that shared interests and a healthy respect for privacy are not mutually exclusive. There is a good chance of having someone to grow old with, to share friends and memories and walks in the rain with, someone to absorb the hush of a household where children no longer reside and to make it resonate with the joys of recaptured time together.

Gail Sheehy, *Passages*

On the positive side, the cross presents a basic affirmation about God. It says that on the cross God himself is crucified. The Father suffers the death of his Son and takes upon himself all the sorrow and pain of history. This ultimate solidarity with humanity reveals God as a God of love in a real and credible way rather than in an idealistic way. From the ultimate depths of history's negative side, this God of love thereby opens up the possibility of hope and a future.

Jon Sobrino, *Christology at the Crossroads*

All goodness and truth are yours, O Lord.
May no evil estrange us from you,
*   nor error darken our vision*
*   of your purpose.*
Help us to discern your justice
*   and to understand your will.*
In adversity and prosperity,

let the promise of your presence
  put strength into our souls.
Help us so to trust you
  that we may not be afraid,
but may work with you
  in the service of the world,
  proving your love by our own,
through Jesus Christ our Lord.
Amen.

Terry Falla, *Be Our Freedom, Lord*

A Benediction
The grace of the Lord Jesus Christ, the love of God, and the communion of the Holy Spirit be with all of you. Amen.

2 Corinthians 13: 13, NRSV

15

Grace for little people

The kingdom of heaven is like a landowner who went out early in the morning to hire labourers for his vineyard. After agreeing with the labourers for the usual daily wage, he sent them into his vineyard. When he went out about nine o'clock, he saw others standing idle in the marketplace; and he said to them, 'You also go into the vineyard, and I will pay you whatever is right.' So they went.

When he went out again about noon and about three o'clock, he did the same. And about five o'clock, he went out and found others standing around; and he said to them, 'Why are you standing here idle all day?' They said to him, 'Because no-one has hired us.' He said to them, 'You also go into the vineyard.'

When evening came, the owner of the vineyard said to his manager, 'Call the labourers and give them their pay, beginning with the last and then going to the first.' When those hired about five o'clock came, each of them received the usual daily wage. Now when the first came, they thought they would receive more; but each of them also received the usual daily wage.

And when they received it, they grumbled against the landowner, saying, 'These last worked only one hour, and you have made them equal to us who have borne the burden of the day and the scorching heat.' But he replied to one of them, 'Friend, I am doing you no wrong; did you not agree with me for the usual daily wage? Take what belongs to you and go; I choose to give to this last the same as I give to you. Am I not allowed to do what I choose with what belongs to me?

Or are you envious because I am generous?' So the last will be first, and the first will be last.

(Matthew 20: 1–16 — NRSV)

In any Third World city, day labourers can be observed waiting for someone to come along and hire them. In Calcutta, I saw a row of men with paint brushes and cans waiting on a traffic island in the middle of a busy inter-section: later in the day some of them were still waiting there. The greatest migration in the world's history is taking place in our times: landless rural poor are drifting into the cities and, for many of them, the precarious ex-istence of day labouring is all they can do to survive.

I met Pedro and Isabella in a *favela* outside Fortaleza in north-east Brazil. They had five surviving children (from nine live births) — all malnourished. She sewed dresses on a machine lent her by World Vision; he waited every day in one of the town's marketplaces for work. Two nights out of three he would trudge home ('home' was a few bits of plastic and corrugated iron in a swamp) without any money. Those nights, the children probably wouldn't eat and Isabella would give them little rolled-up wads of moistened newspaper sprinkled with sugar. These had no nutritional value, but the children might not cry so much from hunger and keep others awake. . .

When grapes in Palestine were ready to be harvested about the end of September, it had to be done quickly before the rains came and spoiled the crop. Any pickers were welcome — even if they could give only an hour. The whole enterprise was a race against time.

This story by Jesus is usually titled, 'The Parable of the Labourers in the Vineyard'. Perhaps, it ought to be called 'The Parable of the Generous Landowner'. All the workers, including those hired for just one hour, received the same wage — the usual denarius (or 'penny' in the KJV) paid for a full day's work. The first workers were 'contracted' to receive a day's pay; there is no mention of a contract or agreement with those hired later.

The vineyard owner seems a bit eccentric. He hires workers just before sundown and, when the sun has set, he pays them a full day's wage! He pays less attention to 'productivity' issues than to the workers' motivations and needs. In international trade, there are 'most favoured nations' clauses, but in terms of trade union thinking, this sort of varied treatment of workers is not on. It's not *fair*!

The employer first paid those who had worked only about an hour and, when the others noted they received a fair day's wage for only that small amount of labour, they must have done some quick calculations to figure how much more than a denarius they would receive. Imagine their chagrin and anger when they all received the same (in stress literature, it's the 'disparity between expectations and reality'!). No wonder they grumbled: working under the hot Palestinian sun is hard work.

But the employer explains that he treated those recruited earlier with justice (verse 13) and the last group with generosity (verse 15). So it's not that justice and fair play do not matter: it all depends on what the arrangement was and on the magnanimity of the employer. He is free to run his farm how he chooses; he can stay within legal agreements or give more if he wants to. The landowner operates by standards of grace, not of merit. The reversal of fortunes is on the basis, not of deserving, but on a gracious concern for the needy.

The landowner, of course, represents God. The story is not about economics or industrial relations, but about God's justice and his grace, about law and mercy. God's grace and mercy are open to all: but for some it's his justice which governs the relationship — they are so legalistic in their thinking that they cannot conceive of a gracious system where rewards are measured on some other basis than whatever is appropriate for 'services rendered'.

Even though the last to arrive may not 'deserve' the same generosity, God has the freedom and the desire to bestow unmerited goodness on his children. Jesus' message of God's grace is nonsense to those who build a religious system on meritorious works.

William Barclay quotes a saying of the rabbis: 'Some enter the kingdom in an hour; others hardly enter it in a lifetime,' and then adds one of his favourite pictures of the holy city in the Book of Revelation. It had twelve gates: those on the east faced the dawn; you can enter the kingdom early in your life. Other gates on the west face the setting sun: some come to Christ late in life.

But no matter when it happens, early or late, all God's children are precious to him. When an old person dies, 'full of days' and honour, or a young person is snatched from life too early, both receive the same welcome. From God's perspective, neither has ended life too late or too soon.

Now, this story contains a truth which is at the heart of Jesus' religion. Many religious Jews did not regard tax-collectors and other disreputables and outcasts whose company Jesus enjoyed as equally deserving of God's love as they were. When some of these Jews later became Christians, the churches to whom Matthew addressed his Gospel might have thought the same thing: why are these heathen Gentiles getting in on the act and displacing us? God is generally thought to have favourites — people like us. Of the 22 000 Christian denominations in the world, of course ours is more right than the other 21 999, and we are more favoured than others.

And the problem is in every local church, too. In a television culture, corporate worship is changing. Baby boomers don't like 'liturgies-as-usual': the old way of doing church is dry, dull, boring, repetitive, irrelevant. But those who have borne the 'burden and the heat of the day' and held the church together through hard times are not about to surrender their precious church to these younger people with their new songs.

The parable also teaches something about our motivation for being a Christian. We belong to God, love God and serve God not for pay or any other reward, but from a heart-response of love. God doesn't reward people simply because they work hard or long or cleverly. The service we render, the gift we give, is received with love by God despite its size or prettiness: what counts is our motive.   It's the spirit in which our gift is given or our work done that counts.

As Wordsworth put it in his 'Inside of King's Chapel, Cambridge': 'Give all thou canst; high heaven rejects the lore/ Of nicely calculated less or more.'

So that's why the first are last and the last first. Many who are poor in this world are great in the kingdom; many who are rich will be poorest in the kingdom. If we serve for reward, we are in great danger of losing it; if we serve without thought of reward, we will be honoured with it, forever.

❧

This parable teaches the amazing grace of a Lord who lifts 'lasts' — the less effective, less fruitful little people and spiritual latecomers — into places of honour. Lasts become firsts in this story, not because they have done enough good works, but because they have a good Lord — a Lord who invites them into his field at all, even at the latest possible hour, and who then rewards them as though they had done a full day's work.

Frederick Dale Bruner, Matthew

God's love cannot be portioned out in quantities nicely adjusted to the merits of individuals. There is such a thing as the twelfth part of a denarius. . . But there is no such thing as a twelfth part of the love of God.

T.W. Manson, The Sayings of Jesus

There is an element of human tenderness in this parable. There is nothing more tragic than [someone] who is unemployed, whose talents are rusting in idleness because there is nothing to do.   . . .The saddest words in all Shakespeare's plays are: 'Othello's occupation's gone.' There in the marketplace stood those men still waiting because no-one had hired them; in his compassion, the master gave them work to do. He could not bear to see them idle, for his heart was touched by the sight of a man with no work to do. . .

The master well knew that if the workman went home

with less [than a full day's wage], there would be a
worried wife and hungry children at home; and therefore
the master went beyond justice and gave them more than
was their due. . . This parable states implicitly two great
truths which are the very charter of the worker — the
right of everyone to work and the right of everyone to a
living wage for that work.

William Barclay, *The Gospel of Matthew*

Many have commented in recent years about the hard
edge of anger building up in our society. Could it be that
when life is reduced to 'you-get-what-you-deserve' and to
economic values alone, hearts contract and compassion
and kindness dry up? Perhaps knowing ourselves as
receivers of astonishing mercy is what opens our hearts
and hands to others.

Anthony B. Robinson, 'Living by the Word'

Some come to the adventure of life eternally young; others
are crippled from the start. Some have negligible hand-
icaps; others have a taint in the blood, a pressure of
environment, a native feebleness of will, an early thwarting
which has left a constant smart on an ever open wound.
One leaps to victory; another stubbornly resists the foe a
hundred times and then succumbs — and only God knows
which of them has truly won the victor's crown!

Those whose strength is sure despise the comrade hired
at the eleventh hour. 'These last' they murmur; and forget
that the 'scorching heat' is harder on the one who waits
despairingly than on the labourer who toils in assurance
of a livelihood! Idleness in appearance may not be idleness in motive. But God's judgments are 'true and
righteous altogether' and it comes to pass that those who
are 'first' in our appraisals are sometimes 'last' in the
verdicts of God.

If only the labourers of the morning hours had offered
a part of their ample wage to comrades who, because of
weakness or 'the inhumanity of man to man' or fettering
circumstance, waited while no-one hired them! Then, they
would have entered into the joy of their Lord and realised

the wise and gentle kingdom in their midst!

George A. Buttrick, *The Parables of Jesus*

There are people who think that, because they have been members of a church for a long time, the church practically belongs to them and that they can dictate and control its policy; such people resent what seems to them the intrusion of new blood into the church or the rise of a new generation who have different plans and different ways. In the Christian church, seniority does not necessarily mean honour.

William Barclay, *The Gospel of Matthew*

All that God gives is of grace. We cannot earn what God gives us; we cannot deserve it; we cannot put God in our debt; what God gives to us is given out of the goodness of his heart, out of his grace; what God gives is not pay, but a gift; not a reward, but a grace.

William Barclay, *The Gospel of Matthew*

When I consider how my light is spent
Ere half my days in this dark world and wise,
And that one talent which is death to hide,
Lodged with me useless, though my soul more bent
To serve therewith my Maker, and present
My true account, lest he returning chide;
'Doth God exact day-labour, light denied?'
I fondly ask. But Patience, to prevent
That murmur, soon replies, 'God doth not need
Either man's work or his own gifts; who best
Bear his mild yoke, they serve him best; his state
Is kingly. Thousands at his bidding speed,
And post o'er land and ocean without rest:
They also serve who only stand and wait.

John Milton

Lord, I have several responses to this unusual story. I want to know how to live compassionately in a world where some can't work and others don't want to work; a world where some are idle through accident, others through choice; where 'structural unemployment' means some will never work at a meaningful job and many do not have a marketable skill or trade; where some employers are selfish and greedy and exploit their workers; or where workers organise themselves for protection, but sometimes abuse their power and strike on a negligible pretext.

Then, there are those willing to work for the kingdom, but are idle, not knowing what to do or not able to do very much. Some are handicapped, some live in desperate circumstances. Who will hire them? They want to serve you, Lord, but don't seem to have the opportunity. Thankyou that the intention is accepted by you as the deed. They will not be forgotten in the appraisals of the kingdom.

But above all, help me not to look down on others who are weaker, less gifted, less knowledgeable. Your grace has reached even me; I did not deserve your favour. I am saved not by doing good works — I could never do enough and I would then suffer from a bloated pride. Nor am I lost for my failure to do good works — I do them from love, not for reward.

A Benediction

So rejoice that you are worthy to reign with Christ in his kingdom, not because you are good, but because you are chosen. May his grace work in your mind and heart to encourage you to be similarly gracious to others. For his glory. Amen.

16

Let your desert bloom

'Go out and stand on the mountain before Yahweh.'
Then Yahweh went by. There came a mighty wind, so
strong it tore the mountains and shattered the rocks
before Yahweh. But Yahweh was not in the wind. After
the wind came an earthquake. But Yahweh was not in
the earthquake. After the earthquake came a fire. But
Yahweh was not in the fire. And after the fire there
came the sound of a gentle breeze.

The Spirit drove him [Jesus] out into the wilderness
and he remained there for forty days, and was tempted
by Satan.

God, examine me and know my heart,
probe me and know my thoughts;
make sure I do not follow pernicious ways,
and guide me in the way that is everlasting.

You did not choose me, no, I chose you; and I commissioned you to go out and to bear fruit, fruit that will
last; and then the Father will give you anything you ask
him in my name.

May the God of our Lord Jesus Christ, the Father of
glory, give you a spirit of wisdom and perception of
what is revealed, to bring you to full knowledge of him.
May he enlighten the eyes of your mind so that you can
see what hope his call holds for you, what rich glories
he has promised the saints will inherit and how infinitely
great is the power that he has exercised for us believers.
This you can tell from the strength of his power at work
in Christ, when he used it to raise him from the dead

and to make him sit at his right hand in heaven.

. . .Let your light shine before others, so that they may see your good works and give glory to your Father in heaven.

Rejoice and be glad, for your reward will be great in heaven.

There is nothing I cannot master with the help of the One who gives me strength.

(1 Kings 19: 11–12; Mark 1: 12–13; Psalm 139: 23–24; John 15: 16; Ephesians 1: 17–20 — all JB; Matthew 5: 16, NRSV; Matthew 5: 12; Philippians 4: 13 — both JB)

The Lord called and I answered him. Or thought I did. I moved out of home, studied for years, graduated, became ordained into his ministry. Warily at first, but afire with the enthusiasm for my chosen profession, I trod his path. Accepted, popular, my life was filled with promise. Yes, the Lord had called and I had answered him.

Then came the crisis. It caught me unawares. After all, I was confident and successful. Where did this cloud of doubt and unknowing come from? Suddenly, my Lord seemed to have deserted me. I could not pray. I experienced anguish, desolation. I was in a desert. My soul was parched and dry. I thirsted for the company of my Lord.

'Where have you gone? Why have you abandoned me when I needed you most? Didn't I give my life to you, give up everything to work for you?'

No-one understood. Least of all did I.

I sat there in the parched waterless desert of spiritual desolation. . . for years, it seemed. Completely stripped. No credibility. No parish. No self. Only a long, cold night, almost without life.

Then, slowly, a faint dawn shimmered on the horizon, with just enough light to kindle hope. Was it a mirage? Or was it the Lord's voice whispering on the gentle breeze? The last small ember of my dying faith glowed faintly, fanned by the breath of the Lord.

'Where did you go? Why did you abandon me when

I needed you most? Didn't I give up my life for you?' questioned my Lord. He disturbed me with my own pleas. What did he mean?

I had nothing left. There was not a thing I could lose. 'I don't understand, Lord. There I was, working for you, doing it right; everyone approved of the great job I was doing.'

'But that's just the point. *You* were doing it. *You* were doing it for *you*. Did I not ask you to be *my* hands, *my* feet, *my* voice to a hungry world? I have brought you to the desert to show you what your efforts amount to, if you continue to do it alone. Nothing. You have felt powerless to change anything in your life here in the desert.

'As you were, you enjoyed a position of standing in the community, you were a leader of people, you were looked up to and praised. When did the bottom fall out of your life? When you felt so confident that you could do it alone. You see, I have chosen you to come higher up. Any number of people can succeed in the world on their own, but I have chosen you to put aside yourself, to become so immersed in me that, looking at you, people will see me. Be my light. Be my channel. Be my hands, my feet, my voice. Your reward will be glorious beyond your imagining.'

∞

I am afraid of saying 'yes', Lord.
Where will you take me?
I am afraid of drawing the longer straw,
I am afraid of signing my name to an unread agreement,
I am afraid of the 'yes' that entails other 'yeses'.
And yet I am not at peace.
You pursue me, Lord, you besiege me.
I run after noise for fear of hearing you, but in a moment of silence you slip through.
I turn from the road, for I have caught sight of you, but at the end of the path you are there awaiting me.
Where shall I hide? I meet you everywhere.
Is it then impossible to escape you?

I am hungry and thirsty,
And the whole world cannot satisfy me.
And yet I loved you, Lord; what have I done to you?
I worked for you; I gave myself for you.
O great and terrible God,
What more do you want?

Michel Quoist, *Prayers of Life*

I fled him, down the night and down the days;
I fled him, down the arches of the years;
I fled him, down the labyrinthine ways
Of my own mind; and in the midst of tears
I hid from him. . .
For, though I knew his love who followed,
Yet was I sore adread
Lest, having him, I must have naught beside.

Francis Thompson, *The Hound of Heaven*

Eye to eye with this man. The street. Many faces.
Pounding in my temples as in a forge.
Nothing adventurous for me. I don't want to offend;
let me keep myself to myself. . .

Karol Wojtyla, *Simon of Cyrene*

I was praying. . . and read the passage about calming of
the storm (Luke 8: 22–25). It was as though the Lord said
to me: 'You know, I have complete control over the
elements. They obey me. But you have free will. You can
choose.' The Lord showed me he would never force me.

Then he gave me an image of a house. I have a great
imagination, which I believe God uses to speak to me. In
this image of the house, I was inside and a man came
knocking at the door. I opened the door and he seemed
to be a very nice man, so I asked him to come in.

I told him: 'See all these rooms. Make yourself at
home, go anywhere you like in my house.' I followed the
man as he walked through all the rooms. There were
many of them and they were very pretty. Suddenly, he
came upon a locked door. On the door in large dark type
was *Private — Do not enter*. He turned to me and, as he

turned, I recognised him to be Jesus. He asked me, 'Briege, why can't I go in this room?'

I replied, 'Come now, Jesus, look at all I've given you. I want to keep a little something for myself.'

I heard him say, in this image, 'You know, Briege, if you do not open that door, you will never know what it means to be truly free.'

I remember looking at the image and saying to myself, 'Now what is in that room?'

The Lord said, 'I'll show you.'

Inside that room was my reputation, what others thought of me. I didn't want Jesus in that room because I was preserving my good name and my reputation. I wanted to follow Jesus, but I wanted control of my life. I wasn't going to be a fool. Anything to do with the cross, with picking up my cross — that was out of the question.

I heard Jesus saying to me, 'I thought you gave me your life.'

Briege McKenna, *Miracles Do Happen*

Lord, I fear my freedom
(which is yet your greatest gift to me
and my greatest glory),
for it alone has the power
to separate me from you.
Do not let this mistrust of myself
become mistrust of you,
or a doubt in me of my love for you,
but let it make me rely
ever more entirely on you,
until you grant me to possess
that perfect love
which, opening myself to you irrevocably,
casts out all fear.

Brian Moore, *Groping Godwards*

The divine action. . . can only take possession of a soul in so far as it is empty of all confidence in its own action.

Jean-Pierre de Caussade,
Self-Abandonment to Divine Providence

Poverty of spirit means *to have no will of my own.* At root it is not surrendering things or my attachment to things, but surrendering my very will. As long as we can choose the things, the attachments, to surrender — even if we choose to surrender all of them — it is still we who are choosing; it is still our will which is in control. As long as it is we who are stripping ourselves, we are not truly poor in spirit. The beatitude which Jesus proclaims is only realised — made real — in us when we have let go of our own will, even our will to become holy!

We have, then, a paradox: To have no will of my own, to be truly poor in spirit, is not to have *no* will, but to have only *one* will. That is why the poor in spirit are not spineless, wishy-washy souls devoid of energy and initiative. They are, in fact, the real doers in the kingdom of God, precisely because they are totally and passionately surrendered to the will of God. Having no will of their own, all their energies can be harnessed to the work of God in the world; all their loves and talents — and limitations, too — can be animated totally by his will.

Thomas H. Green, *When the Well Runs Dry*

Divine activity floods the whole universe; it pervades all creatures; it flows over them. Wherever they are, it is there; it precedes, accompanies and follows them. We have but to allow ourselves to be carried forward on the crest of its waves.

Jean-Pierre de Caussade,
Self-Abandonment to Divine Providence

Jesus, Friend of a lonely heart,
You are my haven,
You are my peace.
You are my salvation,
You are my serenity in moments of struggle and amidst an ocean of doubts.
You are the bright ray that lights up the path of my life.
You are everything to a lonely soul.
You understand the soul even though it remains silent.

You know our weaknesses and, like a good physician,
You comfort and heal, sparing us sufferings —
Expert that you are. Amen.

Sr Faustina Kowalska

O Lord my God
let me totally surrender
myself to you.
Dissolve my will
and replace it with yours.
Dispel all evil spirits
that seek to oppress me
So that freely
I may blossom forth,
Radiating your love to all. Amen.

A Benediction

Dear Pilgrim:
I may have called Moses up to the mountain into my presence,
but I was no less present with all the people when I fed them
manna in the desert. Deprived, they learned to depend on me.
I am asking you also to rely on me, so that when you feel weak,
I can be your strength; when your well runs dry, I can fill you
with the living water of my love, to make your desert bloom.

17

Satisfied servanthood

After this, Jesus and his disciples went out into the
Judean countryside, where he spent some time with
them, and baptised. Now John also was baptising at
Aenon near Salim, because there was plenty of water,
and people were constantly coming to be baptised. (This
was before John was put in prison.)

An argument developed between some of John's disciples and a certain Jew over the matter of ceremonial
washing. They came to John and said to him, 'Rabbi,
that man who was with you on the other side of the
Jordan — the one you testified about — well, he is
baptising, and everyone is going to him.'

To this John replied, 'A man can receive only what is
given him from heaven. You yourselves can testify that
I said, "I am not the Christ but am sent ahead of him."
The bride belongs to the bridegroom. The friend who
attends the bridegroom waits and listens for him, and
is full of joy when he hears the bridegroom's voice. That
joy is mine, and it is now complete. He must become
greater; I must become less. The one who comes from
above is above all; the one who is from the earth belongs
to the earth, and speaks as one from the earth.

'The one who comes from heaven is above all. . . He
testifies to what he has seen and heard, but no-one
accepts his testimony. The man who has accepted it has
certified that God is truthful. For the one whom God
has sent speaks the words of God, for God gives the
Spirit without limit. The Father loves the Son and has
placed everything in his hands. Whoever believes in
the Son has eternal life, but whoever rejects the Son will

not see life, for God's wrath remains on him.'
(John 3: 22-36, NIV)

What will it take to make me satisfied to be simply a servant of Jesus Christ? How can I ever become a faithful follower of Christ, rather than an irritable initiate of earthbound projects?

John the Baptist could be described as the most satisfied servant of Christ. His commitment to Jesus' cause was unwavering: he was a faithful signpost to Christ and he wanted no share of the glory. Yet his personal contact with Jesus was brief: he saw nothing of Jesus' miracles or Jesus' popular ministry. John's satisfaction seemed to be rooted in a clear perception of his own role and the role of Jesus. His sense of joy and completeness seemed to spring from a recognition of God's purposes. His willingness to stand aside and decrease seemed to grow out of his intense commitment to God's plans.

In every declaration he made, John pointed people to Jesus whilst drawing a cloak of increasing obscurity about himself. The man who said he was not the light diffused his diminishing light into the lives of those he loved best as he urged them to go and follow Christ. Selfless heroics take us by surprise so early in the account of Christ's ministry.

John's disciples, destined to spend so much time with the master, still failed to learn the need for sacrifice and unselfish devotion in Christ's lifetime. These disciples who so readily abandoned the redundant baptiser-with-water for the baptiser-with-Spirit would not be able to imitate John the Baptist's abdication of ego until Christ had died and been raised again,until they also had a clear perception of Christ's heavenly redemptive role in glimmering contrast to their own earthbound duties.

How did John learn to die to himself so thoroughly before death overtook him so soon? John, who willingly describes himself as earthbound and limited in his understanding, demonstrates his insights into heavenly priorities by declaring the pre-eminence of Jesus, the son so loved by God. He bills himself as merely a friend of the groom who has watched and waited for his appearance, yet he trumpets boldly Christ's claim to reign.

If I want an example of satisfied servanthood and faithful following, I need look no further than John the Baptist. Perhaps it was the brevity of his life which protected him from the blunders and bloopers of Peter or James and John. Perhaps it was the gravity of his mission and God's great grace for that task which set him so distinctly apart. Yet there is something in this man's attitude to the closure of his ministry which promises peace, integration and hope for those who struggle on in their ministries.

As a servant of Christ, I often experience disappointment and great dissatisfaction. In these troughs, I am least able to point people clearly to Christ. In these times, I need something for me: a dose of glory, recognition — or at least some faithful friends to stick with me if my ministry seems to be in decline. As I grow older, I become increasingly impatient with an ego that will not die and my own plans, priorities and agenda which spring up from my desk demanding attention like a schoolboy with all the answers.

Where does this frustration come from? The demands of others and my idealised view of self. Sometimes, I aspire to be too much like Christ in his wisdom and counsel and others want me to be like him in devotion to their causes and pain. I try to increase, squeezing Jesus out of the picture.

If I take myself in hand, I can remind myself that I am only another appointed signpost. Whether my ministry flourishes or fails, my relationship to Jesus cannot change, because its foundation is the great triumph of his ministry. If I can get hold of John's perspective of the Lord and keep my own paltry task in view, then I can share some of John's satisfaction in serving.

❧❧❧

'The great mistake made by most of the Lord's people is in hoping to discover in themselves that which is to be found in Christ alone.' These words of Arthur W. Pink focus on a key issue in living by grace. Most of us have the tendency that Arthur Pink identified: to seek within ourselves what is to be found in Christ alone.

Jerry Bridges, *Transforming Grace*

How, then, can a young man with limited experience, undeveloped sympathies, an impatient temper, a longing for attention, a love of self-expression and a passion for ideas become a true shepherd of his people? First of all, let him study afresh the life of the ideal Shepherd and then let him, day by day, both by prayer and self-sacrificing deeds, endeavour to build up in himself the mind of Christ.

Charles Jefferson, *The Minister as Shepherd*

First, since the organisation of the Christian church as an institution is so physically real and apparently understandable, I begin to imagine that the most important task for me as a Christian is to manage this institution and make it succeed for God's purposes. So I put my organisational mind to this task, only to find that this becomes a destructive error because my mind becomes focused almost exclusively on the procedures of government and the preservation of the institution of the church.

Earl Palmer, *Integrity In a World of Pretense*

It is an immense irony when the very practice of our work results in abandoning our work. In the course of doing our work we leave our work. But in reading, teaching and preaching the scriptures it happens: we cease to listen to the scriptures and thereby undermine the intent of having scriptures in the first place.

Eugene H. Peterson, *Working the Angles*

The process of transformation, however, demands our death. We must die to become like Christ. We must die to live, lose ourselves to find ourselves, renounce what we have to inherit the world (Luke 9: 22-36). The whole notion of becoming new persons is so utterly preposterous, so far beyond reasonable imagination, that only by dying to the idea of ever achieving it will we ever receive it. It is God's plan. It must be his doing, not ours.

We can understand why the requirements of discipleship stagger the mind. We always get more than we bargain for. Initially, we embraced the Christian faith for a particular reason. We felt guilty, anxious or timid, and we found forgiveness, peace or confidence in the gospel. We all entered the Christian life through one of its many doors. But the door through which we walked is only the beginning. We found forgiveness, but God intends to make us forgiving. We discovered peace, but God sends us into the tumult. We gained confidence, but God commands us to be servants. God keeps pushing us farther than we ever wanted to go. He will push us all the way to Christlikeness.

Jerry Sittser, *The Adventure*

Father, make us faithful signposts to the faithful one. Thankyou for the life of Christ who is our righteousness and thankyou for the sanctifying power of the Holy Spirit at work in our lives to make us more like our Lord and saviour. Teach us, Lord, to love our servanthood despite all its earthly limitations and frustrations. While we want to be more like Jesus, we know that Christ alone can truly nurture people. While we want to be instruments of your peace and grace in the lives of those we serve, teach us never to grasp for the glory which belongs to you alone.

A Benediction
Lord, let us launch into this day and this week with a new determination to point people to Jesus, as we serve them for your sake. Amen.

18

When God says: 'No!'

Will the Lord reject forever? Will he never show his favour again? Has his unfailing love vanished forever? Has his promise failed for all time? Has God forgotten to be merciful? Has he in anger withheld his compassion?

'As the heavens are higher than the earth, so are my ways higher than your ways and my thoughts than your thoughts,' declares the Lord.

As for God, his way is perfect. . . It is God who arms me with strength and makes my way perfect.

Though the fig tree does not bud and there are no grapes on the vines, though the olive crop fails and the fields produce no food, though there are no sheep in the pen and no cattle in the stalls, yet I will rejoice in the Lord, I will be joyful in God my Saviour.

'You do not want to leave too, do you?' Jesus asked the Twelve. Simon Peter answered him, 'Lord, to whom shall we go? You have the words of eternal life. We believe and know that you are the Holy One of God.' Then Jesus replied, 'Have I not chosen you, the Twelve? Yet one of you is a devil!'

Going a little farther, he fell with his face to the ground, and prayed, 'My Father, if it is possible, may this cup be taken from me. Yet not as I will, but as you will.'

Praise be to God, who has not rejected my prayer or withheld his love from me!

(Psalm 77: 7-9; Isaiah 55: 9; Psalm 18: 30a,32; Habakkuk 3: 17,18; John 6: 67-70; Matthew 26: 39; Psalm 66: 20 — all NIV)

Sometimes it is hard to remember that God is sovereign, particularly when his ideas and ours do not yet coincide. When we pray and expect a particular intervention of God's power, but it seems to be missing, then we become sad and hurt and bewildered. When we hurt, our emotions are thrown off balance and our eyes are only able to see what we feel.

It is hard to hold onto the truth. 'The Lord is my shepherd, I have everything I need' (Psalm 23: 1). But the dark threads of God's weaving just seem to get darker. We want to pull them out and replace them with gold.

Instead of improvement, we see deterioration. We are disappointed and do not understand what God seems to be doing, or at least allowing. Our heads hold some truths to which we try to cling, but where we live is a maelstrom of hurt and anger and non-understanding. God is Person. We will know him as Person, or we will not know him at all. There will be anger, frustration, hurt, tears — and certainly joy.

Some of us have had to say to this God we must know as Person: 'We *know* you love us — but God, it doesn't *feel* very much like it. Everything seems to point to the opposite. How can these things be happening if you who care are in charge? It seems to be night all the time! Are you *really* here in the dark?'

If we listen, God will turn us right side up when he says something like: 'I do not ask if you *understand*; I ask you, "Do you *love* me?"' And if this dissolves us into tears, maybe the frustration and anger and hurt will begin to dissolve, too.

Once, when many people stopped following Jesus because it had become too hard, Jesus asked his disciples: 'Will you also go away?' Where *else* is there to run except to the God who loves us, whether we *feel* it or not, whether we *know* it or not — to the God who loves us whether we *believe* it or not, for that matter. That God only ever wants our highest good is true. The crucifixion and the resurrection are the grounds for knowing that.

But when our tears and darkness hide our highest good, the only way through is to run, clinging to him. 'My soul has run clinging to you; on me has your right hand laid hold' (Psalm 63: 8).

But somehow, it takes us time to get our thinking and emotions to agree with the truth and to do that — to run, clinging to him. We feel more like running in the opposite direction; we feel like locking God out.

God comes to us *even* when we lock him out. Jesus has promised to be with us always. His promise is that we can trust, even when God seems to be saying: 'No!'

While we are praying, we are seeking that God should display his power — his, to use the Greek word, *dunamos*. One English word derived from that is 'dynamite'. We pray, and expect the dynamite of God's power to be displayed in meeting the need as we perceive it. We expect God to 'fix it' because we know that he can.

Yet he often seems to be saying, 'No!'

Sometimes, we must come to the place where we need to recognise God's *dynamos* at work, not as dyna*mite*, but as dyna*mo*— controlled energy empowering, enabling us to go on despite the presenting problem.

Whether we see God's power as dynamite or dynamo, he is still the One who says *not*: 'Do you understand?', but: 'Do you love me?'

❧❧❧

God's purposes are bigger and better than anything you can ask for in this present moment. Therefore, in his great love and mercy, he will not settle for the little solutions you demand. . . When your wants are strained through the fabric of God's larger truths, then what is real will precipitate out.

Robert Wise, *When There is no Miracle*

We are called to serve with a willing mind just where we are and just as things are. We may not be able to see the meaning of anything, or to catch the least glimpse of the gladness of before. . . He trusts us to trust. He loves the offering of a willing mind.

Amy Carmichael, *Whispers of his Power*

When some beloved voice that was to you
Both sound and sweetness, faileth suddenly,
And, silence, against which you dare not cry
Aches round you like a strong disease and new -
What hope? What help? What music will undo
That silence to your sense. . .
Speak Thou, availing Christ! — and fill this pause.

Elizabeth Barrett Browning, 'Sustitution'

I asked for strength that I might achieve;
He made me weak that I might obey.
I asked for health
that I might do greater things.
I was given grace
that I might do better things.
I asked for riches that I might be happy;
I was given poverty that I might be wise.
I asked for power
that I might have the praise of men;
I was given weakness
that I might feel the need of God.
I asked for all things that I might enjoy life;
I was given life that I might enjoy all things.
I received nothing that I asked for,
all that I hoped for,
My prayer was answered.

G. & M. Rosell, *Shoe Leather Faith*

The exciting thing about Augie was the instant obedience
and absolute trust he showed toward me. Whenever we
entered a show ring he would quietly dance and prance
in one place, never pulling on the reins, ears flicking
backward and forward in anticipation of my command. I
never had to tug his head; I just held this snaffel bit firmly
against his mouth, keeping the reins low and taut. Whenever I wanted him to move ahead, all it took was a slight
tightening of my knees against him and — flash! — off
he would go. . . because he trusted my judgment, he loved
to do my will.

. . .Augie's response to me did not hinge on his approval

of the course. . . What counted was that he knew me. . . We had built a relationship and I had proven myself to him over and over again. . . demonstrating myself trustworthy. . . When someone set fire to my father's barn. . . we covered [the horses'] eyes with blankets before leading them past the roaring flames and out to safety. . . Here these humans were covering their eyes with a blanket that ordinarily went on their backs and asking them to follow us when they could not even see. . .

In that confusing moment. . . they trusted us to care for them as we had always done. There was no rebelling, no challenging of our wisdom or authority and, as a result, we were able to save their lives.

How unlike these simple animals we are! They put tremendous confidence in their masters, mere human beings, yet the great God who has chosen to save and redeem us at such a precious price does not [always] have our trust. . .

What causes this senseless lack of faith? It is our failure to realise just how much God has already done to prove himself to us. . . he has proved his intentions! When he covers our eyes with the blanket of a limited under-standing, surely he deserves to be given the benefit of the doubt. . . He deserves our trust.

Joni Eareckson & Steve Estes, *A Step Further*

To these earliest days belongs also the story of her prayer that God would change the colour of her brown eyes and give her blue instead: '. . .the bewilderment that even now I can remember as if it were yesterday. . . Without a shadow of a doubt that my eyes would be blue in the morning I had gone to sleep. The minute I woke I pushed a chair to the. . . looking glass. . . full of eager expectation and saw — mere brown eyes. I don't remember how the words came: 'Isn't *No* an answer?'

. . .At the age of three she began to learn a lesson which she never forgot. . . even silence is an answer, that our gracious Lord may sometimes say 'Wait' or even 'No' rather than 'Yes', but that he is never heedless of our prayers:

Will not the End explain
The crossed endeavour, earnest purpose foiled
The strange bewilderment of good work spoiled,
The clinging weariness, the inward strain,
Will not the End explain?

Frank Houghton, *Amy Carmichael of Donhnavur*

I walked to a nearby lake one afternoon and for the first time realised that what seemed like an ordinary childhood accident might become the end of this small winsome little life. . . .I started sobbing uncontrollably. I have prayed. I did believe. . . Why? I wanted to scream and curse everything in the universe. . .

Think back to a time when you prayed for help during a hard situation. Did God answer your prayer the way you wanted him to? Or did he turn a 'deaf ear' to your plea? . . .When God doesn't relieve you of pain — emotional or physical — do you feel like he doesn't like you any more or that there is something wrong with your faith? What does Romans 8: 38-39 say about God's love? . . .The lack of a miracle is only a signal that the time is not ripe and that God's best moment is not yet ready to be fulfilled.

Robert Wise, *When There Is No Miracle*

And shall I pray Thee change Thy will, my Father
Until it be according unto mine?
But no, Lord, no, that never shall be, rather,
I pray Thee blend my human will with Thine. . .

Frank Houghton,
Amy Carmichael of Dohnavur

Lord, when my prayers are like a gibber plain,
and my soul like spinifex —
drench me with a downpour of mercy!
. . .and show me again what love can make
with two pieces of wood and a few nails.

Bruce Prewer, *Australian Psalms*

A Benediction

In darkness and in light, in trouble and in joy, help us to trust your love, to serve your purpose and to praise your holy Name; . . .May we live by faith, walk in hope and be renewed in love, until the whole world reflects your glory and you are all in all. Even so, come Lord Jesus. Amen.

An Australian Prayer Book

19

The inscrutable sovereignty of God

The general principles: My thoughts are not your thoughts, neither are your ways my ways, says the Lord. O house of Israel, can I not do with you as this potter has done? says the Lord. Who can resist his will?

The promise to Abram of people and land: Go from your country and your kindred and your father's house to the land that I will show you. And I will make of you a great nation. Know of a surety that your descendants will be sojourners in a land that is not theirs, and will be slaves there, and they will be oppressed for four hundred years; but. . . afterward they shall come out with great possessions.

No longer shall your name be Abram. . . for I have made you the father of a multitude of nations. I will make you exceedingly fruitful; and I will make nations of you, and kings shall come forth from you. . . And I will give to you and to your descendants after you. . . all the land of Canaan, for an everlasting possession; and I will be their God.

The promise repeated to Isaac and Jacob: There was a famine in the land. . . and Isaac went to Gerah. The Lord appeared to him and said, 'Do not go down to Egypt. . . to you and to your descendants I will give all these lands. . . I will multiply your descendants as the stars of heaven.'

Jacob left Beersheba. . . and he dreamed. . . the land

on which you lie I will give you and your descendants; and your descendants shall be like the dust of the earth.

So his name was called Israel. And God said to him 'I am God Almighty, be fruitful and multiply. . . a company of nations. . . and kings shall spring from you. . . and I will give the land to your descendants after you.'

And God spoke to Israel in visions of the night. . . 'Do not be afraid to go down to Egypt; for I will there make of you a great nation.'

The descendant promise fulfilled: The descendants of Israel were fruitful and increased greatly; they multiplied and grew exceedingly strong; so that the land was filled with them. Now there arose a new King over Egypt, who did not know Joseph. . . But the more they were oppressed, the more they multiplied.

The land promise fulfilled: The time that the people of Israel dwelt in Egypt was four hundred and thirty years. And. . . on that very day, all the hosts of the Lord went out from the land of Egypt.

And while all Israel were passing over on dry ground, the priests who bore the ark of the covenant of the Lord stood on dry ground in the midst of the Jordan, until all the nation finished passing over the Jordan.

So Joshua took the whole land. . . and Joshua gave it for an inheritance to Israel according to their tribal allotments. And the land had rest from war.

And now the Lord your God has given rest to your brethren, as he promised them; therefore turn and go to your home in the land where your possession lies, which Moses the servant of the Lord gave you on the other side of the Jordan.

For the Lord has driven out before you great and strong nations; and. . . no-one has been able to withstand you to this day. One man of you puts to flight a thousand, since it is the Lord your God who fights for you.

'I gave you a land on which you had not laboured, and cities which you had not built, and you dwell therein; you eat the fruit of vineyards and oliveyards which you did not plant.'

(Isaiah 55: 8; Jeremiah 18: 6; Romans 9: 19; Genesis 12: 1-2; 15: 13-14; 17: 5-6,8; 26: 1-4; 28: 10,12-14; 35: 10-12; 46: 2-3; Exodus 1: 7,8,12; 12: 40-41; Joshua 3: 17; 11: 23; 22: 4; 23: 9-10; 24: 13 — all RSV)

Abraham must have passed on the promise he had been given by God. In any case, God himself reinforced it with a special revelation. And Isaac undoubtedly passed it on to Jacob/Israel, and again God confirmed it directly. Did Abraham pass on, though, the extra revelation of Genesis 15 that the fulfilment would only come through 400 years of slavery in a foreign land? Neither Isaac nor Jacob give any hint that they knew.

The natural explanation of the promise up to the time of Jacob's departure for the south was that the increase in numbers and the promise of land would take place naturally precisely in the place where they were. Jacob, after all, had departed as a single man, and twenty years later returned with two wives and twelve children. This seemed to fulfil the promise. Could they not stay? The answer was negative in the strategy of God.

The promise that Abraham (and Isaac) had was clear and direct. Abraham obviously trusted God — who else would have been willing to offer up his only son as a sacrifice? But Abraham's faith did not just rest on odedience over Isaac, or in an implicit faith that if necessary 'God was able to raise [people] even from the dead' (Hebrews 11: 19), but also, and perhaps most extraordinarily, that he was convinced that God was in control of time. Abraham was prepared to wait over his long life — and beyond — for God to fulfil his purposes. He had left Haran at 75, Isaac was born at 100 and he died at 175 when Isaac was 75 years old and Jacob 15.

Isaac had a similar faith that God was fulfilling his promises over time. He died at 180 when Jacob was 120, about the time Joseph became Prime Minister of Egypt at 30.

Isaac's whole life was lived without seeing the promise of land come true, though he would have seen his twelve grandchildren when Jacob returned and could have guessed that the next generation (his great-grandchildren) was when the promise would start to come true. What faith to wait so long for God to act!

That same faith of God working over time was given to Joseph, too. His father Israel died (at 147) when he was 57, and he lived in Egypt another 53 years before he too died (at 110). The seventeen years that Jacob lived in Egypt and the subsequent 53 for Joseph total 70 years, but another 360 were to pass before they left Egypt. Abraham's 100 years since leaving Haran, Isaac's 105 till he died after his father's death, 10 more years for Jacob to reach Egypt, and 430 years there total 645 years — and *still* no land, though the Israelites were perhaps by then two million strong.

If that isn't enough, then follows the journey across the Red Sea, the forty years' wait in the wilderness and the fight for ownership of the Promised Land, proving their right to belong. The length of the conquest is not known, though it took at least five years, judging from Caleb's age (Joshua 14: 7-10) and it was 'a long time afterward, when the Lord had given rest to Israel' that Joshua prepared to die. This 'long time' must have been something like another ten years, making a total of 700 years from the original promise to Abraham to its fulfilment through Joshua of a 'land flowing with milk and honey'.

Seven hundred years in the making! How patient is the Lord! Few things on earth have such a time span. The churches the Norman conquerors built in rural England have lasted such a length of time — to the extent that today one-third of England's 15 000 parish churches are Norman buildings, 700 or 800 years old. The Great Wall of China took centuries to complete. But mostly, our conceptual time span is far less — we measure in decades not centuries, for we are but 'three score years and ten', like the flower of the grass passing away (James 1: 10).

If you look through a magnifying glass at a leaf, you see its detail, still perfectly made and balanced. It is as if we live our lives in that detail, as it were through the microscope. But God has the vantage point of looking at the whole leaf. What then matters if we have to wait an extra day — or month, or year — to learn his purposes? He is dealing with centuries (and in truth with millennia and aeons of time)! God is working his purpose out as year succeeds to year. Of course, one day with the Lord is as a thousand years. Do you fret that your way is not clear? Have patience. He who has the whole world in his hands has your world in his hands, too. At best we see the micro; God works at macro level his glory, his will, his purposes to perform. Trust him!

❦

Crown him the Lord of Years
The Potentate of time;
Creator of the rolling spheres,
Ineffably sublime:
All hail, Redeemer, hail!
For Thou hast died for me:
Thy praise shall never, never fail
Throughout eternity.

Matthew Bridges (1800-94)
and Godfrey Thring (1823-1903)

God. . . has never regretted his gifts and calling, for what he had intended has come to pass. It cannot be affirmed that God willed the unbelief, but because we humans, even the chosen, are as they are, the hardening of Israel was bound to become necessary. In addition, God is never merely passive and indifferent in the face of the obstinacy and disobedience of his people, but suffers through them. In the voice of his Son weeping over Jerusalem we may hear the suffering love of the Father as well.

H.L. Ellison, *The Mystery of Israel*

The God of Abraham praise,
At whose supreme command
From earth I rise and seek the joys
At his right hand.

I all on earth forsake
Its wisdom, fame and power;
And him my only portion make,
My shield and tower.

Thomas Olivers (1725-99)

There's a divinity that shapes our ends, Rough-hew them
how we will.

Shakespeare, *Hamlet*

Somebody placed the shuttle in your hands; somebody
who had already arranged the threads.

Dag Hammarskjöld, *Markings*

God is content to wait because He reigneth; man must be
content to wait because he believeth.

Isobel Kuhn, *Second Nite People*

Because God knows the number of our days and their
purpose, he wants to direct us so that we can come to old
age without regret. He wants us to come to the day of
our death knowing that we have done the work God gave
us to do, enabling us to say, as Jesus did, 'It is finished'.
(John 19: 30).

Janice Wise, 'Needed: Grace for Growing Old'

Be not afraid of going slowly, be only afraid of standing
still.

Anonymous

God give me work till my life shall end,
  and life till my work be done.

Anonymous

There is a point at which everything becomes simple and
there is no longer any question of choice, because all you
have staked will be lost if you look back. Life's point of
no return.

Dag Hammarskjöld, *Markings*

He is before all things
And in him all things consist
Oh wondrous power!
To create such a nature
To control such a creation,
To share with our unworthiness.
He will come after should we wish it —
But to our eternal loss.
On, no, never, Saviour. For before us, he directs us
And life with love
Stretches out in the blueness
of eternity.

Peter Brierley

Focus on minimising or eliminating the many activities in your day that take up so much of your time yet produce such a small part of your overall result. If you think you don't have enough time to spend with your family, begin to eliminate the activities in each week that contribute little to your productivity. You can find time for your family and still get all the important things done as well.

Myron Rush, *Burnout*

I cannot tell how he will win the nations,
How he will claim his earthly heritage,
How satisfy the needs and aspirations
Of East and West, of sinner and of sage.
But this I know, all flesh shall see his glory,
And he shall reap the harvest he has sown,
And some glad day this sun shall shine in splendour,
When he the Saviour, Saviour of the World, is known.

William Young Fullerton

A grocer was down in the cellar of his shop, when he noticed his small son standing at the edge of the open trap door. He called up, 'Here I am, sonnie, jump down.' But the boy hesitated. 'I can't see you, Daddy.' Up came the answer, 'No, but I can see you; trust me and jump and I will catch you,' which he did.

Anonymous

Amid all the changes and chances of this mortal life God abides, God reigns, God rules. His kingdom will be set up, his purposes shall be realised, his will must be done. Let us take heart as servant after servant of God passes into the unseen. Let us take large views of the future and not be tempted to concentrate attention solely upon our own narrow little life in the present. 'I die, but God will surely visit you' (Genesis 50: 24). It is this assurance of God's unchanging presence and undeviating purpose that alone can keep the heart peaceful, restful, trustful and hopeful amid all the vicissitudes of life.

W. H. Griffith Thomas,
Genesis: a devotional commentary

If only we knew how to look at life as God sees it, we should realise that nothing is secular in the world, but that everything contributes to the building of the Kingdom of God. To have faith is not only to raise one's eyes to God to contemplate him; it is also to look at this world — but with Christ's eyes.

Michel Quoist, *Prayers of Life*

Almighty God,
Whose chosen servant Abraham
faithfully obeyed your call
and rejoiced in your promise
that, in him, all the families of the earth should be
        blessed:
Give us a faith like his,
that, in us, your promises may be fulfilled;
through Jesus Christ our Lord.

Alternative Service Book,
Third Sunday before Advent

Almighty God,
Who alone can bring order
to the unruly wills and passions of sinful people:
give us grace
to love what you command

and to desire what you promise,
that in all the changes and chances of this world,
our hearts may surely there be fixed
Where lasting joys are to be found;
through Jesus Christ our Lord.

Alternative Service Book
Fourth Sunday after Easter

A Benediction

May the God of time take us as we are and make us what he
wants us to become; may the Lord Jesus, creator and upholder
of the universe, enable us to rest in his eternal providence; and
may the Holy Spirit grant us the faith to trust when we doubt,
to move forward when we cannot see, and to rejoice when all
seems lost.

'Faithful is he who calls you, who also will do it.' **Amen.**

I Thessalonians 5 verse 24, RSV

20

Doing the unthinkable

Now when Jesus learned that the Pharisees had heard, 'Jesus is making and baptising more disciples than John' — although it was not Jesus himself but his disciples who baptised — he left Judea and started back to Galilee. But he had to go through Samaria. So he came to a Samaritan city called Sychar, near the plot of ground that Jacob had given to his son Joseph. Jacob's well was there, and Jesus, tired out by his journey, was sitting by the well. It was about noon.

A Samaritan woman came to draw water and Jesus said to her, 'Give me a drink.' (His disciples had gone to the city to buy food.) The Samaritan woman said to him, 'How is it that you, a Jew, ask a drink of me, a woman of Samaria?' (Jews do not share things in common with Samaritans.) Jesus answered her, 'If you knew the gift of God, and who it is that is saying to you "Give me a drink," you would have asked him, and he would have given you living water.'

The woman said to him, 'Sir, you have no bucket, and the well is deep. Where do you get that living water? Are you greater than our ancestor Jacob, who gave us the well, and with his sons and his flocks drank from it?' Jesus said to her, 'Everyone who drinks of this water will be thirsty again, but those who drink of the water that I will give them will never be thirsty. The water that I will give will become in them a spring of water gushing up to eternal life.'

The woman said to him, 'Sir, give me this water, so that I may never be thirsty or have to keep coming here to draw water.'

Jesus said to her, 'Go, call your husband, and come back.' The woman answered him, 'I have no husband.' Jesus said to her, 'You are right in saying, "I have no husband"; for you have had five husbands, and the one you have now is not your husband. What you have said is true!'

The woman said to him, 'Sir I see that you are a prophet. Our ancestors worshipped on this mountain, but you say that the place where people must worship is in Jerusalem.' Jesus said to her, 'Woman, believe me, the hour is coming when you will worship the Father neither on this mountain, nor in Jerusalem. You worship what you do not know; we worship what we know, for salvation is from the Jews.

'But the hour is coming, and is now here, when the true worshippers will worship the Father in spirit and truth, for the Father seeks such as these to worship him. God is spirit and those who worship him must worship in spirit and truth.' The woman said to him, 'I know that Messiah is coming' (who is called Christ). 'When he comes, he will proclaim all things to us.'

Jesus said to her, 'I am he, the one who is speaking to you.'

(John 4: 1–26, NRSV)

The account of Jesus' meeting with the Samaritan woman at Jacob's well is a dramatic illustration of Jesus doing the unthinkable. Here is a Jewish rabbi socialising with a woman — a Samaritan woman! — in public. That might not sound like such a big deal to us, but the woman herself was taken by surprise and John says the disciples were absolutely astonished when they arrived on the scene. They didn't dare say anything to Jesus — or to the woman — but John leaves us in no doubt that this behaviour was unthinkable as far as the woman and the disciples were concerned.

Jesus saw the possibility that men and women could be in a natural, caring relationship of equality with each other;

that ethnic and religious differences need not prevent people from caring for each other; and that the least 'spiritual' among us can serve God as well as anybody else. Jesus was a doer of the unthinkable.

Most of us do not really understand Jesus in this way. We have grown up with a 'gentle Jesus, meek and mild', who would never ruffle anybody's feathers, who would never offend anybody, and who would always staunchly support the government, the hierarchy, law and order, democracy, comfortable middle-class values and the status quo. Not so the Jesus of John's Gospel!

Jesus lived in a time and was the product of a tradition in which the relationships of a wife to a husband or a daughter to a father were defined in terms of the property rights of the man. That demeaning concept of dependency and inferiority determined and permeated the whole of male-female relationships and the status of women.

In this incident at Jacob's well, Jesus demonstrated that there was another possibility. He would be turning his back on his own precious tradition and, at the very least, be re-interpreting it in a controversial, new way. He would incur the wrath of the upholders of the status quo; he would astonish and perplex his friends; he would be open to misunderstanding, including by the woman; perhaps, he would become the subject of gossip and scandal.

The Samaritans were an ancient people who had been forcibly settled in Samaria during the Assyrian exile and, because of their syncretistic worship practices, the Jews of Jesus' day regarded them contemptuously as apostates.

Tragically, our world has been very slow to see the possibility Jesus saw — and so has the Christian church. Look at this century alone. The German church in the main supported Hitler; the Dutch Reformed Church in South Africa provided the theological rationale and the basic institutional support for apartheid. Racism found a comfortable home in the white churches of the US at least until the 'sixties. Official church support has been readily available, often on both sides, for every bloody war since the Boer War ushered in the twentieth century.

Sadly, Jacob's well today, instead of being a milestone

on the road to a new world of justice and peace, is a symbol of the ethnic and religious differences which divide the human family.

Finally, Jesus saw that the least 'spiritual' among us can serve God. Whatever else can be said about the unnamed woman at Jacob's well, you would hardly describe her as a towering spiritual giant who was an obvious candidate to step up to the diamond and take first strike for the disciple band! Of course not! That is John's whole point in including this incident in his Gospel — and he is the only Gospel writer to do so.

John is wanting to make that point through the witness of a despised, much-married Samaritan woman currently living in a *de facto* relationship, who wants to argue, perhaps evasively, about whether true worship should be here or there, 'many . . .came to believe in Jesus. . . (as) the Saviour of the world' (verses 39 and 42).

And the delightful thing to me is that it all began when *he* asked *her* for a drink. Not, I believe, because he saw her as a target for evangelism — there is no evidence of that in the text — but because he was tired and thirsty and needed a drink.

We have drawn some important lessons from this fascinating account — and there are many more we could learn — but the simple, basic reality is that Jesus comes to any and all of us, whoever we are, better than the Samaritan woman or worse, and asks, 'will *you* give me a drink?' Who among us can turn him down?

❧

It was high noon, and hot at that. The little group of men had been for several hours on the dusty road. And some of them were hungry, and had gone to seek for such food as might be available (verse 8). But this was Jacob's well; and Christ elected to remain there in that place of memories, alone with God. Moreover he was wearied and glad to rest.

Hearing that, many look up and turn toward him with a quickened interest and a new sudden hope. The popular conception of the coming Messiah was of a mighty conqueror, ruthlessly crashing his way to irresistible victory. But there are multitudes for whom a tired Christ must understand, might help, as no other could.

It is so easy for one outside of a trouble, himself wholly secure, to toss good advice from the safe distance of his own immunity to poor souls struggling desperately with what is likely to overwhelm them; so easy — and unhelpful! Did not Carlyle once protest that Emerson, shut in that quiet nook of a life of his, into which no breath of the tidings of the world's unhappinesses was allowed to blow lest that might ruffle the placidity of his existence and vex him, seemed to him like a complacent person, himself keeping well out of the least touch of spray, throwing chatty and cheerful remarks to a swimmer battling for his very life in huge and angry waters, and with the breath being battered out of him?

If a homely illustration is in order, to one of the three or four best people I have known, suddenly without warning there came a day of disaster when her whole life was disorganised. She said no word, made never a whimper of complaint, but bent everything in her being to a valiant attempt to straighten things.

There dropped in a pious person, clad in soft furs and with not one wrinkle in her luxurious existence, who, hearing how things were, murmured comfortably out of her own immense security, 'Isn't it sweet to know that it is all in the plan?' My friend knew it was in the plan, and had with steady eyes accepted it as such. But she confided to me later, 'That good soul will never know how nearly it was also in the plan that I should fairly slap her!'

[The Bible] takes pains to bring home to us Christ's oneness with us; and people recognising that will listen to him, feeling that he has the right to speak. Thus, those who labour and are heavy laden can see for themselves that he is carrying burdens far heavier than their own, and might well be able to show them how to bear theirs with something of his own unfaltering courage and quietheartedness.

A. J. Gossip, *Exposition of the Gospel by St John*

The well of Jacob lies at the foot of Mount Gerizim, the centre of Samaritan worship. It is one of the historic sites in Palestine that we are reasonably certain of. The 'sixth hour' would probably have been about noon, reckoning from daybreak. It was an unusual time for women to come to a village well for water. Perhaps the Samaritan woman had a sudden need, or perhaps she did not care to meet the other women of the community. In consideration of her general character, the other women may have shunned her.

Undoubtedly, the woman was surprised to find a man sitting by the well and doubly surprised to be addressed by a Jew. Jesus' initial approach was by a simple request for water, which would presuppose a favourable response. One would hardly refuse a drink of cold water to a thirsty traveller in the heat of the day. The request did have a surprising element, however, for no Jewish rabbi would have volunteered to carry on a public conversation with a woman, nor would he have deigned to drink from a Samaritan's cup, as she implied by her answer.

There was a trace of sarcasm in the woman's reply, as if she meant, 'We Samaritans are the dirt under your feet until you want something; *then* we are good enough!' Jesus paid no attention to her flippancy or to her bitterness. He was more interested in winning the woman than in winning an argument. He appealed to her curiosity by the phrase 'If you knew.' He implied that, because of the nature of his person, he could bestow on her a gift of God that would be greater than any ordinary water.

His allusion was intended to lift her level of thinking from that of material need to spiritual realities.

Merrill C. Tenney, *The Gospel of John*

Good theology begins with 'The Lord our God, the Lord is One' (Deuteronomy 6: 4) and quickly adds 'Jesus is Lord' (Romans 10: 9, 1 Corinthians 12: 3). Theology reflects on God as creator of all being (the ecological dimension), God as redeemer concerned with history (incarnation) and God as Spirit (imparting grace through the life and word of the redeemed community).

Jesus is both fully divine and fully human. Western Christians have been more preoccupied with Christ's divinity: he is 'very God of very God'; Third World theology with his humanity: God's solidarity with suffering 'nonpersons'.

If Jesus came back in the flesh again, where would we find him and what would he be doing? Jesus is the supreme theologian of our faith (Kenneth Bailey). A good theology agrees with Jesus' emphases — particularly about love and justice. (Actually, love and justice are the same: justice is love in action, seeking the wholeness and well-being of another.)

Rowland Croucher, 'Every Christian
Should be a Good Theologian'

Most of us spend most of our time thinking what is do-able and doing what is thinkable. It is all so predictable, so practical, so right — and a lot of the time so downright *boring*. What the world needs, as John F. Kennedy — and others — so eloquently reminded us, is, not so much people who see things as they are and ask 'why?', but people who see things as they could be and ask 'why not?'

The people who see things as they could be and ask 'why not' are the agents of change, the pioneers of a new world — in exploration, in science, in medicine, in every field of human enterprise and endeavour. Sometimes, they are patient, persevering types of people working quietly away to fulfil their dreams; sometimes, they are impatient to bring into being what they see, but what others cannot yet envisage. Almost always, they pose a threat to the custodians of the status quo and often they pay dearly for their ideas.

Harold Henderson

He (a church official) was one of those grim-looking men who sometimes hold office in the church. (Nobody doubts their integrity, but nobody wants to be like them.) All the lines of his face seemed to run down at acute angles, as though he lived all the while with an unpleasant odour under his nose. . .

It is an undoubted fact that many people outside the churches think that, if they become Christians, they will become miserable. They think that life in Christ is less and less rather than more and more. They think that it is giving up most of the things which make glad our hearts. . . Who could help being radiant with God living in them? The best Christians have surrendered their wills and their minds to Christ.

W. E. Sangster, *The Secret of Radiant Life*

Certainly Jesus had some unkind things to say about the 'scribes and pharisees' but most of them were sincere upholders of the historic traditions of the people of God. I don't mean to be offensive or to denigrate the Bible, but the 'scribes and pharisees' were 'The Bible says' people of their day, who could quote you chapter and verse for every conceivable prejudice they held.

Jesus' main problem with them was not that they were insincere (though, of course, some of them inevitably were), but that they were sincerely misguided. They were blindly leading the blind into an ever-increasing bondage to things as they were, whether they could tell them why or not, whereas Jesus saw things as they could be and asked 'why not?'

Harold Henderson

In many respects especially in the church, we have not advanced very far beyond the traditions Jesus set aside at Jacob's well.

The church today is seriously divided over the question of the ordination of women, to take a concrete example. The divisions in the Episcopal churches around the world over this question are bitter and deep. This issue is probably the most serious threat to the ecumenical movement and its commitment to Christian unity around the world. Rome and the Orthodox churches are so implaccable in their opposition to the ordination of women priests that meaningful dialogue on the question is very difficult, if not impossible.

I am reminded of Pope John Paul II's bold assertion that

there could never be women priests in the Catholic church because there were no women among the disciples; and of the response by an Episcopal bishop that there were no Polish Catholics among the disciples either!

Harold Henderson

Jesus, in Western cultures we may not be surprised at your talking to a woman like this in public, but we would be surprised, probably, at the answers to these questions: If you, Lord, came to our town or suburb, where would we find you? What would you look like? Who would you be with? What would you be doing? What would you be talking about?

Jesus, I wonder how 'respectable' you would be? I wonder if you would be nominated for the office of a bishop? What injustices in our world would attract your ire? Who would choose to follow you as your disciples and how much would you ask them to give up?

Lord Jesus, I am looking forward to meeting this Samaritan woman in heaven and I have some questions for her: 'What did you think when this Jewish male asked you for a drink? Why did you stay around and talk to him? When you knew that he knew all about your private life, how did you feel? What did he ask you to do about the de facto relationship you were in? Why did you want to introduce all your village-friends to Jesus? What kind of person did you become after this encounter?'

Lord, in the byways and highways of life I, too, have opportunities to do with and for others what you did with and for this woman-stranger. Help me to be sensitive to these opportunities and, regardless of the opinions of 'religious frowners', to be as loving and accepting as you were. In other words, Jesus, I want to be like you! Amen.

A Benediction
Go into the world, carrying the gospel of peace. Do in your world what Jesus did in his, and may you spread his love to those you meet, most of whom desperately need a big dose of it! And may the blessing of God, Father, Son and Holy Spirit enrich you now and forever. Amen.

By the rivers of Babylon — there we sat down and there we wept when we remembered Zion. On the willows there we hung up our harps. For there our captors asked us for songs, and our tormentors asked for mirth, saying 'Sing us one of the songs of Zion!' How could we sing the Lord's song in a foreign land?

These are the words of the letter that the prophet Jeremiah sent from Jerusalem to the remaining elders among the exiles, and to the priests, the prophets and all the people, whom Nebuchadnezzar had taken into exile from Jerusalem to Babylon. This was after King Jeconiah and the queen mother, the court officials, the leaders of Judah and Jerusalem, the artisans and the smiths had departed from Jerusalem.

The letter was sent by the hand of Elasah son of Shaphan and Gemariah son of Hilkiah, whom King Zedekiah of Judah sent to Babylon to King Nebuchadnezzer of Babylon. It said: Thus says the Lord of hosts, the God of Israel, to all the exiles whom I have sent into exile from Jerusalem to Babylon: Build houses and live in them; plant gardens and eat what they produce. Take wives and have sons and daughters; take wives for your sons and give your daughters in marriage, that they may bear sons and daughters; multiply there and do not decrease. But seek the welfare of the city where I have sent you into exile and pray to the Lord on its behalf, for in its welfare you will find your welfare.

(Psalm 137: 1–4; Jeremiah 29: 17 — both NRSV)

Here's a contrast. The exiles lamented, 'By the waters of Babylon, we sat down and wept.' What was their concern? 'How shall we sing the Lord's song in a foreign land?' Their experience was one of depression and nostalgia. The prophet's word was, by contrast: build, plant, marry, procreate, extend a generation, multiply, do not decrease, seek the welfare of the city for, in its welfare, you will find your welfare. The approach of the exiles was negative. The other approach, the word of the Lord from Jeremiah, was positive, forward-looking, others-centred.

The captives' contemporaries were saying to them, albeit in mockery and jest, 'sing us your songs, witness to us'. What was their response? A theological reflection about old times, old days, old ways and good times in Jerusalem. Their religion was territorial — that's where God was. It depended on the good times and the memory, the festivals and the sacrifices, the temple occasions, the excitement.

In exile, they lost all that and were left with God alone. They didn't realise or recognise the power that they had and so their focus was the songs of Zion — how they should sing them, used to sing them, felt when they sang them, will never, ever sing them again and what they ought to do so that they can start singing them again. That answer was simple — go back to Jerusalem.

On the other hand, Jeremiah says, 'The emphasis should not be on what you have lost, on the songs of Zion. The emphasis should be on the city of exile.'

These exiles were told God had sent them to that strange place, from Jerusalem to Babylon. Our exile, too, is part of the central strategy of God and the work of the kingdom of God. This is where we are meant to be, in the world. The world is where we are meant to be: not Mars, not the moon — not today anyway — and not heaven, not just yet, but the world.

We don't have to be afraid of the world. While in exile, we are told to build houses, to live in them, to plant gardens, to eat their produce, to take wives and husbands, to give daughters and sons in marriage, to bear sons and daughters, to multiply and so on. The emphasis is not on looking back, but is on looking forward; it is not on straining for what we have lost, but on reaching out to where God is leading us.

So we have a mandate. We're not just to live as residents, but also as missionaries seeking the welfare of the city where God has sent us into exile, praying to the Lord on its behalf. Our welfare as a Christian community is bound up with the welfare of the world in which we live.

We are to be residents and resident aliens. Both belong together, because you cannot be a missionary unless you are fully immersed, baptised and incarnate in the culture.

It was Archbishop William Temple who some time ago said that the church is the only organisation which exists for the benefit of its non-members. You wouldn't think so if you look at the profile of most churches. Their organisation, their priorities, the things that excite them revolve around themselves. They seek another kind of welfare — peace. That kind of peace is a bogus peace; it's a sham peace.

The only kind of peace is that which comes as a consequence of seeking God's will, which is to seek the welfare of the city in which we live.

Bonhoeffer said a similar thing: 'The church is the church only when it exists for others.' We are here to serve others. Jesus lived and died for a world of human sinners, not for himself. We are here for them, as his disciples, and we have no option but to follow him.

Then, there is the beautiful Hebrew word 'welfare', *shalom*. It's a beautiful, Old Testament 'salvation word' and it expresses the true meaning of what peace is.

For the individual, it means total humanisation, harmony with ourselves and all created things. It means an integrated life with health of body, heart and mind, harmony with nature, openness to others, joy in God. *Shalom* leaves the recipient with the view that life is good and adequate, with nothing to wish for. *Shalom* means love, mutuality and sharing. In society, it means justice, dignity, God's justice. *Shalom* is the opposite of oppression and violence, suffering and selfishness. It means the state of being a caring trustee of the creation.

Shalom means doing in our world what Jesus did in his.

There are different kinds of Jesus, of course. For example, I love the Jesus who is the Rose of Sharon, the bright and morning star, the Lily of the Valley. . . 'Jesus how lovely you are!' That is a very comfortable Jesus to live with; it's the Jesus of what I call the 'ballad'.

But what we find difficult to live with is the Jesus who is the friend of publicans and sinners, prostitutes and lepers; the Jesus who delivers demoniacs and the blind and the lame; the teacher whom the poor heard gladly; the one who is the champion of the scum of the earth. We find the Jesus a little too hard to handle who scatters the proud, liberates the poor, lifts up the lowly, puts down the mighty from their thrones. . . Give us the ballad any day rather than the Jesus of the battle hymn.

This Jesus bids us to give up all for him, because he has done the same for us.

❦

Justice is basic to Christian perspectives on economic life. Justice is rooted in the character of God. 'For the Lord is righteous, he loves justice' (Psalm 11: 7, NIV). Justice expresses God's action to restore God's provision to those who have been deprived and to punish those who have violated God's standards. . .

Poverty was neither part of God's original creation, nor will poverty be part of God's restored creation when Christ returns. Involuntary poverty in all its forms and manifestations is a result of the fall and its consequences. Today, one in every five human beings lives in poverty so extreme that their survival is daily in doubt. We believe this is offensive and heartbreaking to God. . .

Justice may also require socio-political actions that enable the poor to help themselves and be the subjects of their own development and the development of their communities. We believe that we and the institutions in which we participate are responsible to create an environment of law, economic activity and spiritual nurture which creates these conditions.

The January 1990 Oxford Declaration on
Christian Faith and Economics

The church is involved politically if it does nothing: it is voting for the *status quo*. It has been said that all it takes for evil to triumph is that good people do nothing. The villains in Jesus' parables were seldom men who did things they ought not to have done; usually they were men who left undone the things they ought to have done. The rich man let Lazarus lie unhelped at his gate, the servant made no use of his talent — these received his severest condemnation.

The opposite of love is not hate, but indifference. Churches are bearers of traditions concerning ultimate meaning and value and are already organised, so they are ideal mediating groups in our society.

If charity begins at home, then a church will ask: 'What needs exist in our neighbourhood and what resources do we have to meet them?' Day-care facilities, a food box in the foyer, a counselling centre (with fees related to ability to pay), housing for the homeless or elderly, writing letters to keep elected officials honest — these are some beginnings. Above all, let us build '*shalom* churches', where the values we preach to the world are incarnated in the faith community.

However, charity is not justice. A charitable act is a somewhat spontaneous, temporary, non-controversial response to an accident or tragedy. Conditions of injustice are not accidents. They are never 'acts of God', but acts of men. To relieve victims of injustice demands that the root causes of injustice be addressed and removed. Charitable acts must not be a substitute for this more controversial pursuit. Giving a pneumonia sufferer a box of tissues may be of some comfort, but it is irrelevant to the victim's recovery, which depends on other factors.

Rowland Croucher, *Recent Trends Among Evangelicals*

Australia's leading copyrighter said of advertising that it operates on the assumption that emotions are a greater motivation than logic. He is right in terms of advertising, because they aim at the gut. They bypass the head because if you thought about it, you wouldn't believe half the garbage that they spill out. We would see through it straight away. They aim for the gut — and you know what happens when you have a pain in the gut: you want to respond to it.

But there is a positive side to that, because I believe that when the Holy Spirit grabs hold of our gut feelings and reflex reactions and begins to change them, that is the point of conversion. Remember, when we are actually responding unconsciously in a different way, we know that something has taken place. Transformation and confirmation: the Spirit *confirming* in our gut feelings those things that are right and *transforming* those things that are wrong.

Morris Stuart

A parable I constructed a few years ago came out of the idea that the Englishman's home was his castle. So many churches, so many Christian communities behave as if they live in one: first the drawbridge, then the moat which surrounds it, then the strong tower, then the battlements with the sentries who walk up and down warning of the dire and dirty state of the world outside and encouraging those people inside to piety, to perseverance. Most often I think it's cosmophobia, fear of the world. This is 'fortress mentality'.

And in that 'fortress mentality', divorced from the world, things like warm fellowship, expository preaching and a whole host of other good things abound, but to all intents and purposes they exist in a kind of splendid isolation. In the midst of this atmosphere exists all kinds of unsavoury things like party spirit, conflict, disagreement and jealousy.

Suddenly, somebody emerges and that person is called a prophet. Now the prophet is one who has been up to the battlements and has started to re-interpret what the sentries were telling the people. 'Yes,' he says, 'there is a world out there, but it is a world in need and we have a divine obligation to reach it.' So they think, 'That's a good idea.'

He comes back down and the clarion call goes out. The troops are summoned, trained, prepared, stoked up and excited then. Just as they're ready, down comes the drawbridge, out go the troops complete with their evangelical maxim guns, grab them, run back in, pull up the drawbridge. They thrill at the new life for a while and then it's back to business as usual.

Morris Stuart

The rap!

[Refrain]: Seek the welfare of this city,
Seek the welfare of this land,
Walking with you hand in hand, Lord,
Help me understand your plan.
We're pilgrims in the city,
We're exiles in the land;
We marry, we tarry,
We farm the land,
We have sons and daughters,
Take husbands and wives —
Why?
Because we'll be here for the
rest of our lives, So

[Refrain]: Seek the welfare of this city,
Seek the welfare of this land,
Walking with you hand in hand, Lord,
Help me understand your plan.
The city is pretty, the land is grand,
Its gods are many on every hand;
Its magic, its money, its mayhem,
Its murder, and sister kills sister,
And brother kills brother. So

[Refrain]: Seek the welfare of this city,
Seek the welfare of this land,
Walking with you hand in hand, Lord,
Help me understand your plan.
Now, who made the city, who made the land,
Who measured the waters in the hollows
Of his hand,
Who stilled the waters, who calmed
the storm?
It was God a'mighty, with a strong arm,
So what's the problem?

[Refrain]: Seek the welfare of this city,

> Seek the welfare of this land,
> Walking with you hand in hand, Lord,
> Help me understand your plan.
>
> Morris Stuart

Lord, today I feel like Jesus in the wilderness, tempted by the devil. Satan is offering an easy way, but Lord, you are calling me to another lifestyle altogether.

The easy way involves 'settling down', enjoying life, having friends who are like me and reinforce my values, 'getting on' and so on.

On the other hand, I hear Jesus offering me a cross. I cannot be his follower without carrying a cross. In a world of pain and savagery, poverty and hunger, war and oppression, Jesus offers me a role in being for this world what he was for his.

But, Lord, they're hard, stark options! Haven't I studied hard, worked hard, to deserve an easy life? It's not my problem, surely, that those others were born there rather than here. . .

My son, my daughter, I know it's hard. But this is the way I trod and I call upon you to tread it still. What would you want from better-off others if you were poor, oppressed, starving, sick? I am simply asking of you to be my hands and feet, voice and heart in a world without shalom.

Okay, Lord, I will follow you, wherever you go. Give me strength to live for you, to obey you and to love for you. Amen.

A Benediction

May you go with God's peace, God's shalom, to enjoy his beautiful creation and to restore its brokenness, heal its woundedness and fight its injustices. And the blessing of God — Father, Son and Holy Spirit — be with you. Amen.

Who's on trial?

They took Jesus to the high priest; and all the chief priests, the elders and the scribes were assembled. Peter had followed him at a distance, right into the courtyard of the high priest; and he was sitting with the guards, warming himself at the fire. Now the chief priests and the whole council were looking for testimony against Jesus to put him to death; but they found none. For many gave false testimony against him, and their testimony did not agree.

Some stood up and gave false testimony against him, saying, 'We heard him say, "I will destroy this Temple that is made with hands, and in three days I will build another, not made with hands."' But even on this point their testimony did not agree.

Then the high priest stood up before them and asked Jesus, 'Have you no answer? What is it that they testify against you?' But he was silent and did not answer. Again the high priest asked him, 'Are you the Messiah, the Son of the Blessed One?' Jesus said, 'I am; and "you will see the Son of Man seated at the right hand of the Power," and "coming with the clouds of heaven."'

Then the high priest tore his clothes and said, 'Why do we still need witnesses? You have heard his blasphemy! What is your decision?' All of them condemned him as deserving death. Some began to spit on him, to blindfold him, and to strike him, saying to him, 'Prophesy!' The guards also took him over and beat him.

As soon as it was morning, the chief priests held a consultation with the elders and scribes and the whole council. They bound Jesus, led him away, and handed him over to Pilate. Pilate asked him, 'Are you the King of the Jews?' He answered him, 'You say so.' Then the chief priests accused him of many things. Pilate asked him again, 'Have you no answer? See how many charges they bring against you.' But Jesus made no further reply, so that Pilate was amazed.

(Mark 14: 53–65; 15: 1–5, NRSV)

Why did the authorities hate Jesus so much? It's hard to imagine what they could have had against him. He was not violent in his speech or actions. He was a law-abiding citizen. There was nothing that he had done which could possibly have been described as criminal. It is quite understandable that they didn't *agree* with him. But that is a different matter. You can disagree with a person — with what they teach, with what they do — and that doesn't mean that you hate them.

It is all a bit of a mystery. There are many explanations. There are various hints that we find in the Gospels and, perhaps, the truth involves a number of things.

Mark says quite clearly in our reading that the authorities were jealous of Jesus. Pilate knew that the chief priests had only handed Jesus over to him because they were jealous or envious. But there would seem rather little about Jesus over which the authorities could be envious. Jesus had nothing. People get envious of someone who has more power, more fame, more possessions than they have.

In terms of this world's possessions, Jesus had nothing and the high priests had everything. Jesus had no money, not even a place to lay his head. He had no position. He was hardly famous, even if many people around Galilee and Judea had heard of him and of his miracles. Certainly, Jesus would not have been known outside his own country. He did not attract wealthy and educated patrons.

There appeared nothing that the high priests could be

envious about. Unless it was his popularity. There were times when Jesus appeared to have quite a considerable popular following. People were listening to him. On Palm Sunday, a great crowd had gathered as he rode into Jerusalem on a donkey. They had shouted, waved palm branches and sung songs.

But it really was nothing. These were just the peasant people, not the people that the high priests would want to impress anyway.

I suspect that there was something in the fact that Jesus was setting the new religious tone for the nation. Jesus was being hailed as a religious leader. People were turning to him for answers to their religious needs. This was indeed the task of the high priests. They should have set the spiritual standards, but people had little respect for them. They were not men of high spiritual calibre.

There has always been the theory that the authorities were worried about a disturbance. Perhaps, they really did expect Jesus to make a move and try to overthrow the whole system — not just the Temple and its hierarchy, but the whole Roman system as well. Perhaps, they decided that it would be better if they moved first, in case Jesus did something which would cause a bloodbath in Jerusalem. Perhaps, they really hadn't heard what Jesus had been saying to them — that his kingdom was not of this world.

Whatever the explanation for the attitude of the authorities, it probably came down to power. They were frightened of losing control. They were frightened that they could not tell people what to do; that their position as religious leaders would be under threat. They were worried that they would lose popular support; that Rome would get upset with them if they did not keep the peace, and they would be replaced. Rome wasn't kind and patient with its puppets.

Finally, it comes down to the fact that the authorities, like most of us, were concerned about themselves, about their own livelihoods, their own prestige, their own positions. They weren't criminal types. They were ordinary people — like you and me — anxious to keep the peace and the status quo. . . for their own sakes.

And they brought the disturber to trial.

But who was on trial here? Was it really Jesus who was on trial as he faced the council of the seventy, called rather unexpectedly late in the evening?

No, the trial was really an illusion. In fact, it was the council that was on trial that night. Their own fates would be decided by what they did that night.

It is always the same, when an authority that is genuine and legitimate meets some self-appointed judges. Jesus is the criteria by which we are all judged. It can be no other way.

❧❦❧

Trafalgar Square is one of the important landmarks in London: the place where pigeons gather and where Lord Nelson looks blindly out on the busy traffic from a great and lofty perch. In one corner of Trafalgar Square is a brass plaque, which is the actual standard for imperial measurement. The distance marked on the plaque is exactly one foot. The plaque in Trafalgar Square cannot be wrong, because it is the criterion by which every other measurement is judged. If you bring a ruler there and find it disagrees with the marks in Trafalgar Square, you will know that your ruler is wrong. . . however much you paid for it.

Jesus is the final criterion against which we are all measured. For the priests to bring him to trial was to put themselves on trial.

The musical composer, Bach, is never on trial before the concert audience. It is the audience which awaits his sentence. The prince of sculptors, Michelangelo, is never on trial before the art class: it is they who must accept his verdict.

So it is with Jesus, here. He towers above his captors in every spiritual and moral sense. He is not on trial before these little men, these self-interested, selfish creatures. They have put themselves on trial before him. And when all is said and done, the last chapter composed, the final sentence written, only his verdict stands eternally.

Philip Hughes

One may recognise, also, in the sins of the Sadducees, the danger which threatens spiritual leaders: that they may become more concerned with their 'church politics' and ecclesiastical machinery than with the souls of the people. Ambition can intrude into any highly organised church. Place-seeking and hankering do not belong only to lay life.

The ordained are not secured by their ordination from a thirst for power and a subtle jockeying for place. God alone knows how much self-seeking is covered with the garments of religion, but sinful persons ought to recognise the danger and match every 'advancement' that comes to them with more time spent in secret prayer.

It is when ecclesiastics actually assume temporal power that the worst tragedies of all occur. Roman Catholic historians themselves have written of the ghastly iniquities of the Papal States, and no informed Protestant can forget Calvin's major share in burning Michael Servetus. These are instances, like the Sadducees, of ecclesiastics turned statesmen. The world conquered the Spirit in them. Such men are often more bigoted, self-seeking, unyielding and merciless than a person without religion at all.

Finally, we should remember from this study of the Sadducees that we have a special duty to pray for those in authority over us. The exercise of power, especially for the conscientious, is hard, burdensome, responsible and dangerous. Lord Acton, in an oft-quoted phrase, says that 'power always corrupts and absolute power corrupts absolutely'.

We have a duty, therefore, to pray for those who bear office — in church and state as well. It is laid upon us in the scriptures. It is laid upon us by a little honest reflection and a little Christian love. They are bearing great burdens. They could make mistakes with most fearful consequences. They will have much to answer for at the last.

Pray for them!

W. E. Sangster, *They Met at Calvary*

Today, in one sense, Jesus is on trial before our civilisation. Many are examining him to determine whether he has any place in this world so different from his. Diligent probers are rendering their verdict in the words Matthew Arnold uses of Goethe, 'Thou ailest here and here.' But in the deepest and final sense it is not Jesus on trial. Our whole civilisation is on trial before his judgments. If we fail to meet them, if in our blindness we condemn him to be merely a peripheral figure in our world, we 'shall all likewise perish'. Albert Einstein put the nature of that trial vividly when he said, in answer to a question, 'I do not know what weapons will be used in World War III. But I do know what will be used in World War IV — stone clubs.' Unless we are 'members one of another', we will not be members of anything.

A second aspect of this trial which calls for continual remembrance is that Jesus was confronting the religious institution of his time and nation. That fact presents searching questions to all religious institutions of every age, particularly to the churches of Christ. Why did the religious institution fail so terribly in its hour of visitation? Are there any causes of that failure which may be present in institutions which bear Christ's own name, his church?

One hardly needs to put the question. To begin with, the Jewish religious establishment had substituted itself for God's purpose in his revelation to the Jewish people. The great prophetic heritage of Israel had become quite secondary to the fortunes of an entrenched institution. That has often happened to Christian churches. It can easily happen. When it does happen, where the prosperity and security of the institution bulk larger than its prophetic responsibility, the church takes its place with the Sanhedrin as an obstruction to God's will, rather than as an instrument of it.

Those are terrible words of Stephen Spender's: 'The church blotting out the sun.' It can happen.

Halford E. Luccock, *Interpreter's Bible*

First, we watch the Pharisees and scribes plotting to entrap him. They seek to 'ensnare him in his talk'. Why, what has he done to them? What has he done! What has he not done? In Dr Gore's phrase: 'He has challenged the Pharisees to change their fundamental ideas and methods in matters of religion; and when have high ecclesiastics been ready to accept this challenge from a "mere layman"?' If Jesus is right, they are wrong. If Jesus is proved right, they are proved wrong. If Jesus wins the people to his side, their job is done, their influence has gone, their prestige vanished. That *they* should repent probably only occurred to a few like Nicodemus and Joseph of Arimathaea.

Besides, their very living was threatened. Josephus says that 20,000 priests ministered in the Temple. Some would serve the Temple for only one week in the year, but they would take a full year's wages. To Roman taxes, priestly taxes were added. Annas and Caiaphas controlled, not only taxation, but the Temple market. They had country estates on which the animals sacrificed in the Temple were reared. All other animals were rejected. All other sales were prohibited. They determined the rate of exchange. Their avarice, corruption, luxury, gluttony and oppression were a byword among the people.

Are they going to change their way of looking at life? Are they going to become as little children? Is there any chance of their becoming meek and lowly in heart? Not they! Men love darkness rather than light because their deeds are evil. The scribes and Pharisees worked in the dark; they kept the people in the dark. Light is the enemy of darkness. Light 'showed them up,' as we say. They must extinguish the Light at all costs — and the quicker the better. They were afraid of him.

No wonder! Some of them had seen his supernatural deeds as he went about his Father's business. They were afraid of what the people would do to them if they touched him yet. But listen to what they say. 'If we let him alone, all will believe on him; and the Romans will come and take away both our place and our nation.' What a tribute that is to him from the mouths of his enemies!

Leslie D. Weatherhead,
The Plain Man Looks at the Cross

Lord Jesus Christ, Son of God, Son of Mary, who lived a perfect life among us but was maligned, persecuted and finally 'tried' and put to death for being the kind of person who shames us all. . . Lord, you are on trial still, and we are on trial in all kinds of ways.

The scholars are putting you 'on trial': some of them have been Satan's instruments to sow doubts in the minds of the faithful.

Ecclesiastical leaders are putting you 'on trial': they often do not understand that the greatest power on earth is not wielded by weapons of war. . .

Actually, Lord, everybody on this planet is on trial and you are everybody's judge. We are judged in what we do and what we do not do for you, who comes amongst us still in the persons of the poor. We are judged in what we say and do not say, as we condemn you in others. We are judged every moment in what we think and do not think — our thoughts and our motives are under your constant scrutiny.

So Lord, I submit to you as a willing servant. Jesus my judge, I commit myself to following your royal law of love.

In a world of strutting and pompous leaders who think they are ultimately in charge of events, help me to follow your way and to do your will and, at the last, meet you joyfully and with a clear conscience. For your glory. Amen.

A Benediction
And may Jesus, before whom everybody will one day 'bow the knee', empower you to do his will in a world that is continually under his judgment. Amen.

23

Poured out for the many

While they were eating, Jesus took a loaf of bread, and after blessing it he broke it, gave it to the disciples, and said, 'Take, eat; this is my body.' Then he took a cup and after giving thanks he gave it to them, saying, 'Drink from it, all of you; for this is my blood of the covenant, which is poured out for many for the forgiveness of sins.'

Now before the festival of the Passover, Jesus knew that his hour had come to depart from this world and go to the Father. Having loved his own who were in the world, he loved them to the end. The devil had already put it into the heart of Judas son of Simon Iscariot to betray him. And during supper Jesus, knowing the Father had given all things into his hands, and that he had come from God and was going to God, got up from the table, took off his outer robe and tied a towel around himself. Then he poured water into a basin and began to wash the disciples' feet and to wipe them with the towel that was tied around him. . .

'For I have set you an example, that you also should do as I have done to you. Very truly, I tell you, servants are not greater than their master, nor are messengers greater than the one who sent them.'

(Matthew 26: 26–28; John 13: 1–5, 15 and 16 — both NRSV)

The sacrament of Holy Communion is sometimes called in various Christian traditions the Mass, the Eucharist, the Lord's Table, the Lord's Supper or the Breaking of Bread.

Holy Communion has occupied a large place in the life of the church as a whole, a much larger place than is the usual practice in the Methodist tradition, for example. Often the observance of Holy Communion has been the vehicle and the focus for elaborate, ritualised celebration — as in the Roman, Orthodox, Anglican and Lutheran traditions. That is helpful for those who find the Lord more readily in eucharistic rituals than otherwise.

What is interesting is that Jesus began what we have come to know as the observance of Holy Communion, not as a separate piece of religious ceremonial, but in the context of a family meal which he shared with his disciples. The meal was part of the ancient Jewish passover tradition, but it was — and was meant to be — a family meal as distinct from other elements in the traditional observance of Passover.

The officiating priest raises the bread and then the wine above his head and consecrates the Sacred Host. You don't necessarily agree that the bread and the wine are being transformed into the body and blood of Christ, but you *do sense and respond to the real presence of Christ* — just as a good salvationist does at every family meal!

Suppose that, by some mischance, the synoptic Gospels — Matthew, Mark and Luke — had been lost and we were entirely dependent on the Gospel of John as our model for celebrating Holy Communion. There would be no bread and wine because John makes no reference to these in his account of the last Passover meal Jesus shared with his disciples before his death. Read John 13: 1–5, 15 and 16 and see if you can nominate the symbols we would use instead of bread and wine.

As you can see, if we had only John's account, we would use, not bread and wine, but a towel and a basin! Holy Communion would be a *footwashing* ritual! It might be pretty embarrassing for some of us, given the shape and odour of our feet. But then, who said the disciples' feet were carefully manicured and perfumed?

The Pope engages in a symbolic, public footwashing as part of the Vatican's Easter observance each year, but Mennonites include footwashing in their ritual on a regular basis. A Mennonite friend of mine assured me that it is a wonderful exercise in humility, service and fellowship. It is hard for the kinds of bickering and division all too common in churches (not this one, of course!) to survive when you are humbly washing one another's feet as regularly as you share the bread and wine of Holy Communion together.

As we come to the Table of the Lord, it is worth remembering that Jesus takes things that are commonplace and makes them sacred; that he chooses ordinary people like the disciples — uncertain, hesitant, promising more than they can deliver, all of whom with one possible exception would forsake him in fear a few days later — as the first partakers of his body and blood 'poured out for the many'.

Let us sense and know the real presence of Christ in this sacred observance as I did in the cathedral in Barcelona, even though I could not understand the words. Christ is more than words; he is *the Word* who comes to us in a special way in the bread and the wine of Holy Communion, and the towel and the basin of humble service we offer to each other and to the world.

He comes to us, too, as our servant, willing to wash our feet and calling us to follow him in humble service of each other so that when we depart from the Holy Table our grudges, our superiorities, our animosities are washed away by the one whose life is 'poured out for the many'.

❧

Jesus taught a lot about service by washing his disciples' feet. In our highly urban culture where we wear closed shoes and socks and drive in automobiles, washing feet is not an especially effective way to express service. We read about what Jesus did; we get the basic insight that it is important to serve others; and then we try to interpret that in our culture.

Maybe we read to an old person or mow somebody's lawn. For me, 'washing feet' might be to prepare coffee for my wife each morning.

Richard Foster,
'An Introduction to Spiritual Disciples'

Jesus didn't normally wash his disciples' feet. They could well do that themselves. There was no need for Jesus to waste his time on that. There were other things that were far more important. Jesus spent his time doing what was in the greatest interest of his disciples, not running round doing what his disciples wanted him to do.

Sometimes, in family life, in society, we can end up just pleasing the desires of others. There is a big difference between that and really doing what is in the best interests of others. We are not nice and subservient to others for the sake of being nice and subservient. That is not what Jesus' example is all about.

There is still a lingering image in family life of the wife who runs around and serves everyone else. She is the slave of the household. She looks after her husband; she cares for her children. But is it all in the real interests of her family. . . or is it just playing a role? Is she really serving them in order to make them free, independent, to help the family members to grow? Or is she just being used — by the rest of the family members. . . however willing she is?

Philip Hughes, 'Washing One Another's Feet'

Today is Resurrection Sunday. My first Easter in prison. Surely, the regime can't continue to keep almost 10 000 political prisoners in its gaols! In here, it is much easier to understand how the men in the Bible felt, stripping themselves of everything that was superfluous. Many of the prisoners have already heard that they have lost their homes, their furniture and everything they owned. Our families are broken up. Many of our children are wandering the streets, their father in one prison, their mother in another.

There is not a single cup. But a score of Christian prisoners experienced the joy of celebrating communion — without bread or wine. The communion of empty hands. The non-Christians said: 'We will help you; we will talk quietly so that you can meet.' Too dense a silence would have drawn the guards' attention as surely as the lone voice of the preacher. 'We have no bread, nor water to use instead of wine,' I told them, 'but we will act as though we had.'

'This meal in which we take part,' I said, 'reminds us of the prison, the torture, the death and final victory of the resurrection of Jesus Christ. The bread is the body which he gave for humanity. The fact that we have none represents very well the lack of bread in the hunger of so many millions of human beings. The wine, which we don't have today, is his blood and represents our dream of a united humanity, of a just society, without difference of race or class.'

I held out my empty hand to the first person on my right and placed it over his open hand — and the same with the others: 'Take, eat, this is my body which is given for you; do this in remembrance of me.' Afterward, all of us raised our hands to our mouths, receiving the body of Christ in silence. 'Take, drink, this is the blood of Christ which was shed to seal the new covenant of God with us. Let us give thanks, sure that Christ is here with us, strengthening us.'

We gave thanks to God and, finally, stood up and embraced each other. A while later, another non-Christian prisoner said to me: 'You people have something special which I would like to have.' The father of the dead girl came up to me and said: 'Pastor, this was a real experience! I believe that today I discovered what faith is. Now, I believe that I am on the road.'

Thomas G. Pettepiece, *Visions of a World Hungry*

This sacrament is the sacrament of memory. It is a simple fact that in the New Testament the only definite instruction regarding the sacrament of the Lord's Supper is: 'Do this in remembrance of me.' Here is the centre of the whole matter. First and foremost, we do this in order that we may remember Jesus Christ.

It will be said by some at once that this is an inadequate view of this sacrament. But is it? Do we really realise what memory means? It is almost impossible to remember *simpliciter*. We always remember for some purpose or to some effect. Memory never operates in a vacuum. . .

1. We remember to realise again what our blessed Lord has done and suffered for us. It is easy to forget. It is easy to lose the cutting-edge of emotion and realisation. It is easy to forget that Jesus Christ suffered and died for us and, even when we remember, it is easy to remain unmoved. But in the sacrament, with its vivid picture, realisation of what Jesus Christ did and suffered for us is rekindled and reborn.

2. This is to say that first we remember what Jesus Christ has done for us. The second step follows naturally. We remember in order once again to appropriate the benefits of Jesus Christ. We remember once again to receive. 'This is my body *for you*.' We need to receive again and again, for we sin again and again. . .

3. But there is something still more to be said. We have been speaking of remembering. But we are not remembering someone who is dead and gone, someone who lived and who died and who left a memory. We are not remembering someone whose place was in the past and who lives only in the pages of a history book. We are remembering someone who was crucified, dead and buried — and who rose again. We are remembering someone who is gloriously alive. And therefore we remember Jesus Christ in the sacrament in order to encounter Jesus Christ.

The memory turns into an experience and an encounter. . .

4. All this must end in still another act on our part. It must end in renewed dedication. Here is where the other meaning of the word '*sacramentum*' must come in. It means a soldier's oath of loyalty to his emperor and that the sacrament must be for us, too. As Arthur said of his knights:

> I made them lay their hands in mine
> And swear to reverence the king.

No experience such as we have described can end in anything other than a renewed pledge to the one whom we have encountered or experienced. It must surely be impossible to leave the sacramental table without a deeper devotion to the blessed Lord whom we meet there.

We may end with the one fact which makes the Lord's Supper a permanent necessity in the Christian church. T.C. Edwards, in his commentary on I Corinthians, makes the point. The Lord's Supper is the unchanging statement of that which is unchanging in Christianity. The centre of Christianity is what Jesus did. The Lord's Supper in its dramatic picture states that just as it is. Preaching talks about it; theology interprets it and conceptualises it. The sacrament announces it.

'Ideas mark the progress, sacraments the fixity of Christianity. . . Doctrines develop, sacraments continue and help to anchor theological thought to its moorings. Paul does not hesitate to develop new truth, but he does not ever institute a new sacrament.' The Lord's Supper is the permanent dramatic pronouncement of the unchanging divine action in Jesus Christ, which theology interprets and reinterprets continuously.

William Barclay, *The Lord's Supper*

Here, O my Lord, I see Thee face to face;
　　Here would I touch and handle things unseen,
Here grasp with firmer hand the eternal grace,
　　And all my helplessness upon Thee lean.

Here would I feed upon the bread of God,
　　Here drink with Thee the royal wine of heaven;
Here would I lay aside each earthly load,
　　Here taste afresh the calm of sin forgiven.

This is the hour of banquet and of song;
　　This is the heavenly table spread for me;
Here let me feast and, feasting, still prolong
　　The hallowed hour of fellowship with Thee.

Too soon we rise: the symbols disappear;
　　The feast, though not the love, is past and gone;
The bread and wine removed, but Thou art here,
　　Nearer than ever; still my shield and sun.

I have no help but Thine; nor do I need
  Another arm save Thine to lean upon;
It is enough, my Lord, enough indeed;
  My strength is in Thy might, Thy might alone.

Feast after feast thus comes and passes by,
  Yet passing, points to the glad feast above,
Giving sweet foretaste of the festal joy,
  The Lamb's great bridal feast of bliss and love.

Horatius Bonar

O God, our Father, we thank you for this sacrament;
  For all who down the centuries at this table have found
  the light that never fades;
  the joy that no-one takes from them;
  the forgiveness of their sins;
  the love which is your love;
  the presence of their Lord:
    We thank you.
For all the means of grace;
  For the church to be our mother in the faith;
  For your book to tell us of your ways;
  For the open door of prayer which you have ever set
  before us:
    We thank you.
For the memory of the unseen cloud of witnesses who
  compass us about;
And for the presence still with us of those who are an
  inspiration:
    We thank you.
  That you have made us as we are;
  For the dream that will not die;
  That somehow we cannot sin in peace;
  That even in the mud we are haunted by the stars:
    We thank you, O God.
For Jesus Christ our blessed Lord:
  That he who knew no sin was made sin for us;
  that he came to seek and to save that which was lost;
  that he gave his life a ransom for many;

that he was obedient even to death, the death of the cross;
that having loved his own he loved them to the end:
    We thank you.
That he lived;
that he died;
that he rose again;
that he is with us to the end of time and beyond; and
that he is with us here today:
    We thank you. Amen.

                   William Barclay, *The Lord's Supper*

A Benediction
May God, Father, Son and Holy Spirit send you into the world,
with the light of God's hope in your eyes and the fire of his
love in your hearts. Amen.

The cross is Christ's — and ours

And whoever does not take up the cross and follow me is not worthy of me. Those who find their life will lose it, and those who lose their life for my sake will find it.

Then he said to them all, 'If any want to become my followers, let them deny themselves and take up their cross daily and follow me.' Whoever does not carry the cross and follow me cannot be my disciple.

For Christ did not send me to baptise but to proclaim the gospel, and not with eloquent wisdom, so that the cross of Christ might not be emptied of its power.

By his death on the cross Christ destroyed their enmity; by means of the cross he united both races into one body and brought them back to God.

The people who are trying to force you to be circumcised are the ones who want to show off and boast about external matters. They do it, however, only so that they may not be persecuted for the cross of Christ.

Through the Son, then, God decided to bring the whole universe back to himself. God made peace through his Son's death on the cross and so brought back to himself all things, both on earth and in heaven.

Let us keep our eyes fixed on Jesus, on whom our faith depends from beginning to end. He did not give up because of the cross; on the contrary, because of the joy that was waiting for him, he thought nothing of the disgrace of dying on the cross, and he is now seated at the right-hand side of God's throne.

So far as the Law is concerned, however, I am dead — killed by the Law itself — in order that I might live for God. I have been put to death with Christ on his cross, so that it is no longer I who live, but it is Christ who lives in me. . .

. . .erasing the record that stood against us with its legal demands. He set this aside, nailing it to the cross.
(Matthew 10: 38–39; Luke 9: 23; Luke 14: 27; 1 Corinthians 1: 17 — all NRSV; Ephesians 2: 16; Galatians 6: 12; Colossians 1: 20; Hebrews 12: 2; Galatians 2: 19–20 — all GNB; Colossians 2: 14 — NRSV)

So often as I sit in church, my eyes stray to the wooden cross and this becomes the focal point of my thoughts. The words of the prayers, the preaching and the hymns flow around me, but I listen then I drift away, and central to all my being is that cross.

Look: see two pieces of roughly-cut timber, joined together to form a 'T'. They were once part of some majestic tree, but now comprise a thing of fear, hatred, torture and death, stained with the blood of an innocent body.

Take time to look at this ugly monument to death and see beauty — the beauty of life, love, joy and peace, the beauty of spilt blood washing us clean from our sins and giving us a chance to start anew.

Look at the dark-stained timber. See light, light pulsating, drawing us in ever closer to the cross and what it stands for. Feel its force drawing you closer and closer, until you are completely enveloped in the light and yet, at the same time, the light is going out from the cross, sending us with it, reaching out to others, drawing them into its light.

The cross is the centrepiece of our lives. It represents both that which is ugly and also that which is beautiful.

The cross calls us — and we must not try to resist this compelling attraction. But we must not stop there; we must go out in the 'power of the cross' and do what God has called us to do. This cross is my cross and yours, too, and we bear it, carry it. May the Lord help us to carry this load with the humility and love with which Jesus carried his. Showing Christ's love to all people everywhere is hard. Everywhere there are crosses, ugly and beautiful.

Jesus had his cross; it is also ours. Sometimes it is heavy. It is always hard, but it is also a 'healing cross'. Must Jesus bear the cross alone, and all the world go free? No, there's a cross for you and me. . .

❧❧

In the cross of Christ I glory,
towering o'er the wrecks of time;
all the light of sacred story
gathers round its head sublime.
Through the cross, Christ's love empowers us:
worldliness and self deny;
by his Spirit it inspires us
him, through love, to glorify.
When the woes of life o'ertake us,
hopes deceive and fears annoy,
never shall the cross forsake us,
from it shines our peace and joy.
Bane and blessing, pain and pleasure,
by the cross are sanctified;
peace is there that knows no measure,
joys that through all time abide.
In the cross of Christ I glory,
towering o'er the wrecks of time;
all the light of sacred story
gathers round its head sublime.

John Bowring

Lord, you stretch at full length on the cross.
There.
Without a doubt, it is made for you.
You cover it entirely and, to adhere to it more surely,
    you allow men to nail you carefully to it.
Lord, it was work well done, conscientiously done.
Now you fit your cross exactly, as the mechanic's
    carefully filed parts fit the engineer's blueprint.
There had to be this precision.

Michel Quoist, *Prayers of Life*

Unfortunately, the cross as a symbol has been used and misused by so many nominal Christians down the centuries that its original historical meaning has been completely lost. When the barbaric Crusaders came to invade the Middle East, they came with bright red crosses painted on their shields and wielding swords in their hands. Any thinking follower of Jesus must feel ashamed remembering those armies.

Of course, the common people did not have the New Testament in their own language in those days, otherwise history might have turned out differently. How surprised they would have been to read the actual teachings of Jesus and see what he said about war and violence! When just *one* of his followers (Peter) lifted his sword to defend Jesus at the time of his arrest, Jesus told him to put his sword away. Spiritual battles cannot be fought with physical weapons.

The Crusaders and their political leaders believed that Christianity is about defending pieces of land, about holy sites. But in fact the kingdom of God is not about geography, about places, at all.

Bruce Farnham, *The Way of Jesus*

The cross came as no surprise to Jesus. From the beginning of his life to the end of his life he knew that it was coming. All through his life we can trace his consciousness of the cross.

William Barclay, *Jesus Christ for Today*

Look at Jesus. The world did not pay any attention to him. He was crucified and put away. His message of love was rejected by a world in search of power, efficiency and control. But there he was, appearing with wounds in his glorified body to a few friends who had eyes to see, ears to hear and hearts to understand. This rejected, unknown, wounded Jesus simply asked, 'Do you love me, do you really love me?'

He whose only concern had been to announce the unconditional love of God had only one question to ask: 'Do you love me?'

Henri Nouwen, *In the Name of Jesus*

Seated in my study one day and reading the biblical story of Jesus Christ going to Calvary, I felt a quality of his life and the beauty of his commitment gripping my heart. What moved me so much was not that he loved God; it was rather that he loved people! He loved them unto death.

There was a strange and compelling beauty in Jesus Christ which I felt was connected to that simple fact. He was a man of great integrity and such beautiful simplicity and profound intelligence. His love for people was unconditional and he never selfishly preserved himself from the consequences of his commitments. I felt a terrible lack of a similar love within myself. Likewise, I sensed a corresponding lack of such expressed love in the church.

I had been a Christian for many years and professed my faith in Christ. I had bent my mind to follow his teachings, as I understood them, and yet I sensed a great vacuum in my soul. How could a selfish man ever move to such a dimension of love? It seemed totally and psychologically impossible.

Len Evans, *Love Love Love*

Christianity is not a friendly society, much less a friendly society floated on tea. Its symbol is not a cushion, but a cross. A cross! What do any of us know of a cross? People talk about bearing their cross when they mean getting on with their mother-in-law, or bearing a twinge of rheumatism that they get through coming home from the pictures in the wet. A cross! A cross is a bloody thing. But Jesus uses the word. And he uses it of *all* who would follow him. He uses it of me and of you. He invites us to a friendship, but its demands are inexorable.

Leslie Weatherhead, *The Transforming Friendship*

You have given everything. You 'have emptied yourself, taking the form of a slave; you have humbled yourself by accepting death, death on a cross'. Your body has been fully given for me; your blood has been fully poured out for me. You who are love have not held back anything for yourself, but have let all your love flow from your heart to make it bear fruit in me.

Henri Nouwen, *Heart Speaks to Heart*

Lord, your goal was the cross. For us you embraced death so that we could be free, free to live a life of love, love for you and for all your creation.

In faith, Lord, help us to reach the goal that you have for us, let us never be ashamed of your cross and all that it means, but with confidence and joy let us proclaim, 'Our Lord is alive!' Amen.

A Benediction
God the Father make you holy in his love;
God the Son enrich you with his grace;
God the Holy Spirit strengthen you with joy;
The Lord bless you and keep you in eternal life.
Amen.

Theme: Growth. . .

to live God's way

Consider Assyria, a cedar of Lebanon, with fair branches and forest shade, and of great height, its top among the clouds.

The waters nourished it, the deep made it grow tall, making its rivers flow around the place it was planted, sending forth its streams to all the trees of the field.

So it towered high above all the trees of the field; its boughs grew large and its branches long, from abundant water in its shoots.

All the birds of the air made their nests in its boughs; under its branches all the animals of the field gave birth to their young; and in its shade all great nations lived.

It was beautiful in its greatness, in the length of its branches; for its roots went down to abundant water.

The cedars in the garden of God could not rival it, nor the fir trees equal its boughs; the plane trees were as nothing compared with its branches; no tree in the garden of God was like it in beauty.

I made it beautiful with its mass of branches, the envy of all the trees of Eden that were in the garden of God.

Ezekiel 31: 3-9, NRSV

25

Discipline is (still) a key Christian virtue!

The end of all things is near; therefore be serious and discipline yourselves.

Moab has been at ease from his youth,
settled like wine on its dregs;
he has not been emptied from vessel to vessel,
nor has he gone into exile;
therefore his flavour has remained
and his aroma is unspoiled.

Therefore the time is surely coming, says the Lord, when I shall send him decanters to decant him, and empty his vessels, and break his jars in pieces. Then Moab shall be ashamed. . .

You once lived, following the course of this world, following the ruler of the power of the air, the spirit that is now at work among those who are disobedient. All of us once lived in the passions of our flesh, following the desires of flesh and senses, and we were by nature children of wrath, like everyone else. But God, who is rich in mercy. . . made us alive together with Christ.

If anyone is in Christ, there is a new creation: everything old has passed away; see, everything has become new!

Let us run with perseverance the race that is set before us, looking to Jesus the pioneer and perfecter of our faith, who. . . endured the cross.

Do you not know that in a race the runners all compete, but only one receives the prize? Run in such a way that you may win it. Athletes exercise self-control in all things; they do it to receive a perishable wreath, but we an imperishable one. So I do not run aimlessly, nor do I box as though beating the air; but I punish my body and enslave it, so that after proclaiming to others I myself should not be disqualified.

For [Christ's] sake I have suffered the loss of all things, and I regard them as rubbish, in order that I may gain Christ. . . I want to know Christ and the power of his resurrection and the sharing of his sufferings.

Therefore, lift your dropping hands and strengthen your weak knees, and make straight paths for your feet. . .

(1 Peter 4: 7; Jeremiah 48: 11–13; Ephesians 2: 2–4; 2 Corinthians 5: 17; Hebrews 12: 1–2; 1 Corinthians 9: 24–27; Philippians 3: 8 and 10; Hebrews 12: 12–13 — all NRSV)

In October 1982, a twenty-five-year-old woman finished the New York marathon. That was 'no big deal' — until you learn that Linda Down had cerebral palsy and was the first woman ever to complete the 42.2 kilometre race on crutches. Down she fell half a dozen times, but kept going until she crossed the finishing line, eleven hours after she started. Her handicap limited her speed, but not her determination.

Moab, says the old translations, had been at ease from his youth, 'settled on his lees'. Problem was, Moab was undisciplined; Moab had never been disturbed. In those days, excellent wine was made by pouring it from vessel to vessel, making sure not to disturb the dregs. If the fermented juice stayed still too long, it took on the flavour of the dregs. The wine became bitter. It would also smell like the dregs, a rotten smell. And it would take on the colour of the dregs. When we settle down in indiscipline, this is what happens to us. . .

All of life illustrates this basic point: without con-centrated discipline, we do not achieve anything worthwhile. The horse follows its own erratic directions until it is disciplined; the athlete won't any more win medals on athleticism alone; steam or gas — or the mighty Niagara waters — won't produce power until they are concentrated, focussed, 'disciplined'. There is an ancient saying: 'Those who rule their spirit are better than those who take a city.'

We won't live worthwhile lives until we are disciplined; only when we are mastered (by Christ) will we be free; only when we have a worthwhile goal will we have direction. The battle is won when the soldier is utterly committed and is motivated by self-sacrifice.

We do battle constantly with the 'unholy trinity' — 'the desire of the flesh', 'the lust of the eyes', 'the pride of life'. We need 'won't' power as well as will power. The ancient Chinese philosopher Mencius said, 'You must decide on what you will not do, and then you will be able to act with vigour in what you ought to do.'

There is an old saying: 'To my God, a heart of flame; to others, a heart of love; to myself, a heart of steel.' When Gladstone was asked the secret of his success, he replied in one word, 'concentration'. Which reminds me of the problem of James M. Barrie's character, Sentimental Tommy, who struggled so hard to make up his mind: 'It's easy to you that has just one mind, but if you had as many minds as I have. . .!'

The best-disciplined people know their life-goals, their intermediate goals and things that ought to be done today, this week, this year. The violinist, Yehudi Menuhin, said: 'To play great music you must keep your eyes on a distant star.' Do not let the urgent crowd out the important.

Disciplined people make big sacrifices to achieve their goals. After one of Paderewski's performances, a fan said to him, 'I'd give my life to play like that.' The brilliant pianist replied, 'I did.'

But remember there is a difference between being *driven* and being *called*. Driven people are very busy trying to impress others; the called want to impress their Lord. Driven people live out the drama of their lives according to a script written by others; called people do what they are commissioned to do by God: their 'rewards are in heaven'.

If we are in a people-helping profession, there is a real temptation in our drivenness to so strive to see people grow and change, that we ourselves are 'running on empty', giving out emotionally more than we are receiving.

Do you know the old story of the two lighthouse keepers? They lived on an isolated island. Neighbours kept coming to borrow oil for their lamps and the keepers generously gave it to them. One day, they themselves ran out of oil and, when the lighthouse lamp went out, many ships were wrecked on the rocks. The keepers had been too generous with their resources and hadn't replenished them. Jesus needed to say 'no' to people's demands to find rest and refreshment alone in the desert — so do we. Spend (or 'waste') time with God each day; take a day off each week, religiously; program a retreat every year; find a spiritual director.

Mark Twain once said habits can't be thrown out the upstairs window. They must be coaxed down one step at a time. If your inner life is not disciplined, practise becoming so — one step at a time.

And do not be discouraged. When Martin Luther got depressed, he would repeat to himself two Latin words: *Baptizatus sum*— 'I have been baptised.' In effect, he was saying: 'Whatever is happening around me and within me, God is still there. His seal is on me forever.'

An unknown person, hiding in a bunker in Cologne during the bombing raids of World War II, wrote on the wall: 'I believe in the sun even if it is not shining: I believe in God even if he is silent: I believe in love even if it is hidden.'

An old hymn, sung now mostly by Christians in the Third World says it all:

I would be true, for there are those who trust me;
I would be pure, for there are those who care;
I would be strong, for there is much to suffer;
I would be brave, for there is much to dare.

The effective Christians of history have been men and women of great personal discipline. The connection between the words 'disciple' and 'discipline' is obvious. . . The progress of the church has been hindered not so much by our talk and our creeds as by our walk, our conduct, our daily living. . . Having found the life which is in Christ, strict discipline leads to a full-orbed, rich and complete, deeply satisfying life.

❧❀❧

First, there is mental discipline: you can control the thoughts that enter your mind. . . Second, the body: let us pray as Jeremy Taylor once did, 'Let my body be a servant of my spirit, and both body and spirit servants of Jesus.' Third, the tongue is to be brought under control: we should ask ourselves three questions before we speak: Is it true? Is it kind? Does it glorify Christ? Fourth, we must discipline our emotions. The apostle James had never heard of Freud, but he knew something of human nature. He asked: 'Where do wars and fightings come from? Do they not come from the cravings that are at war within you?' [James 4: 1].

Billy Graham, 'Christian Discipline'

Lack of self-discipline is an increasing problem of our time. The emphasis today is on liberty as opposed to authority. Personal freedom is claimed as a right and uninhibited self-expression is seen as a necessity for fulfilled living. . .

Clearly established goals and strong motivation are essential components of self-discipline. We need to know where we are heading in life and why we want to get there. Then, self-discipline becomes the means of achieving the desired goal. Discipline is the rudder of life — giving direction and purpose to living. . .

Thomas Carlyle said that 'genius is the capacity for taking infinite pains'. Very few of us come into the genius category. However, most of us have certain expectations in life. Our need is to have realistic expectations, reasonable goals and determined motivation. These possibilities are held together and become reality through self-discipline. Nothing is achieved without effort. There is no easy way to achievement in any area of living.

Paul Rees says, 'The highest forms of self-expression are to be found not in the lotus gardens of self-gratification, but in the gymnasium of self-renunciation.'

Ron Elbourne, 'Parson's Pitch'

Last week I read an interesting interview with Elton Trueblood, the great Quaker Christian philosopher. He says: 'I have become aware of two separate dangers: the futility of empty freedom, and the fruitlessness of solo effort. Hence my concern for discipline, and that is how the Yokefellow Movement emerged. For years, I have been impressed with the powers of the Christian orders. They were strong precisely because of their corporate discipline. Hope lay in the creation of orders and, for a quarter of a century now, much of my thought and energy have gone into the Order of the Yoke. We engage in daily prayer, daily scripture reading, weekly worship, proportionate giving and study.'

Rowland Croucher

Effective executives do first things first and they do one thing at a time. . . There was Mozart, of course. He could, it seems, work on several compositions at the same time, all of them masterpieces. But he is the only known exception. The other prolific composers of the first rank — Bach, for instance, Handel, or Haydn, or Verdi — composed one work at a time. They did not begin the next until they had finished the preceding one, or until they had stopped work on it for the time being and put it away in the drawer. Executives can hardly assume that they are 'executive Mozarts'.

Peter Drucker

Well-known commentator Eric Severeid said that the best lesson he ever learned was the principle of the next mile: 'During World War II, I and several others had to parachute from a crippled Army transport plane into mountainous jungle on the Burma/India border. It was several weeks before an armed relief expedition could reach us and then we began a painful, plodding march out to India. We were faced with a 140-mile trek over mountains in August heat and monsoon rains. In the first hour of the march, I rammed a boot nail deep into one foot; by evening I had bleeding blisters the size of fifty-cent pieces on both feet. Could I hobble 140 miles? Could the others, some in worse shape than I, complete such a distance? We were convinced we could not. But we could hobble to that ridge, we could make the next friendly village for the night. And that, of course, was all we had to do. . .'

> Donald McCullough, 'Time for Things that Matter'

When Phillips Brooks entered the divinity school where he was trained, he was shocked at the situation he found. There were students of rare evangelical fervour who prayed like steam-engines in the prayer meeting. But the next day in the classroom they showed with painful clarity that they had not learned their Greek. 'The boiler had no connections with the engine' was his comment.

> A. Skevington Wood, 'The Need for Discipline'

Every moment was planned and used purposefully, never frittered away. How else in the midst of a very busy, burdened life could he have produced almost forty books on a wide variety of subjects, and every one a gem, fruit of careful study and thought and prayer, to be a spiritual challenge and a spiritual blessing to thousands upon thousands?

He made time for prayer, time for reading, time for meticulous preparation for countless sermons and seminars. I have heard 'Jo' preach many times, and I have heard one or two sermons more or less repeated, but I have never once listened without sensing a fresh touch from the Lord and gone away blessed. He had time for family and friends and time for just a little recreation. All was fitted in so that he never seemed in a hurry or unduly pressured.

> David Stewart, writing of J. Oswald Sanders

In one way or another, increasing numbers of Christians

are observing the season of Lent. Its value is obvious. Lent is an opportunity to discipline our discipleship, to exercise our spiritual muscles, to put iron into our blood. It is not merely a time for giving up — giving up some luxury or indulgence in the interests of spiritual fitness.

This is not to be despised, of course, although the luxuries and indulgences should probably be given up permanently anyway. It is, rather, a time for tightening up — for tightening up the ties that bind us to Christ and his church. There should be nothing negative about the right use of Lent, but everything positive. That is why J.B. Phillips' inspired paraphrase of Hebrews 12: 12 speaks with so much relevance; 'So tighten your loosening grip.'

John N. Gladstone, 'How is Your Grip on Life?'

His precept was glorified by his example,
While for thirty-three years
He moved among the teachers and students of
Harvard College
And wist not that his face shone.

On a tablet in memory of Dr Peabody,
in the chapel at Harvard University.

One of the evidences, Lord, of your Spirit's work in our lives, is self-control. Help us, as Paul encouraged his son Timothy, to be 'disciplined for the purpose of godliness' (1 Timothy 4: 7).

Lord, sometimes our lives are undirected, disorganised, lacking in self-discipline. We are not really free because we cannot command ourselves. We are occasionally like wild horses, untamed, allowing ourselves to run free wherever we will, rather than where you want us to go.

Lord Jesus, you invite us, your followers, to deny ourselves, take up our cross daily, and follow you: no discipline, no discipleship. As we accept your disciplines, so we are your disciples.

Lord, teach us to 'count our days, that we may gain a wise heart' (Psalm 90: 12): help us to discipline our time.

May we offer ourselves as a living sacrifice, acceptable for your service: help us to discipline our bodies.

Bring all our thoughts into the captivity of your will: teach us to discipline our minds.

May our relationships be tempered by love: please help us to discipline our emotions.

May we be workers who do not need to be ashamed; pray-ers who are diligent in seeking spiritual strength from the divine source; servants who delight to do our Master's will; soldiers ready for the inevitable battle; athletes finely-tuned to excel in the race of the spiritual life. Amen.

A Benediction

May you have no plans but God's plans for your life. May you be a disciple, a learner, a follower of Jesus all your life. May God's will truly become your 'magnificent obsession'. May your prayer, every day, be 'Your will be done in my life, as it is done in heaven.'

The blessing of God, Father, Son and Holy Spirit, strengthen you this day, and all your days. Amen.

26

Comes the sharp pruning

And the Lord God planted a garden in Eden, in the east. . . And out of the ground the Lord God made to grow every tree that is pleasant to the sight and good for food, the tree of life also in the midst of the garden, and the tree of the knowledge of good and evil.

You brought a grapevine out of Egypt; you drove out other nations and planted it in their land. You cleared a place for it to grow; its roots went deep, and it spread out over the whole land.

Let me sing for my beloved a love song concerning his vineyard: My beloved had a vineyard on a very fertile hill. He dug it and cleared it of stones, and planted it with choice vines; he built a watchtower in the midst of it, and hewed out a wine vat in it; and. . . he looked for it to yield grapes, but it yielded wild grapes. . .

And now I will tell you what I will do to my vineyard. I will remove its hedge, and it shall be devoured; I will break down its wall, and it shall be trampled down. I will make it a waste; it shall not be pruned or hoed, and briers and thorns shall grow up; I will also command the clouds that they rain no rain upon it. For the vineyard of the Lord of hosts is the house of Israel.

But when he saw many Pharisees and Sadducees coming for baptism, he said to them, 'You brood of vipers! Who warned you to flee from the wrath to come? Bear fruit that befits repentance, and do not presume to say to yourselves, "We have Abraham as our father"; for I tell you, God is able from these stones to raise up children to Abraham. Even now the axe is laid at the root of the trees; every tree therefore that does not bear good fruit is cut down and thrown into the fire.'

I am the true vine, and my Father is the vindresser.

Every branch of mine that bears no fruit, he takes away, and every branch that does bear fruit he prunes that it may bear more fruit. You are already made clean by the word which I have spoken to you.

Abide in me, and I in you. As the branch cannot bear fruit by itself, unless it abides in the vine, neither can you, unless you abide in me. I am the vine, you are the branches. Those who abide in me, and I in them, bear much fruit, because apart from me you can do nothing. Whoever does not abide in me is thrown away like a branch and withers; branches are gathered, thrown into the fire and burned. If you abide in me and my words abide in you, ask whatever you will and it shall be done for you. By this my Father is glorified, that you bear much fruit, and so prove to be my disciples.

We have had earthly fathers to discipline us and we respected them. Shall we not much more be subject to the Father of spirits and live? For they disciplined us for a short time at their pleasure, but he disciplines us for our good, that we may share his holiness. For the moment all discipline seems painful rather than pleasant; later it yields the peaceful fruit of righteousness to those who have been trained by it.

And this is my prayer, that your love may overflow more and more with knowledge and full insight to help you determine what is best, so that in the day of Christ you may be pure and blameless, having produced the harvest of righteousness that comes through Jesus Christ for the glory and praise of God.

Awake, O north wind, and come, O south wind! Blow upon my garden that its fragrance may be wafted abroad. Let my beloved come to his garden, and eat its choicest fruits.

(Genesis 2: 8a–9, RSV; Psalm 80: 8, GNB; Isaiah 5: 1–2, 5–7a; Matthew 3: 7–10; John 15: 1–4 — all RSV; John 15: 5–6, NRSV; John 15: 7–8, RSV; Hebrews 12: 9–11, Philippians 1: 9–11; Song of Solomon 4: 16 — all NRSV)

The grapevine had almost taken over a large area of our garden, arching across the path, tendrils waving in the air, rank, untidy and out of control. Thinking to get rid of it, we pruned it severely so that only a stump was left. But, come summer, the grapevine flourished as never before! The harsh pruning gave it a stimulus to new life and lush growth.

Not only did we learn a lesson in viticulture, but we were reminded of the activities of the divine Gardener, the vinedresser who breaks off and throws away the useless branches and prunes the fruitful branches so that they will bear more fruit. We are pruned through the Word and our experience of remaining united to the vine. The promise of Jesus is abounding fruitfulness as we remain united to him. Without him, we cannot bear fruit. Without that essential union, we wither and are cast aside, unfruitful and worthless.

The characteristic feature of our 'vine-being' is that we receive answers to all our requests, as we ask in the name of Jesus and in line with God's will. God is glorified in our abundant fruitfulness and the fruits of love and obedience are the marks of true discipleship.

There was more to be learned in the lesson of the grapevine. We thought to kill it or to cut if off so closely to the ground that it could never come back to its previous abundance. We were wrong. The harsh pruning made it flourish as never before. We are faced with the conclusion that *the plant most severely pruned by the gardener is the one which will bear the most beautiful blossoms and the most abundant fruit.*

Is that, then, a key to understanding some of the hurts and disappointments of life? The pruning may have been painful, but if we know it is happening at the hands of the divine Gardener, we are better able to accept it or *suffer*, in the true sense of the word, that which God purposes for our fruitfulness.

As [the vine] grows, it is not free to heaven,
But tied to a stake; and if its arms stretch out,

It is but crosswise, also forced and bound.
Then, it blooms and
  makes all the land lovely in spring time.
Comes the sharp pruning and
  it strips it bare of all its innocent pride
And wandering garlands, and cuts deep and sure
And in its loss and pain it wastes not;
But yields itself with unabated life
More perfect under the despoiling hand.
Then, as soon as the grapes are ripe, they are
  gathered and taken to the winepress,
Until the blood-red rivers of the wine
Run over and the land is filled with joy.

But the vine stands stripped and desolate,
Having given all.
And soon
It is cut back to the very stem,
Despoiled, disfigured, left a leafless stock
All through the dark that shall come.
And all the winter-time the wine gives joy
To those who else were dismal with the cold;
But the vine stands out amidst the cold.
And next year, it is ready to give itself again.

Hubert Northcott, The Gardens of the Lord

The Old Testament was the shadow of that noble bud which God in the eternal plan had decided to bring forth from the Virgin Mary. This bud is the Son of God. He is the radiant sun that brightens the whole world. He is the true vine who provides us with the best wine, when as a result of his generous grace, we recognise the glorious shape of his divinity through the garment of his humanity, and when we have learned in wisdom the true teaching of a pure faith.

Hildegard of Bingen,
Book of Divine Works: with Letters and Songs

At home, the flowers have begun to blossom, pruning time has come (Song of Solomon 2: 12). The flowers of our heart, Philothea, are good desires. As soon as they appear, we must take a pruning-knife and cut away all dead and superfluous works. Before marrying an Israelite, an alien girl had to lay aside the garb of a captive, shave her head and pare her nails close (Deuteronomy 21: 12). Similarly, those who aspire to the honour of being a spouse of Christ must put off the old [nature] and put on the new (Ephesians 4: 22) forsaking sin; then pare down and shave away whatever hinders union with God.

St Francis de Sales, *Introduction to the Devout Life*

How good you are, my God, to have broken everything around me, to have annihilated in such a way everything that would have prevented me living for you alone, giving me an ever deeper feeling of the futility and falseness of the life of the world, and of the vast distance there is between the perfect life, the life of the gospel, and the life we lead in the world. You gave me a tender and increasing love for you, O Lord Jesus, and a taste for prayer, trust in your word, a profound awareness of the duty of almsgiving, a longing to imitate you. . . and a thirst to give you the greatest sacrifice I am capable of making for you, by leaving forever the family which had been all my joy, to live and die far away from it.

Charles de Faucauld,
Come Let Us Sing a Song Unknown

A tree is mature only when it is bearing fruit. Until then, it is immature. A person is immature until he or she is outgoing and sharing. And how does a tree bear fruit? By struggling, trying, working itself up into a lather, by tense anxiety, by trying harder? No. It bears fruit as it takes in from soil and sun and atmosphere — it bears fruit by receptivity.

Jesus said: 'As the branch cannot bear fruit by itself, unless it abides in the vine, neither can you, unless you abide me.' 'As the branch cannot bear fruit by itself' — that verse is the death knell to all attempts at maturity by self-tinkering, striving for self-salvation. All these attempts leave you centred on yourself and, when you are centred on yourself, you are immature, however religious you may be and however psychological you may be. Something has to break the tyranny of self-preoccupation and only a mighty influx of love from Christ can do that.

E. Stanley Jones, *Christian Maturity*

There have been no cataclysmic experiences; only a progressively enriched experience. . . In this process of enlightenment, first of all there was brought under my notice, vividly and repeatedly, the truth of 'the soul's union with Christ'. I can still remember the thrill, both intellectual and spiritual, with which I received it. I rejoiced to learn that, as a believer, I was joined to my Lord in a holy union of love; that I was in Christ and that Christ was in me; that no union on earth was more real than this mystic union with Christ.

In the possession of this scriptural doctrine, I found a potent secret of inner control. I saw that because of Christ's indwelling, I had Christ's own life within me, a life which had known experience on earth and, though tempted in all points as we are, had been without sin.

Under the guidance of wise masters of the inner-life, I adopted a new spiritual technique. I stopped praying for my own self to be controlled. Instead, I prayed for grace to cease from myself and to allow Christ to live his own life through me. Instead of praying in times of stress, 'Lord, keep me calm,' I prayed, 'Lord, entrench me in your calm. Not now my weakness made strong, but my weakness abandoned and your strength, a strength tested and triumphant in like circumstances, permitted to express itself through my surrendered personality.'

That was gain indeed. It was not only an immediate enrichment; it was also the opening up of a new world of possibility. . . by consciously abiding in Christ, horizons were widened for me.

G.H. Morling, *The Quest for Serenity*

Father, if the hour has come to make the break,
help me not to cling, even though it feels like death.

Give me the inward strength of my redeemer, Jesus Christ,
to lay down this bit of life and let it go,
so that I and others may be free
to take up whatever new and fuller life
you have prepared for us, now and hereafter. Amen.

J.V. Taylor, *A Matter of Life and Death*

Merciful Lord, grant to your faithful people pardon and peace,
that they may be cleansed from all their sins and serve you with
a quiet mind; through Jesus Christ our Lord. Amen.

A Benediction
May the God of peace who brought again from the dead our
Lord Jesus, the great shepherd of the sheep, by the blood of the
eternal covenant, equip you with everything good that you may
do his will, working in you that which is pleasing in his sight,
through Jesus Christ; to whom be glory for ever and ever.
Amen.

Where is God?

Philip said to him, 'Lord, show us the Father, and we
will be satisfied.' Jesus said to him, 'Have I been with
you all this time, Philip, and you still do not know me?
Whoever has seen me has seen the Father. How can
you say, "Show us the Father"? Do you not believe that
I am in the Father and that the Father is in me? The
words that I say to you I do not speak on my own; but
the Father who dwells in me does his works. Believe
me that I am in the Father and the Father is in me; but
if you do not, then believe me because of the works
themselves. Very truly, I tell you, the one who believes
in me will also do the works that I do and, in fact, will
do greater works than these, because I am going to the
Father.'

(John 14: 8–12, NRSV)

Many of my friends outside the church have confided that
a primary struggle with belief in God is their lack of
experience of him. Where is God, they ask? The difficulty
of belief does not rest on questions and rationality. The
idea of God makes a good deal of sense, they say. The
problem essentially is as old as human consciousness; that
is, why does God not show his face? Our modern way
of asking this question is: Where is the proof of God;
what are the empirical facts or data; or where does God
fit into the explainable universe of relativity and quantum
mechanics?

Perhaps our image of God is unhelpful. The culturally
pervasive view of an almighty, wholly other, antiseptic

God, in fact, blinds us to the reality of God's activity in creation and the evolutionary process. If we take the approach outlined above, we are like tourists who holiday in a country with an alien culture and come away unchanged, with their presuppositions and prejudices of that culture intact.

A different paradigm is required to begin the discovery of God in reality. The lifestyle, ministry, death and resurrection of Jesus of Nazareth has the power to transform the old presuppositions. Once we appreciate and begin to integrate the way God worked through Jesus in the Gospel stories, we will catch a glimpse of God's face. The answer to our initial question, 'Where is God?' is: in Jesus we discover that God is at work in the world through people's acts of justice, mercy and love. What good news this is. What an unexpected or even alien image of God this is: God who is constantly with us, nurturing us, loving us and continually giving us the opportunities to be agents of human salvation.

Recently, an accident occurred at an industrial plant in Melbourne. As with many such incidents, it did not make the headlines. A maintenance crew began work on some high pressure gas lines. Whenever such work was to be carried out, a stringently followed shut-down procedure ensured that the gas was cleared from that particular section. The procedure was always double-checked. The head technician who was overseeing the operation was highly qualified and had done the task hundreds of times. Somehow, this day, the checking was not quite complete and gas remained in just one of the many lines that had been isolated for work.

A nineteen-year-old apprentice began work on this line. He started to cut through it with the oxy. The flame broke through — simultaneously, there was a flash of blinding light, a muffled eruption and unbearable heat as the oxygen was sucked up into the fireball.

As the gas ignited, the young man jumped from the scaffolding which was several metres high. He landed heavily on the mezzanine below. His workmates later remarked that it was a miracle that he had not been incinerated. With the agility and lightning reactions that only the youthful have, he had escaped death. He spent several weeks in hospital recovering from severe concussion, broken bones, breathing difficulties and burns.

Responsibility for the accident ultimately lay with one person — the head technician. This job had become an important part of her life. She was devastated at the result of her mistake. Almost as soon as the young man had been dischargd from the hospital, he wanted to see the person responsible. The Churches of Christ chaplain organised a time for them both in his office. Both parties had requested his presence. At first, there was an earth-shattering silence as they faced each other. The woman lent heavily against a table, trembling from guilt, anxiety and sorrow. No-one could speak.

Then it came. Just as the woman was about to utter some faint response, the young man grasped her by the hand and said: 'It's okay. . . there's no hard feelings. It was an accident. . . it could have happened to anyone. There's nothing to feel bad about.' He stepped back, released her hand and, from underneath his coat on a chair, produced a bunch of flowers and a box of chocolates. He held them out to her. She could not bring herself to take them. He said: 'Look, I'm okay. I'm just worried about you. You must feel awful.' Her eyes welled with tears and, at the chaplain's prompting, she took the gifts.

Where, then, is God? God is at work doing the most extraordinary things in the most ordinary places!

❧❦

A drunk was looking for something on the sidewalk one night under a street light. He groped along the ground, feeling the cement, occasionally grabbing the pole for support. A passer-by asked what he was looking for. 'Lost my wallet,' the drunk replied. The passer-by offered to help him look, but with no success.

'Are you sure you lost it here?' he asked the drunk.

'Course I didn't,' the drunk replied. 'It was half-a-block back there.'

'Then why aren't you looking back there?'

'Because,' answered the drunk with baffling logic, 'there ain't no street lights back there.'

Searching is important, but it doesn't do any good unless we search in the right places.

Billy Graham, *How to be Born Again*

But at the very heart of religion lies this quite unique notion of something of which we cannot conceive at all without seeing at the same time that it must be.

To put this in more expressly religious terms, there is substance in the view that the sceptic and agnostic do not so much find themselves unconvinced that in fact there is a God as fail to see what is meant by 'God'; and we cannot first tell them what we mean and then proceed to show that God is also real. If they can be induced to see what we mean when we speak of God, they will at one and the same time be convinced of his existence; and this is not without considerable importance for religious propaganda in all its forms.

H.D. Lewis, *Our Experience of God*

What is God like? People have always asked this question. It is particularly serious for someone who is certain of God's existence, but even more for someone who doubts this. For whether God exists depends for many on what he is like. . .

Nowhere more clearly has it become manifest to me than in Jesus' life and work, suffering and dying, that this God is a God for us, a God who is wholly on our side. Not a fear-creating, theocratic God 'from above'. . . but a *benevolent, compassionate* God 'with us below'. No, the God who has manifested himself to me in Jesus is not a cruel, despotic, legalistic God. . . but a God encountering me as redeeming love, a God who has identified himself with me in Jesus, who does not demand, but bestows love — *who is himself wholly love.*

'God is love. God's love for us was revealed when God sent into the world his only Son, so that we could have life through him.'

Hans Kung, *Does God Exist?*

Is Australia the South Land of the Holy Spirit? Most Australians, in their inimitable way, would shy clear of such a flowery description. But like the Aborigines who have known this country as 'land of the Spirit' since the time of the Dreaming, many white Australians today find spiritual value in the very terrain their ancestors found so terrifying. There are deep springs of spiritual values, too, underlying the so-called secular society. They are simply waiting to be baptised by a church generous enough to recognise that they are of God.

Muriel Porter, *Land of the Spirit?*

When I read the Gospels, I read them as an Aboriginal. There are many things in the gospel that make me happy to be Aboriginal, because I think we have a good start.

So many of the things Christ said and did and the way he lived make me think of the good things in our way of life. Christ did not get worried over material things. In fact, he looks down on them as things that get in the way and make it hard to get to our true country.

Deacon Boniface Perdjert,
'The Community of Believers'

Neither Feuerbach's philosophical interpretation, nor Marx's class struggle, nor Freud's psychoanalysis can decide whether there is a divine reality independent of our thinking, willing mind and society. If God does not exist, these theories can explain why we should have a false belief in God; but they cannot finally decide whether God is real or not. If God exists, we have an answer to the origin and purpose of the world and of humanity. The existence of God is proposed as a matter of trust which has its basis in reality. There can be no stalemate between 'yes' and 'no' to God. Faith in God can be demonstrated rationally in the audacity of its practice. Fundamental trust and trust in God belong together.

Eric Osborn, 'Rational Faith'

To experience compassion and to identify with the suffering of others — as well as with their joy — is to experience the divine One who suffers and rejoices in each person.

Matthew Fox, *The Coming of the Cosmic Christ*

When I was young, I thought of God as a grandfatherly figure, which made God very accessible. Now, inside me is an almost imageless conception, a dark light or a light darkness. I find God through the clues given in Jesus Christ — that God is caring and compassionate, that God has deep feelings about us. And God is always available.

You know the wonderful story of Elijah, where the prophets of Baal call to Baal, but Baal doesn't answer when they call. And Elijah says, 'Maybe your God is deaf. Call loudly. He is asleep, or he is on a journey, or he has gone to the john.'

Desmond Tutu, 'Who is God?'

The world of particle physics is more like a crossword than a clockwork mechanism. Each new discovery is a clue which finds its solution in some new mathematical linkage. As the discoveries mount up, so more and more cross-links are 'filled in' and one begins to see a pattern emerge.

At present, there remain many blanks on the crossword, but something of its subtlety and consistency can be glimpsed. Unlike mechanisms, which can slowly evolve to more complex or organised forms over time, the 'crossword' of particle physics comes ready-made. The links do not evolve; they are simply there in the underlying laws. We must either accept them as truly amazing brute facts, or seek a deeper explanation.

According to Christian tradition, this deeper explanation is that God has designed nature with considerable ingenuity and skill, and that the enterprise of particle physics is uncovering part of this design. If one were to accept that, the next question is: To what purpose has God produced this design?. . .

The apparent 'fine-tuning' of the laws of nature necessary if conscious life is to evolve in the universe then carries the clear implication that God has designed the universe so as to permit such life and consciousness to emerge. It would mean that our own existence in the universe formed a central part to God's plan.

Paul Davies, *The Mind of God*

If I did believe in a god, I'd believe in one with a sense of humour, one you could joke with. I'd applaud his prodigious originality, and the humour expressed in the incongruities of creation. Anyone who, for example, created sex is clearly a consummate practical joker.

But the fundamentalists, like the Boers, are a humourless bunch. Theirs is the Old Testament God of vengeance, discipline, law and order. They see God as a grumpy old [so-and-so] glaring balefully down at an unworthy world, just aching to demolish it, to judge and to pulverise. The only pleasure they seem to feel is self-righteous indignation. Their brand of Christian soldiering evokes the brutality of the Crusaders and the Cossacks.

Phillip Adams, *Adams versus God*

If we make the leap of faith which thinks of God as present in every circumstance, speaking to us in the beauty and humour and sadness of human life, challenging us in its pains and sorrows and calamities so as to make us lay hold of things that do not pass away, then we shall find God everywhere and the whole earth will be full of his glory.

Leslie Weatherhead, *How can I find God?*

In no case is God a 'what' that one may peep at close up or at a distance and value or disparage as one pleases. God is a 'who'.

And he is not who he is 'for me' or 'for you' (according to our ideas of him), but in his own reality and truth, above both you and me for all people, for the whole world. And hence also for you and for me!

. . .Thus he is 'our', 'your' and 'my' Creator and Lord, who judges and has mercy on us, our Father and Redeemer. It is thus that he revealed and reveals himself in the history of Israel and in Jesus Christ, to which witness is given in scripture.

Think carefully about each of these words, yet not according to your own opinion, but as you try to read the Bible and pray a little. Each of these words is a pointer to God himself.

Karl Barth, *Letters*

Loving God, we give thanks that you are the creator and sustainer of all creation. Yet there are times when we cry out: where are you, God? We give thanks that you have revealed your true nature through Jesus of Nazareth and that you continue to reveal yourself in the Spirit of the risen Christ. You are Immanuel. You are always with us, especially in our darkest times, in the pain and suffering of the world. Help us, Lord, we pray, to develop the wisdom to experience you in the unexpected, in the ordinary as well as the spectacular.

Give us courage to have faith,
Support us in our doubt,
Nurture us in our weakness,
Grant us insight in the turmoil of life.

Help us to see the divine in each other and in all of creation. Give us the wisdom to trust, love and have compassion, despite sin and suffering. In Jesus' name, we pray. Amen.

A Benediction

And now may you go with faith in God, through Jesus Christ. May you know his strength through weakness, his love through joy and tragedy, his grace through sin and his call through our humanity. In the name of God the Father/Mother, Jesus the Son and the Holy Spirit. Amen.

28

Coals of fire

You have heard that it was said, 'You shall love your neighbour and hate your enemy.' But I say to you, love your enemies and pray for those who persecute you, so that you may be children of your Father in heaven; for he makes his sun rise on the evil and on the good, and sends rain on the righteous and on the unrighteous. For if you love those who love you, what reward do you have? Do not even the tax collectors do the same? And if you greet only your brothers and sisters, what more are you doing than others? Do not even the Gentiles do the same? Be perfect, therefore, as your heavenly Father is perfect.

You shall not take vengeance or bear a grudge against any of your people, but you shall love your neighbour as yourself: I am the Lord.

When an alien resides with you in your land, you shall not oppress the alien.

You shall not abhor any of the Edomites, for they are your kin. You shall not abhor any of the Egyptians, because you were an alien residing in their land. The children of the third generation that are born to them may be admitted to the assembly of the Lord.

O that you would kill the wicked, O God, and that the bloodthirsty would depart from me — those who speak of you maliciously, and lift themselves up against you for evil! Do I not hate those who hate you, O Lord? And do I not loathe those who rise up against you? I hate them with perfect hatred; I count them my enemies. Search me, O God, and know my heart; test me and know my thoughts. See if there is any wicked way in me, and lead me in the way everlasting.

Honour your father and mother; also, you shall love your neighbour as yourself.

He said to him, '"You shall love the Lord your God with all your heart, and with all your soul, and with all your mind." This is the greatest and first command- ment. And a second is like it: "You shall love your neighbour as yourself."'

The commandments, 'You shall not commit adultery; You shall not murder; You shall not steal; You shall not covet'; and any other commandment, are summed up in this word, 'Love your neighbour as yourself.'

If, however, you bite and devour one another, take care that you are not consumed by one another.

If your enemies are hungry, give them bread to eat; and if they are thirsty, give them water to drink; for you will heap coals of fire on their heads, and the Lord will reward you.

Then Jesus said, 'Father, forgive them; for they do not know what they are doing.' And they cast lots to divide his clothing.

(Matthew 5: 43–48; Leviticus 19: 18, 33; Deuteronomy 23: 7–8; Psalm 139: 19–24; Matthew 19: 19; 22: 37–39; Romans 13: 9; Galatians 5: 15, Proverbs 25: 21–22; Luke 23: 34 — all NRSV)

The capacity to love is the key spiritual quality. God loves us in an unqualified way. The fact that we sin does not affect his love. Its essence lies in the nature of God as a lover rather than the nature of the loved. We do not entice love out of God; he freely gives it.

And our spiritual growth will be indicated and measured by our capacity to love, irrespective of the at- tractiveness of the object of our loving.

Jesus, as the hard end of his commandment that we love our neighbour, said very clearly that our neighbour includes our enemy. For someone to be our enemy does not necessitate that they be a lifelong antagonist or be bent on destroying us or doing us some harm. Our 'enemy' in Jesus' terms is anyone who does not love us — anyone who does not have goodwill towards us or our interests at heart.

Therefore our 'enemy' could well be someone who has a different lifestyle or different beliefs and values. Our enemy may be someone whom we once loved deeply and/or who loved us, but there has been a falling out with resultant disappointment and probably hurt. Our enemy may be someone with whom we compete — someone whom others think is close to us, not knowing the jealousy which has crept into the relationship.

To be willing and able to love those who don't love us is a miracle. It requires grace. It gives better than justice (love for love) and becomes proactive.

What a wonderful release it would be for us to be freed from the need to get as much as we give and to be able to love even those who actively or passively do not have goodwill towards us — to be active rather than reactive. To be growing in this area is surely an important part of what Jesus meant by having 'life to the full'.

I find it more likely that this miracle can be a part of my living if I deliberately seek to understand the other rather than starting at a self-preserving distance and judging. It is not that this empathy is the basis of any capacity that we might have to love our neighbour, but rather that it gives God a chance, through his Spirit in us, to begin or continue the miraculously freeing work of giving us a loving heart.

It might be the hard end of Christianity in one sense, but in another it is the essential basis — even the barometer — of our spiritual walk.

❧

God does not simply *have* love; he *is* love. If *giving* and *sharing* with another is the character and essence of love, then God is love. He can acquire nothing, because he is God. He needs nothing, because he is God. He has all goodness and all riches within himself.

But goodness is self-diffusive; it seeks to share itself. So the infinite goodness which is God seeks to communicate, to diffuse, to share itself. . . with you. . . with me. . . with all of us.

John Powell, *Why Am I Afraid to Love*

Indeed, the Jewish-Christian norm of [brotherly/sisterly] love is entirely different from fairness ethics. It means to love one's neighbours — that is, to feel responsible for and one with them — while fairness ethics means *not* to feel responsible and one, but distant and separate; it means to respect the rights of one's neighbours, but *not* to love them.

It is no accident that the Golden Rule has become the most popular religious maxim today; because it can be interpreted in terms of fairness ethics, it is the one religious maxim which everybody understands and is willing to practise. But the practice of love must begin with recognising the difference between fairness and love.

Erich Fromm, *The Art of Loving*

Under the cross of Christ, a way has been found to overcome all enemies by drawing them into the sphere of God's love.

William Klassen, *Love of Enemies: The Way to Peace*

The love of Christians is to be like the love of God that produced it (and thus a love for outsiders) rather than a different kind of love (confined to those in the fold).

Leon Morris, *Testaments of Love*

I remember a mini-paradigm shift I experienced one Sunday morning on a subway in New York. People were sitting quietly — some reading newspapers, some lost in thought, some resting with their eyes closed. It was a calm, peaceful scene.

Then suddenly, a man and his children entered the subway car. The children were so loud and rambunctious that instantly the whole climate changed.

The man sat down next to me and closed his eyes, apparently oblivious to the situation. The children were yelling back and forth, throwing things, even grabbing people's papers. It was very disturbing. And yet, the man sitting next to me did nothing.

It was difficult not to feel irritated. I could not believe that he could be so insensitive as to let his children run wild like that and do nothing about it, taking no responsibility at all. It was easy to see that everyone else on the subway felt irritated, too. So finally, with what I felt was unusual patience and restraint, I turned to him and said, 'Sir, your children are really disturbing a lot of people. I wonder if you couldn't control them a little more?'

The man lifted his gaze as if to come to a consciousness of the situation for the first time and said softly, 'Oh, you're right. I guess I should do something about it. We just came from the hospital where their mother died about an hour ago. I don't know what to think and I guess they don't know how to handle it, either.'

Can you imagine what I felt at that moment? My paradigm shifted. Suddenly, I *saw* things differently, I *thought* differently, I *felt* differently, I *behaved* differently. My irritation vanished. I didn't have to worry about controlling my attitude or my behaviour; my heart was filled with the man's pain. Feelings of sympathy and compassion flowed freely.

'Your wife just died? Oh, I'm so sorry! Can you tell me about it? What can I do to help?' Everything changed in an instant.

Stephen R. Covey,
The 7 Habits of Highly Effective People

To our most bitter opponents we say: 'We shall match your capacity to inflict suffering by our capacity to endure suffering. We shall meet your physical force with soul force. Do to us what you will and we shall continue to love you. We cannot in all good conscience obey your unjust laws, because non-cooperation with evil is as much a moral obligation as is cooperation with good. Throw us in gaol, and we shall still love you. Send your hooded perpetrators of violence into our community at the midnight hour and beat us and leave us half dead, and we shall still love you.

'But be assured that we will wear you down by our capacity to suffer. One day we shall win freedom, but not only for ourselves. We shall so appeal to your heart and conscience that we shall win *you* in the process, and our victory will be a double victory.'

Love is the most durable power in the world. This creative force, so beautifully exemplified in the life of our Christ, is the most potent instrument available in humankind's quest for peace and security.

Martin Luther King, Strength To Love

Three nights later, our home was bombed. Strangely enough, I accepted the word of the bombing calmly. My experience with God had given me a new strength and trust. I knew now that God is able to give us the interior resources to face the storms and problems of life.

Let this affirmation be our ringing cry. It will give us courage to face the uncertainties of the future. It will give our tired feet new strength as we continue our forward stride toward the city of freedom. When our days become dreary with low-hovering clouds and our nights become darker than a thousand midnights, let us remember that there is a great benign Power in the universe whose name is God, and he is able to make a way out of no way and transform dark yesterdays into bright tomorrows.

This is our hope for becoming better people. This is our mandate for seeking to make a better world.

Martin Luther King, Strength To Love

Father,
I thank you for the inclusive nature of your love. Forgive me for rejecting expressions of your love. I am grateful that my preoccupation with self and my preoccupation with competitiveness, which has blinded me to your reaching out to me, has not discouraged or daunted your loving.

May I open myself to be loved by you. I have hesitated because I don't always understand or comprehend that there is such a reality as an accepting, forgiving love. I have been hurt by those who have seemed as if they care about me, but have needed to get more than they could give. It's risky to try again, but I pray that through your Spirit I may be willing.

I pray for the capacity to love others as I am loved by you. May I seek to understand others rather than judging them unfairly. I look today to you to give me a spirit of love such that even those who define themselves as my enemies will experience your goodwill through me. Amen.

A Benediction

Go forth into the world in peace; be of good courage; hold fast to that which is good; render to no-one evil for evil; strengthen the faint-hearted; support the weak; help the afflicted; give honour to everyone; love and serve the Lord, rejoicing in the power of the Holy Spirit.

And the blessing of God Almighty, the Father, the Son, and the Holy Spirit, be upon you, and remain with you for ever. Amen.

29

Freedom from shame

They heard the sound of the Lord God walking in the garden at the time of the evening breeze, and the man and his wife hid themselves from the presence of the Lord God among the trees of the garden. But the Lord God called to the man and said to him, 'Where are you?' He said, 'I heard the sound of you in the garden and I was afraid, because I was naked; and I hid myself.'

In you, O Lord, I seek refuge; do not let me ever be put to shame; in your righteousness deliver me. I sought the Lord and he answered me, and delivered me from all my fears. Look to him and be radiant; so your faces shall never be ashamed.

But God chose what is foolish in the world to shame the wise; God chose what is weak in the world to shame the strong. For I am not ashamed of the gospel; it is the power of God for salvation to everyone who has faith, to the Jew first and also to the Greek. [Look] to Jesus the pioneer and perfector of our faith, who for the sake of the joy that was set before him endured the cross, disregarding its shame, and has taken his seat at the right hand of the throne of God.

Guard me as the apple of the eye; hide me in the shadow of your wings.

(Genesis 3: 8–10; Psalm 31: 1 and 34: 4–5; 1 Corinthians 1: 27; Romans 1: 16; Hebrews 12: 2; Psalm 17: 8 — all NRSV)

Christian theologians have a 2000-year-old theology of guilt, but have been slow to develop a theology of shame. Shame is often subsumed under guilt and, while one often feels shame because of guilt, there is also a widespread experience of shame that is not directly guilt-related. Whereas guilt relates to what we do, shame has to do with who we are.

Many who have been sexually abused know well the experience of shame. In counselling, abused persons often feel a need for forgiveness — whereas they themselves have been sinned against. The primary emotion being experienced is shame, not guilt. Too often, people use guilt language which doesn't quite fit in order to express their shame experiences.

There is both appropriate and inappropriate shame. When shame is related to genuine guilt, the experience of shame is entirely appropriate. Indeed, it may be the experience of shame which will prompt the person to apologise and to seek forgiveness. It may be the fear of feeling shame that will motivate people to choose wisely in moral situations.

All shame-related experiences are very difficult to 'own', to ourselves or to another. Shame experiences cause us to feel exposed — exposed to others, exposed to God and exposed to ourselves. The self-exposure of shame is usually of a self that we would prefer not to see. When this exposure occurs, it is immediate and all-consuming. Whereas with guilt we may have premeditated the incident which is guilt-producing, with shame the incident occurs without warning. What is a shameful experience for one person may not be so for another.

The remedy for shame is the experience of grace. Our instinctive response to shame is to push it aside and try to escape the painful emotion. To appropriate God's grace, we need to come into his presence, exploring with him the details of the shame experience. As we expose our shame to God in prayer, we gain God's perspective on our shame experiences and know God's gracious acceptance of us.

Shame is a universal experience. In an increasingly bureaucratic society, many people are experiencing shame that is caused by not meeting the expectations they have of themselves or which others place upon them. These shaming experiences leave people with a sense of 'non-okayness' about themselves and is sometimes difficult to put into words.

This sense of felt inadequacy is often more salient for people than any feeling of wrongdoing. When people have the sense of not being good enough, they don't relate this inner wrongness to moral guilt and don't easily relate to guilt theology. A theology of shame is required to meet this special need.

Donald Capps, exploring the dynamics of shame, affirms the need for 'mirroring' as the antidote for shame. Mirroring is more than empathy. Mirroring will recognise the need to be admired and to admire in order to overcome deeply rooted feelings of self-depletion.

The concept of mirroring is encapsulated in the image of the parent with a young child. The parent will smile, speak lovingly and reassuringly to the child and, in this numinous experience, children are learning that they are cherished and have worth and significance.

The numinous experience of God's acceptance of and delight in us is affirmed in our adoration and worship of God. As we come into his presence, the Lord delights to meet with us, he calls us by name and he assures us that we are precious to him.

❧❧

'And night shall be no more; they need no light or lamp or sun, for the Lord God will be their light and they shall reign for ever and ever' (Revelation 22: 5). This is no grandiose fantasy, but the assurance that we are the gleam in God's eye, that we are God's beloved in whom God is well-pleased and that we therefore have no reason to fear that our life-world will lose its colour, for it will always be bathed in the light of God's lustre.

Donald Capps, The Depleted Self

The feeling of shame is about our very selves — not about some bad thing we did or said, but about what we are. It tells us that we are unworthy. Totally. It is not as if a few seams in the garment of ourselves need stitching; the whole fabric is frayed. We feel that we are unacceptable. And to feel that is a life-wearying heaviness. Shame-burdened people are the sort whom Jesus had in mind when he invited the 'weary and heavy laden' to trade their heaviness for his lightness.

Lewis B. Smedes, *Shame and Grace*

It was there, at the bottom, that I discovered clear traces of grace. My desolation inexplicably gave way to comfort. I felt held and undergirded and accepted and loved. It was only afterward, as I thought about it, that I realised that what I experienced was the grace of God. I had heard the words: you are accepted. My feelings echoed: I am accepted. I heard no recordable voice. I felt no physical sensation. But I felt that I was accepted and would not be rejected, was held and would not fall, was loved and would never be unloved.

Lewis B. Smedes, *Shame and Grace*

The dialectic of concealment and exposure is only a sign of shame. Yet shame is not overcome by it; it is, rather, confirmed by it. Shame can be overcome only when the original unity is restored, the person is once again clothed by God.

Dietrich Bonhoeffer, *Ethics*

A common mistake among evangelical Christians is to confuse humility with humiliation and to think that pride can be overcome through self-contempt. Humility enhances our humanity and makes us more like Christ, whereas humiliation diminishes our humanity and tempts us to forget that we are made in the image of God.

Anthony Campolo, *Seven Deadly Sins*

A peasant. . . formed the habit of slipping into a certain church at a certain time of day with clockwork regularity. There, day by day, he would sit and, apparently, do nothing. The parish priest observed this regular, silent visitor. One day, unable to contain his curiosity any longer, he asked the old man why he came to the church, alone, day in, day out. . .

The old man looked at the parish priest and, with a loving twinkle in his eye, gave this explanation: 'I look at him. He looks at me. And we tell each other that we love each other.'

Joyce Huggett, *Listening to God*

Becoming aware of the dynamics of shame that permeates our society allows one to approach theology and ministry in new ways. Shame is related to the deepest places in our souls. Shame cuts to the heart. In its healthy forms, shame helps to shape and inform the heart. In its distorted forms, it can misshape or break the heart. Shame has collective expressions as well. It affects our politics, our economics, our conduct of international affairs and our approach to nature. Pastors and theological educators need to develop an understanding of shame as part of our practical theological work.

James W. Fowler, 'Shame: Toward a Practical Theological Understanding'

I suggest that the painful experience of shame is not to be avoided or renounced, but instead made the core of our identity as Christians. Why the core of Christian identity? Because in shame we experience the pain of self-exposure, and the core of Christian identity is to be 'exposed before God'. The point of Christian identity is not to put our shameful self behind us, but to allow it to be exposed, again and again, to God.

Donald Capps,
Life Cycle Theory and Pastoral Care

In prayer, especially solitary prayer, we enter into intimate conversation with God. In this conversational setting, we are able to 'tell the story' of our shameful experiences, including all details. . . With God as our conversation partner, we can tell the story without fear that it will be judged trivial or unimportant, because we are confident that the God who is known through the Passion understands the depth of our pain.

As the story unfolds, we are able to probe its meaning

without reserve or self-censorship that occurs when we relate these experiences to another person.

Donald Capps,
Life Cycle Theory and Pastoral Care

Gracious Lord, it is good to come into your presence and to worship you. We rejoice that you know us by name and welcome us as ones who are precious to you.

Lord, there are many times when we experience shame. When we are guilty and feel ashamed, help us to acknowledge our guilt and to come to you for forgiveness. When we have failed to live up to our own standards and experience shame, help us to accept ourselves for the people we are. When we have been hurt by others who have taken from us our worth and value, help us to remember that you love us and accept us as we are.

Lord, forgive us when we have been the ones who have shamed others by our words or attitudes. Forgive us when we have done this because of our own insecurity and need for appreciation. Lord, help us to be sensitive and caring to the needs of others and seek to mirror to them that they are special, accepted and loved.

May we always live in the knowledge that you are a gracious God who reaches out to us constantly with the love of your Son, Jesus our Lord. Amen.

A Benediction
The Lord bless you and keep you; the Lord make his face to shine upon you and be gracious to you; the Lord lift up his countenance upon you and give you peace.

Numbers 6: 24–26, NRSV

Seasons of the soul

For everything there is a season, and a time for every matter under heaven.

So God blessed the seventh day and hallowed it, because on it God rested from all the work that he had done in creation.

As long as the world exists, there will be a time for planting and time for harvest. There will always be cold and heat, summer and winter, day and night.

I will give you your rains in their season, and the land shall yield its produce and the trees of the field shall yield their fruit.

They are like trees planted by streams of water, which yield their fruit in its season and their leaves do not wither. In all that they do they prosper.

As a deer longs for flowing streams, so my soul longs for you, O God. My soul thirsts for God, for the living God. When shall I come and behold the face of God? My tears have been my food day and night, while people say to me continually, 'Where is your God?'

These things I remember as I pour out my soul: how I went with the throng, and led them in procession to the house of God, with glad shouts and songs of thanksgiving, a multitude keeping festival. Why are you cast down, O my soul, and why are you disquieted within me? Hope in God; for I shall again praise him, my help and my God.

My soul is cast down within me; therefore, I remember you from the land of Jordan and of Hermon, from Mount Mizar. Deep calls to deep at the thunder of your cataracts; all your waves and your billows have gone over me. By day the Lord commands his steadfast love and at night his song is with me, a prayer to the God of my life.

Seek the Lord while he may be found, call upon him while he is near.

I will make them and the region around my hill a blessing; and I will send down the showers in their season; they shall be showers of blessing.

Yet he [God] has not left himself without a witness in doing good — giving you rains from heaven and fruitful seasons and filling you with food and your hearts with joy.

In this you rejoice, even if now for a little while you have had to suffer various trials.

(Ecclesiastes 3: 1; Genesis 2: 3 — both NRSV; Genesis 8: 22, GNB; Leviticus 26: 4; Psalms 1: 3; 42: 1–8; Isaiah 55: 6; Ezekiel 34: 26; Acts 14: 17; 1 Peter 1: 6 — all NRSV)

All of us have highs and lows in our lives — times when everything is going well and times when we seem disaster-prone. Often good fortune is mirrored by inner elation, or outward crisis echoed by deep depression. These seasons of the soul may be shortlived, or seemingly endless. During the highs, we frequently feel self-congratulatory and capable of conquering the world. During the lows, we either wallow in self-pity, or seek help and refuge from God (or in some alternative like alcohol). Among the crises that may provoke a spiritual or emotional low are things that remind us of our mortality, like sickness or bereavement.

Several times, I have gone to hospital for surgery. Although there was little risk to my life, I must confess each such experience served as a salutary reminder of the uncertainty of life and of my own mortality. On occasions like this, I often find a measure of comfort and encouragement in the prayerful reading of the Psalms.

On one occasion, I had been wrestling mentally with the problem of our (and my) tendency to seek divine help in times of crisis, but to ignore God when things are going well. Is religion merely 'the opium of the people', as Karl

Marx maintained, or is it a response to a loving creator — a legitimate recognition of mortality and expression of need for One who is infinitely greater than we are?

As I read Psalm 42 — one of my favourites — I came across the significant sixth verse: 'My soul is cast down within me; therefore, I remember you. . .' Clearly, for the psalmist, there was a legitimate and natural connection between *feeling low* and *remembering God*. Obviously, we should thank and praise God for our blessings and joys. But it is better to remember God during our lows — even if with an element of self-interest — than to turn to substitutes or wallow in self-pity.

Following another stay in hospital for surgery (for skin cancer on my forehead), I went through a period of acute trauma — I was convinced not only that I was terminally ill, but that my death would be a particularly unpleasant one. For three days I lived a nightmare, when God's love and Christ's death for me — which had always been such a comfort — seemed academic, unrelated to me and my situation. I found myself identifying intimately with Jesus' cry of dereliction upon the cross: 'My God, my God, why have you forsaken me?'

On another occasion more recently, in quite different circumstances, I have found this 'dark night of the soul' (to borrow St John of the Cross' phrase) repeated. In retrospect, I thank God for these experiences, traumatic as they were. They taught me much about God, myself and other people. But I must admit that I also thank God for bringing me through these experiences and restoring to me the joy of his salvation.

I have found in my reading of the Psalms echoes of both the depths and heights I encountered during and after these traumas. I thank God that there is a Psalm for every season of the soul.

ᘓᗋᘒ

Spring is the season of planting and sowing, of new growth and new beginnings. It is a time of vigour and freshness. In the springtime of life, we are young and newly independent. We have thrown off the restraints of childhood and teen years. We are free to set our own goals and make our own choices. The whole of life stretches ahead. We look forward to the expansiveness of summer. Autumn and winter are far away.

Summer is the season of warmth, abundance and fulfilment. It can also be hot and exhausting. In the summer of life, we are at full stretch — at home, at work and in the community — enjoying the richness of life. Time presses: yet we need to make space for rest, for relaxation and for reflection. This is also the opportunity to weigh the options still open to us and to negotiate change, where it is appropriate, while we can.

Autumn is the time of harvest. It is a mild and mellow season, but gales may come, warning of winter's approach. In middle life, as summer gives way to autumn, we begin to reap the harvest of the goals we set in the first half of life. But there is still time to sow for a second harvest. Storms may warn of coming loss and our own mortality. We carry the responsibility now, as the older generation.

Winter closes in around us. It restricts, yet the narrowing of possibilities offers its own special bonus of satisfaction. The earth may be cold and still, but there is warmth and growth within. In our own season of winter, we shed the restraints and ties of earlier years and we can enjoy a new expansion of spirit. In old age, we can experience secret growth and the warmth of kindness and love, received and given.

Mary Batchelor, *Celebrating the Seasons of Life*

He [God] is prepared to do a little overriding at the beginning. He will set them [new Christians] off with communications of his presence which, though faint, seem great to them, with emotional sweetness and easy conquest over temptation. But he never allows this state of affairs to last long. Sooner or later he withdraws, if not in fact, at least from their conscious experience, all those supports and incentives. He leaves the creature to stand up on its own legs — to carry out from the will alone duties which have lost all relish. It is during such rough periods, much more than during the peak periods, that it is growing into the sort

of creature he wants it to be. Hence, the prayers offered
in the state of dryness are those which please him best.

C.S. Lewis, *The Screwtape Letters*

There was a time — my heart is humbled still whenever
I recall — when you, great God of grace, first burst into
my life, forgiving all. It was a sacred moment that, when
in the springtime of your love, I saw a world made new:
an aching void was filled, a troubled hypocrite was healed,
a rebel reconciled to you.

Then came the summer of your love when, while my
childlike heart was tender still, your many revelations
swept across my soul — your urgent, awesome love an
eager, trusting heart to fully fill.

Next came the autumn of your love, when you invited
me to stand on my own feet, within your grace; I thought
that I could stand without your help and had to learn that
I would fall flat on my face.

The winter of your love came then — the fervour of
my first intent was frozen in my veins; and though I
followed formally your way, I found it only echoed back
my pains.

Lord, will you not send spring again to thaw my heart
and heal my pain, refresh me with your love?

Until that day I'll live in hope and trust that, by your
grace, I'll cope till spring comes from above.

Christopher Venning,
'Seasons of Your Love'

Nothing is so beautiful as Spring —
When weeds, in wheels, shoot long and lovely and lush;
Thrush's eggs look little low heavens, and thrush
Through the echoing timber does so rinse and wring
The ear, it strikes like lightnings to hear him sing;
The glassy peartree leaves and blooms, they brush
The descending blue; that blue is all in a rush
With richness; the racing lambs too have fair their fling.
What is all this juice and all this joy?
A strain of the earth's sweet being in the beginning
In Eden garden — Have, get, before it cloy,

Before it cloud, Christ, lord, and sour with sinning,
Innocent mind and Mayday in girl and boy,
Most, O maid's child, thy choice and worthy the winning.

Gerald Manley Hopkins, 'Spring'

It is the heart that is not yet sure of its God that is afraid
to laugh in his presence.

George Macdonald

Learn to commit your soul and the building of it to One
who can keep it and build it as you never can. Attend
then to Christ, the Holy Spirit, the kingdom and the cause,
and he will look after your soul.

Peter Taylor Forsyth, *The Work of Christ*

When God lovingly draws [you] into a dark night of the
soul. . . be grateful that God is. . . drawing you away
from every distraction so that you can see him.

Richard Foster, *Celebration of Discipline*

The Christian way of life does not take away our loneliness. . . but perhaps the painful awareness of our loneliness
is an invitation to transcend our limitations and look
beyond the boundaries of our existence.

Henri Nouwen, *The Wounded Healer*

It is not the sunny side of Christ that we must look to,
and we must not forsake him for want of that; but must
set our face against what may befall us, in following on,
till he and we pass through the briars and bushes on the
dry ground. Our soft nature would be borne through the
troubles of this miserable life in Christ's arms. And it is
his wisdom, who knoweth our mould, that his bairns go
wet-shod and cold-footed to heaven.

Samuel Rutherford

He whispered, 'My precious child,
I love you and will never leave you
never, ever, during your trials and testings.
When you saw only one set of footprints

it was then that I carried you.'

Margaret Fishback, 'Footprints'

Where does a pilgrim shelter in the winter, Lord,
from storm and stress? Inside himself, or thee?
How can he lay aside his staff and sword when
weariness he feels and dangers all around can see?
Yet if he rest not, darker dreams may fly abroad
and threaten equilibrium, and even sanity.
And so he turns to thee, in fear of being ignored,
but casts himself down hopefully.

Our God will not abandon us
to dark despair
whether the storms rage ceaselessly,
or weather still be fair:
though oft unseen, unfelt,
the shelter of God's love is there.
So, weary pilgrim, draw aside a while
and seek his rest,
knowing that he created you,
and he knows best the healing
that you need within yourself
to be most blessed.

Christopher Venning,
'Pilgrimage and Rest'

---

*You, Lord, give perfect peace to those who keep their purpose
firm and put their trust in you.*

Isaiah 26: 3, GNB

*Lord, my mind is cluttered with dirty dishes, unmade beds,
soiled laundry, weed-filled flower beds, uncut lawn, overdue
promises, unpaid bills. Won't you tidy me this morning?*

Doris Carlson

*I was a child
playing hide and seek with you
and you caught me hiding
in the silliest saddest places*

behind old grudges
under a ton of disappointments
tangled in guilt
smothered with success
choking on sobs
that nobody heard.
You found me
and whispered my name
and said 'You're it!'
and I believe you meant it.

From a wall in Chula vista, California

Lord God:
We ask you to help us to celebrate the seasons of the soul.
In times of renewal, may we have a song of praise to sing to you like the birds in spring.
May we bask in the summer of your love when it comes, so we will have warmth to give to others.
In the autumns of our lives, may we pray while the sun shines, so that with your help we may experience a rich harvest of the soul.
And when winter comes at last, may we fall asleep in your grace so spring will bring a gentle awakening to the eternal freshness of your loving presence.
May Christ's cross be to us forgiveness in this life and a bridge to the next. And may we always love as you have loved us and forgive as you have forgiven us.
Through Jesus Christ our Lord. Amen.

A Benediction
May God guide your comings and goings:
May the Father fill you with his Spirit, and make you fruitful;
May Jesus Christ be your companion on life's journey, and bring you encouragement;
And may the Holy Spirit bring you help and healing at each point of need.
May God give you joy and strength in all the seasons of the soul,
Through Jesus Christ our Lord. Amen.

Building the Christian community

As God's chosen ones, holy and beloved, clothe your-selves with compassion, kindness, humility, meekness and patience. Bear with one another and, if anyone has a complaint against another, forgive each other; just as the Lord has forgiven you, so you also must forgive. Above all, clothe yourselves with love, which binds everything together in perfect harmony. And let the peace of Christ rule in your hearts. . .

Love is patient; love is kind; love is not envious or boastful or arrogant or rude. It does not insist on its own way; it is not irritable or resentful; it does not rejoice in wrongdoing, but rejoices in the truth. It bears all things, believes all things, hopes all things, endures all things. Love never ends.

So when you are offering your gift at the altar, if you remember that your brother or sister has something against you, leave your gift there at the altar and go; first be reconciled to your brother or sister and then come and offer your gift.

I ask not only on behalf of these, but also on behalf of those who will believe in me through their word, that they may all be one. As you, Father, are in me and I am in you, may they also be in us, so that the world may believe that you have sent me. The glory that you have given me I have given them, so that they may be one, as we are one.

Let us therefore no longer pass judgment on one another, but resolve instead never to put a stumbling block or hindrance in the way of another. . . Let us then pursue what makes for peace and for mutual upbuilding.

(Colossians 3: 12–15; I Corinthians 13: 4–8; Matthew 5: 23–24; John 17: 20–22; Romans 14: 13 and 19 — all NRSV)

By what process can a congregation, made up of many different individuals, become a community? In many instances, a radical reorientation must occur before real community can be established and maintained. We have to find a new way of being the church in our day.

There needs to be a reorientation in the congregation from individualism to group identity. We have often been preoccupied with personal preference and individual piety at the expense of community. In the New Testament, images of the church are always *corporate* images: people of God, body of Christ, household of faith, vine and branches, shepherd and flock. This is not to say that we do not value individual identity or the importance of personhood. It is to say that when a number of individuals meet together, there needs to be a willingness to transcend personal preferences for the sake of building real community.

There needs to be a reorientation in the congregation from security and *status quo* to risk and change. Lawrence Richards, in *A New Face for the Church*, identifies three groups of people in any given congregation: the innovators (ten per cent), the conservatives (eighty per cent) and the inhibitors (ten per cent).

This suggests, and experience confirms, that only a small minority are willing to set new goals, dream new dreams, see new visions and move to realise them in the life of the church. Because the great majority are content with things the way they are, there is a high degree of inertia and resistance. But there can be no growth in individuals or community without a willingness to take risks and be open to change.

There needs to be a reorientation in the congregation from organisation and busyness to relationship and being. Time and time again, we hear it said that the church is over-structured, 'over-committeed' and too bureaucratic. We know that we are over-organised and that this inhibits the real life and growth of the church, but we do not seem to have the will to do anything about it.

Lawrence Richards talks about the tension in the church between 'possessed values' and 'operational values'; the difference between what we say we believe about the church and how we actually go about being the church. Our enslavement to structures and organisation is a particular example of this.

We ought to see every time we meet together as an opportunity to experience community and build relationships — and plan all such occasions with that goal in mind. In order for this to happen, there needs to be more time and space in our life together, by freeing up our structures, by delegating responsibility and by trusting people more. We need more time just to be persons together, to meet one another at depth, to share our pilgrimage and our faith more freely with one another.

❧❧

When others look at us in a friendly way, we feel alive and vital. When others recognise us just the way we are, we feel fulfilled. And when we feel accepted and affirmed, we are happy, for we human beings need acceptance just as the birds need air and the fish water. Acceptance is the atmosphere of humanity. Where acceptance is lacking, the air becomes thin, our breathing falters and we languish. Therefore, we are repulsed by the indifferent glance, hurt by disregard and humanly destroyed when others deny us.

Jurgen Moltmann, *The Open Church*

Christianity is a community event. As Christians, we have always believed that the life of faith is not a private enterprise, but a communal venture. Over the past several decades in the church, we have come to renewed awareness of this fact. One of the most significant efforts within the church today is the movement of Christians to understand themselves as the people of God and to experience their relations with one another as a life together in community.

We rejoice in this vision of Christian life, taking hope in its challenge to the formality and bureaucracy that can find their way into church structures. But gradually, many of us have come to sense that this goal of life together as Christians is both a gift and a most difficult ambition.

Evelyn and James Whitehead, *Community of Faith*

That most difficult thing —
to see something
from someone else's point of view.
To let go of ourselves enough
to be able to care,
to let go enough
to be aware,
to let go enough
to sit still and listen
intently —
taking it all in. . .
the problem,
the person,
the others involved,
our own prejudices.
To get inside someone else's skin
and feel what they feel —
their joy, their sorrow —
as though it were our own —
to know.

Ken Walsh, *Sometimes I Weep*

A Christian community is therefore a healing community, not because wounds are cured and pains are alleviated, but because wounds and pains become openings or occasions for a new vision. Mutual confession then becomes a mutual deepening of hope and sharing weakness becomes a reminder to one and all of the coming strength.

Henri Nouwen, *The Wounded Healer*

Two trucks were standing back to back and a truck driver was struggling to get a huge crate from one truck to the other. A passer-by, seeing his desperate situation, volunteered to help. So the two of them huffed and puffed and struggled for well over half an hour with no result at all.

'I'm afraid it's no use,' panted the passer-by. 'We'll never get it off this truck.' 'Off?' yelled the driver. 'I don't want it off. I want it *on!*'

Anthony de Mello, *The Prayer of the Frog*

Generosity proved to be contagious. Once begun, this charity soon extended beyond regimental loyalties to include any man in need. Men started thinking less of themselves, of their own discomforts and plans and more of their responsibilities to others. . .

It was dawning on us all — officers and other ranks alike — that the law of the jungle is not the law for us. We had seen for ourselves how quickly it could strip most of us of our humanity and reduce us to levels lower than the beasts.

Death was still with us — no doubt about that. But we were slowly being freed from its destructive grip. We are seeing for ourselves the sharp contrast between the forces that made for life and those that made for death. Selfishness, hatred, envy, jealousy, greed, self-indulgence, laziness and pride were anti-life. Love, heroism, self-sacrifice, sympathy, mercy, integrity and creative faith, on the other hand, were the essence of life, turning mere existence into living in its truest sense.

Ernest Gordon, *Miracle on the River Kwai*

Lord, we come before you, not alone,
but in the company of one another.
We share our happiness with each other —
and it becomes greater.
We share our troubles with each other —
and they become smaller.
We share one another's griefs and burdens —
and their weight becomes possible to bear.
May we never be too mean to give,
nor too proud to receive.
For in giving and receiving
we learn to love and be loved;

we encounter the meaning of life,
the mystery of existence —
and discover you.

Terry Falla, *Be Our Freedom, Lord*

God of love,
you have been present with us in the past,
made yourself real to us,
loved and forgiven us,
brought your word alive in us,
stimulated and disturbed us,
comforted and strengthened us,
directed and guided us.
We acknowledge in faith and joy that you are
with us now.
We pray that by the end of this day,
through the power of the Holy Spirit,
that we will have changed and grown in some way
pleasing to you,
meaningful to ourselves
and enriching to others.
Through Jesus who loved us and gave himself for us.
Amen.

A Benediction
Peace be to the whole community and love with faith, from God
the Father and the Lord Jesus Christ. Grace be with all who
have an undying love for our Lord Jesus Christ.

Ephesians 6: 23–24, NRSV

32

Grace versus law

And the Lord God made all kinds of trees grow out of the ground — trees that were pleasing to the eye and good for food. In the middle of the garden were the tree of life and the tree of the knowledge of good and evil.

And the Lord God commanded the man, 'You are free to eat from any tree in the garden; but you must not eat from the tree of the knowledge of good and evil, for when you eat of it you will surely die.'

For the law was given through Moses; grace and truth came through Jesus Christ.

The sting of death is sin and the power of sin is the law.

The law is only a shadow of the good things that are coming — not the realities themselves. For this reason it can never, by the same sacrifices repeated endlessly year after year, make perfect those who draw near to worship.

For whoever keeps the whole law and yet stumbles at just one point is guilty of breaking all of it.

It is not those who hear the law who are righteous in God's sight, but it is those who obey the law who will be declared righteous.

[We are] not justified by observing the law, but by faith in Jesus Christ. So we, too, have put our faith in Christ Jesus that we may be justified by faith in Christ and not by observing the law, because by observing the law no-one will be justified.

It was not through law that Abraham and his offspring received the promise that he would be heir of the world, but through the righteousness that comes by faith because law brings wrath.   And where there is no law there is no transgression.   Therefore, the promise comes by faith, so that it may be by grace and may be guaranteed to all Abraham's offspring — not only to those who are of the law, but also to those who are of the faith of Abraham.   He is the father of us all.

All who rely on observing the law are under a curse, for it is written: 'Cursed is everyone who does not continue to do everything written in the Book of the Law.'

Sin shall not be your master, because you are not under law, but under grace.

Christ is the end of the law, so that there may be righteousness for everyone who believes.

I do not set aside the grace of God, for if righteousness could be gained through the law, Christ died for nothing!

Clearly no-one is justified before God by the law, because 'The righteous will live by faith.'

You who are trying to be justified by law have been alienated from Christ; you have fallen away from grace.

For it is by grace you have been saved, through faith — and this not from yourselves, it is the gift of God.

(Genesis 2: 9 and 16–17; John 1: 17; 1 Corinthians 15: 56; Hebrews 10: 1; James 2: 10; Romans 2: 13; Galatians 2: 16; Romans 4: 13–16; Galatians 3: 10; Romans 6: 14; Romans 10: 4; Galatians 2: 21; Galatians 3: 11; Galatians 5: 4; Ephesians 2: 8 — all NIV)

How can we best describe the wonderful grace of God? Christians so often speak of God being gracious to them, referring to his divine favour, yet many may not understand what the grace of God fully entails.

Perhaps the major conflict in the Bible was not God versus Satan, or even good versus evil, but grace versus law.   In the Garden of Eden, humankind was given the choice of the fruit of two trees: the tree of knowledge (the law) and the tree of life (God's grace).   In the New Testament, Jesus violently opposed the Pharisees, who were experts in the law, but had little concept of grace.

It is the most common recurring theme in the epistles of Paul and the root of Jesus' rebuke to Peter. It is made abundantly clear throughout the New Testament that no-one will be declared righteous in God's sight by observing the law. Instead, according to Paul in Ephesians, 'It is by grace you have been saved, through faith.'

Yet Christians continually struggle with legalism in our lives, attitudes and congregations; grace has little long-term impact on their lives or behaviour. Today, legalism amongst Christians might be different in kind to that of the Pharisees or false teachers of the first century, but it is still alive and well, with the same pretensions to be 'biblically based'.

Christians today measure holiness and commitment ac-cording to the regularity of quiet times, witnessing or attending prayer meetings and so on. If they don't do these things as well as they feel they ought, they either castigate themselves or others will do it for them. They are left feeling guilty and depressed and robbed of joy — even less able than before to meet their standards of holiness.

Colossians 1: 6 states: 'All over the world this gospel is bearing fruit and growing, just as it has been doing among you since the day you heard it and understood grace in all its truth.' There are many reasons for the church's empty pews and the lukewarm commitment of the laity. One of these may be that God's people have not understood grace in all its truth. Grace is much more than a doctrine of unmerited favour — though that is part of the truth. We must learn to put aside our trust in fulfilling the law and learn to live by grace.

So what is grace? Grace is true freedom and is the only way that Christians can be free in Christ. Grace is the freedom to be an individual with God — to grow like him according to his specific plan for us without needing to fulfil the impersonal expectations of those under the law. It is the recognition that some are 'hands' and others are 'feet', that it's okay to be an 'elbow' — God's unity is not about sameness. What is true for one Christian at one time is wrong for another — God's sovereign timing overrules all law. Grace is the freedom to grow in faith — to risk looking foolish without fear of censure. Grace is freedom to make innocent mistakes — freedom to step out of the boat onto the water, trusting that we hear his voice correctly and secure in the knowledge that he will catch us if we fall. Grace is learning to proceed at our own pace. Grace is praying for ten and seeing one healed, yet rejoicing for that one and keeping praying. Grace recognises that God is bigger than all of our failures, both doctrinally and practically. Grace is the freedom to seek God's opinion of his word and not limit our faith to the wisdom of others. In short, grace sets us free to let God be God.

Grace is the freedom to truly live, to enjoy God like a child — to experience his love and power and fellowship without feeling the need to be worthy. In essence, as Luke 15: 21–22 says, to live as children of the Father, rather than as hired servants, which is the true desire of God's heart. It frees us from the need to do and allows us simply to be. As Paul says in 2 Corinthians 3: 6: 'For the letter [of the law] kills, but the spirit gives life.'

Most importantly, grace is the freedom to choose, in each and every situation, whether to please God or ourselves. Some will take licence with grace, but that is the risk of liberty; for those whose desire is to please their master, such behaviour is abhorrent. There are no rules where grace rules! Just good or bad consequences from our actions.

❧❧

Most of us have been taught to think of the Old Testament as the law and the New Testament as grace. However, this is not how we have traditionally related to them. The old covenant is the letter, the new covenant is the Spirit.

If we read the New Testament with an old covenant heart, it will only be law to us. We will still have a dead religion in which righteousness is based on compliance with the written commandments rather than on a living relationship with our God. The Bible is a means, not an end. Our goal is not just to know the book of the Lord, but to know the Lord of the book.

Rick Joyner, The Journey Begins

Nothing lasts, except the grace of God by which I stand. In Jesus, I know that I would surely fall away, except for grace by which I'm saved.

Keith Green, Grace by which I Stand

The legalism of the Israelites drove out the presence of God. They kept an outward form of religion, but they let their hearts wander far from God. Legalism always blinds its adherents to the spiritual reality. Legalism drives out the revelatory ministry of the Holy Spirit. Think about that for a minute.

How many legalists have you known?. . . I have heard many people caught in the midst of immorality confess their immorality, but I have never heard a legalist confess legalism. There is something so blinding about that sin. . . Legalism is more than simply following human rules or keeping a correct external behaviour whole, letting our heart run away from God. These are both forms of legalism, but the essence of legalism is trusting in the religious activity, rather than trusting in God. It is putting our confidence in a practice rather than in a Person. And, without fail, this will lead us to love the practice more than the person.

Jack Deere, Surprised by the Power of the Spirit

The tree of knowledge and the tree of life are symbolic of two spiritual lineages or family trees. The Bible, from Genesis to Revelation, is a history of two lineages. . . The tree of knowledge of good and evil is the law. As the Apostle Paul declared: 'The power of sin is the law' (1 Corinthians 15: 56). Satan did not tempt Eve with the fruit of the tree of knowledge just because the Lord had put it off limits. He tempted her with it because the source of his power was rooted in that tree. Furthermore, the Lord did not make it taboo just to test his children. . . he knew it was poison. . . The knowledge of good and evil kills us by distracting us from the One who is the source of life; the tree of life — Jesus.

Rick Joyner, There were Two Trees in the Garden

The revelation of Christ is God's means of transferring to us the spiritual substance, the very nature of Christ. Every time the Lord is revealed, two things occur: we see truth (the reality and purity of God) much more fully than we dreamed possible and we see our need of grace more definitely than before. . . 'Therefore. . . fix your hope completely on the grace to be brought to you at the revelation of Jesus Christ' (1 Peter 1: 13).

Our minds must be fixed on grace, otherwise we will always be overwhelmed and withdrawn from the presence of God. . . we must remind ourselves of God's great mercy and his faithfulness toward us, lest we shrink from him when he commands we draw near. . . He personally receives us to himself, not as perfect beings, but as those whom he seeks to set free.

Francis Frangipane, Holiness,
Truth and the Presence of God

In short, the spirituality and strictness of the law, its severity and its levelling effect, confounding all seeming differences in human characters and stopping every mouth without distinction, are three properties of the law which in our natural state we cannot allow to be good.

These prejudices against the law can only be removed by the power of the Holy Spirit. It is his office to. . . communicate an impression of the majesty, holiness, justice and authority of the God with whom we have to do. . . It is his office likewise to discover the grace and glory of the Saviour, as having fulfilled the law for us. . .

It is not a lawful use of the law to seek justification and acceptance with God by our obedience to it; because it is not appointed for this end or capable of answering it in our circumstances. . . for if righteousness could come by the law, then Christ has died in vain (Galatians 2: 21; 3: 21) . . .The law is lawfully used as a means of conviction of sin. . . The law entered, that sin might abound: not to make us more wicked, though occasionally and by abuse it has that effect, but to make us sensible how wicked we are.

John Newton, *Letters of John Newton:*
The Right Use of the Law

'There were two trees in the Garden'. . . the two trees are a picture of the eternal choice we must make — the choice of whether to embrace a life of relationship with God or one of independence from God. The 'tree of the knowledge of good and evil' offers men and women a chance to go it alone — to obtain and achieve for themselves the necessary elements for 'the good life'. Satan uses that tree to solidify his big lie: 'You have to do to be: If you will eat, you will be like God.' Once the fruit from that tree is eaten, humanity is never released from the need to perform until we die. We are blinded by the need to 'do something'. We not only become performers, but judges of performance — our own and others'.

There are some terrible pitfalls of the 'do to be' mentality.

First, when we succeed in doing something right, we expect God to be pleased and to bless us as a result. Then, if it doesn't happen, we are terribly disillusioned. We also tend to develop pride in accomplishment.

Second, we invariably judge ourselves worthless if we fail. . .

The alternative. . . is the mindset that begins with essence, not performance: who I am, not what I do. And 'who I am' begins with what I was created to be — a person living in intimate communion with God. . . Our lives are most full and satisfying when being defines doing.

Nature defines character. Who we are determines what we do. . . Christians are 'new creatures' — a 'new species' (2 Corinthians 5: 7). We have the nature of Christ in us. . . and this form of life has the capability and desire to live the same way Jesus lived on earth.

Dudley Hall, *Grace Works*

Those in the Puritan movement were devout in their commitment to godly standards. Their problem was that in their human zeal, some of them sought to impose those standards on their natural and spiritual offspring before the Holy Spirit had born those standards in them.

This resulted in some of their followers adhering to those standards outwardly, while inwardly they did not possess the conviction and reality of them. This led to legalism and dead formalism. We walk in a similar tension today. . . We need to experience the liberty of the grace of God while avoiding the pitfalls of being leaders who lack clear biblical New Testament standards of purity and sacrifice. . . We seek to walk in a dynamic tension of maintaining Christian liberty while still being faithful to scriptural standards. The test of whether our standards are legalistic or life-giving is seen in the joy that is released in our hearts.

Mike Bickle, *What About Leadership Standards for the 90s?*

Though it seems a paradox, the law does make grace abound, in the same way darkness makes light shine.

Ray Comfort, *Hell's Best Kept Secret*

Father, I thank you for your unfailing grace that has set me free. I thank you that I am made holy by the sacrifice of your Son. Show me the areas of legalism in my life and grant me grace to surrender them to you without falling into sin. Teach me your ways and restore my joy, that I might truly delight in holiness and righteousness in all the things I do and say. Above all, let me be a minister of your loving grace to others in need, that they may be free.

In Jesus' name, Amen.

A Benediction

Peace to the whole community and love with faith from God the Father and the Lord Jesus Christ. Grace to all who love our Lord Jesus Christ with an undying love.

Ephesians 6: 23–24

Embracing change

Be perfect, therefore, as your heavenly Father is perfect.

Jesus answered him, 'Very truly, I tell you, no-one can see the kingdom of God without being born from above.'

I am the true vine and my Father is the vinegrower. He removes every branch in me that bears no fruit. Every branch that bears fruit he prunes to make it bear more fruit.

I appeal to you therefore, brothers and sisters, by the mercies of God, to present your bodies as a living sacrifice, holy and acceptable to God, which is your spiritual worship. Do not be conformed to this world, but be transformed by the renewing of your minds, so that you may discern what is the will of God — what is good and acceptable and perfect.

So if anyone is in Christ, there is a new creation: everything old has passed away; see, everything has become new!

Then I saw a new heaven and a new earth; for the first heaven and the first earth had passed away, and the sea was no more. . . And I heard a loud voice from the throne saying, 'See, the home of God is among mortals. He will dwell with them as their God; and they will be his peoples, and God himself will be with them; he will wipe every tear from their eyes. Death will be no more; mourning and crying and pain will be no more, for the first things have passed away.'

No-one sews a piece of unshrunk cloth on an old cloak, for the patch pulls away from the cloak and a worse tear is made. Neither is new wine put into old wineskins; otherwise, the skins burst, and the wine is spilled, and the skins are destroyed; but new wine is put into fresh wineskins and so both are preserved.

(Matthew 5: 48; John 3: 3; John 15: 1–2; Romans 12: 1–2; 2 Corinthians 5: 17, Revelation 21: 1 and 3–4; Matthew 9: 16–17 — all NRSV)

Not so many years ago in the Soviet Union, when Christianity was frowned upon, a ten-year-old girl was in trouble at school for standing by her conviction that her Christian faith was something she should devote her life to. She was told that the next day she would be made an example of before the whole school and be critiqued. That night, she asked her church for advice and prayer.

The next day, when she was made to stand before the pupils in a corner of the room, she looked out the window and saw that all the members of her church were silently gathered there, standing with her. For however long she stood there, they stood with her. To her church, she and other children facing similar experiences had proved their Christian maturity. Therefore, with appropriate support, she was encouraged by the church to take her place as a leader and teacher in her church, even though she was so young.

There are many ways we can react to this story. We can, with admiration for the girl, relegate her experience to a particular cultural setting and go on our way as if it has nothing to do with us. On the other hand, we can see this as challenging accepted views about support for one another, the role of children, the nature of leadership, the nature and use of gifts, what Christian maturity is, the roles of women, the nature of teaching and learning — and perhaps others. We are more likely to feel comfortable allowing ourselves to be challenged in this way if we truly believe that the very nature of Christianity is not continuity, but change: change in ourselves, change in others, change in our church, change in society.

I believe it can rightly be argued that the Christian church has existed for 2000 years believing certain fundamental unchanging truths. But these truths involve turning us upside down, not just once at our initial conversion, but throughout our lives again and again as we are confronted by our self-centredness, our greed, our desire for security and comfort, our fear, our single-minded desire for power, sex and money, our arrogance — and a host of other ungodly obsessions. The lesson in this lifetime of critical self-examination can be that change is a constant state for all of us. As someone has paradoxically said, 'The conservative Christian position is change.'

So the appropriate image of the Christian is hand to an ear, listening — listening for the Holy Spirit's prompting, sensitised to that voice coming from perhaps totally unexpected quarters.

A friend of mine says that his purpose in attending a church gathering is to be a different person at the end of the time together than at the beginning. Church should be a transforming experience. But so should everything else. Our work, our home, people we find hard to get on with, mowing the lawn, getting caught in traffic jams, listening to the radio — everything should be seen as containing potential for transformation by the Holy Spirit.

But perhaps the most fertile area for change is solitude, when we give ourselves uninterrupted leisure to listen to the Holy Spirit's perspective on all the experiences of the day, the week, the month that have challenged our preoccupations about ourselves and our world and where we can, in breathless anticipation, open ourselves to the possible changes in perception that God has waiting for us just beyond our line of vision.

⚬✠⚬

Being 'in control' doesn't mean that life will suddenly become orderly and predictable, or that everything will happen to our liking: what it means is that we have seized the initiative; that we have thrown off a victim mentality and decided to accept responsibility for our situation, that we have been prepared to dream of a better future and then take the first tentative steps towards achieving it.

Hugh MacKay, Reinventing Australia

Thirty or forty years ago, fear of the future could be explained on national grounds because of the horrors which the future seemed capable of visiting on us during the years of the Cold War. Today's fear of the future is not so much based on what the future holds as on our inability to chart a confident course through it.

Hugh MacKay, *Reinventing Australia*

Jesus' response to our worry-filled lives is [that he] asks us to shift the point of gravity, to relocate the centre of our attention, to change our priorities. Jesus wants us to move from the 'many things' to the 'one necessary thing'. It is important for us to realise that Jesus in no way wants us to leave our many-faceted world. Rather, he wants us to live in it, but firmly rooted in the centre of all things.

Jesus does not speak about a change of activities, a change in contacts, or even a change of pace. He speaks about a change of heart. This change of heart makes everything different, even while everything appears to remain the same. This is the meaning of 'Set your hearts on his kingdom first . . . and all these other things will be given you as well.' What counts is where our hearts are. When we worry, we have our hearts in the wrong place. Jesus asks us to move our hearts to the centre, where all other things fall into place.

Henri Nouwen, *Making All Things New*

For the Christian, change is the name of the game. Most of us anticipate that as individuals we will change and grow as we progress in our walk with God, and that the growth in maturity will mean changes in the way we live. However, when it comes to our life as a corporate body, as a church, most of us seem to believe that we can grow in maturity as the body of Christ without changing the structures at all — or, at most, with minor tinkerings.

In one of his books, Juan Carlos Ortiz, drawing on the analogy of the human body, points out that we don't expect the clothes of a five-year-old to be suitable for a fifteen-year-old and yet, so often, we expect the struc-tures which give expression to the life of the church to be the same, whether the congregation is five years old or fifty.

Julie Banks

The principle of transfiguration says that nothing, no-one and no situation is 'untransfigurable', that in the very creation, nature waits expectantly for its transfiguration when it will be released from its bondage and share in the glorious liberty of the children of God, when it will not be just dry inert matter, but will be translucent with a divine glory.

The principle of transfiguration avers that an erstwhile persecutor can become the greatest missionary of the truth he once persecuted, that one who denied his Master not once but three times could become the prince of apostles, proclaiming boldly faith in Jesus Christ, when only a short while before he was cowering in abject fear behind locked doors. It is the principle of transfiguration at work when an instrument of the most painful and shameful death can become the life-giving cross, which Christians wear with pride and which is traced over them at significant moments in their life.

Desmond Tutu, The Rainbow People of God

Jesus was masterly at offering the signals needed to reframe the thinking of those he encountered. It illustrates that he was not content with anything less than significant change. And he orchestrated such change in the minds, hearts and bodies of individuals by enabling them to think about things differently, to see the world in a new way, and to experience new openness.

Michael Frost, Jesus the Fool

God's agenda has human beings as its major focus. He is concerned that they should experience the transforming power of Christ's love and live their lives accordingly. But God's agenda is also wider. He is concerned about the whole of society, the whole world and the world that is to come. Clearly, our concerns should also stretch beyond the personal, the family and the church. If God's love is for the whole world, then we should work for change in the whole of our society. But real change can only come when God opens up new possibilities and we are willing to respond appropriately.

Charles Ringma,
Seize the Day with Dietrich Bonhoeffer

Conversion is what happens between birth and death. We are saved every day. We are saved from our self-righteousness, our narrow minds, our own wills, our obstinate clinging. Salvation stands before us at every moment. Our frailty fades into splendour. . . Transformation! This is a wondrous, glorious truth.

Mocrina Wiedekehs,
A Guide to Prayer for All God's People

Love bade me welcome: yet my soul drew back,
Guilty of dust and sinne,
But quick-ey'd Love, observing me grow slack
From my first entrance in,
Drew nearer to me, sweetly questioning
If I lack'd anything.
A guest, I answer'd, worthy to be here:
Love said, You shall be he.
I, the unkind, the ungrateful? Ah, my deare,
I cannot look on thee.
Love took my hand, and smiling did reply,
Who made the eyes but I?
Truth, Lord; but I have marr'd them; let my shame
Go where it doth deserve.
And know you not, says Love, who bore the blame?
My deare, then I will serve.
You must sit down, says Love, and taste my meat.
So I did sit and eat.

George Herbert, 'Love'

O God, you claim me as your partner,
  respecting me,
  trusting me,

tussling with me.
Support me
  as I dare to be vulnerable with you,
encourage me
  as I dare take risks with you,
so together we can transform our world. Amen.

Bridget Rees, 'Partners in Transformation'

Examine me, O God, and change my mind;
test me, and clean my thoughts.
Start the revolution in my life,
create me anew,
and guide me in the way everlasting.

Zephaniah Kameeta, 'Create me anew'

A Benediction

Gracious God, lead us to the company of those who will challenge us to change. Show us ways in which we can become transparently open with ourselves, with others and with you so that that change can come from deep within. Equipped with this insight, show us how we can bless those around us and have a deeper understanding and appreciaton of you and your purposes. Amen.

34

Liberated servants

Fools say in their hearts, 'There is no God.'
They are corrupt, they commit abominable acts: there is no-one who does good.
God looks down from heaven on humankind to see if there are any who are wise, who seek after God.
They have all fallen away, they are all alike perverse; there is no-one who does good, no, not one.
Have they no knowledge, those evildoers, who eat up my people as they eat bread, and do not call upon God?
There they shall be in great terror, in terror such as has not been. For God will scatter the bones of the ungodly; they will be put to shame, for God has rejected them.
O that deliverance for Israel would come from Zion!
When God restores the fortunes of his people, Jacob will rejoice; Israel will be glad.

(Psalm 53, NRSV)

The Christian faith rests on paradoxes. God's own Son exchanged a heavenly robe for a 'nappy'. His power was vested in the weakness of infancy and then in the willing submission of servanthood.

Jesus was able to take both the blame and the punishment which belong to sinful people and make death into life. No follower of Christ can be free without submitting to servanthood.

These concepts can be so familiar to us that we miss their enormous significance unless we probe the contradictions. This paradox, of servanthood making us free, has intrigued me for most of my life. Since childhood, my favourite hymn has been Matheson's 'Make me a captive, Lord,' and I whiled away many long sermons mulling over it.

The hymn explores this paradox with enormous thoroughness. Matheson keeps mixing the imagery of battle — sword and flag, the conqueror, imprisonment, slavery, strife and the resigning of the crown — with images of loving care: 'imprison me within thine arms', 'enslave it with thy matchless love'.

We are reminded by Matheson that fire can be either extinguished or enlivened by the wind. There is a sense in which we risk annihilation as individuals by full surrender to Christ — and yet it is this very surrender that makes us free.

The analogy of the Christian life to marriage is connected with this: we risk losing ourselves by our total commitment to our marriage partner, but we gain in return a liberation which is out of all proportion to that risk of loss. The gain in each case is inexplicable and largely beyond words: it can be a marvel that lasts a lifetime.

Sacrifice hardly rates a mention in the twentieth century. The guiding principles of our hedonistic culture seem to be self-interest and self-definition through career and possessions. They run counter to the ruling paradigms of the Gospels, particularly the calling to be servants and pilgrims passing through.

We are all shaped by our culture to some extent but, as Christ's disciples, we need to test our own presuppositions, prepared for radical changes where we see that our foundation is not in Christ, but in 'me first' secular humanism.

So God offers us the challenge: lose your life to find it; take on Christ's servitude to be free.

Such contradictions, which appear to be mutually exclusive and yet are true at the most profound level, repay our prayerful consideration by renewing our sense that knowing God is at the same time unfathomably complex and utterly simple. This is a truth which nourishes and sustains a lifetime's exploration.

Batter my heart, three person'd God; for, you
As yet but knocke, breathe, shine and seeke to mend;
That I may rise and stand, o'erthrow mee, and bend
Your force, to breake, blow, burn and make me new.
I, like an usurpt town, to another due,
Labour to admit you, but Oh, to no end,
Reason your viceroy in mee, mee should defend
But is captiv'd, and proves weake or untrue.
Yet dearely I love you, and would be loved faine,
But am betroth'd unto your enemie;
Divorce mee, untie, or breake that knot againe,
Take mee to you, imprison mee, for I,
Except you enthrall mee, never shall be free,
Nor ever chast, except you ravish mee.

John Donne, Holy Sonnets

What distinguishes the present moral order. . . from that
of earlier generations?   Simply this: today's secular
*mind*set rests as never before upon a nonbiblical *will*set.

Carl Henry,
The Christian Mindset in a Secular Society

Make me a captive, Lord,
And then I shall be free;
Force me to render up my sword,
And I shall conqueror be.
I sink in life's alarms
When by myself I stand;
Imprison me within thine arms,
And strong shall be my hand.

My heart is weak and poor
Until it master find;
It has no spring of action sure —
It varies with the wind.
It cannot freely move,
Till thou hast wrought its chain:
Enslave it with thy matchless love,
And deathless it shall reign.

My power is faint and low
Till I have learned to serve;
It wants the needed fire to glow,
It wants the breeze to nerve;
It cannot drive the world,
Until itself be driven;
Its flag can only be unfurled
When thou shalt breathe from heaven.

My will is not my own
Till thou has made it thine;
If it would reach a monarch's throne,
It must its crown resign;
It only stands unbent
Amid the clashing strife,
When on thy bosom it has leant
And found in thee its life.

George Matheson

Christians live not for themselves but for others. And they do this freely 'in the freest servitude'. Thus, we also follow the example of Christ, our Lord. Christ gave up his all for us and took the form of a servant. So we should also do for others.

Bernhard Christensen, *The Inward Pilgrimage*

I am no longer my own, but thine. Put me to what thou wilt, rank me with whom thou wilt; put me to doing, put me to suffering; let me be employed for thee or laid aside for thee, exalted for thee or brought low for thee; let me be full, let me be empty; let me have all things, let me have nothing; I freely and heartily yield all things to thy pleasure and disposal. And now, O glorious and blessed God, Father, Son and Holy Spirit, thou art mine and I am thine. So be it. And the covenant which I have made on earth, let it be ratified in heaven.

Renewal of the Covenant with God,
The Book of Offices

'Humble yourselves therefore under the mighty hand of

God, that he may exalt you in due time' (1 Peter 5: 6).

This is tantamount to a promise: if we will bow down, the Lord will lift us up. Humility leads to honour: submission is the way to exaltation. That same hand of God which presses us down is waiting to raise us up when we are prepared to bear the blessing. We stoop to conquer. Many cringe before others and yet miss the patronage they crave; but those who humble themselves under the hand of God shall not fail to be enriched, uplifted, sustained and comforted by the ever-gracious One. It is a habit of Jehovah to cast down the proud and lift up the lowly.

C.H. Spurgeon,
The Cheque Book of the Bank of Faith

Although Christians are thus free from all works, they ought in this liberty to empty themselves, take upon themselves the form of a servant, serve, help and in every way deal with their neighbours as they see that God through Christ has dealt and still deals with them.

Martin Luther, *Christian Liberty*

Lord God, why are we so afraid to give ourselves utterly to you? Do we think that independence from you will make us whole, that we know better than you, our Maker, who we are and what we should become? Or do we fear our little selves will be so subsumed in your largeness as to be utterly insignificant?

Your Son did not offer into your hands such portions of his spirit as you could be trusted with, but all, without reserve, and it was painful. It is painful to us too, Lord, to relinquish our hopes of becoming something without you.

But we recognise your call, daily, and we ask you to help us let go, to let go of a self that is separate from you, that holds back little corners of independence from your care. We accept the risk of relinquishing our central self to you, so that our wheel of life may spin smoothly around you, its centre, no matter how rough the road.

We celebrate the life you make from death, the slavery you transform into freedom, the eternity you carve out of time.

We thank you for the privilege of being yours.
In the name of your son Jesus, Amen.

A Benediction
To him who is able to keep you from falling and to present you
before his glorious presence without fault and with great joy —
to the only God our Saviour be glory, majesty, power and
authority, through Jesus Christ our Lord, before all ages, now
and forevermore! Amen.

Jude 24 and 25, NIV

35

We all have an audience. . .

[Jesus] began to speak first to his disciples, 'Beware of the yeast of the Pharisees, that is, their hypocrisy.'

And whenever you pray, do not be like the hypocrites; for they love to stand and pray in the synagogues and at the street corners, so that they may be seen by others. Truly, I tell you, they have received their reward.

Woe to you, scribes and Pharisees, hypocrites! For you tithe mint, dill and cummin, and have neglected the weightier matters of the law: justice and mercy and faith. It is these you ought to have practised without neglecting the others. You blind guides! You strain out a gnat, but swallow a camel!

Woe to you, scribes and Pharisees, hypocrites! For you clean the outside of the cup and of the plate, but inside they are full of greed and self-indulgence. You blind Pharisee! First, clean the inside of the cup, so that the outside also may become clean.

Woe to you, scribes and Pharisees, hypocrites! For you are like whitewashed tombs, which on the outside look beautiful, but inside are full of the bones of the dead and of all kinds of filth. So you also on the outside look righteous to others, but inside you are full of hypocrisy and lawlessness.

You hypocrites! Isaiah prophesied rightly about you when he said: 'This people honours me with their lips, but their hearts are far from me; in vain do they worship me, teaching human precepts as doctrines.'

But when Cephas came to Antioch, I opposed him to his face, because he stood self-condemned; for until certain people came from James, he used to eat with the

Gentiles. But after they came, he drew back and kept himself separate for fear of the circumcision faction. And the other Jews joined him in this hypocrisy, so that even Barnabas was led astray by their hypocrisy.

Therefore, rid yourselves of all malice and all deceit, hypocrisy, envy and slander of every kind.

(Luke 12: 1b; Matthew 6: 5; 23: 23–28; 15: 7–9; Galatians 2: 11–13 — all NRSV; I Peter 2: 1, NIV)

How often do we hear people say, 'Christians? They're nothing but a bunch of hypocrites.' Sadly, we cannot dispute them. It's true we are hypocritical; but then, so is everybody else. Christians are not necessarily more hypocritical than others; they are just more ashamed of it.

Somehow, we have managed to give the world the impression that we think we are better than everybody else, when what makes us Christians is that we are aware of the fact that we are bad.

It is all too easy, when talking evangelism, to outline desirable Christian behaviour in a manner which indicates that we ourselves actually manage to behave in this way. Other people get the idea that we are holding ourselves up as examples, when in fact the only example of Christian behaviour is Jesus himself.

Everybody is hypocritical. Our society teaches hypocrisy as a way of life. An example is the football fan who stands on the sideline screaming advice to the players, advice which he knows he could not carry out and would not carry out if he could. Or the parent who insists to the bemused child, 'Don't do what I do, do what I say.'

Perhaps some expressions of Christian faith are too much talk and too little action. We talk about serving the poor and yet our churches have billions of dollars of potential to save starving children locked up in buildings, vestments, chalices, candlesticks and other treasures. Some of our churches worship mammon instead of Christ and, worse than that, they are efforts to make Jesus worship mammon. Our Lord lived, died and was resurrected in holy poverty — and yet we try to force him to live on in arrogant wealth. How much more hypocritical can we get?

Part of our fallen human heritage is to be hypocritical, but we cannot combat it until we realise it and admit it; not merely to God, but also to ourselves and to each other. All Christians are hypocrites, because all people are hypocrites. The difference between Christians and non-Christians should be that Christians keep trying to do something about it, whilst the non-Christian is unaware of failing in this way.

Without divine justice, charity and mercy, our churches may be merely congregations of Pharisees. Jesus said that those of us in such congregations are in danger of being 'the children of the Devil'.

So let's try to bring Jesus back into our lives — and into the church and all its works.

❧

Besides the selling of Christian music, Keith was also grieved by all the Christian merchandising going on. Everyday items like clocks, coasters, drinking mugs and wallets were selling for twice their usual price just because some enterprising Christian — or non-Christian — stamped a dove or a fish on them. We'd actually seen ads for Christian doggie sweaters — and even Christian ashtrays!

Then one day, we saw what we felt was the ultimate slap in the face to Jesus. Browsing through a large Christian bookstore, we came across a handmade ceramic piggy bank. Engraved on the side of this plump little pig were the words, 'Jesus saves'. We felt sick at heart.

It seemed that selling Christian products was very big business — not only in Christian bookstores, but at festivals as well. I was with Keith the day someone told us that at one Jesus festival they sold over $98,000 worth of 'Jesus junk' in just a few days! Keith nearly fell over from hearing those two words casually linked together.

'Jesus — and junk?' He said angrily, 'Those must be the two most opposite words in the English language!'

On the one hand, Keith saw Christian ashtrays, doggie

sweaters and piggy banks. And on the other hand, he saw Jesus — like a pure, white rose — crushed beneath tons of garbage and debris, his sacrifice and his heart cry sinking from view.

Melody Green and David Hazard,
No Compromise: The Life Story of Keith Green

I remember one day the hierarchy of the church put on an enormous garden party in one of the big homes. These were delegates from all over the world and there were impoverished people really looking over the fence at the people gorging themselves. On Christmas Eve, there was a party. . . and we sang carols and hymns. Two lines that stuck in my mind at the time we were singing were the lines: 'Christ to the world we bring, The world to Christ we bring.' It all seemed like so much irrelevant and hypocritical nonsense to me.

I walked out of the party, thinking about these things, and went down into the streets where there were scores and scores of people just lying in the gutters asleep. I was sickened by the hypocrisy and irrelevance of it all. . .

Bob Hawke speaking to Terry Lane in
As the Twig is Bent

I live among people the world tells me are kind, pious, Christian people. And they seem to me crueller than the cruellest heathens, stupider than the stupidest animals. I cannot believe that the truth is so. That life is without understanding or compassion. That there are not people generous enough to understand what I have suffered and why I suffer. . . and that, whatever sins I have committed, it is not right that I should suffer so much.

John Fowles, *The French Lieutenant's Woman*

Hypocrisy is a religious catastrophe. . . It is a personality flaw, an error in judgment, and spiritual paralysis. . . Hypocrisy is not something to smile about, but it is something that is absolutely devastating so far as one's religion is concerned. . .

We must stand at the foot of the cross of Calvary and

realise what God has done for us in the Lord Jesus Christ. At the cross we realise how great the grace of God is and we realise, too, how desperately we need it. Hypocrites are proud of all the great religious good works they have done, but when hypocrites stand at Calvary's cross, they see that all of their so-called good works are worthless. They see how great Christ's payment for sin has been and realise that they can do nothing to earn their own salvation. Hypocrisy dies at the cross.

Back to God Hour, 'The Trouble with Hypocrisy'

We all have an audience by whom we play our lives and by whom we are tremendously affected. Who, then, will it be — our peers, who can offer us only bondage and stifling limitation, or the Father, who will lead us more and more to be all we were meant to be? Inevitably, we will take on the image of our audience. Whose image will it be — our peers on earth, or our Father in heaven?

John Claypool, *The Light within You*

Lord, help me in my waywardness; I read your words and yet do not follow them. I shut my ears to your voice and, when I do hear your voice, I do not listen to what you say. I tell others to live lives of Christian example and yet I fail again and again to do so myself.

Father, I am unworthy of your love.

Lord, help me in my weakness; I wander from your way and follow the falsehoods of the world, chasing the illusions of success and dreams of the false happiness of riches — and yet all the while I call myself your child and your servant.

Father, I am unworthy of your sacrifice.

Lord, help me to overcome my pride; I show the world my Christian face and yet, within my mind, I listen to the lies and promises of the evil one. Time and again, I weaken and fall into sinful ways and thoughts.

Father, without you I am nothing. Be my guide and my guardian. Take my life and shape me upon the wheel of your world as potters shape the clay with their hands. Lord, teach me to be true. Amen.

A Benediction

May God our Father guard you and guide you through all the temptations of life. May he gently show you the pathway of truth, the power of repentance and the strength of honest example.

May he protect you when you stray from the way which he has brightly lit for you, when you dart after the trumpery glitter of Satan's tinsel, and may he softly bring you back to his grace and mercy.

May our Lord Jesus walk with you, holding your heart and your mind close to his, that you may leave aside the world's deceits and grow closer to him in thought, in word and in behaviour.

May the Lord's love and resurrected life be always a beacon of truth shining forth from your mind and your life and lighting the path for those who walk in the shadows lit only by the dim glow of worldly delights. May the Lord teach you to be true. Amen.

Love the Lord your God with all your heart and with all your soul and with all your strength. Do not follow other gods, the gods of the peoples around you; for the Lord your God, who is among you, is a jealous God and his anger will burn against you and he will destroy you from the face of the land.

The Spirit lifted me up between earth and heaven and in visions of God he took me to Jerusalem, to the entrance of the north gate of the inner court, where the idol that provokes jealousy stood. . . Then, he said to me, 'Son of man, look toward the north.' So I looked, and in the entrance north of the gate of the altar I saw this idol of jealousy.

They have moved me to jealousy with that which is not God; they have provoked me to anger with their vanities. . .

Love not the world, neither the things that are in the world. . . [For] love is as strong as death, its jealousy unyielding as the grave. It burns like blazing fire, like a mighty flame.

Anger is cruel and fury overwhelming, but who can stand before jealousy?

The acts of the sinful nature are obvious: sexual immorality, impurity and debauchery; idolatry and withcraft; hatred, discord, jealousy, fits of rage, selfish ambition, dissensions, factions and envy; drunkenness, orgies and the like. I warn you as I did before, that those who live like this will not inherit the kingdom of God.

You are still worldly. For since there is jealousy and

quarrelling among you, are you not worldly? Are you not behaving according to human inclinations?

Let us behave decently as in the daytime, not in orgies and drunkenness, not in sexual immorality and debauchery, not in disssension and jealousy. Rather, clothe yourselves with the Lord Jesus Christ and do not think about how to gratify the desires of sinful nature.

(Deuteronomy 6: 5,14–15; Ezekiel 8: 3, 5 — both NIV; Deuteronomy 32: 21; I John 2: 15 — both KJV; Song of Solomon 8: 6; Proverbs 27: 4; Galatians 5: 19-21 — all NIV; I Corinthians 3: 3, NIV/NRSV; Romans 13:13–14, NIV)

Jealousy is something which affects almost all of us at some time or another and is one of Satan's most savage weapons against us. Where does it come from, this surging feeling of pain, rage and hatred, which maroons us in a cell of solitary agony?

It stems from our breaking the Lord's greatest commandment — and at the same time expecting someone else to do the same.

Our love for someone can be so warped that it becomes completely exclusive. It shuts out everything and anything else and then it becomes utterly possessive and self-consuming. We start to expect and demand that the object of such an idolatry devote his/her complete attention, devotion and worship to us — and to us alone. We want absolutely all of her/his mental, emotional and physical worship.

We don't get it; we don't deserve it and we shouldn't have it. We are so blinded by our own solipsism — theories about the self being the only object of real knowledge or that nothing but self exists — that we blame the object of our passion for their inability to be the idol which we are trying to make of them. At the same time, we blame them for their inability to make of us the idol we wish to be to them.

Jealousy comes from one individual trying to usurp the place of God in the mind and heart of another individual. It comes from trying to steal from God what is rightfully his and his alone, namely worship.

To avoid or overcome jealousy, we must give back to God what belongs to him. Worshipping another human being will lead inevitably to disaster; desiring to be worshipped by another human being is a disaster. Giving our worship back to God will bring back the peace and happiness for which we long so desperately. (Jealousy is merely the direct result of ignoring the Manufacturer's Instruction Book.)

Jealousy's cousin, envy, has similar results, though different causes. The big danger in envy is not simply the desiring of what another has, but the feelings about that other person which those desires may engender. There are very short steps between 'Isn't he/she lucky?', 'What has he/she done to deserve that when I haven't got it?', 'What right have they got to have what I can't have?' — and finally, 'I hate those spoiled, stuck-up people!'

God has chosen everyone's place in life and the opportunities which they are given. To be angry at someone simply because they seem to have more of what we want than we do is to rage against God. It is also pretty silly, because it assumes that material advantages take away unhappiness — and that assumption is one of Satan's favourite lies. To envy another's happiness is merely to throw away our own happiness for the sake of indulging in a hateful and profitless emotion.

❧

In the highly complex and competitive world of AIDS vaccine research, no other scientist is using Salk's approach, which involves using a killed form of the AIDS virus, mostly because no other scientist believes it will work. As always, Salk is going it alone — the sceptics and the nay-sayers be damned.

'Of course,' says Salk, 'I know that there are those that are waiting for failure, but my answer to that is that there is no such thing as failure. You can only fail if you stop too soon.'

His life, he says, is a 'consistent pattern' that began early in his career. 'I've been told, by one of my mentors,

"Damn it, Salk, why don't you do things the way everybody else does them?"'

Sheryl Stolberg, 'Jonas Salk'

Envy may be defined as sadness or discontent over the good fortune of a fellow human because that good fortune stands in the way of something we crave for ourselves. People who give in to envy look with undisguised glee at the troubles of their victims and indulge their cruelty by adding to these troubles whenever possible.

Envious persons are painfully and resentfully conscious of some advantage others enjoy; their minds become a breeding-ground for yearnings to secure the same advantage. Envious people nurse a grievance against others whose blessings seem to prove a stumbling block to their own excellence and glory.

'Envy,' said St John Baptist de la Salle, 'is a criminal sorrow for the welfare of our neighbour.'

Florence Wedge, Environs?

Women are more likely than men are to try to make their partners jealous. And when an interloper threatens an intimate relationship, women generally react by trying to save the relationship, while men more often concentrate on saving face.

Virginia Adams, 'Jealous Love'

In all its manifestations, jealousy springs essentially from self-doubt, a lack of self-esteem, feelings of inadequacy — all those things that psychotherapists lump under the heading of 'low self-image'. For example, I asked the men and women I talked with what was one thing their partners might do that would make them most jealous. Only a few nominated sexual infidelity. Most mentioned situations that threatened their self-esteem: If he talked with old friends about things I didn't know, and I felt left out. . . When everybody clusters round her at a party and ignores me. . .

To confront such jealousy — to convert it from a negative to a potentially positive reaction — requires, says psychoanalyst Rollo May, 'turning one's attention to oneself asking: Why is my self-esteem so low in the first place? This question may be difficult, but at least it turns your concern to an area that you can do something about.'

All too often, we permit jealousy to deteriorate into feelings of guilt or self-pity or helplessness. 'Poor me!' is what jealousy says then. But jealousy can be used to motivate us to constructive action: to examine our emotional needs more intelligently; to do something positive about shortcomings; to work harder at a relationship; even to voice an honest cry for help — to say, 'I love you. . . I'm afraid of what's happening and I need you to help me stop it.'

When allowed to go unquestioned, jealousy remains malevolent. Examined in the light of reason, it can be a stimulus to growth.

Norman Lobsenz, 'How to Cope with Jealousy'

Lord, our souls cry out with remorse, for all our lives we have longed so much to be loved and have forgotten you whose love is perfect.

Our hearts have ached for the love of others and have not realised that your perfect love has been ours all along. At times, in the physical demonstration of love, we have given to others the love which we owed to you.

Forgive our foolishness, Lord, for we are weak and sinful.

We have loved so many, not in generous freedom, but demanding their love for us in return.

Forgive us, Lord, for our emotional greed.

We have misunderstood so much — and yet have gloried in our understanding and in the intellect which you have given us.

Forgive us, Lord, for our pride and arrogance.

In our conceit, we have presumed to teach and, as a result of our pride, have inflicted pain and grief upon those who loved us.

Forgive, Lord, our selfishness and lift away the burdens of guilt which our sin has laid upon others.

Lord, grant us your mercy. Amen.

A Benediction

May our heavenly Father look kindly upon us as we strive to overcome the torments of selfish emotions.

May our Lord show us how we can love with open generosity, teach us how to love those who are as little deserving as we are, and shield us from expressing our love in inappropriate ways.

May the Holy Spirit of God guard us from the distortions which twist love into an evil expression of self-admiration; and protect us from the dangers of becoming lost in Satan's confusing webs of sexual lust.

May God teach us how in service we can be thankful for his love — undeserved but perfect — and may he grant us peace and joy in all the turmoils that surround us. Amen.

37

Faith

But the fruit of the Spirit is love, joy, peace, longsuffering, gentleness, goodness, faith. . . Now, faith is the substance of things hoped for, the evidence of things not seen. . . By faith, we understand that the universe was formed at God's command, so that what is seen was not made out of what was visible.

If you have faith as small as a mustard seed, you can say to this mulberry tree, 'Be uprooted and planted in the sea,' and it will obey you. . . I tell you the truth, if you have faith as small as a mustard seed, you can say to this mountain, 'Move from here to there' and it will move. Nothing will be impossible for you.

'Have faith in God,' Jesus answered. 'I tell you the truth, if anyone says to this mountain, "Go, throw yourself into the sea," and does not doubt. . . but believes you. . . it will be done. Therefore I tell you, whatever you ask for in prayer, believe that you have received it and it will be yours.'

In the same way, faith by itself, if it is not accompanied by action, is dead. But someone will say, 'You have faith; I have deeds.' Show me your faith without deeds and I will show you my faith by what I do.

Jesus said to him, 'If you are able! All things can be done for the one who believes.' Immediately, the father of the child cried out, 'I believe; help my unbelief!'

For to one is given by the Spirit the word of wisdom; to another, the word of knowledge by the same Spirit; to another, faith by the same Spirit. . .

(Galatians 5: 22; Hebrews 11: 1 — both KJV; Hebrews 11: 3; Luke 17: 6; Matthew 17: 20; Mark 11: 22–24; James 2: 17–18 — all NIV;

Mark 9: 23–24, NRSV; I Corinthians 12: 8–9, KJV)

When Jesus told us that if we had faith the size of a mustard seed, we could move mountains, he was pointing out that the very tiniest part of the faith available to us carried the most awesome power.

Incredible power from God is available to us if we have enough faith. However, the measure must be qualitative as well as quantitative. When we pray for healing, either for ourselves or for someone else, we need faith — not merely faith that the healing will be granted, but faith in Christ himself and in his competence and abilities.

We must have faith in the fact that, no matter what the apparent result of our prayer, it has been heard and answered according to God's will (which is, after all, what we should have prayed for in the first place). We may not see what we want to see — our beloved may not be returned to health — but, if we have prayed for healing and for the will of God to be done, we must have faith that it will be done and has been done. We must accept and, if we can, welcome the result, all the while persisting in faithful prayer.

If we can command mountains to move and trees to uproot themselves and plant themselves in the sea, empowered by a tiny fragment of the faith which God has made available to us, what might we achieve with a good-sized chunk of it? If instead of a mustard seed-sized faith, we had an apple-sized faith or perhaps a soccer ball-sized faith, what staggering wonders we could achieve.

But what is faith? It is much more than mere belief. After all, the devil has belief: he knows the reality of God and his majesty and power far better than we do. The faith we need is a combination of identification, belief (both in God and of God), hope, confidence, 'understanding without the demand for understanding' and absolute trust.

We begin by becoming aware of who God is. God's identity is only available to us in God's own terms. He says 'I am' or, in extrapolation, 'I am that which exists entire unto itself and without which nothing else exists.' He creates all by the combination of will and very existence. God's Son Jesus is far easier to know, for he came and made himself knowable to us.

To believe means knowing as much of God's nature as he has revealed to us — mainly by studying the life and teachings of Jesus. It means being willing to accept the truth of what he has told us, both about himself and about ourselves. It means cultivating hope, by which I mean belief-backed expectation, and thus to gain confidence in God, his love for us and his power.

To believe means to seek to understand all that God chooses to reveal to us. It is easy to turn away from something which our selfishness finds unpalatable and refuse to accept or comprehend it because we simply don't want to. At the same time, we do not have the right to demand the ability to understand more than God decides is good for us.

We need to combine all of those factors to try to achieve complete trust in God, his love, his power and his plan for us and our lives.

Where does faith come from and how can we obtain it? The answer is that it comes from the same place as everything else does — from God. Faith is a free gift. We get it by asking for it and it is the first and most important thing for which we should pray.

❧❧

Nowhere does the Bible suggest that a person should believe without strong reasons or act blindly with no firm assurance of the outcome. Faith connotes something quite other than wishful thinking. It is the conviction that certain propositions are true. And it has as its primary object a Person. Faith is seeing as opposed to not seeing. It is having certainty as opposed to speculation.

To have faith is to be convinced. But in the process, human faculties are not stifled or ignored. In fact, all systems are go! Facts and reasoning are not enemies of faith, but friends. Nevertheless, faith takes us further than reason ever can. It brings us beyond reason's uncertainties as it is concerned with a self-revealing God. The outcome of knowing him is trusting him and, in this way, the whole of one's life is affected. Attitudes and decisions are taken on the basis of his trustworthiness.

This is not to deny the presence of the famous 'risky' element in faith. However, this is not in the act of faith itself, but in the circumstances of its exercise. All the information which would satisfy natural curiosity is not given to us. We have no promise that faith will unlock every mystery. But though the truth it sees is not exhaustive, it is nevertheless true. There are times when faith will feel that it is walking a tightrope, but it knows that the rope will hold and the walk is worth making.

Anonymous, *Believing is Seeing*

What is faith? It is made up of three things — *knowledge, belief* and *trust*.

Knowledge comes first.

I have to be informed of a fact before I can possibly believe it. We must first hear, in order that we may know what is to be believed.

The *mind* goes on to believe that these things are true. The *soul* believes that God is and that he hears the cries of sincere hearts; that the gospel is from God; that justification by faith is the grand truth which God has revealed in these last days by his Spirit more clearly than before. Then, the *heart* believes that Jesus is verily and in truth our God and Saviour, our Redeemer, the Prophet, Priest and King of his people. All this is accepted as sure truth, not to be called in question.

The difference between common faith and saving faith lies mainly in the subjects upon which it is exercised. Believe the witness of God just as you believe the testimony of your own father or friend.

So far you have made an advance toward faith. Only one more ingredient is needed to complete it, which is *trust*. Commit yourself to the merciful God. Rest your hope on the gracious gospel. Trust your soul on the dying and living Saviour.

Charles H. Spurgeon, 'What is Faith?'

Faith always implies an object — that is, when we believe, we must believe something. That something I call the 'fact'. Let me give you, then, three words — three words that must always be kept in the same order and never rearranged, three words that will point you the way out of uncertainty to a confident Christian life. These words are: fact, faith and feeling. They come in this order and the order is essential. If you confuse them, eliminate one or add to them, you will end up in the mire of despair and continue to grope about in semidarkness, without the joy and confidence of one who can say, 'I know whom I have believed.'

If you are saved from sin, you are saved through a personal faith in the gospel of Christ as defined in the scriptures. Though it may at first seem dogmatic and narrow to you, the fact remains that there is no other way.

Billy Graham, 'Facts, Faith and Feelings'

Faith is the dimension that reaches upward and claims the power of God. The word faith, of course, is by no means an exclusively religious word. We all live by faith in something or someone. It is nonsense to regard faith as an extra, an addendum tagged onto the tail of life, a sort of desperate last resort, rather than a basic necessity undergirding the whole of our existence. Faith fills every horizon and fashions every philosophy. Even so, we often get faith wrong when we think of it in the specifically Christian context.

Some think of it as credulity. H.L. Mencken, the cynical American journalist, defined faith as 'an illogical belief in the occurrence of the improbable'. In Lewis Carroll's *Through the Looking Glass*, the White Queen says, 'Now I'll give you something to believe. I'm just a hundred and one, five months and a day.' 'I can't believe that,' replied Alice. 'Can't you?' said the Queen, pityingly. 'I dare say you haven't had much practice. Why, sometimes I've believed as many as six impossible things before breakfast.'

But Christian faith is emphatically not blind credulity! The first and great commandment is that we should love the Lord our God with all our mind, as well as with our heart, soul and strength. God wants our heads as well as our hearts. To think and to think hard is a Christian duty and to believe without doing so is not a Christian virtue, but superstition.

Others think of faith as credence. It is merely subscription to abstract religious truths — assent to what the Bible and the church teach about God and Christ and the Holy Spirit. Such barren orthodoxy, believing with the 'top' of the mind but not at the bottom of the heart, is not real faith.

Pierpoint Morgan, the American oil millionaire, believed the Bible from cover to cover. Once asked if he believed that the whale swallowed Jonah, he replied that if the Bible said that Jonah swallowed the whale, he would believe it! But his personal life and business conduct were hardly examples of saving faith.

What then is faith? Christian faith abides forever. Not blind credulity; not mere credence. It is the dimension that reaches upward and claims the power of God, that lifts us out of earth's material and temporal boundaries, that links our littleness with God's greatness, our weakness with God's strength.

John Gladstone, 'The Dimensions of Christian Living'

I was talking with a very attractive older couple. The man was seriously ill and they were both seeking some kind of new spiritual reality. The wife, a lovely, intelligent and active woman, said to me very candidly: 'All of my life I've believed in God. I've gone to church. But now I've met some people who get far more out of their Christianity than I do. They have a dimension I never knew was there. And I don't know what more I have to do to get it.'

I pointed to a chair on the porch where we were sitting. 'A carpenter,' I said, 'might make that chair. He might keep it in his house for years, even give it a name and take it to church! But it would always be his creation, never his child. A child is born, not made. All [humans] are God's creatures, but only those who know they are sinners and put their trust in the Lord Jesus Christ as their Saviour and Lord are God's children.'

Leighton Ford

If Christianity were reducible to mere psychology, common factors would show themselves revealing believers to be 'of a kind'. But the hard facts falsify the idea. Who can deny that all temperaments, backgrounds, educational and intellectual levels are well represented among believers? I have personally known extroverts who have gone to hear Christian addresses with the intent of sheer destructive criticism, who have returned humbled possessors of faith in Christ.

Anonymous, 'Believing is Seeing'

Trusting.
You ask how you learn to trust him?
Dear child, you must just let go!
Let go of your frantic worry,
And the fears which plague you so;
Let go of each black tomorrow
Which you try to live today;
Let go of your fevered planning,
He's with you all the way.
Fear not lest your slipping fingers
Let go of your Saviour, too —
Trusting is only knowing
He'll not let go of you.

Martha Snell Nicholson

Lord, I believe. . . help my unbelief. Lord, have mercy on me and give me the gift of faith that my mind and soul may be at peace. Again and again, Lord, in the toils and labours of life I forget to have faith — the frantic pace of my worldly pursuits drives your presence from my mind.

Lord, forgive me and grant me a living (and working) faith.

My worries and fears are swept away on the cooling waves of faith in you. Lord, you are the strength which I lack. You are the security which I struggle to find.

Lord, forgive me for losing myself in the turbulence of worldly matters. Grant me your peace.

These three are left: faith, hope and love. For all three I pray, Lord; for faith that I may learn hope, for hope that in its security I may find love, and for love so that all who surround me will see in my love the expression of my faith.

In the name of Jesus whose willing death for me has given me the right to use his name, I pray. **Amen.**

A Benediction

May God our Father bless you with the safety and peace which only his gift of faith can bring.

May he lift you away from the pains and fears caused by our endless pursuit of earthly success.

May our Lord Jesus fill you with the strength and joy which faith in him provides.

May he walk with you through all the paths of your life and fill you with the awareness of his presence.

May the Holy Spirit empower you and make his faith a visible light in your life.

May he send you your armour of faith to keep you in health, happiness and love all the days of your life. **Amen.**

Eat your heart out

There was once a rich man who dressed in the most expensive clothes and lived in great luxury every day. There was also a poor man named Lazarus, covered with sores, who used to be brought to the rich man's door, hoping to eat the bits of food that fell from the rich man's table. Even the dogs would come and lick his sores.

Jesus said to his host: 'When you give a lunch or a dinner, do not ask your friends, brothers, relations or rich neighbours, for fear they repay your courtesy by inviting you in return. No; when you have a party, invite the poor, the crippled, the lame, the blind; that they cannot pay you back means that you are fortunate.'

The Lord your God is bringing you into a prosperous land of streams and springs, of waters that well up deep in the valleys and hills, of wheat and barley. . . a land where you will eat bread without stint, where you will want nothing, where the stones are of iron, where the hills may be quarried for copper. . .

When you have eaten and had all you want, when you have built fine houses to live in, when you have seen. . . your silver and gold abound and all your possessions grow great, do not become proud of heart. Do not forget your God. Beware of saying in your heart: My own strength and the might of my own hand won this power for me. Remember your God; it was he who gave you this strength.

(Luke 16: 19–21; Luke 14: 12–14; Deuteronomy 8: 7–18)

'I came that you may have life, and have it more abundantly,' Jesus said, 'with a complete wardrobe each, three large meals a day and all the nibbles you want in between' (middle-class translation). No? It doesn't say that? Then, what does Jesus promise to fill us with? What did the early church 'pig out' on?

His last meal with the disciples may not have been a MacSupper. (Options have been limited until the late arrival this century of 'nothing' foods.) Celebrations in first century Palestine certainly featured all-you-can-eat hospitality, but they seem to have been rare. The Gospels tell of our Lord's frequent day-long journeys where thirst was chronic, never mind one's hunger. And there are enough cases of malnutrition during Paul's travels and in Acts to assume first-century waistlines were trimmer than ours.

But does it matter? Are they lesser followers who fancy croissants and butter instead of skim milk yoghurt? Do we lose our inheritance by yielding to Tzatziki temptation? Your answer depends on what you think God means by abundance. But you will have to answer.

Gorging isn't new. Old Testament banquets sound like a Sizzler overdose, and Jesus' image of the rich man wasn't an isolated case. Having tucker on the table when friends drop in is as timeless as it is universal, limited only by what's in the fridge.

When a family walked all day to get to your home, nourishment was more a necessity than an indulgence. The Emmaus Road pair who put bread before Jesus would have been ravenous. And if Martha's catering duties kept her flat out the day Lazarus came back, it might have been because her Lord had travelled for three days to get there. Little would have been available en route.

No recorded event tells of Jesus or the disciples eating more than their body needed. Twentieth-century humans are the only animals who eat when they aren't hungry.

How expensive is it to eat well?

* About $30 000 for a triple bypass. You are free to be a middle-aged gourmet; you can also avoid pain

and illness in old age; but you can't have both.
* Butter and bacon were fine at fourteen, but at forty they're poison.
* Four litres of icecream may cost only $5 in the supermarket, but blood pressure tablets cost a lot more.
* Think about it: will fried fish 'n chips give you a better feeling than avoiding a stroke?
* Is the convenience MacDonald's offers greater than the inconvenience to your schedule of a heart attack?

Physical factors aside, what is eating your fill likely to cost? Answer: a decade or two out of your life, if the habit grows as fast as you do. Jesus emphasised that nobody should become captive to anything except him, certainly not the flesh.

Remember seeing penniless comic-strip characters wearing a barrel because they can't afford clothes? Looks awkward, doesn't it? You can choose whether you want to become one. Can you overcome the temptation to let a barrel of flesh grow around you? Will you be a prisoner inside your own body, too heavy to walk the Emmaus Road? Will the service you owe the kingdom be shortened by the hours needed to rest your frame, by the decades cut off in your untimely demise?

What witness can we give to those addicted to drugs or alcohol if we are addicted to over-eating? We stand a slim chance. How will the starving millions accept our God of love for others if we are visibly self-indulgent? 'It does a fat lot of good!'

'Coke Adds Life' blares the jingle. We know better — Jesus is the giver of life, in this world and the next. But who refreshes us? Does our revival come from the communion cup or a red and white can?

❈❈❈

Is God really interested in what I had for breakfast this morning? When I'm in my local newsagent's trying to choose between forking out for a Mars Bar or a tube of Smarties, should I ask his advice? Is it okay to be overweight or obsessed with diets *and* be a friend of Jesus?

Like sleep, oxygen and water, food is a basic necessity. The rich variety of labourings, tastes, colours and texture reveal something of God's wondrous creativity and the goodness of his gifts. Yet for many, food represents a life of tyranny, an uncontrollable obsession of plain old poison for others. Not to mention those who simply don't have enough. Somewhere along the line we seem to have forgotten to look out for the mark of our creator on the food we eat.

For when Jesus declared to the devil that we cannot live by bread alone, he emphasised the importance of spiritual sustenance, too. If we are to eat properly, in the true sense of the word, then we must put the food on our plates and the drink we drink under the microscope of our Christian faith.

Catherine von Ruhland, *Glorious Food*

You'd think that with all the money, technology and scientific knowledge that is centred in the developed world, we could rely on a diet that kept us in good health. But unfortunately, the reverse is in fact true. Evidence is now mounting that a refined, low-fibre, high-fat diet is linked to an increased risk for certain diseases, including heart disease, stroke, obesity and particular forms of cancer.

Friends of the Earth Handbook

The food industries have been aware of the potential for prestige in food preferences for a long time. Advertising and marketing techniques work to reinforce the sense that certain foods represent a desirable lifestyle. Through their desires and aspirations, many people are manipulated into spending much more than they have to on their food. And that expensive food may not be as nutritious as their normal diet.

The marketing of food and the rather terrifying twist of the concept that 'something of value is worth more' to 'something expensive must be good' has led to the ludicrous extreme of part of the food industry dressing up the packaging of ordinary nutritious foods, increasing the prices and selling 'prestige' health foods. They're selling nutrition, health and prestige all at the same time, but at much more than the food value and the nutrition should cost.

Jean Bacon, *Food Preferences: Nutrition or Prestige?*

In 1973, two-thirds of Colombia's Green Revolution rice was being fed to livestock or going into the production of beer. Increased yields of corn provided the raw material for starting up a chicken feed industry. Did this mean Colombia's undernourished would be eating chicken? For over a quarter of the country's families, buying just two pounds of chicken or a dozen eggs would require an entire week's earnings or more. Much of the increased egg production goes into processed foods such as snacks and mayonnaise sold by multinational food companies to elite urban groups.

R.J. Ledogar, *Hungry for Profits*

And what has happened to the fruits of our own [US] Green Revolution? Although the United States succeeded in increasing corn yields almost three times over, it has not meant the elimination of hunger in America. The increased corn production has gone to livestock — doubling the meat consumption of many Americans who already were taking in more protein than their bodies could use.

F. Lappe & J. Collins, *Food First*

Only God knows the amount of surplus fat the American public carries around, but it has to run in the millions of tons. Add to that the other millions of tons which are lost through dieting annually and regained by backsliding, and the total is mind-blowing.

Stan Mooneyham,
What Do You Say to a Hungry World?

When your mother told you to eat everything on your plate because people were starving in India, you thought it was pretty silly. You knew the family dog would be the only one affected by what you did or didn't do. Since then, you've probably continued to think that making any sort of *ethical* issue of eating is absurd. You ate what your family always ate, altered only perhaps by proddings from the food industry.

Frances Lappe, *Diet for a Small Planet*

O Lord, our creator,
you have provided on this bountiful earth
all kinds of good things for us to enjoy.
But the rich eat too much
and the poor eat too little.
And both groups will,
for different reasons,
meet you earlier than they should.
Help me to view eating and drinking
as sacramental acts.
May I regard food and water as holy.
Give me the discipline to eat and drink
with moderation most of the time,
with festivity occasionally,
and also to fast sometimes.
I pray for the loved ones who today will mourn
the passing of 40 000 children of the poor,
who will die mainly as a result of
poverty-related illnesses.
I also pray for those who imbibe anything overmuch
and are addicted to excessive consumption.
May my life incarnate the values of Jesus
and may he be glorified in my body. Amen.

A Benediction
May your real needs be met, and
your imagined needs be seen for what they are.
May your desires be holy and healthy.
May you glorify God in your spirit, soul and body,
until you meet him (hopefully after a good life, 'full of years').
  Amen.

Theme: Courage. . .

to do God's will

Then Jesus went with them to a place called Gethsemane; and he said to his disciples, 'Sit here while I go over there and pray.' He took with him Peter and the two sons of Zebedee and began to be grieved and agitated. Then he said to them, 'I am deeply grieved, even to death; remain here and stay awake with me.' And going a little farther, he threw himself on the ground and prayed, 'My Father, if it is possible, let this cup pass from me; yet not what I want, but what you want.'

Then he came to the disciples and found them sleeping; and he said to Peter, 'So, could you not stay awake with me one hour? Stay awake and pray that you may not come into the time of trial; the spirit indeed is willing, but the flesh is weak.'

Again he went away for the second time and prayed, 'My Father, if this cannot pass unless I drink it, your will be done.' Again he came and found them sleeping, for their eyes were heavy. So leaving them again, he went away and prayed for the third time, saying the same words. Then he came to the disciples and said to them, 'Are you still sleeping and taking your rest? See, the hour is at hand and the Son of Man is betrayed into the hands of sinners. Get up, let us be going. See, my betrayer is at hand.'

Matthew 26: 36-46, NRSV

39

God in the darkness

As the sun was setting, Abram fell into a deep sleep, and a thick and dreadful darkness came over him. Then, the Lord (spoke) to him. . .

Thou also shalt light my candle; the Lord my God shall make my darkness to be light. Yahweh, you yourself are my lamp; my God lights up my darkness.

The people walking in darkness have seen a great light; on those living in the land of the shadow of death a light has dawned.

At the sixth hour, darkness came over the whole land until the ninth hour. And at the ninth hour, Jesus cried out in a loud voice, '*Eloi, Eloi, lema sabachthani*?' — which means, 'My God, my God, why have you forsaken me?'

When Jacob awoke from his sleep, he thought, 'Surely the Lord is in this place, and I was not aware of it.'

I cried out to God for help; I cried out to God to hear me. When I was in distress, I sought the Lord; at night I stretched out untiring hands. . . I remembered my sons in the night. My heart mused and my spirit inquired: Will the Lord reject forever? Will he never show his favour again? Has his unfailing love vanished forever? Has his promise failed for all time?

When the people saw the thunder and lightning and heard the trumpet and saw the mountain in smoke, they trembled with fear. They stayed at a distance. . . while Moses approached the thick darkness where God was.

(Genesis 15: 12–13, NIV; Psalm 18: 28, (i) Psalms in the Book of Common Prayer, (ii) JB; Isaiah 9: 2; Mark 15: 33–34; Genesis 28: 16; Psalm 77: 1–2 and 6-8; Exodus 20: 18 and 21 — all NIV)

Sometimes God, whom we understand to be all loving, all powerful, interested in each of his children and who promises to be with us always, never leaving us or forsaking us, seems to have withdrawn and left us alone in dense darkness. Suddenly, God seems a stranger whom we do not know any more.

What can we do to help ourselves when we are in that kind of darkness? Either we can choose to remain 'at a distance', like the people of Israel, bewildered and afraid, or, like Moses, we can enter the thick darkness where God is.

The North American Indian trained his child to have courage by having him spend a night alone in the forest, while he himself, unbeknown to the child, kept guard. As he would not be acting on a cruel whim, so the thick darkness where God is is no cruel whim, either.

When God seems withdrawn, he is training us for a hostile world. If we remain 'at a distance', we will not learn or grow as he plans for us to do in his love.

When we are in thick darkness and God does not seem to be there, we need to discipline ourselves deliberately to remember, think about, meditate on the things we know to be true about God. We must not allow ourselves to be tricked into believing only what we think we see. It *might* be dark. God *might* be silent. The wild animals *might* be rustling in the undergrowth. But God has promised in Jesus to be with us all the days and all the day long — and there is no 'use by' date on that promise.

God is there in the darkness, whether we are aware of him or not.

What is your particular darkness at this moment?

Loneliness? When we know Jesus, we need never *stay* lonely. 'Make your home in me, as I make mine in you,' said Jesus in John 15: 4.

Disappointment? It doesn't take much faith to believe in God when he gives us what we want. Real faith is needed when he takes it away — or when what we earnestly prayed for is not granted. We need to know, with unshakeable assurance, that he loves us with an everlasting love and is utterly to be trusted.

Depression? It can be like a thick black cloud where, if God *is* there, we don't seem to be able to find him for ourselves. A person in depression needs to know afresh that God loves them. If they have lost sight of *him*, they can still see *us*. So in their darkness, we need to love them for, in doing so, we are declaring God's love for them.

If we are able to pray — not 'standing at a distance', but *entering* the 'darkness where God is' — we need to fix our minds on the thought expressed in 2 Corinthians 4: 17–18: 'For our light and momentary troubles are achieving for us an eternal glory that far outweighs them all. . . so we fix our eyes not on what is seen' (the darkness, God withdrawn and silent), 'but on what is unseen' (our Father close by, watching over us). 'For what is seen is temporary, but what is unseen is eternal.' This is a case of what we *see* is *not* what we get!

Whatever your 'darkness where God is,' listen to David's assurance in Psalm 18: 28: 'You, O Lord will light my candle; my God turns my darkness into light.'

Whenever the circumstances of life make you feel someone has blown out your candle, know for sure that God *is* there in the darkness with you and assuredly wants to light your candle.

❧❧

When the night is troubled by confusion and crying, we must know whether God is for us or against us. When the sky breaks into pieces that fall at our feet, we need assurance that the heavenly Father's wish is for us to find his strength to sustain our night of difficulty. . . When I first encountered [Jesus], his sense of destiny drew me even closer. . . This was a man who knew where he was going!. . . 'Jesus, you have made sense out of my aimless life. Yet so much of what I have experienced seems to have no purpose. . . Why can't I understand the final reasons for all that I have suffered?'

He picked up the loaf from the table and ripped the bread apart. Holding the torn halves, he stared into my eyes. 'My Father does not let us see life from beginning to end. But we know that his loving hands hold even the pieces that are torn.'

My doubts insisted on one more word. 'But how do I *know* that his love holds the broken portions?'

He laid down the loaves and reached for my hand. . .'You know me, don't you?'

Robert Wise, *When There is No Miracle*

Christian Reger will tell the horror stories if you ask. But he will never stop there. He goes on to share his faith — how at Dachau, he was visited by a God who loves.

'Nietzsche said a man can undergo torture if he knows the *why* of his life,' Reger told me. 'But I, here at Dachau, learned something far greater. I learned to know the *who* of my life. He was enough to sustain me then, and is enough to sustain me still. . . God did not rescue me and make my suffering easier. He simply proved to me that he was still alive and he still knew I was here. . .'

. . .As long as he has his health, Christian Reger will stiffly pace the grounds of Dachau, speaking to tourists in his warm, accented voice. He will tell them what it was like and where God was during the long night at Dachau.

Philip Yancey, *Where is God when It Hurts?*

When God seems absent, he may be closest of all. . . Good Friday demonstrates that God has not abandoned us to our pain. The evils and sufferings that afflict our lives are so real and so significant to God that he willed to share them and endure them himself.

Philip Yancey, *Disappointment with God*

And a light shined in the cell,
And there was not any wall,
And there was no dark at all,
Only Thou, Immanuel.
Light of Love shined in the cell,
Turned to gold the iron bars,
Opened windows to the stars,
Peace stood there as sentinel.
Dearest Lord, how can it be

That Thou art so kind to me?
Love is shining in my cell,
Jesus, my Immanuel.

Amy Carmichael, *Toward Jerusalem*

Barracks 8 was in the quarantine compound. Next to us
— perhaps as a deliberate warning to newcomers — were
located the punishment barracks. From there, all day long,
and often into the night, came the sounds of hell itself.
They were not the sounds of anger or of any human
emotion, but of a cruelty altogether detached: blows land-
ing in regular rhythm, screams keeping pace. We would
stand in our ten deep ranks with our hands trembling at
our sides, longing to jam them against our ears to make
the sounds stop. . .

Fridays — the recurrent humiliation of medical inspec-
tion. . . How there could have been any pleasure in the
sight of these stick-thin legs and hunger-bloated stomachs
I could not imagine. . .

Nor could I see the necessity for the complete undress-
ing. . . But it was one of these mornings while we were
waiting, shivering, in the corridor, that yet another page
in the Bible leapt into life for me. . .

I leaned towards Betsie, ahead of me in the line. Her
shoulder blades stood out sharp and thin beneath her
blue-mottled skin. 'Betsie, they took his clothes, too. . .'

It was the week before Christmas that Betsie woke up
unable to move either legs or arms. . . They placed the
stretcher on the floor and I leaned down to make out
Betsie's words. . . 'Must tell people what we have learned
here. We must tell them that there is no pit so deep that
he is not deeper still. They will listen to us, Corrie,
because we have been here.'

Corrie Ten Boom, *The Hiding Place*

Lord, you are a present help in trouble.
Come, revive,
Redeem,
Restore.
In our darkness come as light,

In our sadness come as joy,
In our troubles come as peace,
In our weakness come as strength.
Come, Lord, to our aid.
Revive,
Redeem,
Restore us.

David Adam, *Tides and Seasons*

---

*Creator God, of light and love, when you seem to be withdrawn
and silent, help us not to stay at a distance, but to run clinging
to you in the darkness, trusting your precious promises, trusting
your love for us.*

*Redeeming Shepherd, grow in us the habit of remembering
that what we see is not all there is.*

*Holy Comforter, thankyou for the comfort you give to us and
for the privilege of sharing that comfort with one another.*
Amen.

A Benediction

O God of the morning, Christ of the hills,
O Spirit who all the firmament fills,
O Trinity blest who all goodness wills,
Keep us all our days.
   Amen.

G.R.D. McLean, *Poems of the Western Highlanders*

The discipline of disappointment

I must go on boasting. Although there is nothing to be gained, I will go on to visions and revelations from the Lord. I know a man in Christ who fourteen years ago was caught up to the third heaven. Whether it was in the body or out of the body, I do not know — God knows. And I know that this man — whether in the body or apart from the body I do not know, but God knows — was caught up to paradise. He heard inexpressible things. . .

I will boast about a man like that, but I will not boast about myself, except about my weaknesses. Even if I should choose to boast, I would not be a fool, because I would be speaking the truth. But I refrain, so no-one will think more of me than is warranted by what I do or say.

To keep me from becoming conceited because of these surpassingly great revelations, there was given me a thorn in my flesh, a messenger of Satan, to torment me. Three times, I pleaded with the Lord to take it away from me. But he said to me, 'My grace is sufficient for you, for my power is made perfect in weakness.'

Therefore, I will boast all the more gladly about my weaknesses, so that Christ's power may rest on me. That is why, for Christ's sake, I delight in weaknesses, in insults, in hardships, in persecutions, in difficulties. For when I am weak, then I am strong.

(2 Corinthians 12: 1–10 — NIV)

What exactly was Paul's 'thorn in the flesh'? Some have suggested a bodily ailment such as malaria, epilepsy or blindness; others something in his circumstances that he felt he could no longer bear. Still others feel it could have been something in his own life and character that constantly reminded him of his sinfulness and which made him cry out, 'I know that nothing good lives in me . . .What a wretched man I am! Who will rescue me from this body of death?' (Romans 7: 18–24). Whatever the thorn was, for Paul it was like a stake sticking into his flesh that hindered his effectiveness and perhaps could ultimately destroy his usefulness for God.

Paul believed the thorn or stake came from God, but Satan was the agent or messenger. God's purpose in allowing it was to teach Paul humility and to keep him from being 'too elated'. Paul longed for it to be removed and prayed on three occasions that God would take it away. But when God said 'No!', he also said, 'My grace is sufficient for you, for my power is made perfect in weakness.' His power (and the word is *dynamis*, dynamite) is made perfect in our weakness (the word is *neurasthenia*).

When Paul received this answer from the Lord he was able to say, 'That is why, for Christ's sake, I delight in weakness, in insults, in hardships, in persecutions, in difficulties. For when I am weak, then I am strong.' The discipline of disappointment in Paul's life enabled him to be content with his lot and to get on with his ministry which became all the richer because God did not remove the thorn — he did something better.

🙠🙡

At times in our lives, the tail winds of joy, triumph and fulfilment favour us and, at times, the head winds of disappointment, sorrow and tragedy beat unrelentingly against us. Shall we permit adverse winds to overwhelm us as we journey across life's mighty Atlantic or will our inner spiritual engines sustain us in spite of the winds? Our refusal to be stopped, our 'courage to be', our determination to go on 'in spite of', reveal the divine image within us. When we make this discovery, we know that no burden can overwhelm us and no wind of adversity can blow our life away. We can stand anything that can happen to us.

Martin Luther King, *Strength to Love*

Who rises from prayer a better person, that one's prayers are answered.

George Meredith, *The Ordeal of Richard Feveral*

God not only says that failure is never the final word, but that your area of weakness will become your area of strength. Where you were weak and learned grace will become a place where you can reach out and touch the lives of others who need the same good news.

Terry Hersey, *Beginning Again*

Accepting one's life means accepting all that one considers to be unfair victimisation, the injustices of fate as well as those of others.

Acceptance of one's nature as it is, with its infirmities and the difficulties they entail, acceptance of them without rebellion, is one of the demands Christianity makes.

Paul Tournier, *The Healing of Persons*

A deep understanding of one's own pain makes it possible for [the hurting person] to convert weakness into strength and to offer this experience as a source of healing to those who are often lost in the darkness of their own misunderstood sufferings. Once the pain is accepted and understood, a denial is no longer necessary and ministry [to others] can become a healing service.

Henri Nouwen, *The Wounded Healer*

Constantly, God is trying to train and fashion us into his will and the process may be painful at times. We must humbly accept that he knows what he is doing and later we will see the value of it.

David Watson, *Fear No Evil*

The same is true of our broken places — where we have been hurt, have fallen and failed, or are afraid. When we bring these to God for his healing, his strength is made perfect through our weaknesses.

This is certainly true in helping other people. They are helped not through our brilliant logic or persuasive speech, but through the sharing of our struggles, disappointments and losses and how, with God's help, we have overcome. It is a case of one beggar who has found bread showing other beggars where they can find bread, too.

Dick Innes, *How to Mend a Broken Heart*

I just don't understand. Are you a loving God or are you a vengeful God? Did you have a reason for me to be raped? Did you really *want* that to happen to me? What reason could be good enough for that kind of pain? I nearly killed myself over it. Do you remember that?

I was only nineteen years old when it happened. God, that's a very young age to have to face that kind of crisis. I didn't even know what the beautiful, loving, sharing kind of sex was supposed to be like when all of a sudden I was violated in an ugly, twisted, sexual way. I was too young for that. I'm still too young to have been through this kind of suffering. All I have been through, Lord! I'm only twenty-two.

I will never understand God, but I can trust him. I cannot expect to be spared pain and suffering, but I can go to God in the midst of it and find comfort and love.

Because I can trust him, I will never again need to ask the question, 'Why me?' I am content to know that God's love is sufficient. In this, I have found healing, a healing that cannot be found outside of his love.

Deborah Roberts, *Raped*

God has not promised skies ever blue,
Flower-strewn pathways always for you,
But he has promised strength from above,
Unfailing sympathy, infinite love.

Source unknown

Losing a mate by death or divorce is miserably sad and
you have a right to indulge in a certain amount of self-pity.
But don't remain in this state too long, for you have a job
to do. Your goal is: recovery from a broken heart [and]
a wounded ego; the rebuilding of a life; the rediscovery
of your own personality; and, last but not least, learning
to live with and like yourself.

Amy Ross Young,
By Death or Divorce. . . It Hurts to Lose

I will restore to you the years
which the swarming locust has eaten.

Joel 2: 25, RSV

We may be in heaviness through many temptations and
trials at this present time and we may be weeping as we
go along. It does not matter. We are promised that the
day will come when 'the Lamb which is in the midst of
the throne. . . shall lead us unto living fountains of water'
and that God himself 'shall wipe away all tears from our
eyes' and we shall be with him in glory everlasting.
That is the Christian way of facing trials. Thank God we
are in his hands. It is his way of salvation and not ours.

D. Martin Lloyd-Jones, *Trials*

When through the deep waters I call you to go,
you will not be swamped by the rivers of woe;
for I will be with you, your troubles to bless,
and sanctify to you life's deepest distress.

When through fiery trials your pathway shall lie,
my grace all-sufficient shall be your supply;
the flame shall not hurt you; my only design
your dross to consume and your gold to refine.

The soul that on Jesus has leaned for repose
I cannot, I will not, desert to its foes:
that soul, though all hell should endeavour to shake,
I'll never abandon and never forsake.

Baptist Praise and Worship

O Lord, I have so much to learn. Sometimes I expect you to smooth my way in life and I feel resentful — towards you, towards people and towards life itself — when things go wrong. I know that's childish and selfish. Forgive me, Lord.

Help me to see that disappointments need not 'get me down', but can be the means of making me a stronger Christian and that I, like Paul, can know that your strength is made perfect in my weakness.

I know, Lord, you are ever reaching out in love to me and that 'my gloom is but the shade of your hand outstretched caressingly'. Thankyou, Lord. With you as my helper, I have nothing to fear. Amen.

A Benediction
May the Lord give us
the serenity to accept what cannot be changed;
the courage to change what ought to be changed;
and the wisdom to distinguish the one from the other.
  Amen.

(Reinhold Niebuhr)

For you are a holy people to the Lord your God; the Lord your God has chosen you to be a people for his own possession out of all the peoples of the earth.

Cursed is he who lies with his father's wife. . . cursed is he who lies with his sister, the daughter of his father or of his mother. . . cursed is he who lies with his mother-in-law.

Absalom the son of David had a beautiful sister whose name was Tamar and Amnon the Son of David loved her. And Amnon was so frustrated because of his sister Tamar that he made himself ill, for she was a virgin, and it seemed hard to Amnon to do anything to her. . . he took hold of her and said to her, 'Come, lie with me, my sister.' But she answered him, 'No, my brother, do not violate me, for such a thing is not done in Israel; do not do this disgraceful thing!' . . .However, he would not listen to her; since he was stronger than she, he violated her and lay with her.

Another has lewdly defiled his daughter-in-law. And another of you has humbled his sister, his father's daughter. . . 'Can your heart endure or can your hands be strong, in the days that I shall deal with you? I, the Lord, have spoken and shall act. . . and you will know that I, the Lord, have poured out my wrath on you.'

No-one is to approach any close relative to have sexual relations. I am the Lord.

O Lord my God, I cried to you for help and you have healed me. . . Sing praises to the Lord, O you, his faithful ones, and give thanks to his holy name. . . Weeping may linger for the night, but joy comes with the morning.

(Deuteronomy 7: 6; 27: 20 and 22–23; 2 Samuel 13: 1–2, 11–12 and 14; Ezekiel 22: 11, 14 and 22 — all NASB; Leviticus 18: 6, NIV; Psalm 30: 2 and 4–5, NRSV)

Like a racehorse wearing blinkers which keep it looking only ahead, the church today has blind spots — areas it doesn't, in general, want to deal with. One such area is the reality of the abuse of incest. Like many others, I pitied those abused, while feeling detached from it; it did not seem real in relation to any of my church friends; it did not seem real in relation to me.

Although Christ became my Saviour when I was ten years old, I grew up with very low self-esteem. I felt worthless, no good at or for anything, and I didn't trust anyone. If anything ever went wrong, I'd always feel that in some way it was my fault. Things began to change as I grew older; I made a conscious choice to trust God and so I began to trust (a little) other people. But my actions flowed from choices of the will, not because I felt them in my heart. Living the Christian life was a constant effort, with the occasional lift of joy in the Lord.

In recent times, anger began to be a problem. Although I could control and hide it, I knew there was a simmering anger just beneath the surface and I began seeking God for its source.

The reality shocked me. I remembered that as a child, I loved and trusted my father more than anyone in the world; I remembered that as a teenager, I was emotionally detached from my father with an indifference that was really hatred; I remembered that as a young adult I chose to love and respect my father as an act of will in obedience to the scriptures — and I began to remember why that was all so.

Flashbacks began to occur of the sexual abuse my father imposed on me, against my will, when I was eleven. The memories were devastating. The anger, the hatred, the self-hatred came bursting to the surface and I wanted to scream with the agony of betrayal. I was rocked to my foundations as I had to confront in myself what had happened. The words 'rape' and 'incest' became very personal words. And where in the church can a Christian look for help?

Over time and with the help of two caring counsellors, I worked through the anger and hatred. God enabled me to forgive my father for what he had done. He helped me forgive myself for what had been forced on me. He showed me his grief at the suffering his precious child had endured in this very sick world. He healed the deep wounds in my psyche and began to show me that there is a future and a hope, in him. My life began anew, for the first time not just from my will, but from an integrated base. How he is worthy to be praised!

I look at people with different eyes, now. From what I have experienced myself, and from wide reading about others' trauma, I now am able to recognise that a major problem exists. And to the church, it is a subject which is not respectable, while the hidden pain of many congregation members is screaming out for release. Jesus said in Luke 5: 31 (NASB): 'It is not those who are well who need a physician, but those who are sick.' The challenge for the church is to care for and minister to its members, particularly those who have been 'sinned against'.

❈❈❈

Sexual abuse exacts a terrible price in the victim's life in terms of shame, contempt and denial. The sins of the perpetrator continue to colour the victim's life through an inability to enjoy relationship, intimacy and hope. The victim's soul feels bound to denial; the heart feels wounded and alone. . .

All abuse is a violation of the sanctity and wholeness of the human soul, but when sexual abuse is perpetrated by a member of one's family or by someone who has gained one's trust, the loss is even more severe. Sexual abuse is always a violation of relationship. The violation always damages the soul, irrespective of the severity, nature of the relationship with the perpetrator, use or nonuse of violence, or duration of the abuse.

Dan B. Allender, *The Wounded Heart*

If you are an incest victim, you are much like the root-bound plant. You may go on for years without any visible symptoms, but eventually surface problems will appear. Often, these are visible as depression, anger, marital difficulties, migraines, anxiety, eating disorders or feeling distant from God. The tendency of well-meaning Christians is to treat the surface symptoms, but that is like trimming up the root-bound plant to make it attractive on the outside. This fails to deal with the real problem. In the meantime, the surface symptoms will reappear, often with greater seriousness than before.

Jan Frank, *A Door of Hope*

Every human experience has a psychological dimension because we approach any new experience with all the psychological baggage we carry from our past experience with significant people. Thus, our experience of God or of Jesus will be affected by our past experience with significant people in our lives as well as our past learning about God and Jesus. Just imagine how the experience of God as Father is influenced by an experience of having been abused physically and sexually by one's own father.

William A. Barry, *Finding God in All Things*

Not all theological questions and doubts are a sign of disbelief, unbelief or rebellion. In many instances, they are symptoms of the need for a deep, inner healing. It is only *after* this takes place that such people are able to reshape their faulty doctrines and properly understand the scriptures.

David A. Seamands, *Healing of Memories*

The basis of all forgiveness, whether it be forgiving ourselves or another person, is Jesus' death on the cross. An individual who refuses to forgive another person is actually cutting oneself off from God's forgiveness. . . Many people carry bitter feelings toward a parent because of incest, divorce, abuse or alcoholism. You were not born to those parents by chance — God hand-picked them for you. No matter how bad a situation was, God can still use it for your good and you need to forgive your parents.

Josh McDowell, *The Secret of Loving*

A [person] who is not yet perfectly dead to self is easily tempted and is overcome even in small and trifling things. And those who are weak in spirit and still a prey to the senses and bodily passions can only with great difficulty free themselves from worldly lusts. Therefore, they are sad when they withdraw themselves and angered when anyone opposes them. Yet, if they obtain what they desire, then conscience is at once stricken by remorse, because they have yielded to their passions which in no way helps them in their search for peace. True peace of heart can be found only by resisting the passions, not by yielding to them.

Thomas à Kempis, *The Imitation of Christ*

Lord, you know the pain of betrayal, when a trusted friend delivered you up to crucifixion; you empathise with those whose trust as a child was betrayed and brutalised. May you teach us, Lord, to respond to people with the compassion you would show if you were here in our place.

As we walk this Christian life and as we travel on our own journeys to healing and wholeness, teach us to be your body as you would have us to be — to truly love one another as you have loved us.

A Benediction
Finally, [brothers and sisters], rejoice, be made complete, be comforted, be like-minded, live in peace; and the God of love and peace shall be with you.

2 Corinthians 13: 11, NASB

42

Cool, calm and corrected

If any want to become my followers, let them deny themselves and take up their cross daily and follow me. For those who want to save their life will lose it, and those who lose their life for my sake will save it.

After you had been enlightened, you endured a hard struggle with sufferings, sometimes being publicly exposed to abuse and persecution, and sometimes being partners with those so treated. For you had compassion for those who were in prison and you cheerfully accepted the plundering of your possessions, knowing that you yourselves possessed something better and more lasting.

You must understand this, my beloved: let everyone be quick to listen, slow to speak, slow to anger; for your anger does not produce God's righteousness.

Love your enemies and pray for those who persecute you, so that you may be children of your Father in heaven.

For I think that God has exhibited us apostles as last of all, as though sentenced to death, because we have become a spectacle to the world, to angels and to mortals. We are fools for the sake of Christ, but you are wise in disrepute. To this present hour, we are hungry and thirsty, we are poorly clothed and beaten and homeless, and we grow weary from the work of our own hands. When reviled, we bless; when persecuted, we endure; when slandered, we speak kindly. We have become like the rubbish of the world, the dregs of all things, to this very day.

If you endure when you are beaten for doing wrong, what credit is that? But if you endure when you do right and suffer for it, you have God's approval.

And not only that, but we also boast in our sufferings, knowing that suffering produces endurance, and endurance produces character, and character produces hope, and hope does not disappoint us, because God's love has been poured into our hearts through the Holy Spirit that has been given to us.

(Luke 9: 23–24; Hebrews 10: 32–34; James 1: 19–20; Matthew 5: 44–45; 1 Corinthians 4: 9–13; 1 Peter 2: 20; Romans 5: 3–5 — all NRSV)

The greatest achievements of Jesus and Paul came when they submitted to being roughed up: Jesus to innocent conviction followed by a humiliating crucifixion; Paul to poverty, imprisonment and degradation. Add to that Peter's grisly death, the stoning of Stephen, John the Baptist's beheading — and the story of our faith seems to be written in blood.

But didn't they handle it well? Extra points for grace under pressure. By their suffering, they achieved more in a day's pain than they could by a lifetime of leisure. The very act of shouldering their burden without grumbling was part of the process of sanctification.

There is a joke about how Australians take up their cross. The story goes that upon hearing the command in a Sunday sermon, we back the station-wagon up to the church and ask the minister to load a cross onto the tailgate. That is symbolic of our varied attempts to avoid burdens, while enjoying God's great blessings. We eat our ice-cream, but leave our spinach on the plate.

Yet Jesus never leaves us. He is closest to us when we hurt. When we submit ourselves to unjust persecution without complaint, for the sake of love and peace amongst God's people, we join the communion of saints.

In one sense, we are invited to welcome ill-treatment and hardship. How we react to it will show all people how deeply God dwells in us. Oppression is one per cent of the evil that's done to us, nine per cent what we think about it, and ninety per cent what we do with it. Jesus didn't become human just to give us eternal life, but as an example of dignity under duress.

Joining his army means we turn the other cheek, forgiving seventy times seven — and amazingly, we find after a while that it doesn't hurt any more! Resistance is painful. Surrender is spiritual maturity. By this, we become his sons and daughters.

❧

'That's another thing I don't understand,' the lieutenant said, 'why you — of all people — should have stayed when the others ran.'

'They didn't all run,' the priest said.

'But why did you stay?'

'Once,' the priest said, 'I asked myself that. The fact is, we aren't presented suddenly with two courses to follow: one good and one bad. We get caught up. . . I didn't believe there was really any cause to run. Churches have been burnt before now. You know how often. . . I thought I'd stay till next month. . . and see if things were better. Then — oh, you don't know how time can slip by.'

Graham Greene, *The Power and the Glory*

Jesus was perfectly aware of what Judas was up to — his hypocrisy, his evil scheme of betrayal. Jesus knew there was a lot going on behind his back.

What would you have done if you were the Lord? I probably would have grabbed Judas by the scruff of the neck and said, 'See here, jerk, I'm fully aware of your evil tricks. There's no way you're going to get away with this.' Then, I would have punched him in the jaw.

What did Jesus do? He washed the man's feet.

If that weren't enough, Christ goes on in that same chapter to remind us: 'I have set you an example that you should do as I have done for you. Now that you know these things, you'll be blessed if you do them.'

Joni Eareckson Tada, *Secret Strength*

In the long pull, those who win the world around them are those whom Jesus calls 'meek' — the controlled, the patient, the honest, the quiet, the forceful, the powerful-but-restrained — disciplined, poised people. Their God-moulded, Christ-shaped, Spirit-dominated lives are like a train that will make many a 'happiness stop'.

Robert H. Schuller, *The Be Happy Attitudes*

Oh joy, that seekest me through pain,
I cannot close my heart to Thee;
I trace the rainbow through the rain
And feel the promise is not vain
That morn shall tearless be.

George Mathieson,
Oh Love that Will Not Let Me Go

Love,
In a microcosm of a moment,
Is enfixed,
Caught,
In the glistening globule,
The teardrop,
Of one who cares.
In all the world there *is* none more beautiful,
None more beloved of God,
Than the one
Who,
Unselfishly,
Cries for joy on behalf of others;
Or cries in pain,
Because of *their* hurts.
Such love is the showing forth
The expression
Of the love of Christ.

Bette Smith

I must attempt to keep on listening even when I am no longer listened to, to keep on being sensitive even when others are insensitive to me, to try — like he did — when reviled, to revile not in return.

Now to be sure, it may not work. In such a stance, I realise I could get run over by the juggernaut and nothing at all would remain to show for so fragile an approach.

But even at that, it would be going down at one's best and not at one's worst by trying to remain human and not get sucked into the swirl of inhumanity. If I have to go down, that is the way I would most prefer to go. . . And by God's help, this is what I most want to do. Will you join me? If there is any hope, this has to be the way!

John R. Claypool, 'Living by the Sword'

From subtle love of softening things,
From easy choices, weakenings —
Not thus are spirits fortified,
Not this way went the Crucified.
From all that dims Thy Calvary,
O Lamb of God, deliver me.

Amy Carmichael

Thankyou, Lord, that hardships are only temporary: part of our sanctification, while your presence protects us from real harm. We know this from all the new, exciting opportunities that enriched our lives following earlier struggles.

Remind us that courage isn't the absence of fear, but planning strategies in spite of it. Knowing that you always bring joy out of pain, we move confidently into the future with positive faith. We praise you for the power of this thought — that trials have the potential to advance us, not damage us. Show us the way out of hardship, free from the cancer of resentment.

With your spirit indwelling in us, Lord, our optimism can overcome today's challenges and we can be confident that tomorrow is radiant because you are already there. Amen.

A Benediction

Go in the security of God's power, knowing that you will sustain no lasting damage. He has already won your victory. When pain is hard to bear, look for Christ revealing himself to you in the person of one whose agony is worse still. Let your fellowship comfort them and so meet Jesus of Gethsemane in person. Amen.

43

Negotiating the rough spots

God. . . girded me with strength, and made my way safe. He made my feet like the feet of a deer and set me secure on the heights. Teach me your way, O Lord, and lead me on a level path because of my enemies. Though the Lord may give you the bread of adversity and the water of affliction, yet your Teacher will not hide himself any more, but your eyes shall see your Teacher. And when you turn to the right or when you turn to the left, your ears shall hear a word behind you saying, 'This is the way; walk in it.'

Strengthen the weak hands and make firm the feeble knees. Say to those who are of a fearful heart, 'Be strong, do not fear! Here is your God. . . He will come and save you.' A highway shall be there, and it shall be called the Holy Way. . . it shall be for God's people; no traveller, not even fools, shall go astray. . . the ransomed of the Lord shall return and come to Zion with singing; everlasting joy shall be upon their heads; they shall obtain joy and gladness, and sorrow and sighing shall flee away.

When you pass through the waters, I will be with you; and through the rivers, they shall not overwhelm you; when you walk through fire you shall not be burned, and the flame shall not consume you. Do not remember the former things, or consider the things of old. I am about to do a new thing; now it springs forth, do you not perceive it? I will make a way in the wilderness and rivers in the desert.

Jesus said. . . 'I am the way, and the truth, and the life. No-one comes to the Father except through me.'

No testing has overtaken you that is nor common to everyone. God is faithful, and he will not let you be tested beyond your strength, but with the testing he will also provide the way out so that you may be able to endure it.

He knows the way that I take; when he has tested me, I shall come out like gold. My foot has held fast to his steps; I have kept his way and have not turned aside. Make me to know your ways, O Lord; teach me your paths. All the paths of the Lord are steadfast love and faithfulness, for those who keep his covenant and his decrees.

(Psalm 18: 32–33; 27: 11; Isaiah 30: 20–21; 35: 3–4, 8 and 10; 43: 2 and 18–19; John 14: 6; 1 Corinthians 10: 13; Job 23: 10–11; Psalm 25: 4 and 10 — all NRSV)

Times of hardship and distress are not foreign to the experience of God's chosen ones. Christianity is not an escape from the harsher realities of life. Yes, the Christian life is full and rich, a life of peace and joy. But the landscape is sometimes rocky and barren, not only green pastures and babbling streams.

When the problems, difficulties and hardships of life come, how do we respond to them? Are they perceived as barriers to our moving on with God and growing in our faith? Or are they a bridge which will take us on to new horizons? If we have swallowed the lie that Christian faith is an insurance policy against the difficulties and traumas of life, then we will question our relationship with the Lord at the very times when it has the potential to be strengthened.

Some well-intentioned Christians may perceive the problems we encounter in life as due to our lack of faith or an inadequacy in our concept of God. They have not correctly read the scriptures or the lives of God's saints through the centuries. Paul reminds us in 1 Corinthians 10: 13 that we will experience all kinds of difficulties and testings and, no matter what our particular situation, it is not unique. Others have faced this problem before us and others still will face it in the future.

Always, God provides for us a way out. We never find ourselves at a precipitous scarp without there being a bridge which will safely take us across the chasm. The bridge doesn't always look inviting. Sometimes it seems no more than a slippery log over a flooded creek or a flimsy suspension structure across a deep chasm. But when we trust ourselves to God, it is always sturdy enough for our need.

When we go to a national park to enjoy its beauty, we appreciate the paths which the rangers have carefully laid out for us. When we stay on these paths, not only do we do less harm to the environment, but the exquisite landscape becomes available to all, not just the athletic few. This is a parable of how God works in our lives.

The park ranger provides a grating for a firm foothold where the way is muddy; a bridge where the way is impassable; a resting place after an arduous climb or where the view is overwhelming. So God provides a way for us through the wilderness of life. The road he calls us to travel may be rocky and heavy-going, but always the Lord blesses us with his presence, provides for our needs on the way and gives the resting places we require to complete the journey.

As we listen for God's guidance, watch for his way and trust and obey him even when we don't see the full picture, we will find ourselves on the path he has for us. Having negotiated certain parts of our journey successfully, the Lord will often then use us as bridges in the lives of others as they, too, walk the paths that the Lord sets before them.

❧❧

There are times in life
when we are called to be bridges —
not a great monument spanning a distance
and carrying loads of heavy traffic,
but a simple bridge to help one person
from here to there

over some difficulty,
such as grief, fear, loneliness;
a bridge which opens the way
for ongoing journey.
When I become a bridge for another,
I bring upon myself a blessing,
for I escape from the small prison of self
and exist for a wider world,
breaking out to be a larger being
who can enter another's pain
and rejoice in another's triumph.
I know of only one greater blessing
in this life and that is
to allow someone else
to be a bridge for me.

Joy Cowley, 'Aotearoa Psalms'

I believe
no pain is lost.
No tear unmarked,
no cry of anguish
dies unheard,
lost in the hail of gunfire
or blanked out by the padded cell.
I believe that pain
and prayer
are somehow saved,
processed,
stored,
used in the divine economy.
The blood
shed in Salvador
will irrigate the heart
of some financier
a million miles away.
The terror,
pain,
despair,
swamped
by lava, flood or earthquake

will be caught up
like mist and fall again,
a gentle rain
on arid hearts
or souls despairing
in the back streets
of Brooklyn.

Sheila Cassidy, *Sharing the Darkness*

When people who were never particularly strong become strong in the face of adversity, when people who tended to think only of themselves become unselfish and heroic in an emergency, I have to ask myself where they got these qualities which they would freely admit they did not have before. My answer is that this is one of the ways in which God helps us when we suffer beyond the limits of our own strength.

Life is not fair. The wrong people get sick and the wrong people get robbed and the wrong people get killed in wars and in accidents. Some people see life's unfairness and decide, 'There is no God; the world is nothing but chaos.'

Others see the same unfairness and ask themselves, 'Where do I get my sense of what is fair and what is unfair? Where do I get my sense of outrage and indignation, my instinctive response of sympathy when I read in the paper about a total stranger who has been hurt by life? Don't I get these things from God? Doesn't he plant in me a little bit of his own divine outrage and injustice and oppression, just as he did for the prophets of the Bible? Isn't my feeling of compassion for the afflicted just a reflection of the compassion he feels when he sees the suffering of his creatures?'

Our responding to life's unfairness with sympathy and with righteous indignation, God's compassion and God's anger working through us, may be the surest proof of all of God's reality.

Harold S. Kushner, *When Bad Things Happen to Good People*

As I look down, I can see Dr Mary Verghese coming down the road, busily wheeling her wheelchair, ready for her morning's work. But as I see her in the distance, I love to look not so much at her, but through the other window where I see deformed, crippled, paralysed patients waiting for their examination and treatment. I love to see their faces as Mary comes around the corner.

Before her coming, I look at these boys — in their despondency, their despair, their apathy — and then I see Mary coming, still with the deep scar across her face where it was once cut open. As she comes round the corner, wheeling her chair without any assistance, I see light come to the faces of the leprosy patients. They see somebody there who has come to life out of death, somebody who even now is only partially alive, but who has dedicated her life, strength, skill, love — all her compassion — to their needs.

They see somebody who is more paralysed than they will ever be, somebody who has more disability than they will ever have, yet she has won through to a high degree of skill. All of that skill she has put at the feet of the Master on behalf of the people who are suffering and who need her.

Some of my friends may hesitate to tell you about my weak moments. It will be a mistake if you paint a picture of continuous victory. That will be far from the truth. It is the story of God's abundant grace working in a very ordinary human being in spite of and through her many weaknesses and failures.

Dorothy C. Wilson, *Take My Hands*

'Yes, you *are* beautiful, Jesus of the City of Joy,' Kovalski was to write that evening in the notebook he used as a diary, 'as beautiful as the crippled leper you sent me today with his mutilated body, his sores and his smile. It was you I saw in him, you who are the incarnation of all pain and anguish, you who experienced Gethsemane, who sweated blood, who knew what it was to be tempted by Satan, abandoned by the Father, brought down, discouraged, hungry, thirsty — and lonely.

'Jesus of Anand Nagar, I tried to care for that leper. Every day, I try to share in the plight of the poor. I bow my head with those who are crushed and oppressed like "grapes in a press and their juice has squirted onto my garments and my clothing has been stained". I am not guiltless, nor am I a saint. I am just a poor fellow, a sinner like all the rest. Sometimes, I am crushed or despised like my brothers in the slum, but with the deep certainty in my heart — that you love me. I also have another certainty — that no-one can take away the joy that fills me, because you are truly present, here in the depths of this wretched slum.'

Dominique Lapierre, *The City of Joy*

Somehow again, the freshness of Christ's love has become very close to me on the brighter edge of sadness and the failure of my integrity as a Christian. I am able to hear individuals and am strongly motivated to work with small groups of people, finding out how to live and love on the adventure with Christ.

I am beginning to see that the renewed motivation God can give us to help others seems to come as a result of our facing our own sin, confessing and making what restitution we can, and thanking him for forgiving us and granting a new start. Then, when we set out in gratitude to find and do his will, our loving can be empowered by the energy God has given us to live again on the other side of failure. And I believe this process of renewal and reborn motivation to love takes place again and again in a growing Christian's life.

Keith Miller, *The Passionate People*

'You have not passed this way before,' it may be; but today it is your happy privilege to prove, as never before, your loyal confidence in Jesus by starting out with him on a life and walk of faith, lived, moment by moment, in absolute and childlike trust in him.

You have trusted him in a few things and he has not failed you. Trust him now for everything and see if he does not do for you exceeding abundantly, above all that you could ever have asked or even thought — not according to your power or capacity, but according to his own mighty power, working in you all the good pleasure of his most blessed will.

Hannah Whitall Smith,
The Christian Secret of a Happy Life

Lord:
You have never waited for us to become perfect before showing us the measure of your love, or commissioning us to serve you in our world.

We dare to believe you are always calling us to a new venture, pointing us to new horizons in ministry and never ceasing to do so.

Create in us a clean heart, O God, and renew a right spirit within us. Stir into flame the gifts you have given and the faith to use them without reserve.

Help us to know the freedom to move into the unknown and the untried, to see the opportunities of the new day and to serve our present age with compassion, imagination and courage.

For in giving and receiving, we learn to love and be loved; we encounter the meaning of life and the mystery of existence — and discover you. Amen.

Terry Falla

Open our eyes more, Lord,
to the wonder and beauty of your creation;
Open our ears more, Lord,
to hear your call of love;
Open our lips more, Lord,
to sing your praises;
Open our hearts more, Lord,
that we may walk, more surely, the Way, the Truth and the Life with Jesus the Christ, as companion, Saviour and guide.
And so find our freedom,
the courage to be,
and our highest joy,
in his service.

Llew Evans

A Benediction
May we know the gracious leading of God, trust in his provision for us and find the paths that lead to fullness of life.   Amen.

Caught in a web

If one member suffers, all suffer together with it; if one member is honoured, all rejoice together with it.

The thought of my affliction and my homelessness is wormwood and gall! My soul continually thinks of it and is bowed down within me. But this I call to mind and therefore I have hope. The steadfast love of the Lord never ceases. His mercies never come to an end. . . 'therefore, I will hope in him.'

Why are you cast down, O my soul, and why are you disquieted within me? Hope in God: for I shall again praise him, my help and my God.

For our struggle is not against enemies of blood and flesh, but against the rulers, against the authorities, against the cosmic powers of this present darkness, against the spiritual forces of evil in the heavenly places.

For just as by one man's disobedience the many were made sinners, so by the one man's obedience, the many will be made righteous. . . Where sin increased, grace abounded all the more.

'Truly I tell you, just as you did it to one of the least of these who are members of my family, you did it to me.'

(1 Corinthians 12: 26; Lamentations 3: 19–22 and 24; Psalm 42: 11; Ephesians 6: 12; Romans 5: 19–20; Matthew 25: 40 — all NRSV)

'Would you do everything in your power to stop someone from committing suicide?'

The question took me by surprise and, judging from the responses around the room, I guessed many others present were also unprepared for that start to our day.

Professor Bryan Tanney from the University of Calgary, Canada, is a world figure in the area of suicide intervention. He was leading a workshop for people engaged in fields of care which are associated with suicide. He went on to say: 'I must do all I can to prevent any other person committing suicide. Suicide is preventable.'

Suicide is an issue in many countries and cultures. It is also a symptom of the fragmented societal environments we have created. It can be the outcome of many experiences which leave a person without hope. A major cause is aloneness — not loneliness, but a feeling of being so alone that there appears to be no purpose in continuing.

Young males, in particular, are caught in the web of aloneness. This might be because they feel inferior in some significant life-skills area. It might be because they do not easily articulate the struggles they have with the major issues in their lives. One man who suicided and whose funeral I conducted was so self-enclosed about the issues of his life that nobody in his family or among his friends could tell me anything about him.

A person's perspective on what is happening in his or her life is vital to having a sense of hope. Without realistic hope, all is lost. Richard Winter, in *The Roots of Sorrow*, indicates that having hope was the key for David and Jeremiah to the door out of the blackness of depression and fear.

Our society is, at many points, a desert crowded with people who are alone, some of them desperately alone: a solo mother on twenty-four-hour duty for her children; a woman or man who carries the weight of having been sexually or physically abused; a person who is HIV-positive or has AIDS; a person whose parents divorced, either recently or years ago, who has feelings of responsibility for the divorce, rejection by one or both parents, or a deep unmet ache for the parent who is no longer present; and a person who appears to be functioning well in life, but who is in deep emotional crisis and pain.

Gerard Egan says that 'learning takes place when options are increased'. The whole society of which we are a part has a challenge to offer useful options to people who are stuck, alone, in the crowded desert.

The funeral of a young man who had suicided was attended by about two hundred young adults. Together with his mother, I tried to tackle the task of exploring options for life. Several members of our parish attended in order to be available to talk with anyone who may have wanted that support.

Several of the young man's friends asked for time with us to discuss the questions his suicide forced them to address. We have had the privilege of entering relationships with these women and men and have begun to walk with them along a painful desert road through their grief, anger and confusion. A major part of our interactions has been to consider options for life and to encourage them to care for each other in ways that enhance those options.

Gerard Egan writes: 'Counselling has value only to the degree that it leads to valued outcomes in the client's day-to-day life.' This must certainly be true for the work we do as Christ's church in sharing with people in their pain and in their struggles to hold onto meaning and value for life.

Life is a balance
between tensions and freedoms,
highs and lows,
and all that blows us
this way and that;
so God
give us some wisdom,
a positive view
to balance this life
on the truth that is you.

Milton J. Drake, 'Life is a balance'

Each year, one adult in 250 attempts suicide and about one in 10 000 succeeds. In this country and in the USA and Canada, suicide is now the second most common cause of death after accidents in the fifteen- to thirty-four-year-old age-group.

Richard Winter, *The Roots of Sorrow*

In Australia, Canada and other Western countries, four times as many males commit suicide as females. The highest risk age group are the fifteen- to thirty-year-olds. What is it that makes men more likely to suicide than women? Men are much more alone than women. How do we get men to be more interactive about the major issues in their lives?

Professor Bryan Tanney

Suicide seldom — if ever — has simple causes. It may be tempting to identify a self-inflicted death with a specific event which triggered it. We might note that financial ruin preceded a banker's suicide or that the natural death of the husband prompts the wife to kill herself. Ordinarily, however, we will find that such events are the last straw in a sequence of things which may have been mounting for years.

Bruce Turley, *Being There for Others*

One November day two geese, somehow separated from the family to which they belonged, settled down on a small beach behind a tavern in Tiburon, California. Tiburon is a sophisticated village across the Golden Gate from San Francisco, with pleasure craft filling its small, sheltered harbour. The two geese quickly won the interest of the bartenders and the waitresses and the people who keep their boats in the marina below the Main Street shops and restaurants.

Soon, it was discovered that one goose was blind and that the other, a gander, had bravely sacrificed his migratory freedom to stay behind and keep his mate company. Thus emerges another demonstrated characteristic of geese: *they keep company with the fallen.*

From this metaphor, drawn from the earth and skies filled with geese in migration, comes an inescapable confrontation with the witness of the Bible about the vocation of the church in the world: *keeping company with the fallen!*

Browne Barr, *High Flying Geese*

Sometimes, a person's most urgent need in the midst of crisis is simply for someone to be there with them. This demonstrates the ministry of presence — of being with people in the darker, more difficult experiences of their lives. It lives out the biblical image of God who chooses to become involved in others' suffering, entering into it with them and sharing their pain.

Bruce Turley, *Turning Points*

In technological society, people are anonymous and yet they want to be known. There is a longing for acceptance and yet many are stranded by isolation and damned by the prejudices which lurk in the minds of their neighbours. The secular outlook exalts human ability to bear and solve problems. But people recognise that many burdens they are called to bear are so heavy that they need spiritual and social resources in dealing with them.

Bruce Turley, *Expanding Horizons of Care*

A [person's] concern, even in. . . despair over the worthwhileness of life is spiritual distress, but by no means a mental disease. It may well be that interpreting the first in terms of the latter motivates doctors to bring their patients' existential despair under a heap of tranquilising drugs. It is their task, rather, to pilot the patient through their existential crisis of growth and development.

Viktor Frankl, *Man's Search for Meaning*

Interpret my life, God,
when the party is ended
and I run out of life-wine,
yet my time's not expended.
Interpret my life, God,
in the life-light of Jesus,
for my past and my future
find in you my life nurture.
Interpret my life, God,
create my new story,
the new feast of meaning,
the new wine of life dawning.

Turn my water to life, God —
make your gospel my story;
take the life I here offer
and create my new meaning.

Milton J. Drake, *Interpret my Life God*

Seeing how connected we all are to a human family system
that passes along dysfunction and pain not only helps us
to forgive those who have wronged us; it also helps us to
forgive and accept the darkest and most shamed parts of
ourselves. This helpful insight, however, is not enough
by itself. Such acceptance must be experienced before we
can practise it. Humans are social beings and, as
psychiatrist Irving Yalom has said emphatically, 'It is the
relationship that heals.'

Joanne Ross Feldmeth & Midge Wallace Finley,
We Weep for Ourselves and our Children

The faith that God is at work in human life is not a release
from our responsibility, but the reason for our working in
hope — not suspending the clinical skills which have become valued tools of pastoral practice, but certainly
transcending them.

Gene Bartlett, *The Authentic Pastor*

We come to expect that Jesus will include individuals who
have been pushed to the margins of society. He will
ignore local prejudices, criticise wooden legalism and
elevate women above their socially assigned station in life.
He will insist that institutions serve rather than enslave
people. He will heal lives and challenge people about
their social responsibilities. He has a respect for tradition
and yet he is not imprisoned by it. We find him
knowledgeable and direct in his assessment of a person's
past and yet his primary interest is in new beginnings.

Bruce Turley, *Expanding Horizons of Care*

Transform
the splinters of my soul
into rainbows,

born of many tears,
through which your sun
now shines.

Milton J. Drake, 'Rainbows'

Christian hope works toward encouragement rather than despair in the long run. It is not founded on compulsive striving toward unrealistic and unattainable goals. Its starting point, rather, is the unqualified acceptance of people as they are, granting them recognition — not because of their achievements, but in spite of them. From there, it encourages and enables people to eliminate the restless striving for attention. This is possible because, as we have said, in a truly Christian community, people are respected for being persons [not for being successful] and are made to feel that they belong.

Bruce Turley, Being There for Others

Peace of God
permeate me,
fill me.
Stress and strain
tear at mind and body.
Bring your peace alive
in me.
Bring your peace alive
for all who walk alone
life's crowded deserts,
that they will know the hope
you bring.
God of peace
permeate us
fill us. Amen.

Milton J. Drake, 'Under Stress'

A Benediction
The peace of God, which surpasses all understanding, guard your hearts and your minds in Christ Jesus. Amen.

Philippians 4: 7, NRSV

45

God and the Hebrew midwives

Therefore, they set taskmasters over them to oppress them with forced labour. They built supply cities, Pithom and Rameses, for Pharaoh. But the more they were oppressed, the more they multiplied and spread, so that the Egyptians came to dread the Israelites. The Egyptians became ruthless in imposing tasks on the Israelites, and made their lives bitter with hard service in mortar and brick and in every kind of field labour. They were ruthless in all the tasks that they imposed on them.

The king of Egypt said to the Hebrew midwives, one of whom was named Shiphrah and the other Puah, 'When you act as midwives to the Hebrew women, and see them on the birthstool, if it is a boy, kill him; but if it is a girl, she shall live.' But the midwives feared God; they did not do as the king of Egypt commanded them, but they let the boys live.

So the king of Egypt summoned the midwives and said to them, 'Why have you done this and allowed the boys to live?' The midwives said to Pharaoh, 'Because the Hebrew women are not like the Egyptian women; for they are vigorous and give birth before the midwife comes to them.'

So God dealt well with the midwives; and the people multiplied and became very strong. And because the midwives feared God, he gave them families. Then, Pharaoh commanded all his people, 'Every boy that is born to the Hebrews you shall throw into the Nile, but you shall let every girl live.'

(Exodus 1: 11–22 — NRSV)

Many of you perhaps were shaped the way I was in terms of where you learned your first Exodus story. I didn't get mine in Sunday school, because I didn't go to Sunday school. I got my total mental furniture from Cecil B. DeMille movies. It's impossible that Moses looks like anything except Charleton Heston. Once, I saw Charleton Heston in a grocery store and thought, *What's Moses doing in this grocery store?*

When we think about where the Exodus experience begins, most of us, I think, tend to believe it begins with the story of Moses. It began in a different place, in a surprising place — in a place, I think, that has lessons for all of us.

Scholars tell us that midwives in Israel were barren women. In a culture within which having children and a family was the ordinary way to build a life, to obtain respect, to know the blessing of God, these barren, somewhat marginal women found their place in this community as those who helped other women bring forth that new life. Part of their daily work, their daily routine, what they got up in the morning to do, was to help — to bring forth life.

And then came the order. Notice that it came from one who had the official authority to give it. He was the legal power in that place — and these midwives were slaves, fully under the authority of this king.

So the order comes down: 'Kill the boys.' The girls could be kept as house servants, slaves, but 'kill the boys — and do it in such a way that it doesn't look like we did it'. Then two ordinary women, who probably were illiterate, said 'no'.

That took courage. Where did it come from? 'They feared God.' They had a fundamental conviction that while there was a Pharaoh, there was a God over Pharaoh and, while they must give account to the human authorities and powers, they must give account to One over all human authorities and powers. They feared God and they said 'no'.

Then Pharaoh summoned them. Can you feel what it must have been like to have the soldiers march to your little hovel in the slave quarters and push their way into the place, and say, 'You! Come!' and then to stand before the Pharaoh and have him say, 'Why did you do that?'

It's interesting: the scholars through the centuries, from the early church fathers down through the Reformers to contemporary days, have spent most of their commentary space wrestling over the issue of whether or not the midwives lied, missing the whole point of the narrative, which is that the midwives disobeyed.

They had carefully framed their answer (given in verse 19) — and I think the writer intends us to enjoy a joke at Pharaoh's expense. But there is a truth here: the Egyptian women, because of the slave culture, were pampered city women. The Hebrew women were hardworking slaves, strong and vigorous, who probably didn't have as much trouble. But if they always had their babies before the midwives arrive, why were there midwives?

What was God's response? So God was kind to the midwives and the people increased. . . 'And because the midwives feared God, he gave them families of their own.'

The fear of God.

I want to say just a small thing, but I think it's very deep. In our increasingly secular culture and in our increasingly secular selves — because we are part of this culture, it is in us even as we seek to be open to the transforming power of God — we are tempted to believe or act as if there were no God to be feared. We have all heard the sermon or address that claims with beguiling if misplaced simplicity: 'Friends, you really don't have to be afraid of God. God is our friend. He's loving. He's nice.'

Yet, we *do* have to be afraid of God. God is the Holy One. God is the Just One. God is the Judge. We also know him as our lover, but he is no less judge for being that.

Notice that these midwives were not from the spiritual professions. They had jobs right in the middle of the society and, in their job, they were governed by the fear of God.

When the fear of God is gone, the decisions of daily life are threatened.

What did these women have? They had courage. Where did that courage come from? It came from a conviction that there was a God to whom we give an account, a God that honours us when we obey him, a God who means good for people and will have his way in the world. And so they acted rightly.

I have one other suspicion. It's not in the text. There were two of them and I think it's possible that part of their courage came from the fact that when they sought to do their daily work, there was another one who stood alongside of them. Shiphrah had Puah. Puah had Shiphrah. And when they were threatened, they could say, 'Well, at least when we go before Pharaoh, we'll go together.'

The church that has long thought of itself as gathered and scattered needs to understand that, in the scattered-ness of our daily work, we need companions — companions of conviction and faith and courage, who can help us do what God calls us to do.

God honoured them. In fact, the names of these two ordinary women, Shiphrah and Puah, have been preserved for over three thousand years. God uses ordinary people to say 'no' when 'no' needs to be said.

❧❦

The reality of cruel oppression and the oppression itself is heightened as the oppressor fears the very one who is being oppressed. This is a pattern built into the human experience. You could go all around the world today and I could exegete this passage — the story of oppression.

In South Africa or Sudan or any place that you wanted to name, the oppressor comes to fear the one who is being oppressed. Then, the screws are tightened and the stakes are raised and the oppressor moves from ruthless injustice — hard labour — to attempted genocide. And, as is common with patterns of oppression, the genocide then is to be carried out by persons from within the oppressed community. In the Exodus story, the genocide is to be carried out by two ordinary women.

Roberta Hestenes

As a child, I did not regard the stories of the Bible in a human, helpful sense. Its heroes were always depicted to me as so grand and perfect that I felt no kinship with them at all. I was fascinated by their exploits, but it didn't occur to me to look on them as fellow strugglers and thus resources in my own struggles. To me, the great names of the Bible were creatures of another order of being. And it was not until I learned to humanise these heroes and to see them the way the Bible depicts them that they became helpful companions alongside me.

I heard Keith Miller, an extraordinarily helpful twentieth-century Christian, make this very point. He was underlining the fact that the Christian life is not easy and that all of us experience fear and fall down at times in trying to follow God's will. Miller said that the story of the Bible is not an account of super men and women doing heroic things out of abnormal resources, but rather a story of chicken-hearted folk like you and me who did not give up when they failed, but somehow 'kept on keeping on' and dared to put the keys of their future into the hands of a merciful God even when they were afraid.

Courage is not the capacity never to be afraid. As Karl Baker reminds us, 'Courage is fear that has said its prayers.' This is what biblical heroes, rightly understood, can teach us.

John Claypool, 'Humanising Our Heroes'

Courage is derived from inner strength. People are courageous when they have deep inner resources which sustain their daily living. In Markus Barth's book, *The Broken Wall*, he has this pertinent statement: 'Christians can "take it", for they realise that God, in his patience, wisdom and love, knows how things are.' They know also what is yet to come. The saints, therefore, need not fear the future. The days may be bad, but still they are not so bad.

The most courageous people I have met are those who are sustained by these inner spiritual resources. Their lives are like productive fields nourished by underground springs.

True courage is not lack of fear that can lead to fool-hardiness. True courage recognises fear, reluctance and hesitancy, but has the resources to overcome them.

Thomas Fuller said that 'fear can keep you out of danger, but courage can support in it'. Jean Paul Richter put it this way: 'Courage consists not in blindly over-looking danger, but in seeing it and conquering it.'

Ron Elbourne, 'Going Strong for the Top'

Isn't it strange that some people think they can be on profanely intimate terms with God? When you listen to them talking about him, you get the impression that he is just something of a good friend to them, almost like a chum or a pal. They seem to have virtually no feeling of awe and reverence towards him. A notorious actress in Hollywood says publicly that 'God is such a dear'.

And a popular song calls him 'the man upstairs'. What a horrible indignity! How can anyone be so dreadfully naive about God? And yet many people are. Otherwise, how can you explain the popularity of that song? It evidently expressed their religious emotions very well. They would probably have no use for the inspired psalm which begins with those words: 'The Lord reigneth: let the people tremble. . .'

Peter Eldersveld, 'The Fear of God'

What happens if there is no fear of God? If there is no fear of God, our horizon shrinks and our measurement of right and wrong becomes utilitarian: 'What's in it for me? What will I gain? Can I get ahead? Will this make a difference?' We may even ask: 'What can I get away with?' or 'Who will know?'

More and more, I find those kinds of equations shaping our behaviour as a society and even as a church. We become vulnerable and susceptible to pressures to conform to the wrong values, to give in to power even when that power is used for destructive or evil purposes, to live a lie, and to deny our calling. When we're called to be helpers, we turn into hurters because power told us to.

I thought of the construction worker who cuts a corner in building a building because 'Who will know?', the construction [contractor] who arranged to water the cement so that the profit margin on the contract would be larger, the pastor watching the pornographic movie in the hotel a long way from home because 'Who will know?', or the skipper of the Valdez.

But not just the skipper of the Valdez. What I thought about was: *How many people on the Valdez knew that the man had a drinking problem and said nothing?*

Roberta Hestenes

Not long before his own untimely death in 1973, Daniel Day Williams was preaching in the chapel of Union Seminary and ended with these words: 'There is a secret in the Christian life. It is the secret of being willing to let go of all our particular prescriptions of how God ought to deal with us. Without this, we have not really learned what divine love is. The Christian spirit in the face of death is, "Whether we live or whether we die, we are the Lord's. Our life is hid with Christ in God." I believe that God will do with my life and with every life what an infinitely wise and caring God can and will do with it. And this is enough not only to live by, but to die by as well.' Amen.

John Claypool, 'Courage and Death'

Lord:
Help me to understand that it isn't what life does to me that matters, but what I do to life.

Give me courage to face whatever I fear and the strength of will to conquer it.

Give me a strong determination to do your will, whatever the cost.

May I have firm inner convictions about what is right and what is wrong and choose, by a kind of reflex instinct, to do what is good, noble and right.

Thankyou for heroes and heroines of faith who have done this before me. Some survived the anger of unjust authorities; some didn't. Some lived to fight another day; others paid the supreme sacrifice for their noble deeds.

So, Lord, when my moral courage is failing, my emotional and physical strength is weak, and my spirit is vacillating between good and evil, equip me with spiritual armour to fight on in your strength, until the victory is won.

You're on my side and that's all that matters.

Thankyou. Amen.

A Benediction

May you know, deep down, that if God is for you (and he is), whoever or whatever is against you is much, much weaker! May you live obediently, with courage and integrity, even when life is hard. May you fear no-one or no thing, other than God, who will give you the strength to endure.

Alleluia! Amen.

46

God wrap me up

Teach me your way, O Lord; lead me in a straight path because of my oppressors. Do not hand me over to the desire of my foes, for false witnesses rise up against me, breathing out violence. I am still confident of this: I will see the goodness of the Lord in the land of the living. Wait for the Lord; be strong and take heart and wait for the Lord.

Praise the Lord, O my soul; all my inmost being praise his holy name. Praise the Lord, O my soul, and forget not all his benefits. He forgives all my sins and heals all my diseases: he redeems my life from the pit and crowns me with love and compassion. He satisfies my desires with good things, so that my youth is renewed like the eagle's.

Do you not know? Have you not heard? The Lord is the everlasting God, the creator of the ends of the earth. He will not grow tired or weary, and his understanding no-one can fathom. He gives strength to the weary and increases the power of the weak. Even youths grow tired and weary, and young men stumble and fall; but those who hope in the Lord will renew their strength. They will soar on wings like eagles; they will run and not grow weary, they will walk and not be faint.

Therefore, I urge you. . . in view of God's mercy, to offer your bodies as living sacrifices, holy and pleasing to God — which is your spiritual worship. Do not conform any longer to the pattern of this world, but be transformed by the renewing of your mind. Then, you will be able to test and approve what God's will is — his good, pleasing and perfect will.

Let us not become weary in doing good, for at the proper time we will reap a harvest if we do not give up. Therefore, as we have opportunity, let us do good to all people, especially to those who belong to the family of believers.

I know what it is to be in need and I know what it is to have plenty. I have learned the secret of being content in any and every situation, whether well fed or hungry, whether living in plenty or in want. I can do everything through him who gives me strength.

Since, then, you have been raised with Christ, set your hearts on things above, where Christ is seated at the right hand of God. Set your minds on things above, not on earthly things. For you died and your life is now hidden with Christ in God. When Christ who is your life appears, then you also will appear with him in glory.

(Psalm 27: 11–14; Psalm 103: 1–5; Isaiah 40: 28–31; Romans 12: 1–2; Galatians 6: 9–10; Philippians 4: 12–13; Colossians 3: 1–4 — all NIV)

We should be soaring to spiritual heights like eagles — and yet. . . we find ourselves fluttering about with sparrows and starlings a couple of metres from the ground.

One reason why we fail to soar is that we feel we've been treated badly in life. We've been given a bad hand. As a result, we spend far too much time 'shoulding on ourselves', as John Powell puts it graphically.

Jewish writers did not try to prove God's existence. They took it for granted, like the air they breathed. Isaiah and other prophets simply reminded people of how God was able to comfort his people and restock their depleted supplies of spiritual strength.

Isaiah opens what we title chapter 40 with a message of comfort. 'Comfort, yes, comfort my people!' Isaiah's people badly needed comfort. Their days were full of change and crisis. Commerce was in chaos and kingdoms all around were collapsing. Governments rose and fell, it seemed, with the change of the wind. The security of the past crumbled around them as old standards were shed and new fads and fancies swept in.

The reaction of many to these changes was to complain that God had let them down. Where was the God of their forbears? To which Isaiah was virtually saying: 'Where he has always been!' He has not left you. He has not forsaken you. He is alive and well.

So Isaiah is commanded by the Most High to comfort his people. The chapter rises to a dynamic peak at the end. While the people may feel faint, the strength of almighty God is not waning. He gives strength to the fainting. Only one thing is required in order to receive this strength from on high — faith.

Little has changed on the world scene — perhaps only the names of the countries and the names of the leaders. 'The more things change, the more they remain the same.' And yet God stays steady, unchanging. 'The creator of the earth neither faints, nor is weary' (Isaiah 40: 28).

We grow weak and weary, just like Isaiah's people. Even the strongest of us feel like giving up: 'Even the youths shall faint and be weary and the young men shall utterly fall.'

Now comes Isaiah's staggering promise: 'But those who wait on the Lord shall renew their strength.'

English historian John Rowntree discovered his eyesight was failing when he was approaching the height of his career. His doctor told him he would soon be totally blind. Rowntree said later that he came out of the doctor's rooms and took a few moments standing on the street to compose himself. He wrote: 'I suddenly felt the love of God wrap me up as though an invisible presence enfolded me and a joy filled me such as I had never known before.'

To be going blind, to be faced with darkness before one's bright hopes for the future could be fulfilled, to stand on the edge of suffering and despair and yet to know the love of God, is to experience what Paul calls the love from which nothing can separate. It's a love that remains constant regardless of how weary we feel. Even in the dark, God's gentle touch holds us steady. Trust him!

Today's leader stands conspicuously alone and vulnerable.

Whatever difficulties and dangers are imposed on us — whether corporate, political, family, or personal — we're going to have to solve them on our own. No cunningly designed program, no sleight of hand accounting, no 'quick fix' is coming to save us.

Today's generation of leaders can't recall the pseudo-superiority resulting from our victories in World War II. We don't have instant ingredients that need only a pot, water, heat and a few seconds to cook. As H.L. Mencken wrote: 'There's always an easy solution to every problem . . . neat, plausible. . . and wrong!'

Enlightened leadership today speaks of solving problems as only one alternative. They understand that removing mountains is seldom feasible, so they must decide whether to tunnel through, go around, or climb over.

Tom Haggai with Richard L. Federer,
How the Best is Won

Fear of ultimate failure is almost a fear of succeeding too well — of going so far you overreach yourself. We fear the great height because we don't believe we can stay up there, and the fall back down will be too painful, too humiliating. Plan for one success at a time instead of anticipating where it will all lead. Remember that you can always stop at any point — if you should.

But in fact if you believe you have any ability at all, and if you let that belief move you to try to achieve something, the very effort will strengthen the belief, your confidence will grow and, because confidence itself is an asset, your chances of achievement will increase. And as you do strive and achieve, your fear of the great height will diminish. Regard your fear of it as an illusion of childhood, like the little boy's impression that his father is gigantic. When you're that size yourself, it will seem only natural.

George Weinberg, *Self Creation*

We are mentally closer to the seventeenth century than our predecessors of the nineteenth, who believed in continuous progress and British domination and regarded England as safe for ever from the threat of despotism and the shadow of medieval barbarity. Having lived for a decade and a half upon the edge of totalitarian night, with conscription at home replacing the press gang and cries assailing our ears from concentration camps abroad, we can no longer boast that our society has outgrown the savagery of our ancestors.

In a different guise, we fight the same battles against the same Apollyon, whether we call it the totalitarian state, or describe it, like John Bunyan, by the simpler name of sin. And now, as then, our most reliable armour is a national Christian tradition which has no connection with power and a great deal with resistance to power.

It was established for us by such men and women as the seventeenth century nonconformists, whose only power was the power of the spirit. They bought our freedom at the price of their own and, driven by conscience, repeatedly broke oppressive laws which finally yielded to their fearless opposition.

Vera Brittain, *In the Steps of John Bunyan*

I believe in Jesus and doubtless this is quite acceptable to all and sundry; it is only when I spell out what I mean by the confession that hackles arise and barriers are erected. Yet there can be no doubt that Jesus Christ is not simply a figure of history; he has torn history asunder and has influenced and shaped cultures and nations for almost two thousand years. Long ago, they crucified him and down through the generations many attempts have been made to banish his name from the lips of [his followers] and yet he is still in the midst of all of life, challenging and judging.

John Wilson, *Pity My Simplicity*

Clearly, our efforts to find new solutions will continue. If of little value for the present generation, they may eventually benefit a wiser and more sober human race. Yet the inability of technology to invest human life with an ultimate meaning and purpose should in these days, more than ever, cause us to look to God and to see our role from his perspective. When we do this, we not only find renewed vitality for the tasks at hand but, more important, we begin to see our way through the hungry multitudes pressing at our doorstep. For it seems that God is telling us simply to share with them whatever we have and, when it runs low, to try to get more and, when there is no more, to leave the issue to him.

He is telling us to enter into their suffering without concern for the outcome. He is reminding us that, as much as we have done for the least of these our brethren, we have done unto him. We cannot, as some do, restrict the interpretation of 'brothers/sisters' to mean fellow-Christians alone. We wince when we hear Christians refer to much of the agony of mankind as the judgment of God; it may be, but it is not for us to say or even to think.

Thomas Hale, *Don't Let the Goats Eat the Loquat Trees*

It is very difficult for any of us to see ourselves without someone to hold up a mirror for us. Certainly, depression has an important message for us about the necessity of change. We may need to pay attention to our job, lifestyle, living accommodation or some other external circumstance which needs to be changed. It may be a message about the quality and nature of the relationships we make which are somehow less than fulfilling. Or we may need to change our attitude to some fact that we cannot alter.

Myra Chave-Jones, *Coping with Depression*

Loving Lord, I easily grow weary. When I think I'm riding the crest of a spiritual wave, I get dumped in the shallows and my life seems full of the sand and grit of despair. My body and my mind fail. So often I attempt to rise to the need and I discover I am weary beyond measure.

My strength gets sapped so easily. My hope dissipates and I feel I cannot go on. There is so much I want to accomplish in life. So many demands. Please teach me I only have one life to live on earth and that only what's done for Christ will last.

Dear Lord, may I rest in you. Teach me to rely on your strength for Jesus' sake. Amen.

A Benediction
May our gracious Lord give you strength for your journey and power sufficient for your work. Amen.

God's secret

Where shall wisdom be found? And where is the place of understanding?

The secret things belong to the Lord our God; but the things that are revealed belong to us and to our children for ever, that we may do all the words of this law.

For my thoughts are not your thoughts, nor are your ways my ways, says the Lord. For as the heavens are higher than the earth, so are my ways higher than your ways and my thoughts than your thoughts.

For he has made known to us in all wisdom and insight the mystery of his will, according to his purpose which he set forth in Christ. . . the riches of the glory of this mystery, which is Christ in you, the hope of glory.

His name shall be called Emmanuel (which means, God with us)

We speak God's wisdom, secret and hidden, which God decreed before the ages for our glory.

All this Jesus said. . . to fulfil: 'I will utter what has been hidden since the foundation of the world.'

Father, I desire that they also, whom thou hast given me, may be with me where I am, to behold my glory which thou hast given me in thy love for me before the foundation of the world.

The precious blood of Christ. . . foreordained before the foundation of the world.

Come, O blessed of my Father, inherit the kingdom prepared for you from the foundation of the world.

He chose us in him before the foundation of the world, that we should be holy and blameless before him.

All who dwell on the earth will worship it, every one

whose name has not been written before the foundation of the world in the book of life of the Lamb that was slain.

For we are his workmanship, created in Christ Jesus for good works, which God prepared beforehand, that we should walk in them.

Think of us. . . as. . . stewards of God's mysteries.

Trust in him at all times, O people; pour out your heart before him; God is a refuge for us.

(Job 28: 12; Deuteronomy 29: 29; Isaiah 55: 8–9; Ephesians 1: 9; Colossians 1: 27b; Matthew 1: 23; 1 Corinthians 2: 7; Matthew 13: 34–35 — all RSV; John 17: 24, RSV/KJV; 1 Peter 1: 19–20, KJV; Matthew 25: 34; Ephesians 1: 4; Revelation 13: 8; Ephesians 2: 10; I Corinthians 4: 1; Psalm 62: 8 — all RSV)

In the old King James version of the Bible, the word 'wait' occurs 101 times, 'trust' occurs 184 times and 'understand/understanding' occurs 298 times. The simple deduction from such numbers might be that, in God's economy, trusting and understanding are twice/three times more important than waiting — or just simply, *more* important if the mathematics are left out. Our relationship and our knowledge of God are valued more highly than the speed with which God acts. This is never easy to grasp in the busy twentieth century, with doubtless an even busier twenty-first century ahead.

That relationship, however, has been prepared from before the foundation of the world. Before God created the universe 'and all that therein is', he knew his Son would have to suffer and die. And yet he still went ahead and created it! Most of us would have taken the other option.

Before the foundation of the world, God chose you and me. That's fantastic! God said, in effect, looking at the billions created since the beginning, 'That one there, the whole family here, that group for three generations, that cluster over there, this one in that century, that group in that country, those who live in this region, these who speak that language — all these I will choose for my kingdom, prepared before the foundation of the world.'

Such knowledge is too great for me, said Job. God knew our parents, our grandparents, our great-grandparents, our great-great-grandparents — and so on all the way back. He knew the one who was born illegitimately and the one who died in childbirth. He planned it all and, through that maze of all mazes, he chose. . . you, and he chose me.

Enough? No, there's more! He not only chose us, but, *before the foundation of the world*, he also knew 'the good works that we should walk in'. He knew the intimate details of our lives as well! That's incredible! And we get worried when we don't see what he's doing? We can't wait for the unfolding of his purposes?

He asks us to trust him — he who has the whole world in his hands has our world in his hands, also. We may not understand what he is doing — we are to be much more concerned with our relationship with him and the good we do to others. And if we have to wait awhile? Brother, sister, let us have patience. Whatever in the world God is doing, be sure that it is God, our God, who is doing it. In Christ, he is 'waiting' too, until the kingdoms of this world become his kingdom, the new heaven and the new earth are formed and he returns to take his own to be with him for ever.

Those who lived in Jesus' time had had to wait until the message of the prophets came to pass. They had to wait until God's secret became visible, the incredible 'Christ in you, the hope of glory'. If they waited centuries, cannot we wait days? God's secrets *are* revealed; his will has been made known and he is working his purposes out until the day when 'the earth shall be filled with the knowledge of the Lord, as the waters cover the sea'.

***

Greece said, 'Be moderate; know yourself.' Rome said, 'Be strong; order yourself.' Confucianism says, 'Be superior; correct yourself.' Buddhism says, 'Be disillusioned; annihilate yourself.' Hinduism says, 'Be separated; merge yourself.' Islam says, 'Be submissive; bend yourself.' Modern materialism says, 'Be industrious; enjoy yourself.'

And modern dilettantism says, 'Be broad; cultivate yourself.'

Christianity, on the other hand, says, 'Be Christ-like; give yourself.'

Sam Shoemaker, *Extraordinary Living for Ordinary Men*

'I said to the man who stood at the gate of the year: "Give me a light that I may tread safely into the unknown." And he replied, "Go out into the darkness and put your hand into the hand of God. That shall be to you better than light and safer than a known way."'

To look is one thing. To see what you look at is another. To understand what you see is a third. To learn from what you understand is still something else. But to act on what you learn is what really matters.

Anonymous

Those who are negligent awaken in the morning by considering what they are going to do; and those who are wise by considering what God will do with them.

An anonymous Muslim mystic

Put your trust in God and keep your powder dry.

Oliver Cromwell

Choose for us, God, nor let our weak preferring
Cheat us of good Thou hast for us designed:
Choose for us, God; Thy wisdom is unerring,
And we are fools and blind.

'Still Will We Trust'

I do not know what next may come across
   my pilgrim way;
I do not know tomorrow's road, nor see beyond
   today;
But this I know — my Saviour knows the path
   I cannot see
And I can trust his wounded hand to guide and care
   for me.

I do not know what may befall of sunshine or of pain;
I do not know what may be mine of pleasure or of pain;
But this I know — my Saviour knows and
    whatso'er it be
Still I can trust his love to give what will be
    best for me.

I do not know what may await or what the morrow
    brings;
But with the glad salute of faith I hail its opening wings;
For this I know — that in my Lord shall all
    my needs be met
And I can trust the heart of him who has not failed
    me yet.

Anonymous

Climb if you will, but remember that courage and strength are nought without prudence, and a momentary negligence may destroy the happiness of a lifetime. Do nothing in haste, look well to each step and from the beginning think what may be the end.

Edward Whymper

Be sure if God sends you on a stony path, he will provide you with strong shoes.

Anonymous

Almighty God:
you have created the heavens and the earth
and made us in your own image.
Teach us to discern your hand in all your works,
and to serve you with reverence and thanksgiving;
through Jesus Christ our Lord,
who with you and the Holy Spirit,
reigns supreme over all things,
now and for ever.

Lord God:
the protector of all who trust in you,

without whom nothing is strong, nothing is holy:
increase and multiply upon us your mercy,
that with you as our ruler and guide,
we may so pass through the things temporal
that we finally lose not the things eternal.
Grant this, heavenly Father,
for the sake of Jesus Christ our Lord.

Merciful God:
you have prepared for those who love you
such good things that surpass our understanding.
Pour into our hearts such love towards you
that we, loving you above all things,
may obtain your promises,
which exceed all that we can desire;
through Jesus Christ our Lord.   Amen.

A Benediction
May the God of hope fill you with all joy and peace in believing,
so that by the power of the Holy Spirit you may abound in
hope.   Amen.

Romans 15: 13

48

My knapsack on my back

He said, 'My presence will go with you and I will give you rest.'

'Be strong and bold; have no fear or dread. . . because it is the Lord your God who goes with you; he will not fail you or forsake you.'

'I hereby command you: be strong and courageous; do not be frightened or dismayed, for the LORD your God is with you wherever you go.'

. . .and be content with what you have; for he has said, 'I will never leave you or forsake you.'

My friends, if anyone is detected in a transgression, you who have received the Spirit should restore such a one in a spirit of gentleness. Take care that you yourselves are not tempted. Bear one another's burdens and in this way you will fulfil the law of Christ. For if those who are nothing think they are something, they deceive themselves. All must test their own work; then that work, rather than their neighbour's work, will become a cause for pride. For all must carry their own loads.

(Exodus 33: 14; Deuteronomy 31: 6; Joshua 1: 9; Hebrews 13: 5; Galatians 6: 1–5 — all NRSV)

Our family is grown now, yet the memories of our children's early childhood days are as vivid to me as today's sunshine. One vibrant memory takes me walking through the wonderful forests of Costa Rica, where we saw all sorts of plants and trees growing along the tracks and we were sometimes fortunate to have as a travelling companion a guide who could give to each plant, bush or tree its particular botanical name. As we walked, we would sometimes sing: 'I love to go a wandering, along the mountain track, and as I go, I love to sing, my knapsack on my back. Valderi! Valdera! Valderi! Valdera-ha-ha-ha-ha-ha-ha!'

We loved to carry those knapsacks of goodies to munch on if we grew hungry and coats to wrap up in if the weather turned cold. We never considered those knapsacks were burdens when we were taking a mountain walk, surrounded by the overwhelming magnitude and unashamed opulence of God's creation. No, burdens were what we were forced to carry when things didn't go well for us; burdens felt heavy. Knapsacks, on the other hand, contained our own special things and did not seem heavy at all.

Many years later, as I was strolling through biblical terrain, a friendly guide helped me identify some words and ideas, seeing them with new eyes and calling them by their proper names. And my heart began to sing just as it had while walking the mountain tracks of Central America.

This time, we were walking through some well-known verses in Galatians 6, when I spotted something I hadn't properly understood: 'Bear one another's burdens. . .'; but then there is a seemingly opposite proposition outlined several verses later: '. . .carry your own load'. Many, many times I'd heard about bearing another person's burden, but I could not recall anyone mentioning, in this context, the need for me to carry my own load. What did 'load' mean, I asked? Was it just another meaning for 'burden'? And then my friendly guide gave me the correct word: 'Load, here, means knapsack!'

Valderi!

Each person has their own personal knapsack to carry; I have mine and you have yours. I take responsibility for mine. You take responsibility for yours. I need to be level-headed about the whole business, quietly accepting the humble reality of carrying my own load in my own knapsack, without fanfare or seeking the spotlight, without looking for the pity or sympathy of passers-by. The

Galatians text doesn't indicate that carrying another person's burden is more 'spiritual' than carrying one's own load, yet every sermon I've heard on this text has *always* focussed on burden-bearing for others and neglected load-carrying for oneself.

Would there be a little less burden-bearing if there was a little more knapsack-carrying, I wondered?

Even so, I am called to help others carry their temporary burdens for a while, to come alongside as their companion along the way. Yet in doing so, I can't take off my own uniquely-shaped knapsack in order to bear the burden of another person. The trick is for us each to flex our muscles in such a way that together we can manage two loads and one burden — you with your loaded-up knapsack, I with my loaded-up knapsack — and both of us bearing the additional burden for a while.

I want to redress the imbalance that has leaned toward seeing burden-bearing for others as a more sacred trust than load-carrying for oneself.

Valdera!

God is the One who is (and will always be) with us in all our wanderings along all our mountain tracks with our knapsacks on our backs. There is not one single bit or piece inside my knapsack or inside your knapsack that is not enfolded in God's love, wrapped in God's grace, saturated in God's mercy. I've begun to sing: 'Valderi! Valdera!' with new vigour and a great sense of joyful release.

It's not heavy; it's my knapsack.

❧❧

No matter what happens, keep on beginning and failing. Each time you fail, start all over again and you will grow stronger until you find that you have accomplished a purpose — not the one you began with, perhaps, but one that you will be glad to remember.

Helen Keller, *Teacher*

When I gaze at the ancient mountains,
their huge strength steadies my trembling.
The strength of the Lord made the galaxies,

and shaped this dear old planet.
You can never stumble out of his care;
he who loves you never falls asleep.
The One who looks after you is awake,
always alert to the cries of his children.
Your God cares for you,
closer than your own right hand.
Even the fiery sun will not harm you,
nor the barren face of the moon.
God will keep you going in hard times;
he'll treasure your very being.
When you leave for work in the morning,
and when you return home at evening,
he will surely be with you,
this day and for ever.

Bruce D. Prewer, Australian Psalms

What next? Why ask? Next will come a demand about which you already know all you need to know: that its sole measure is your own strength.

Forward! Thy orders are given in secret. May I always hear them — and obey.

Forward! Whatever distance I have covered, it does not give me the right to halt.

Forward! It is the attention given to the last steps before the summit which decides the value of all that went before.

Dag Hammarskjöld, Markings

The path to your door
Is the path within:
Is made by animals,
Is lined by flowers,
Is lined by thorns,
Is stained with wine,
Is lit by the lamp of sorrowful dreams:
Is washed with joy,
Is swept by grief,
Is blessed by the lonely traffic of art:
Is known by heart,
Is known by prayer,

Is lost and found,
Is always strange,
The path to your door.

Michael Leunig, *Common Prayers Collection*

One morning early, I was, as it were, woken up by prayer.
I began to say my morning prayers, but it was as if my
tongue was tied and I was overcome with the desire
simply to repeat the Jesus Prayer. I began to repeat it and
was immediately happy. My lips moved effortlessly of
their own accord.

I passed the whole of that day in a state of joy. It was
as though I was detached from everything and I felt as if
I was in another world. I went to see [the spiritual
director] and gave him a detailed account of all this.
When I had finished, he said: 'God has given you the
desire to pray and the capacity to do so without effort.'

From then on, how happy I was! What joy to feel
within me the fervour of my prayer.

Whenever I went into a church, I burned with love for
Jesus.

My solitary hut seemed like a magnificent palace and I
did not know how to thank God for having such an
excellent [spiritual director] to a poor sinner like myself.

But unfortunately I had not much longer to take advantage of his direction: my beloved master died at the
end of the summer.

And so I found myself alone once more.

The summer came to an end and the garden produce
was gathered in. The farmer gave me two silver roubles
in payment. I filled my knapsack with bread for the
journey and went back to my wandering life.

But I was no longer poor, as I had been previously.
Invoking the name of Jesus made my travelling a joyous
affair and everywhere I met with kindness. It seemed that
everyone was predisposed to love me.

So here I am on the road once more, constantly reciting
the Jesus Prayer which is dearer and more precious to me
than anything else.

God knows what has taken place within me; I do not.

I only know that I am happy and that I now understand
what the apostle meant when he said: 'Pray constantly.'

Carlo Carretto, *The Desert and Beyond*

Great is Thy faithfulness, O God my Father,
There is no shadow of turning with Thee;
Thou changest not, Thy compassions, they fail not;
As Thou has been Thou forever will be.

Great is Thy faithfulness! Great is Thy faithfulness!
Morning by morning new mercies I see;
All I have needed Thy hand hath provided,
Great is Thy faithfulness, Lord unto me!

Summer and winter and springtime and harvest,
Sun, moon and stars in their courses above
Join with all nature in manifold witness
To Thy great faithfulness, mercy and love.

Pardon for sin and a peace that endureth,
Thine own dear presence to cheer and to guide,
Strength for today and bright hope for tomorrow,
Blessings all mine, with ten thousand beside!

Thomas Chisholm, 'Great is Thy Faithfulness'

Amazing and wonderful God:
I want to thank you for being with me all along my journey
of yesterday and today; and that you will remain with me
through every tomorrow. My own particular knapsack is known
to you and, though I sometimes try to hand it over to someone
else to carry, I'm gradually realising it is mine. I truly believe
that every bit and piece in my knapsack is soaked and saturated
in your grace, mercy and love, but I need your reminders of
that truth during those times when self-pity rears its mean little
head.

Thankyou, too, for the companions along the way who have
waved and cheered me on, noticing my courageous efforts to
carry my loaded-up knapsack. I've twisted an ankle sometimes
and I've also tripped and even fallen flat on my face and my

companions have put courage into my heart. I have taken detours and later regretted them, but they don't give up on me.

Thankyou, too, for other companions who have helped bear my extra burdens from time to time. During such moments of grief and loss, these companions of mine have prayed, supported and loved me; and during times of physical weakness and vulnerability, they have worked and helped and served me.

Can anything be more wonderful and amazing than your faithfulness and theirs?

A Benediction

May you have a new discovery of the faithfulness of God with your every step along your journey. May you find courage, strength and determination to carry your own load with joy, learning also to flex your muscles in such a way that you can bear another's burdens when the need arises.

May you go with a song in your voice, knowing that our amazing and wonderful God sings with you as you go forward together. Amen.

49

With all your mind

So God created humankind in his own image, in the image of God he created them; male and female he created them.

Then my tongue shall tell of your righteousness and of your praise all day long. Oh, how I love your law! It is my meditation all day long.

Those of steadfast mind you keep in peace — in peace because they trust in you.

You shall love the Lord your God with all your heart, and with all your soul, and with all your mind.

So then, with my mind I am a slave unto the law of God, but with my flesh I am a slave to the law of sin. Let the same mind be in you that was in Christ Jesus.

Devote yourselves to prayer, keeping alert in it with thanksgiving. Rejoice always, pray without ceasing, give thanks in all circumstances; for this is the will of God in Christ Jesus for you. Do not quench the Spirit.

(Genesis 1: 27; Psalm 35: 28; Psalm 119: 97; Isaiah 26: 3; Matthew 22: 37; Romans 7: 25; Philippians 2: 5; Colossians 4: 2; 1 Thessalonians 5: 16–19 — all NRSV)

Educational psychologists assure us that English-speaking people of average intelligence are able to process words at the rate of 800 per minute or more.

That's a frightening thought for those of us who teach or preach, because few of us can speak much faster than 200 words per minute. Also, textbooks on oral presentations recommend no more than 150 words per minute for public speakers. This means that people in our audiences can still process an additional 600 words per minute while listening to us.

But it's a comforting thought for those of us who read. Once we learn to read at around 800 words per minute, our minds become fully occupied and we have no capacity for other thoughts to crowd in. We become totally involved in what we are reading.

Recently, when an Eastern guru came to Melbourne, crowds of Australians paid $400 to attend meditation intensive weekends at fashionable conference centres. A friend of mine took leave for several days to attend. Afterwards, my friend said that the guru was able to meditate, continually, without ceasing — even when doing other things. The guru was able to continue in meditation, I was told, even when washing dishes, when gardening or when addressing crowds, as well as in moments of solitude.

As I understand the capacity of the mind to handle words, I could see that this was possible. Later, when addressing a group of clergy and community workers, I told this story and suggested that if this leader of an Eastern religious group could be in a state of continuous meditation, surely we who are Christian could be in a state of continuous prayer. Surely, we can pray as we wash the dishes, as we garden, as we work on the car, as we teach and as we preach — as well as when we are alone in a quiet place.

When St Paul told the Thessalonians to pray without ceasing he, maybe, didn't just mean not to miss their morning or evening prayers. Our minds really can handle several different thoughts at once and 800 or more words per minute. We can pray whilst doing other things.

When defining the greatest commandment as loving your God with your heart and soul, Jesus added the words 'with all your mind'. We who are made in his image should use our minds to the fullest capacity of their created potential. We can pray, whatever else we are doing — even when reading. Maybe you are praying at the same time as you are reading this! We need never cease praying. So we truly understand what it is to live a life of prayer. All that we do becomes dedicated to our Lord and, 'without ceasing', we love him with all our mind.

❧

More things are wrought by prayer
Than this world dreams of. Wherefore let thy voice
Rise like a fountain for me by night and day.
For what are men better than sheep or goats
That nourish a blind life within the brain,
If, knowing God, they lift not hands of prayer
Both for themselves and those who call them friend?

Tennyson, *Morte D'Arthur*

We are always completely, and therefore equally, known to God. That is our destiny whether we like it or not. But though this knowledge never varies, the quality of our being known can. . . Ordinarily, to be known by God is to be, for this purpose, in the category of things. We are, like earthworms, cabbages and nebulae, objects of divine knowledge. But when we (a) become aware of the fact — the present fact, not the generalisation — and (b) assent with all our will to be so known, then we treat ourselves, in relation to God, not as things, but as persons. We have unveiled.

Not that any veil could have baffled his sight. The change is in us. The passive changes to the active. Instead of merely being known, we show, we tell, we offer ourselves to view.

C. S. Lewis, *Letters to Malcolm: Chiefly on Prayer*

The theme of our generation is: 'Get more, know more, do more' instead of 'Pray more, be more, serve more.'

Billy Graham

The idea of living and communicating is to have fun even when you are not. Your life is in your own hand and you can do it — your way.

Phil Boas, *Truth & Lies*

Prayer is not a machine. It is not magic. It is not advice offered to God. Our act, when we pray, must not, any more than all our other acts, be separated from the continuous act of God himself, in which alone all finite causes operate.

C.S. Lewis, *Fern-seed and Elephants*

I keep in touch with Jesus
And he keeps in touch with me,
And so we walk together
In perfect harmony;
There's not a day that passes,
There's not an hour goes by,
But that we have sweet fellowship,
My precious Lord and I.

Margaret W. Brown, *Youth Favorites*

Here in the quietness, Lord, we are part of each other.
Closer than lovers and loving close.
Thanks, Lord, for being part of me — not just now,
But in the hurly burly of life;
For being present in the children's smile,
The old man's whine, the mother's care;
For being where others are, Lord.
But most of all,
For once,
Being human.
Amen.

Roger Bush, *Prayers for Pagans*

Lord, I know that you are present in all places and in all time. I know that you are always aware of where I am, what I am doing and what I am thinking. Help me to so understand the mental capabilities of my mind that I may be continuously aware of you. Keep me in constant touch with you. Teach me how to be in a state of continuous prayer, wherever I am and whatever I am doing.

As I so pray, Lord, so must I act in accordance with your will for me.

Lord, you have made me in your image and given me a mind which is able to keep me in touch with you. Help me to realise that potential. Help me, too, to share these skills with others that they may also exercise their skills of continuous prayer, that we may all glory in your creation and be as you made us to be. Even as the disciples prayed, this, too, is our request: Lord, teach us to pray, without ceasing, in your name, and for your sake. Amen.

A Benediction
Go 'in prayer'. May God the creator enable you to develop your intellectual abilities; may Christ give you an understanding of your potential; and may the Holy Spirit assist you to worship continuously — with all your mind, to the glory of God and with his everlasting blessing. Amen.

The paradox of death

Turn, O Lord, save my life; deliver me for the sake of your steadfast love. For in death, there is no remembrance of you; in Sheol, who can give you praise?. . . For I am convinced that neither death, nor life, nor angels, nor rulers, nor things present, nor things to come, nor powers, nor height, nor depth, nor anything in all creation, will be able to separate us from the love of God in Jesus Christ our Lord.

Death and life are in the power of the tongue and those who love it will eat its fruits. Do not invite death by the error of your life, or bring on destruction by the works of your hands; because God did not make death and he does not delight in the death of the living. For he created all things so that they might exist; the generative forces of the world are wholesome, and there is no destructive poison in them, and the dominion of Hades is not on earth. For righteousness is immortal.

For all our days pass away under your wrath; our years come to an end like a sigh. The days of our life are seventy years, or perhaps eighty, if we are strong; even then their span is only toil and trouble; they are soon gone and we fly away.

Wretched man that I am! Who will rescue me from this body of death?. . . Jesus said to her, 'I am the resurrection and the life. Those who believe in me, even though they die, will live, and everyone who lives and believes in me will never die.'

(Psalm 6: 4–5; Romans 8: 38–39; Proverbs 18: 21; The Wisdom of Solomon 1: 12–15; Psalm 90: 9–10; Romans 7: 24; John 11: 25–26 — all NRSV)

My first funeral in an inner city Melbourne community was more like a baptism: that is, a baptism of fire for me. I had been given the dubious honour of officiating the service for ol' Jock. I felt doubtful because I could not afford to 'stuff up', in the words of an eloquent adviser. Jock, you see, just happened to be a patriarch for the Anglo working-class families in the area.

I used to come across Jock quite frequently at the Bayview pub (aptly named in an Aussie way because there was neither bay nor view). Jock was no angel. Day after day he was perched on, or in the process of falling off, his bar stool. He had lived a hard life. I guess his intoxicated state served as an escape from the tragedies in his life. Jock had not been in touch with his real family for thirty years. He had sailed from Scotland to Sydney in 1950. He arrived with one suitcase and a row of wristwatches up each arm. He sold a couple of watches for the train trip to get work at Port Melbourne.

The day for the funeral arrived. Most of the community were there. The funeral director was amazed at the turnout. I'll never forget the half dozen brilliant white stretch limos arriving, having ferried people across from the Bayview. No expense was spared for Jock (the wake lasted for two days). It was all to be a lavish affair funded by the 'battlers' of Kensington. He was one of their own. The community had become his surrogate family and Jock was one of its favourite sons because he had been 'true blue', a mate you could depend on. It was a time of sorrow and celebration.

The epitome of this paradox was the open casket with Jock laid in state, complete with peaked cap, Footscray football team scarf and guernsey, clasping his favourite 'stubbie' holder.

This community handled death in their own way. Some coped better than others. All felt the anxiety, fear, sorrow and awe that our mortality engenders. The negative and destructive (that is, sinful) side of this culture was exposed in its alcoholic and analgesic response to death.

On the other hand, there was a spontaneous, life-affirming reaction to Jock's death. People with few resources gave of their time and money freely. While they mourned Jock, they gave thanks for his life and his 'spirit' that was somehow still with them. These ordinary human experiences, fears and hopes became the connecting link for me to proclaim that death is not the end of the story.

❧

We die 'like the animals'. There can be no doubt about that. But what remains as an open question is: 'Where does dying bring us? Into a nothingness or into an absolutely final reality?'

Hans Kung, *Eternal Life?*

What can be called revelation can only be what actually abolishes death. For what else could it be? Could it be a remarkable knowledge about God and the world? Of what help is all that I know in face of death? Could it be moral achievement and the creation of culture? All this is subject to death, just as I am myself, first of all. Could it be 'experiences'? They do not save me from death. The 'numinous', then? Indeed, what is that but death itself? No, revelation can only be the gift of life through which death is overcome.

Rudolph Bultmann, *Existence and Faith*

The idea of the immortality of the soul is quite foreign to the Old Testament. It only entered later from the Greek world into Hellenistic Judaism. . . the Old Testament invariably confines human life to this earth. The departed live in shadowy existence in Sheol.

Rudolph Bultmann, *Primitive Christianity*

Death belongs integrally to human life. It is an essential element in our being. It is not only part of our heritage, but also part of our hope. Without death we could not be human, but we can diminish our humanity by the way we approach death. The deepest search in life — and our ultimate source of joy — is the search to find and develop our own proper and true humanity. When this search is thwarted, it becomes the source of our deepest frustrations.

Understanding and coming to terms with death is itself a way of understanding and coming to terms with the human, with life.

The converse is equally true. The failure to come to terms with death involves a failure truly to appreciate life and such a failure must be of the deepest concern to the church which seeks to celebrate life and to promote the human.

Graeme Griffin, *Death and the Church*

In contemporary America, the attempts to deprive death of its reality are just as frantic as they ever were in any culture. On the one hand, there are funeral customs — the embalming of bodies, the expensive caskets designed to delay as long as possible decay and decomposition, soft music piped into the tombs. Then, there is the deep-freezing of bodies, in the hope that one day medicine will have discovered a cure for the victim's disease and there can take place a joyous (?) resurrection.

It is of course natural to fear death or to be anxious in the face of death. But this is very different from constructing a vast cultural illusion (to say nothing of a highly profitable industry) to help us forget about death or to persuade ourselves that it is unreal.

John Macquarrie, *Existentialism*

The feeling of the vanity of the passing world kindles love in us, the only thing that triumphs over the vain and transitory, the only thing that fills life again and eternalises it. . . And love, above all when it struggles against destiny, overwhelms us with the feeling of the vanity of this world of appearances and gives us a glimpse of another world, in which destiny is overcome and liberty is law.

Miguel de Unamuno, *The Tragic Sense of Life*

Death be not proud, though some have called thee
Mighty and dreadful, for, thou art not soe,
For, those, whom thou think'st thou dost overthrow,
Die not, poore death, nor yet canst thou kill mee;
From rest and sleepe, which but thy pictures bee,

Much pleasure, then from thee, much more must flow,
And soonest our best men with thee doe goe,
Rest of their bones, and soules deliverie.
Thou art slave to Fate, chance, kings, and desperate men,
And dost with poyson, warre, and sickness dwell,
And poppie, or charmes can make us sleepe as well,
And better than thy stroake; why swell'st thou then?
One short sleepe past, wee wake eternally,
And death shall be no more, Death thou shalt die.

John Donne, Holy Sonnets: Divine Meditations

What I learned about dying is that I am called to die for
others. The very simple truth is that the way in which I
die affects many people. If I die with much anger and
bitterness, I will leave my family and friends behind in
confusion, guilt, shame or weakness. When I felt death
approaching, I suddenly realised how much I could influence
the hearts of those whom I would leave behind. . .

I realised on a very deep level that dying is the most
important act of living. It involves a choice to bind others
with guilt or to set them free with gratitude. The choice
is a choice between a death that gives life and a death
that kills.

Henri Nouwen, Beyond the Mirror

If I believe in an eternal life, I know that this world is not
the ultimate reality, conditions do not remain as they are
for ever, all that exists — including both political and
religious institutions — has a provisional character, the
division into classes and races, poor and rich, rulers and
ruled, remains temporary; the world is changing and chan-
geable.

If I believe in an eternal life, then, it is always possible to
endow my life and that of others with meaning. A meaning
is given to the inexorable evolution of the cosmos out of the
hope that there will be a true consummation of the individual
and society, and indeed a liberation and transfiguration
of creation, on which lie the shadows of transitoriness,
coming about only through the glory of God himself.

Hans Kung, Eternal Life?

Our universe is a wounded universe — divided, suffering, with great despair and poverty, where there are many signs of death, division and hatred. But all these signs of death are taken up in the cross of Jesus and transfigured in the resurrection. Our hope is that the winter of humanity will gradually be transformed to the bursting forth of love, for it is to this that we are called.

> Jean Vanier, *Be Not Afraid*

Death is unique. It is the one aspect of reality humans cannot look full in the face. Death is the ultimate paradox: it exposes a fundamental contradiction between the legacy of our genes and the legacy of our experience. This is why humans are flawed and divided creatures.

Most people deny that the fear of death plays a negative role in their psychology. 'I never think about death' is a common comment. But this kind of response lies on the surface of mentality; the underlying reality is different. One only has to watch the face of a man who has been told he is seropositive for AIDS to see how the mere suggestion of death shakes the pillars of life. Foreknowledge of imminent death invades the most personal part of us, threatening the sanctum of our very identity, the self, with extinction.

> Darryl Reanney, *The Death of Forever*

It has been observed that the anxiety of death increased with the increase of individualisation and that people in collectivistic cultures are less open to this kind of anxiety. . . But the very fact that courage has to be created through many internal and external (psychological and ritual) activities and symbols shows that basic anxiety has to be overcome even in collectivism.

> Paul Tillich, *The Courage to Be*

In facing one's own death, one finds a rather clear distinction between three possible attitudes in dying. First, there is the attitude that death is a biological necessity and that no further sense can be made of it. . . At the opposite extreme to this attitude is the one that denies death in the name of religious faith. There is an attitude of hide-and-seek about death. It assumes for the believer there is no real death. . .

The third attitude is one that combines the atheist's ruthless awareness of the inscrutable finality of death with the believer's all-consuming response of praise and gratitude to God, whose being and love is reflected in the believer's own maturity of being that overflows for others. It is the attitude of one who dies knowing that we do not really know what resurrection or heaven means or in what sense we personally participate in it, 'what is in it for us', but facing death with total trust in God and making a total surrender of oneself to God.

Monika K. Hellwig, *What Are They Saying about Death and Christian Hope?*

Very truly, I tell you, unless a grain of wheat falls into the earth and dies, it remains just a single grain; but if it dies, it bears much fruit.

John 12: 24

Loving creator, redeeming God, we offer our gratitude for life. We thank you for the experiences of life in all its mysterious mix of splendour and tragedy. Help us, in our finitude, in our egocentricism, to come to terms with our own destructiveness and ultimately our own mortality.

God, we realise that you really are the ground of reality. The cosmos is only possible because, in your wisdom, you created it so. We are thrust into existence and have no say in the matter. We live our lives with temporal freedom and limited control, but ultimately we exist because of the cosmic resources you have provided. Then, we are taken from this life and again we have no say. Death is inevitable.

Lord of heaven and earth, give us the courage to accept that our own death is part of life. Give us the wisdom to live life in the light of death. In your strength, once we begin the process of confronting our fears, help us to begin to appreciate the giftedness, the beauty and the sacredness of life. Thankyou for the example we have in Jesus of Nazareth, who gave his life so bravely. Through the event of Calvary, we know that in death there is life, both now and for eternity. Into your hands we again commit our life and death. In Jesus' name. **Amen.**

A Benediction

May you go in peace, with the assurance of God's love which will be with us for eternity. May you know of God's deep concern for every aspect of our lives: in our loving, in our anger, in laughter, in pain, in crying, in contentment, in anxiety.

May you be a shining light of God's love to all; in the name of God, both Mother and Father, Jesus the Son and the Holy Spirit. **Amen.**

51

Hope has its reason

For surely I know the plans I have for you, says the Lord, plans for your welfare and not for harm, to give you a future with hope. The Lord appeared to us in the past saying: 'I have loved you with an everlasting love; I have drawn you with loving-kindness. I will build you up again and you will be rebuilt. . .'

From ages past no-one has heard, no ear has perceived, no eye has seen any God beside you, who works for those who wait for him. Turn away from mortals, who have only breath in their nostrils, for of what account are they? For thus said the Lord God, the Holy One of Israel: In returning and rest you shall be saved; in quietness and in trust shall be your strength. Then, you will know that I am the Lord; those who hope in me will not be disappointed.

Blessed be the God and Father of our Lord Jesus Christ! By his great mercy, he has given us a new birth into a living hope through the resurrection of Jesus Christ from the dead and into an inheritance that is imperishable, undefiled and unfading, kept in heaven for you, who are being protected by the power of God through faith for a salvation ready to be revealed in the last time. We have this hope, a sure and steadfast anchor of the soul. And now faith, hope and love abide.

(Jeremiah 29: 11 — NRSV; Jeremiah 31: 3–4 — NIV; Isaiah 64: 4; 2: 22; 30: 15 — NRSV; Isaiah 49: 23 — NIV; 1 Peter 1: 3–5; Hebrews 6: 19; 1 Corinthians 13: 13 — all NRSV)

Without hope, life is difficult, if not impossible. An experiment was done in the University of North Carolina with two rats. They were each placed in a container half full of water. The first container was sealed and the creature, instinctively realising that there was no hope, gave up swimming and drowned in three minutes. The second container was not sealed and there remained a possibility of escape and survival. That rat swam for thirty-six hours straight before dying of exhaustion.

Prisoners of war have had much the same experience. Those who maintained hope that one day they would be released and who knew there were people at home who loved and cared for them were able to survive, whereas those without hope died in the atrocious conditions.

People often say of one who is critically ill, 'Where there's *life*, there's hope.' But the reverse is probably more true: 'Where there's *hope*, there's life.'

There is nothing more debilitating than hopelessness. When people are given a vision — a hope for what might be — they have found their lives transformed. A Christian principal of a school was contemplating how to respond to a lad who was always causing trouble in the classroom. The boy's background was difficult and he had no motivation to study. Once more the boy was called to the principal's office. When he came in, the principal took his hands in his, looked at them and said, 'You have good, thin hands — the hands of a surgeon.' Nothing more was said. The boy was dismissed. But his behaviour began to change and he did, indeed, become a skilled surgeon. He was given a vision of hope for what could be.

Jeremiah had a message of hope for the Hebrews in exile. Other prophets were bringing the false hope of a quick return to their homeland; Jeremiah's message was for them to establish their home in this foreign, despicable place. For even here, God knew the plans he had for his people, plans which involved a future and a hope.

Yet the fullness of the Christian hope is not evident until the New Testament. For the richness of our hope is in and through Jesus Christ. Recently, I was in the Blue Mountains (near Sydney) in early spring. I've never before experienced the profusion of colour with the new growth on the trees and the mosaic of spring blossom. The place was alive with hope, with vibrancy, with new life.

Through the resurrection of Jesus, our hope is vibrant with life. No longer can 'hope' ever be a vague, ambiguous word. Now 'hope' is sure and firm — an anchor for the soul. 'Faith, hope and love abide' (1 Corinthians 13: 13) and, while the greatest of these is love, hope is also Christ's gift: now, in even the most trying and difficult circumstances of life; and, in the future, the sure hope of life beyond the grave. Alleluia!

❧

You see, this Christian hope is not a psychological, subjective state that afflicts Christian people. Quite the contrary. Christian hope is rooted in the certainty of objective facts. They are the facts of revelation concerning Jesus Christ. The Bible proclaims that Jesus Christ has accomplished a work of victory so significant that it has changed the course of human history.

Joel Nederhood, *Happiness without Hope*

So right at the beginning of this study of Christian hope, I wish to dissociate it firmly from that distorted form of Christian hope which loses sight of this world and our life in the world in order, ostrich-like, to become immersed in a beyond. Christian hope is a total hope and it touches on all aspects of human life, both individual and social. As a total hope, it is not limited or nullified by death.

Indeed, I would have no hesitation in calling it a 'supernatural' hope, in the sense that it looks for possibilities beyond those which we know in our everyday 'natural' existence. But a truly total hope is a hope so large and many-sided that we impoverish and misrepresent it if we lay all the stress on its supernatural and other-worldly aspects.

John Macquarrie, *Christian Hope*

Christian hope rests on God, not on a person or luck or fate. And it is a dynamic, transforming quality, reaching forward from the present with its fears and frustrations to a future bright with the promises of a faithful God. Without this hope, life is reduced to a purposeless struggle. Hope reaches forward and claims the ongoing purpose of God.

John Gladstone, 'The Dimensions of Christian Living'

As long as people accept the challenge and responsibility of life, they have hope. Their work, their study, their family are all lived in hope and they constantly commit themselves to the future and look for fulfilment in the future. Hope must have very deep roots in our humanity, for over and over again we find to our surprise that people whom we expected to be overwhelmed by disasters and disappointments and made a prey to despair are, in fact, still projecting their lives into the future and still striving forward in quiet hope.

So it has been from the beginning for, although the shadow of evil and death has fallen over every life, it has been met by hope and belief in a promise of better things. . . For the roots of hope, we have to look beyond the natural order, and we find them ultimately only in God.

John Macquarrie, *The Humility of God*

Hope. . . means. . . a continual looking forward to the eternal world. . . It does not mean that we are to leave the present world as it is. If you read history, you will find that the Christians who did most for the present world were just those who thought most of the next. . . It is since Christians have largely ceased to think of the other world that they have become so ineffective in this. Aim at heaven and you will get earth 'thrown in': aim at earth and you will get neither.

C.S. Lewis

What oxygen is for the lungs, such is hope for the meaning of life.

Emil Brunner

Suffering taught him patience, patience taught him experience, experience taught him hope.

Soren Kierkegaard, 'Purity of the Heart is to Will One Thing'

I had asked God to tell me Why? He gave me no answer to this question. Instead he gave me . . .infinite love for my present need, . . .step-by-step guidance for my future walk.

How much anguish I might have saved myself years later if I had remembered this! If I'd thought back to the time of this first great bereavement, when instead of explanations, he gave me himself.

Catherine Marshall, *Light in My Darkest Night*

A genuine hope is always vulnerable and, if the vulnerability is taken away, hope has degenerated into optimism.

John Macquarrie, *Christian Hope*

Hope, of course, contains no guarantee. It does not make things easy, but gives strength to undertake the difficult. It is very important, indeed, to notice that there is a great difference between hope and optimism. Hope is humble, trustful, vulnerable. Optimism is arrogant, brash, complacent. Hope has drawn the pang of suffering and has perhaps even felt the chill of despair. The word 'hope' should not be lightly spoken by people who have never had any cause for despair. Only one who has cried '*de profundis*' can really appreciate the meaning of hope.

John Macquarrie, *The Humility of God*

Put your ear to the ground
and identify the noises around you.
Predominant are
anxious, restless footsteps,
frightened footsteps in the dark,
footsteps bitter and rebellious.
No sound as yet
of hope's first footsteps.
Glue your ear to the ground again.
Hold your breath.
Put out your advance antennae:
The Master is on his way.

Most likely he will not get here
when things are going well,
but in bad times
when the going's unsure and painful.

Dom Helder Camara, *A Thousand Reasons for Living*

---

*I am moved today, Lord, in thinking how completely you
have provided for the restoration of everything that
has fallen in humankind.
I am often downcast, Lord,
because of factors that flow from that fall:
I am ashamed of my sin or my cowardice or
my foolishness;
People assail me or criticise or don't understand me;
So I lose confidence
or hope or faith that things will work out.
But today, hope rises.
I'm reminded that you not only love,
save, forgive and redeem,
but you lean over to take me in your arms.
You stretch forth your hands
to take my crestfallen spirit and,
Lord, you lift up my head!
Like a father assuring a heartbroken child,
like a mother comforting a bruised and frightened child,
you lift up my head!
And I hear you speaking to me from your word,
'I am your glory and the lifter up of your head.'
Thank you.
In Jesus' name.
Amen.*

Based on a prayer from D. Eastman & J. Hayford,
Living & Praying in Jesus' Name

A Benediction
*May the God of hope fill you with all joy and peace as you
trust in him, so that you may overflow with hope by the power
of the Holy Spirit.* Amen.

52

Waiting in hope

Wait for the Lord; be strong and take heart and wait for the Lord.

We wait in hope for the Lord; he is our help and our shield. In him, our hearts rejoice, for we trust in his holy name. May your unfailing love rest on us, O Lord, even as we put our hope in you.

I wait for the Lord, my soul waits, and in his word I put my hope. My soul waits for the Lord more than watchmen wait for the morning.

Yet the Lord longs to be gracious to you; he rises to show you compassion. For the Lord is a God of justice. Blessed are all who wait for him.

Now there was a man in Jerusalem called Simeon, who was righteous and devout. He was waiting for the consolation of Israel and the Holy Spirit was upon him. . . There was also a prophetess, Anna, the daughter of Phanuel, of the tribe of Asher. . . she never left the temple, but worshipped night and day, fasting and praying. Coming up to them at that very moment, she gave thanks to God and spoke about the child to all who were looking forward to the redemption of Israel.

We know that the whole creation has been groaning as in the pains of childbirth right up to the present time. Not only so, but we ourselves, who have the first fruits of the Spirit, groan inwardly as we wait eagerly for our adoption. . . the redemption of our bodies. For in this hope we were saved. But hope that is seen is no hope at all. . . But if we hope for what we do not yet have, we wait for it patiently.

(Psalm 27: 14; Psalm 33: 20–22; Psalm 130: 5–6; Isaiah 30: 18; Luke 2: 25 and 36–38; Romans 8: 22–25 — all NIV)

Waiting is not a very popular attitude. Most people consider it a waste of time. Perhaps, this is because our culture is intent on going somewhere in a hurry! Waiting is like being in limbo between where we are and where we want to go.

Even in our life with God, we don't find waiting very easy. How often do we find ourselves asking God, 'How long. . .? How long before you answer my prayer? How long before revival comes? How long before you send healing to me?' And waiting is frequently made more difficult by our fear of what may be or our doubt that waiting will result in joy.

The psalmists constantly remind us that it is good to wait upon the Lord. Waiting usually means remembering what God has done in the past and the promises he has made with regard to the future. Likewise in Isaiah, the prophet writes of waiting in hope for God to act.

In the first two chapters of Luke, there are four outstanding pictures of people who wait in a special way: Zechariah and Elizabeth, then Mary, then Simeon and finally Anna. All these people were people of promise or hope, waiting for the redemption of Israel and prepared to trust themselves into the awesome hands of God.

The early church waited for Pentecost and then continued to wait on God for his gracious actions. I think Paul sums it up when he wrote that the Lord's people wait as eagerly as creation for what is still to come. The Holy Spirit is a foretaste of what is still to come. Like creation, we yearn for our full redemption.

It becomes apparent that, in both the Old and New Testaments, waiting and hoping are closely related. Because God has been active in the past and is active in the present, we look forward to that activity continuing. So hope is a future thing — with present reality! Waiting in hope is the working out of 'the presence of the future' in our lives today.

One of the most profound forms of prayer is simply stilling our souls in the heart of divine love and waiting quietly for the Spirit to do his work.

There will be times when we shall not be able to do anything more: when we come to the end of our resources; when indeed we have things done to us! Waiting in hope is especially relevant for those times. Jesus came to a time when he allowed people to do things to him. He went to the cross and, when he was most helpless, most vulnerable, God was at work in great power. Waiting in hope will create such possibilities for us.

❧

What oxygen is for the lungs, so is hope for the meaning of life.

Hope means the presence of the future or, more precisely, it is one of the ways in which what is merely future and potential is made vividly present and actual to us.

Hope is the positive, as anxiety is the negative, mode of awaiting the future. Through anxiety and hope [we relate ourselves] to the future in passive expectation.

Emil Brunner, Eternal Hope

Martin Luther King tells of a successful car pool which ran for eleven months. Now, it looked as though it would not be able to continue. He went to the weekly meeting to break the news:

When the evening came, I mustered sufficient courage to tell them the truth. I tried, however, to conclude on a note of hope. 'We have moved all of these months in the daring faith that God is with us in our struggle. The many experiences of days gone by have vindicated that faith in a marvellous way. Tonight, we must believe that a way will be made out of no way. . .'

[Next day] in anxiety and hope, I read these words in the court release: 'The United States Supreme court today unanimously ruled bus segregation unconstitutional in Montgomery, Alabama.'

> My heart throbbed with inexpressible joy. The darkest hour of our struggle had become the first hour of victory.
>
> Martin Luther King, 'A Knock at Midnight'

Who could believe in a God who will make everything new later if it is in no way apparent from the activity of those who hope in the One who is to come that he is already beginning to make everything new now?

Edward Schillbeeckx, *God the Future of Man*

Waiting is active. Most of us think of waiting as something very passive, a hopeless state determined by events totally out of our hands. . . But there is none of this passivity in scripture. Those who are waiting are waiting very actively. They know that what they are waiting for is growing from the ground on which they stand.

That's the secret. The secret of waiting is the faith that the seed has been planted, that something has begun. Active waiting means to be present fully to the moment, in the conviction that something is happening where you are and that you want to be present to it. A waiting person is someone who is present to the moment, who believes that this moment is *the moment*. . .

Much of our waiting is filled with wishes. . . and easily gets entangled in those wishes. For this reason, a lot of our waiting is not open-ended. Instead, it is a way of controlling the future. . . But Zechariah, Elizabeth and Mary were not filled with wishes. They were filled with hope. Hope is something very different. Hope is trusting that something will be fulfilled, but fulfilled according to the promises and not just according to our wishes.

Henri Nouwen, 'A Spirituality of Waiting'

One of the most profound forms of prayer is simply stilling our souls in the heart of divine love and waiting quietly for the Spirit to do his work. . . This is the moment in which our busyness with thoughts and words, our compulsion for achieving good works, our illusions of being indispensable, are all unmasked. . . When we have let go our clever agendas and become empty and quiet before God, the Spirit will achieve what is really important in us. He will comfort and heal, release us from destructive habits, move us to new patterns, challenge and energise us and make us useful for God's kingdom.

Marjorie Thompson, *Wasting Time with God*

Our waiting on God is not simply passive, however; it is active. God's life requires nurturing and attentive care in order for it to come to birth through us. The wisdom of our pregnant bodies tells us as much. I will never forget my amazement, the first time I was pregnant, at the fact that the gestation taking place asked so much of me. . . That little life within had taken control over the whole of myself and its needs suddenly took priority over many otherwise necessary and interesting priorities. . . This sense of being caught up with the whole self, of being asked actively to nurture what is growing within, is a characteristic of the spiritual life as well.

Wendy Wright, 'Wreathed in Flesh and Warm'

The image of God in which we are made is the image of *this* God — who, in loving, exposes himself to be the object no less than the subject of that which happens in the world; and so the presence of the image of God in us is, in principle, to be discerned no less in his passion than in his activity and achievement. We humans are, in principle, no less 'god-like' when we are waiting upon the world than when we are working upon, and achieving within, the world.

W. H. Vanstone, *The Stature of Waiting*

They who wait,
who stand stock-still
amid the whir of wheels,
refusing to be crushed,
can never be enslaved;
cannot be bound to a relentless clock
swung round and round,
hearing no other sound

but time's tick-tock.
They who wait
become imbued with strength,
swing the wide reach of sky
on sure, swift wings;
run with exuberance
through sun-splashed fields;
walk on with single purposed feet,
walk on, and do not faint.

Myra Scovel, *The Weight of a Leaf*

Lord God:
What a blessing memory is! I exercise this precious gift now
to remember the ways in which you have come to your people
through the ages.
God of creation, you have given us a wonderful system of
galaxies and you sustain it by the power of your hand. You have
given to us planet Earth, a marvellous jewel with its beauty and
plenty.
God of redemption, you have shown yourself to be faithful to
your covenant made first with the Jews and then, through Jesus
Christ, with all humankind. You have redeemed me and have
remained faithful to your promises.
Help me to wait in hope. Because you have been faithful in
the past and your promises are sure for the future, then surely
I can depend on you in the present.
I confess that often I rush ahead of you and seek to do your
work for you! After all, I belong to an impatient generation
which wants everything NOW. Will you help me to slow down
and really listen to what you are saying? I want to serve you,
but I also want to travel at your pace and find myself much
closer to you.
Thankyou for the hope you have given to me based on the
constancy of your faithfulness. May 'bright hope for tomorrow'
be shed into my life each day so that I can live in the security
which comes through waiting on you in hope.
In Christ's name. Amen.

A Benediction
May the God of hope help us in our attentive waiting.
May God the Father give us the freedom to wait in hope,
May God the Son continue his work of redemption in us,
May God the Spirit be our companion each day,
For the glory of the Triune God.   Amen.

Postlude

To live a spiritual life, we must first find the courage to enter into the desert of our loneliness and to change it by gentle and persistent efforts into a garden of solitude. This requires not only courage, but also a strong faith. As hard as it is to believe that the dry, desolate desert can yield endless varieties of flowers, it is equally hard to imagine that our loneliness is hiding unknown beauty. The movement from loneliness to solitude, however, is the beginning of any spiritual life because it is the movement from restless sense to restful spirit, from the outward-reaching cravings to the inward-reaching search, from the fearful clinging to the fearless play.[1]

All nature is meant to make us think of paradise. Woods, fields, valleys, hills, the river and the sea, the clouds travelling across the sky, light and darkness, sun and stars remind us that the world was first created as a paradise for the first Adam and that, in spite of his sin and ours, it will once again become a paradise when we are all risen from death in the second Adam. . .

But if we seek paradise outside ourselves, we cannot have paradise in our hearts. If we have no peace within ourselves, we have no peace with what is all around us. Only the one who is free from attachment finds that creatures have become friends. When we are pure, they speak to us of God.[2]

Endnotes

1. Henri Nouwen, *Reaching Out*, Collins Fount, 1980, p.35
2. Thomas Merton, in *The Shining Wilderness: Daily Readings*, Aileen Taylor (ed.), Darton, Longman & Todd, 1988, p.3

Abbreviations

Abbreviations of versions of the Bible used in this book

Barclay:	William Barclay, *The New Testament: A New Translation*, Collins, 1969
GNB:	*Good News Bible*, The Bible in Today's English Version, The American Bible Society, 1976
JB:	*Jerusalem Bible*, Darton, Longman & Todd, 1968
KJV:	*The Holy Bible*, King James Version, 1611
NASB:	*New American Standard Bible*, The Lockman Foundation, 1963
NIV:	*Holy Bible, New International Version*, International Bible Society, 1973
NRSV:	*New Revised Standard Version Bible*, OUP, 1991
RSV:	*Revised Standard Version*, Thomas Nelson, 1952
TLB:	*The Living Bible*, Tyndale House, 1971

Bibliography
Other sources used in weekly readings

WEEK 1
St Augustine of Hippo,
Confessions, in *A Library of Fathers
of the Holy Catholic Church*, J.G. &
F. Rivington, 1836, p.153
Charles de Foucauld, *Silent
Pilgrimage to God*, Jeremy Moiser
(trans.), Darton, Longman & Todd,
1974, p.85
St Francis of Assisi, *The Little
Flowers of St Francis*, Raphael
Brown (trans.), Image Books, 1958,
p.317
St Francis de Sales, *The Elements of
the Spiritual Life*, SPCK, 1934, p.243
Hannah Hurnard, *Hinds' Feet in
High Places*, Olive Press, 1979,
p.152
Michel Quoist, *Meet Christ and
Live!*, Gill and MacMillan, 1973,
pp.54–55
Helen Steiner Rice, *Prayerfully*,
Hutchinson, 1972, pp.13, 15

WEEK 2
Edward Henry Bickersteth,
Salvation Army Song Book, SA
National HQ, 1987, No.564
Dietrich Bonhoeffer, *Life Together*,
SCM, 1954, p.122
Richard Foster, *Celebration of
Discipline*, Hodder & Stoughton,
1978, pp.84, 126, 128
George Fox, in Richard Foster,
Celebration of Discipline, Hodder &
Stoughton, 1978, p.126
Washington Gladden, *Salvation
Army Song Book*, SA National HQ,
1987, No.519

Henri Nouwen, *Out of Solitude*,
Ave Maria, 1975, p.26
Edwin McNeill Poteat, *The
Interpreter's Bible*, Abingdon, 1955,
Vol.4, p.244
Teresa of Avila, in Richard Foster,
Celebration of Discipline, Hodder &
Stoughton, 1978, p.121
W.W. Walford, *Salvation Army
Song Book*, SA National HQ, 1978,
No.633

WEEK 3
Rudolph Bultmann, *Jesus and the
Word*, Fontana, 1958, p.144
Athol Gill, *Life on the Road: The
Gospel Basis for a Messianic
Lifestyle*, Lancer, 1989, p.39
Hans Kung, *On Being a Christian*,
Fount, 1980, pp.191, 200, 211
David Millikan, *The Sunburnt Soul*:
*Christianity in Search of an
Australian Identity*, Lancer, 1981,
p.107
Jurgen Moltmann, *The Power of the
Powerless*, SCM, 1983, p.89
Edward Schillebeeckx, *Jesus: An
Experiment in Christology*, Fount,
1983, p.139 (see also p.202f.)
Eduard Schweizer, *Jesus Christ:
The Man from Nazareth and the
Exalted Lord*, SCM, 1987, p.64
Paul Tillich, *The Shaking of the
Foundations*, Penguin, 1963,
pp.157, 164
Leslie D. Weatherhead, *The
Transforming Friendship*, Epworth,
1946, pp.25–26

WEEK 4
Neil Adcock, unpublished sermon
St Augustine of Hippo, in *Oxford
Dictionary of Quotations*, p.22
Dietrich Bonhoeffer, *Letters and
Papers from Prison*, Fontana,
pp.99,100
Roger Conner, 'American Alliance
for Rights and Responsibilities', in
Christopher Gleeson, *Striking a
Balance*, Hodder & Stoughton,
1993, p.6
Antoine de Saint-Exupery, *Wind,
Sand and Stars*, Penguin, 1966
Christopher Gleeson, *Striking a
Balance*, Hodder & Stoughton,
1993, pp.1, 3
Robert Herrick, 'Hesperides — To
Virgins', in *Oxford Dictionary of
Quotations*, p.247
G. Studdert Kennedy, 'To Patrick',
in *The Unutterable Beauty*, Hodder
& Stoughton, 1970, p.82
George Matheson, *Australian
Hymnbook*, Sydney, William
Collins, 1977, No.528

WEEK 5
Catherine de Hueck Doherty,
Poustinia, Ave Maria, 1974, pp.21,
22, 75
James C. Fenhagen, *Ministry &
Solitude*, Beacon Hill, 1981, pp.84,
85
Richard Foster, *Prayer: Finding the
Heart's True Home*, Hodder &
Stoughton, 1992, p.66
Joyce Huggett, *Listening to God*,
Hodder & Stoughton, 1986, p.34
Henri Nouwen, *Making All
Things New*, Harper & Row, 1981,
p.69
Eugene H. Peterson, *Earth & Altar*,
IVP, 1985, p.16
Charles Ringma, *Dare to Journey*,
Albatross, 1992, Reflection 78
Stephen Rossetti, 'The Pure Gold
of Silence', in *Spiritual Traditions
for the Contemporary Church*, Maas
and O'Donnell (eds), Abingdon,
1990, p.75

WEEK 6
Ruth Burrows, *To Believe in Jesus*,
Sheed and Ward, 1978
Leslie F. Brandt, *Meditations Along
the Journey of Faith*, Concordia,
1986
Keith Clark, *Being Sexual . . . and
Celibate*, Ave Maria, 1986
Catherine Marshall, *A Closer Walk*,
Hodder & Stoughton, 1986
Thomas Merton, *New Seeds of
Contemplation*, New Directions,
1961
John Henry Sammis, in *The
Hymnal*, The Baptist Federation,
Canada, 1973, No.542

WEEK 7
St Ambrose, in H.R. Mackintosh,
*The Christian Experience of
Forgiveness*, Fontana, 1961, p.14
Frederick Buechner, *Wishful
Thinking*, Collins, 1973, p.2
John N. Gladstone, 'Magnificently
Charismatic', unpublished sermon
Donald Guthrie, *New Testament
Theology*, IVP, 1981, pp.579–580
Dag Hammarskjöld, in Michael
Hollings, *Hearts Not Garments*,
Darton, Longman & Todd, 1982,
p.82
Tony Kelly, 'Free to Forgive',
National Outlook, February 1984,
p.18
H R Mackintosh, *The Christian
Experience of Forgiveness*, Fontana,
1961, pp.12, 35
A New Zealand Prayer Book,
Collins, 1989, pp.121–122
Norman Vincent Peale, *Thought
Conditioners*, Foundation for
Christian Living, p.24
W.E. Sangster, *The Secret of Radiant
Life*, Hodder & Stoughton, 1961,
p.245
Lance Shilton, 'Loving Yourself',
New Life, 14 November 1991, p.10
Lewis Smedes, 'Forgiveness: The
Power to Change the Past',
Christianity Today, 7 January 1983,
p.26
Jill Smolowe, 'Lives in Limbo',

Time, 16 December 1991, p.94
Kenneth Swanson, *Uncommon Prayer*, Ballantine, 1987, p.206
Simon Tugwell, 'The Beatitudes' in *Modern Spirituality, an Anthology*, John Garvey (ed.), Darton, Longman & Todd, 1985, pp.65–67

WEEK 8
Augustine, *Homilies on the First Epistle of John* in *Nicene and Post-Nicene Fathers*, Vol VII, Eerdmans, 1978, pp.477f, 481
John Calvin, *Institutes of the Christian Religion*, Vol.1, Westminister, p.500 (II, xv, 5)
Alan Cole, *The Gospel According to St Mark*, IVP, 1983, p.58
Jonathan Edwards, *The Religious Affections*, Banner of Truth, (1746) 1986, p.129
Edwin Hatch, in *New Songs of Praise*, Baptist Press, 1976, No.227
Matthew Henry, *Commentary*, Volume 6, Fleming H. Revell, p.1071
D.M. Lloyd-Jones, *The Puritans: Their Origins and Successors*, Banner of Truth, 1987, p.293
Charles Spurgeon, *The Metroploitan Tabernacle Pulpit*, Vol.XLII, 1896, p.260
Joseph Templeton, 'Oh, for a new anointing', in *Elim Choruses*, Victory Press, No.720
John Watsford, *Glorious Gospel Triumphs*, Charles Kelly, 1900, p.318f.

WEEK 9
Thomas Keating, *Open Mind, Open Heart: The Contemplative Dimension of the Gospel*, Amity House, 1986, p.137
Sam Keen, *To a Dancing God*, Harper & Row, 1970, p.22
Thomas R. Kelly, *A Testament of Devotion*, Quaker Home Service, 1941, p.27
Henri Nouwen, *Reaching Out*, Collins, 1976, p.136

M. Basil Pennington, *Centred Living: The Way of Centering Prayer*, Doubleday, 1986, pp.94–95
John Powell, *Fully Human, Fully Alive: A New Life through a New Vision*, Argus Communications, 1976, p.183
Adrienne Rich, *The Diamond Cutters and other Poems*, Harper & Row, 1955, p.43
Joyce Rupp, *May I Have this Dance?*, Ave Maria, 1992, p.82
Rainer Maria Rilke, *The Selected Poetry of Rainer Maria Rilke*, Stephen Mitchell (ed. and trans.), Picador, 1982, p.293
Sheldon Vanauken, *A Severe Mercy*, Hodder & Stoughton, 1977, p.49
Macrina Weiderkehr, *A Tree Full of Angels: Seeing the Holy in the Ordinary*, Harper & Row, 1988, pp.5–6

WEEK 10
Leonardo Boff, *Jesus Christ Liberator: A Critical Christology for Our Time*, Orbis, 1984, pp.78–79
Charlotte Bronte, *Jane Eyre*, Penguin, 1976, pp.105–106
Ronald Conway, *The Rage for Utopia*, Allen & Unwin, 1992, p.84
Terry Falla, 'The Call of Freedom has been Sounded,' in *Be Our Freedom, Lord: Responsive Prayers and Readings for Contemporary Worship*, Lutheran, 1989, p.21
Athol Gill, *Life on the Road: The Gospel Basis for a Messianic Lifestyle*, Lancer, 1989, p.52
Franky Schaeffer, *Addicted to Mediocrity: 20th Century Christians and the Arts*, Crossway, 1982, pp.65–66
Edward Schillebeeckx, *Jesus: An Experiment in Christology*, H. Hoskins (trans.), Collins, 1983, pp.145–146
Gail Sheehy, *Passages: Predictable Crises of Adult Life*, Bantam, 1984, pp.54–55
Steve Turner, 'Spiritus', in *Up to*

Date: Poems 1968–1982, Hodder & Stoughton, 1983, p.166

WEEK 11
Frederick W. Danker, 'Laughing With God', *Christianity Today*, January 6, 1967, p.16
Jessica Milner Davis, reported by Geoff Holland, 'Keep Rejoicing', *Victorian Baptist Witness*, July 1992, p.2
Graeme Garrett, 'My brother Esau is an hairy man', an encounter between the comedian and the preacher, *St Mark's Review*, Autumn 1989, pp.3, 10
F.W. Harvey, 'From "Ducks"', in *The Lion Book of Christian Poetry*, p.94
Philip Hughes, 'Humour', an unpublished sermon, in Peter McKinnon, 'We interrupt this service for a good belly laugh', *On Being*, May 1984, pp.20–21

WEEK 12
James Dobson, *Emotions: Can You Trust Them?*, Phoenix, 1980, p.186–187
Mark R. Littleton, *A Place to Stand*, Multnomah, 1986, p.38
Max Lucado, *God Came Near*, Anzea, 1989, p.89
Leith Samuel, *There Is An Answer*, Christian Focus Publications, 1990, pp.24–25
Gary Smalley and John Trent, *The Language of Love*, Focus on the Family, 1988, p.27
R.C. Sproul, *In Search of Dignity*, Regal, 1983, p.78
Charles Swindoll, *Second Wind*, Multnomah, 1977, p.69

WEEK 13
William Barclay, *The Gospel of Matthew*, Saint Andrew, 1975, Vol.1, p.318
Frederick Buechner, *Telling Secrets*, Harper Collins, 1991, pp.1–2, 33
C.H. Dodd, *The Interpretation of the Fourth Gospel*, CUP, 1968, p.364
Dag Hammarskjöld, *Markings*, Faber and Faber, 1966, p.87
Dominique Lapierre, *The City of Joy*, Arrow, 1986, p.77
C.S. Lewis, *A Grief Observed*, Faber and Faber, 1966, p.50
John Macquarrie, *Principles of Christian Theology*, SCM, 1977, p.362
Dale Moody, *The Word of Truth*, Eerdmans, 1981, p.491
Henri Nouwen, *A Letter of Consolation*, Gill and MacMillan, 1983, p.59
Wayne E. Oates, *Anxiety in Christian Experience*, George Allen and Unwin, 1958, p.59
Clive L. Rawlins, *William Barclay: The Authorized Biography*, Eerdmans, 1984, p.509

WEEK 14
Leonardo Boff, *Jesus Christ Liberator: A Critical Christology for our Time*, Orbis, 1984, p.207
Charlotte Bronte, *Jane Eyre*, Penguin, 1976, p.101
Terry Falla, 'The Promise of Your Presence', in *Be Our Freedom, Lord: Responsive Prayers and Readings for Contemporary Worship*, Lutheran, 1989, p.123
Neil Finn, 'As sure as I am', *Woodface* album, Crowded House, 1991
Athol Gill, *Life on the Road: The Gospel Basis for a Messianic Lifestyle*, Lancer, 1989, p.148
Edward Schillebeeckx, *Jesus: An Experiment in Christology*, H. Hoskins (trans.), Collins, 1983, p.145
Gail Sheehy, *Passages: Predictable Crises of Adult Life*, Bantam, 1984, p.506
Jon Sobrino, *Christology at the Crossroads: A Latin American Approach*, SCM, 1984, p.371
Bruce Turley, *Turning Points: Invitations to Growth and Healing*, JBCE, 1985, p.31

WEEK 15
William Barclay, *The Gospel of Matthew*, Saint Andrew, 1959, Vol.2, pp.247–249
Frederick Dale Bruner, *Matthew*, Volume 2: The Churchbook, Word, 1990, p.723
George A. Buttrick, *The Parables of Jesus*, Richard R. Smith Inc., 1930, p.165
T.W. Manson, *The Sayings of Jesus*, SCM, 1975, p.220
John Milton, 'When I Consider How My Life is Spent', in *Seven Centuries of Poetry in English*, John Leonard (ed.), OUP, 1987, p.351
Anthony B. Robinson, 'Living by the Word', *Christian Century*, August 25, 1993, p.815

WEEK 16
Jean-Pierre de Caussade, *Self-Abandonment to Divine Providence*, Collins, 1977, pp.14, 36
Thomas H. Green, *When the Well Runs Dry — Prayer beyond the Beginnings*, Ave Maria, 1981, pp.169, 171
Faustina Kowalska, *Devotion to the Divine Mercy and Selected Prayers from the Diary of the Servant of God Sister Faustina Kowalska*, Divine Mercy, 1991, pp.55–56
Briege McKenna, with Henry Libersat, *Miracles Do Happen*, Veritas, 1987, p.11
Brian Moore, *Groping Godwards*, Alba House, 1974, p.33
Michel Quoist, in Sheila Cassidy, *Audacity to Believe*, Collins, 1978, p.82
Francis Thompson, extracts from 'The Hound of Heaven', in Sheila Cassidy, *Audacity to Believe*, Collins, 1978, pp.71–72
Karol Wojtyla, *Easter Vigil and Other Poems*, Jerzy Peterkiewicz (trans.), Arrow, 1980, p.44

WEEK 17
Jerry Bridges, *Transforming Grace*, Navpress, 1992, p.110

Charles Jefferson, *The Minister as Shepherd*, Living Books for All (Asian Edition), 1984, p.33
Earl F. Palmer, *Integrity in a World of Pretence*, Insights from the Book of Philippians, IVP, 1992, p.41
Eugene H. Peterson, *Working the Angles: The Shape of Pastoral Integrity*, Eerdmans, 1987, p.61
Jerry Sitter, *The Adventure*, IVP, 1985, p.87

WEEK 18
Elizabeth Barrett Browning, 'Substitution', in *Masterpieces of Religious Verse*, James Dalton Morrison (ed.), Harper & Row, 1948, p.201
Amy Carmichael, *Whispers of His Power*, Triangle, 1982, p.189
Joni Eareckson & Steve Estes, *A Step Further*, S. John Bacon, 1979, pp.81–85
Frank Houghton, *Amy Carmichael of Dohnavur*, SPCK, 1953, pp.6, 72, 262
Bruce Prewer, *Australian Psalms*, Lutheran, 1980, p.67
'Shoe Leather' Faith, G. and M. Roscel (comp.), St Paul, 1960, selection No.212
Robert Wise, *When There Is No Miracle*, Regal, 1977, pp.18–19, 47, 55, 61

WEEK 19
Peter Brierley, unpublished work based on Colossians 1, verse 17
Christian Praise, Tyndale, 1957, Nos 11, 87
H.L. Ellison, *The Mystery of Israel*, Paternoster, 1966, pp.94–95
W.H. Griffith Thomas, *Genesis: A Devotional Commentary*, Religious Tract Society, 1910, pp.199–200
Dag Hammarksjöld, *Markings*, Faber, 1966, pp.70, 122
The Hymnal, The Baptist Federation of Canada, 1973, No.1
Isobel Kuhn, *Second Nite People*, Overseas Missionary Fellowship, 1982, p.124

Michel Quoist, *Prayers of Life*, Gill and MacMillan, 1954, p.10
Myron Rush, *Burnout*, Scripture Press, 1989, p.13
Shakespeare, *Hamlet*, Act 5, scene 2, line 10
Janice Wise, 'Needed: Grace for Growing Old', *Decision* magazine, July/August 1990

WEEK 20
Rowland Croucher, 'Every Christian Should Be a Good Theologian', in *The Best of Grid*, World Vision of Australia, 1993, p.197
A.J. Gossip, 'Exposition of the Gospel According to St John', *The Interpreter's Bible*, Vol.8, 1952, pp.520–521
Harold Henderson, from an unpublished sermon, 'Doing the Unthinkable'.
Merrill C. Tenney, 'The Gospel of John', in *The Expositor's Bible Commentary*, Regency Reference Library, 1981, pp.54–55
W.E. Sangster, *The Secret of Radiant Life*, Hodder & Stoughton, 1957, pp.58–63

WEEK 21
Rowland Croucher, *Recent Trends Among Evangelicals*, John Mark Ministries, 1992, pp.53–54
Oxford Declaration on Christian Faith and Economics, January 1990, in *The Best of Grid*, Rowland Croucher and Grace Thomlinson (eds), World Vision of Australia, 1993, p.242
Morris Stuart, unpublished sermon

WEEK 22
Philip Hughes, unpublished sermon, 'The Judge on Trial'
Halford E. Luccock, 'Exposition of Mark 14:53', *Interpreter's Bible*, Abingdon-Cokesbury, 1951, pp.887–888
W.E. Sangster, *They Met at Calvary*, Epworth, 1956, pp.30–31
Leslie D. Weatherhead, *A Plain Man Looks at the Cross*, Independent Press, 1945/1957, pp.40–41

WEEK 23
William Barclay, *The Lord's Supper*, SCM, 1967, pp.110–113, 118–119
Horatius Bonar, *Baptist Hymn Book*, Psalms and Hymns Trust, 1964, No.316
Richard Foster, 'An Introduction to Spiritual Disciplines', in *Practical Christianity*, La Vonne Neff et al (eds), Tyndale House, 1988, p.295
Philip Hughes, 'Washing One Another's Feet', unpublished sermon
Thomas G. Pettepiece, in *A Guide to Prayer for Ministers and Other Servants*, The Upper Room, 1983, p.143

WEEK 24
William Barclay, *Jesus Christ For Today*, Tidings, 1973, p.76
John Bowring, 'In the Cross of Christ I Glory', *Australian Hymn Book*, 1979, No.265
Len Evans, *Love, Love, Love*, Logos, 1978, p.44
Bruce Farnham, *The Way of Jesus*, Lion, 1986, p.145
Henri Nouwen, *Heart speaks to Heart*, Ave Maria, 1989, p.35
Henri Nouwen, *In the Name of Jesus*, Darton, Longman & Todd, 1989, p.23
Michel Quoist, *Prayers of Life*, Gill & MacMillan, 1963, p.29
Leslie D. Weatherhead, *The Transforming Friendship*, Epworth Press, 1967, p.60

WEEK 25
Rowland Croucher, unpublished sermon.
Peter Drucker, in Donald McCullough, 'Time for Things That Matter' in Maxie Dunnam et

al, *Mastering Personal Growth*,
Multnomah, 1992, p.146
Ron Elbourne, 'Parson's Pitch',
Waverley Gazette, Melbourne,
26/3/1980
John N. Gladstone, 'How is Your
Grip on Life?', unpublished
sermon
Billy Graham, 'Christian
Discipline', sermon on 'The Hour
of Decision', 1960
Donald McCullough, 'Time for
Things That Matter', in Maxie
Dunnam et al, *Mastering Personal
Growth*, Multnomah, 1992,
pp.146–147
David Stewart, in *The Reaper*, Bible
College of New Zealand, October
1992
A. Skevington Wood, 'The Need
for Discipline', *The Christian*,
September 21, 1962, p.6

WEEK 26
Charles de Foucauld, *Come Let us
Sing a Song Unknown*, Dimension,
1983, pp.12–13
St Francis de Sales, *Introduction to
the Devout Life*, Michael Day
(trans.), Everyman's Library, 1961,
p.17
Hildegard of Bingen, *Book of
Divine Works: with Letters and
Songs*, Matthew Fox (ed.), Bear &
Co., 1987, p.352
E. Stanley Jones, *Christian
Maturity*, Hodder & Stoughton,
1958, p.23
G.H. Morling, *The Quest for
Serenity*, Young & Morling,
pp.31–32
Hubert Northcott, *The Gardens of
the Lord*, SPCK, 1963, pp.100–101
J.V. Taylor, *A Matter of Life and
Death*, SCM, 1986, p.67

WEEK 27
Philip Adams, *Adams versus God*,
Nelson, 1985, p.19
Karl Barth, *Letters: 1961–1968*,
Eerdmans, 1981, pp.55–56
Paul Davies, *The Mind of God:*

*Science and the Search for Ultimate
Meaning*, Penguin, 1992, p.213
Matthew Fox, *The Coming of the
Cosmic Christ*, Collins Dove, 1991,
p.155
Billy Graham, *How to be Born
Again*, Hodder & Stoughton, 1989,
p.14
Hans Kung, *Does God Exist?*,
Collins, 1980, pp.619, 695
H.D. Lewis, *Our Experience of God*,
Collins, 1974, p.46
Eric Osborn, 'Rational Faith',
Pacifica, October 1993, Vol.6, No.3
Deacon Boniface Perdjert, 'The
Community of Believers', *The
Bible through Asian Eyes*, Masao
Takenaka and Ron O'Grady (ed.),
Pace, 1991, p.168
Muriel Porter, *Land of the Spirit?
The Australian Religious Experience*,
WCC Publications, 1990, p.100
Desmond Tutu, 'Who is God?', in
Life Magazine, December 1990,
pp.49–50
Leslie Weatherhead, *How Can I
Find God?*, Hodder & Stoughton,
1933, pp.172–173

WEEK 28
Stephen R. Covey, *The 7 Habits of
Highly Effective People*, The
Business Library, 1989, pp.30–31
Erich Fromm, *The Art of Loving —
An Enquiry into the Nature of Love*,
Harper & Row, 1956, p.130
Martin Luther King, *Strength to
Love*, Fontana/Collins, 1970,
pp.54-55,113
William Klassen, *Love of Enemies
— The Way to Peace*, Fortress,
1984, p.88
Leon Morris, *Testaments of Love —
A Study of Love in the Bible*,
Eerdmans, 1981, p.220
John Powell, *Why am I Afraid to
Love*, Argus Communications,
1972, p.11

WEEK 29
Dietrich Bonhoeffer, *Ethics*,
Macmillan, 1965, p.23

Anthony Campolo, *Seven Deadly Sins*, Christian Press, 1987, pp.88–89

Donald Capps, *Life Cycle Theory and Pastoral Care*, Fortress, 1983, pp.89 and 93

Donald Capps, *The Depleted Self*, Fortress, 1993, p.69

James W. Fowler, 'Shame: Toward a practical theological understanding', in *Christian Century*, August 25 — September 1, 1993, p.816

Joyce Huggett, *Listening to God*, Hodder & Stoughton, 1986, pp.63–64

Lewis B. Smedes, *Shame and Grace*, Harper, 1993, pp.6,131

WEEK 30

Mary Batchelor, *Celebrating the Seasons of Life*, Lion, 1990, pp.11, 21, 35, 49

Doris Carlson, 'A Housewife's Prayer', in *Decision*, August 1974, p.15

Margaret Fishback, 'Footprints', Echo Lake Youth Camp, Kingston, Ontario, Canada, 1964 — copyright: Margaret Fishback Powers

Peter Taylor Forsyth, *The Work of Christ*, Collins, 1965, p.61

Richard Foster, *Celebration of Discipline*, Hodder & Stoughton, 1980, p.91

From a wall in the House of Abba coffee house, Chula Vista, California, in *Decision*, August 1974, p.15

Gerard Manley Hopkins, 'Spring', in *Poems and Prose of Gerard Manley Hopkins*, W.H. Gardner (ed.), Penguin, 1953, p.28

C.S. Lewis, *The Screwtape Letters*, Geoffrey Bles, 1942, pp.46–47

George Macdonald, in *Decision*, August 1975, p.13

Henri Nouwen, *The Wounded Healer*, Image Books, 1979, p.84

Samuel Rutherford, *The Loveliness of Christ: From the Letters of Samuel Rutherford 1600–1661*, Ellen S. Lister (comp.), Samuel Bagster, 1958, p.23

Christopher Venning, 'Pilgrimage and Rest: A Sonnet' (1989) and 'Seasons of Your Love' (1977), unpublished poems

WEEK 31

Terry Falla, *Be Our Freedom, Lord*, Lutheran, 1981, p.158

Ernest Gordon, *Miracle On The River Kwai*, Collins/Fontana, 1965, p.91

Anthony de Mello, *The Prayer of The Frog*, Gujarat Sahitya Prakash, 1989, p.152

Jurgen Moltmann, *The Open Church*, SCM, 1978, p.27

Henri Nouwen, *The Wounded Healer*, Image Books, 1972, p.94

Evelyn Whitehead, & James Whitehead, *Community of Faith*, Winston-Seabury, 1982, p.xi

Ken Walsh, *Sometimes I Weep*, SCM, 1973, p.97

WEEK 32

Mike Bickle, 'What about Leadership Standards for the 90s', in *Holiness Unto The Lord Conference (Teaching Notes)*, Mercy Publishing, 1990, p.104

Ray Comfort, in *The Morning Star Journal*, Vol.3, No.2, Morningstar Publicatons, 1993, p.22

Jack Deere, *Surprised by the Power of the Spirit*, Zondervan, 1993, pp.150–151

Francis Frangipane, *Holiness, Truth and the Presence of God*, Advancing Church Publications, 1986, p.27

Keith Green, 'Grace by which I Stand', in *So Ya Wanna Go Back to Egypt*, Last Days Ministries, 1980

Dudley Hall, *Grace Works*, Servant Publications, 1992, p.23–25

Rick Joyner, *The Journey Begins*, Morningstar Publications, 1992, p.196-197

Rick Joyner, *There Were Two Trees*

in the Garden, Morningstar Publications, 1986, p.7–8
John Newton, 'The Right Use of the Law', in *Letters of John Newton*, The Banner of Truth Trust, 1960, p.40

WEEK 33
Julie Banks, correspondence, 1993
Michael Frost, *Jesus the Fool*, Albatross, 1994, pp.73–74
George Herbert, 'Love', in George Herbert, *The Temple*, Seeley and Co., 1906, p.236
Zephaniah Kameeta, 'Create Me Anew', in *Women of Prayer*, Dorothy M. Stewart (ed.), Lion, 1993, p.57
Hugh MacKay, *Reinventing Australia*, Angus and Robertson, 1993, pp.20, 291
Henri Nouwen, *Making All Things New*, Gill and MacMillan, 1982, pp.41–43
Bridget Rees, 'Partners in transformation', in *Women of Prayer*, Dorothy M. Stewart (ed.), Lion, 1993
Charles Ringma, *Seize the Day with Dietrich Bonhoeffer*, Albatross, 1991, May 18 reading
Desmond Tutu, 'Agents of Transfiguration', in *The Rainbow People of God*, Doubleday, 1994
Mocrina Wiedekehs, in *A Guide to Prayer for all God's People*, Reuben P. Job and Norisa Shavekuck (eds), Upper Room Books, 1990, p.94

WEEK 34
Bernhard Christensen, *the Inward Pilgrimage*, Augsburg, 1976, p.52
John Donne, 'Holy Sonnet XIV', in *The Complete Poetry and Selected Prose of John Donne*, Charles M Coffin (ed.), Random House, 1952, p.252
Carl Henry, *The Christian Mindset in a Secular Society*, Multnomah, 1985, p.19
Martin Luther, *Christian Liberty*,

W.A. Lambert and Harold J. Grimm (trans.), Fortress, 1967, p.29
John Matheson, *The Psalms and Church Hymnary*, OUP, No.464
The Book of Offices, Methodist Publishing House, p.132
C.H. Spurgeon, *The Cheque Book of the Bank of Faith*, Marshall, Morgan & Scott, 1971, p.210

WEEK 35
Back to God Hour, 'The Trouble with Hypocrisy', radio sermon
John Claypool, *The Light within You*, Word, 1983, p.50
John Fowles, *The French Lieutenant's Woman*, Pan, 1987, p.24
Melody Green and David Hazard, *The Life Story of Keith Green*, Sparrow Corporation, 1989
Terry Lane, *As the Twig is Bent*, Collins Dove, 1979, p.63

WEEK 36
Virginia Adams, 'Jealous Love', *Psychology Today*, May 1980, p.41
Norman Lobsenz, 'How to Cope with Jealousy', *Readers' Digest*, December 1975, p.38
Sheryl Stolberg, 'Jonas Salk: He found a vaccine for polio. Can he do it for AIDS?', *Sunday Age*, 2 May 1993, p.4
Florence Wedge, *Environs?*, Francisean Publishers, 1967, p.14

WEEK 37
Believing is Seeing, Outreach Apologetics, p.1
Leighton Ford, unpublished sermon
John Gladstone, 'The Dimensions of Christian Living', unpublished sermon
Billy Graham 'Facts, Faith and Feelings', *Hour of Decision*, Billy Graham Evangelical Association, pp.3–4
Charles Spurgeon, 'What is Faith?', *Decision*, 1963, p.3

WEEK 38

Jean Bacon, *Food Preferences: Nutrition or prestige?*, FAO, 1989, p.4

Friends of the Earth Handbook, Jonathon Porritt (ed.), MacDonald Optime, 1987, p.56

F. Lappe and J. Collins, *Food First*, Houghton Mifflin, 1977, p.136

Frances Lappe, *Diet for a Small Planet*, Ballantine, 1971, p.3

R.J. Ledogar, *Hungry for Profits*, IDOC, 1975, p.97

Stan Mooneyham, *What Do You Say to a Hungry World?*, Word, 1975, p.177

Catherine von Ruhland, *Glorious Food*, Marshall Pickering, 1991, p.1

WEEK 39

David Adam, *Tides and Seasons*, SPCK, 1989, p.81

Corrie Ten Boom, *The Hiding Place*, Hodder & Stoughton and Christian Literature Crusade, 1973, pp.181–183, 200–202

Amy Carmichael, *Toward Jerusalem*, SPCK, 1977, p.114

G.R.D. McLean, *Poems of the Western Highlanders*, SPCK, 1961, p.75

Robert L. Wise, *When There Is No Miracle*, Regal, 1978, pp.37,97-98

Philip Yancey, *Disappointment With God*, Harper, 1988, pp.252–253

Philip Yancey, *Where is God When It Hurts?*, Pickering and Inglis, 1981, pp.95–97

WEEK 40

Baptist Praise and Worship, OUP, 1991, No.380

Terry Hershey, *Beginning Again*, Thomas Nelson, 1986, p.163

Dick Innes, *How to Mend a Broken Heart*, Albatross, 1991, p.100

Martin Luther King, *Strength to Love*, Hodder & Stoughton, 1964, p.84

D. Martin Lloyd-Jones, 'Trials', in *Spiritual Depression*, Pickering & Inglis, 1965, p.232

George Meredith, *The Ordeal of Richard Feveral*, Charles Scribner's Sons, 1905, p.75

Henri Nouwen, *The Wounded Healer*, Image Books, 1972, p.87

Deborah Roberts, *Raped*, Zondervan, 1981, pp.126–128

Paul Tournier, *The Healing of Persons*, Harper & Row, 1965, p.165

David Watson, *Fear No Evil*, Hodder & Stoughton, 1984, p.119

Amy Ross Young, *By Death or Divorce. . . It Hurts to Lose*, Accent, 1976, p.42

WEEK 41

Dan B. Allender, *The Wounded Heart*, CWR, 1991, pp.73–74

William A. Barry, *Finding God in All Things*, Ave Maria, 1991, p.85

Jan Frank, *A Door of Hope*, Here's Life Publishers, 1989, p.23

Thomas à Kempis, *The Imitation of Christ*, Penguin, 1988, pp.33–34

Josh McDowell, *The Secret of Loving*, Here's Life Publishers, 1989, p.77

David A. Seamands, *Healing of Memories*, Victor, 1988, pp.116–117

WEEK 42

Joni Eareckson Tada, *Secret Strength*, Multnomah, 1989, p.277

Graham Greene, *The Power and the Glory*, Penguin, 1940, p.195

Frank Houghton, *Amy Carmichael of Dohnavur*, SPCK, 1954, p.36

Robert Schuller, *The Be Happy Attitudes*, Word, 1986, p.122

WEEK 43

Sheila Cassidy, *Sharing the Darkness*, Darton, Longman & Todd, 1988, p.163

Llew Evans, unpublished prayer

Terry Falla, *Be Our Freedom, Lord*, Lutheran, 1981, p.158

Harold S. Kushner, *When Bad Things Happen to Good People*, Pan, 1981, p.149

Keith Miller, *The Passionate People*, Word, 1979, p.64

Dominque Lapierre, *The City of*

Joy, Arrow, 1986, pp.157–158
Hannah Whitall Smith, *The Christian Secret of a Happy Life*, Pyramid, p.54
Dorothy C. Wilson, *Take My Hands*, Hodder & Stoughton, 1963, pp.183,206

WEEK 44
Brown Barr, *High Flying Geese*, Seabury Press, 1983, pp.63 and 65
Gene Bartlett, *The Authentic Pastor*, Valley Forge, Judson Press, 1978, p.18
Milton J. Drake, 'Life is a Balance', unpublished
Milton J. Drake, 'Rainbows', unpublished
Milton J. Drake, 'Under Stress', unpublished
Milton J. Drake, 'Interpret my Life, God', unpublished
Gerard Egan, *The Skilled Helper*, Books/Cole, 1990, pp.6–7
Viktor Frankl, *Man's Search for Meaning*, Hodder & Stoughton, 1974, pp.104–105
Joanne Ross Feldmeth and Midge Wallace Finley, *We Weep for Ourselves and Our Children*, Harper Collins, 1990, p.141
Professor Bryan Tanney, workshop, 5 July 1994
Bruce Turley, *Being There for Others*, Joint Board of Christian Education, 1976, pp.122, 124–125
Bruce Turley, *Turning Points*, Joint Board of Christian Education, 1985, p.118
Bruce Turley, *Expanding Horizons of Care*, Joint Board of Christian Education, 1979, pp.14, 57
Richard Winter, *The Roots of Sorrow*, Crossway Books, 1986, p.292

WEEK 45
John Claypool, 'Humanising Our Heroes', unpublished sermon
John Claypool, 'Courage and Death', unpublished sermon
Ron Elbourne, 'Going Strong for the Top', *Waverley Gazette*, March 20, 1983
Peter Eldersveld, 'The Fear of God', *Back to God Hour Sermon*
Roberta Hestenes, 'God and the Hebrew Midwives', Preaching Today Tape No.76, 1989, sermon and two quotes

WEEK 46
Vera Brittain, *In the Steps of John Bunyan*, Rich and Cowan, 1987, p.417
Myra Chave-Jones, *Coping with Depression*, Lion, 1981, p.79
Tom Haggai with Richard L. Federer, *How the Best is Won*, Thomas Nelson, 1987, p.17
Thomas Hale, *Don't let the Goats Eat the Loquat Trees*, Marc Europe, 1986, p.257
George Weinberg, *Self Creation*, St Martin's Press, 1978, p.175
John Wilson, *Pity My Simplicity*, Evangelical Press, 1980, p.38

WEEK 47
Oliver Cromwell, in Lord Denning, *The Family Story*, Butterworth, 1981, p.128
King George VI, in his 1937 broadcast to the British Empire
Sam Shoemaker, *Extraordinary Living for Ordinary Men*, Zondervan, 1965, p.31
'Still will we Trust', in John Stott, *Christ the Liberator*, IVP, 1972, p.217
Edward Whymper, a 25-year-old Englishman, who was the first to climb the Matterhorn on 14 July 1865

WEEK 48
Carlo Carretto, *The Desert and Beyond*, Darton, Longman & Todd, 1987, pp.236–237
Thomas Chisholm, *The Hymnal*, Aylesbury, 1978, No.73
Dag Hammarskjöld, *Markings*, Alfred A Knopf, 1965, pp.129, 145
Helen Keller, *Teacher: Anne Sullivan Macy — A Tribute by the*

Foster-child of her Mind,
Doubleday, 1955, p.156
Michael Leunig, *Common Prayers
Collection,* Collins Dove, 1993, p.62
Bruce D. Prewer, *Australian
Psalms,* Lutheran, 1979, p.66

WEEK 49
Margaret W. Brown, 'I keep in
touch with Jesus', *Youth Favorites
by Singspiration,* Zondervan,
No.125
Phill Boas, *Truth & Lies: A
Communication Frame,* Magic
Mouse Communication, 1982, p.89
Roger Bush, 'The Darkened
Church', *Prayers for Pagans,*
Hodder & Stoughton, 1968
Billy Graham, *The Wit and Wisdom
of Billy Graham,* World's Work,
1968, p.70
C.S. Lewis, *Letters to Malcolm:
Chiefly on Prayer,* Geoffrey Bles,
1964, p.32
Fern-seed and Elephants, Fontana,
1975, p.102
Alfred, Lord Tennyson, 'The
Morte D'Arthur', *The Poetical
Works of Alfred, Lord Tennyson,*
Ward, Lock & Co., p.81

WEEK 50
Rudolph Bultmann, *Existence and
Faith,* Collins, 1973, pp.82–83
Rudolph Bultmann, *Primitive
Christianity: In its Contemporary
Setting,* Collins, 1964, p.52
John Donne, Holy Sonnets:
Divine Meditations (6), in *The
Metaphysical Poets,* Helen Gardner
(ed.), Penguin, 1985, p.85
Graeme Griffin, *Death and the
Church: Problems and Possibilities,*
Dove, 1978, pp.10–11
Monika K. Hellwig, *What are they
Saying about Death and Christian
Hope?,* Paulist Press, 1978, pp.64–66
Hans Kung, *Eternal Life?,* Collins,
1985, pp.61, 281–282
John Macquarrie, *Existentialism,*
Penguin, 1973, pp.154–155
Henri Nouwen, *Beyond the Mirror,*

Collins, 1990, pp.48-49
Darryl Reanney, *The Death of
Forever: A New Future for Human
Consciousness,* Longman Cheshire,
1992, p.1
Paul Tillich, *The Courage to Be,*
Collins, 1974, pp.50–51
Miguel de Unamuno, *The Tragic
Sense of Life,* J.E.C. Flitch (trans.),
Harper and Brothers, 1954, p.39
Jean Vanier, *Be Not Afraid,* Gill
and MacMillan, 1975, p.145

WEEK 51
Emil Brunner, in *3000 Quotations
on Christian Themes,* Baker Book
House, 1975, p.180
Dom Helder Camara, *A Thousand
Reasons for Living,* Darton,
Longman & Todd, 1981, p.80
John Gladstone, 'The Dimensions
of Christian Living', unpublished
sermon
Sören Kierkegaard, *Purity of the
Heart is to Will One Thing,* Harper
& Row, 1956, p.209
C.S. Lewis, in *The Quotable Lewis,*
Tyndale House, 1989, pp.305–306
John Macquarrie, *The Humility of
God,* SCM, 1978, pp.10, 11, 13
John Macquarrie, *Christian Hope,*
Mowbray, 1978, pp.1–2, 110
Catherine Marshall, *Light in my
Darkest Night,* A Chosen Book,
1989, p.20
Joel Nederhood, 'Happiness
Without Hope', *The Back to God
Hour*

WEEK 52
Emil Brunner, *Eternal Hope,*
Lutterworth, 1954, pp.7–8
Martin Luther King, 'A Knock at
Midnight', in *Strength to Love,*
Fontana, 1974, pp.65–66
Henri Nouwen, 'A Spirituality of
Waiting', *Weavings,* Vol.II, No.1,
The Upper Room, 1987, p.9
Edward Schillbeeckx, *God the
Future of Man,* Sheed and Ward,
1969, p.183
Myra Scovel, *The Weight of a Leaf,*

Westminster, 1970, p.48
Majorie Thompson, 'Wasting
Time with God', *Weavings*, Vol.IV,
No.2, The Upper Room, 1989, p.32
W.H. Vanstone, *The Stature of
Waiting*, Darton, Longman &
Todd, 1982, p.100
Wendy Wright, 'Wreathed in
Flesh and Warm', *Weavings*, Vol.II,
No.1, The Upper Room, 1987,
pp.23–24

Contributors

Personal profiles of contributors

The following profiles describe our contributors as at the time of original publication. Since then, their life situation may have changed.

Neil Adcock recently retired as pastor of the Canberra Baptist Church, where he has ministered since 1981. He has been involved in many sections of the media, especially radio. In Canberra, he frequently preached on national occasions, including parliamentary services. He and his wife, Joan, have three married children and six grandchildren.

Sue Algate is an ordained minister in the Uniting Church in Australia, serving in parishes in Queensland. She has degrees in Arts and counselling and has a special interest in grief counselling.

Geoff Blackburn is an associate pastor at the Diamond Valley Baptist Church, Victoria, Australia. For many years, he was editor-in-chief of the Australian Baptist Board of Christian Education. He is married to Jessie and has two adult sons.

Peter Brierley has been, until recently, director of MARC Europe, a World Vision-sponsored leadership training organisation headquartered in London. Peter is one of England's leading statisticians. He worships at an Anglican church in Kent.

Barry Chant is an author, speaker and teacher, and has written books on theology, church history and family life, and children's stories. He is founder and president of Tabor College, a multidenominational training centre in Australia. He and Vanessa have three children and eight grandchildren.

Genevieve Cooke studied creative art as a mature-aged student, while working part-time and raising three children single-handedly. Her current voluntary work to promote the faith life in her church community allows her some freedom to express her faith through her favourite literary medium.

Rowland Croucher has pastored churches in New South Wales, Victoria and Canada. For the past twelve years, he has ministered to clergy, church leaders and their spouses, first with World Vision, now with John Mark Ministries. He is also convenor of a ministry and research project among ex-pastors. He and Jan are a 'clergy couple' with four children.

Paul Davies works as a science teacher at a Sydney high school. He and his wife Sarah have recently begun to attend Ryde Baptist Church.

Ed Dickinson is a professional public speaker and a tutor of verbal communication skills. He is a Life Member of the Inter-Church Trade & Industry Mission, Victoria, and a member of the Victorian Baptist Lay Preachers' Association. He and his wife Gwen have been involved in inner-city ministries in Newmarket, Victoria.

Milton Drake, a Churches of Christ minister, has served in parishes in four states and is now minister in the Uniting Church's Kedron parish in Queensland. He and his wife Laureen conduct retreats for clergy and non-clergy. They have two adult daughters.

Mike Esbensen is Churches of Christ Pastor at North Essendon Church of Christ. He is pursuing postgraduate studies in New Testament and tutors at the Churches of Christ Theological College and Whitley Baptist College. He enjoys music, reading, table tennis and seeing movies.

Keith Farmer is married to Margaret and they have three adult children. Keith is the Principal of the Churches of Christ in New South Wales Theological College and lecturer in Pastoral Studies. Previously, he was involved for twelve years in local church pastoral ministry.

Geraldine Foster has a background of nursing and teaching, has studied theology at Melbourne Bible Institute and has been working in pastoral care since 1977. She is currently based at St Matthew's Anglican Church in Prahran.

Ann Garrett is an elder in the Uniting church in Bundaberg, Queensland and teaches Religious Instruction in primary schools. At present, she is studying for her Certificate in Theology. Ann and her husband Frank have four adult children.

Ken Goodlet was editor at Albatross Books. He has been a teacher and school administrator in Malaysia and Australia and attends a home church in the Blue Mountains. He and Jan have four adult sons.

Kevin Gray is corporate treasurer of World Vision Australia. He and his wife Margaret and their three teenage children attend an Anglican church in the Dandenong hills outside Melbourne.

Douglas Gresham was born in the USA to parents who were both writers. After their divorce, with his mother, Joy Gresham and brother, he lived in England, where Joy married the writer, C.S. Lewis. The story of their four years of happiness before her death in 1960 is well-known. Douglas, his wife Merrie and their three sons and two daughters have lived in Perth and Tasmania, before recently returning to Europe, where they live now in Ireland. He is the author of *Lenten Lands*.

John Helm is lecturer-in-charge and carries responsibilities in pastoral studies and spirituality at Burleigh Baptist Theological College, South Australia and has trained as a spiritual director. He and his wife Betty have three married daughters and seven grandchildren.

Harold Henderson was previously an associate in ministry at the Wesley Central Mission, Sydney. Then followed an executive career in World Vision Australia, then World Vision International. With his wife, Ruth, he conducts an English language school in Gainesville, Florida.

Roberta Hestenes has, until recently, been president and

professor of Christian Spirituality at Eastern College, St Davids, Pennsylvania. She is married to John, a research scientist, and they have three adult children. Roberta is the author of several books on teaching and theology, as well as having an international ministry in speaking, preaching and consulting.

Philip Hughes is an ordained Uniting church minister in Victoria, Australia, and has post-graduate degrees in philosophy, education and theology. He has taught in a number of universities and with the Melbourne College of Divinity. He is currently undertaking various projects with the Christian Research Association. Philip is married to Hazel and they have two children.

Jill Ireland, after completing a Master's degree at Oxford on Donne and T.S. Eliot, lived with her husband Stephen, a mining engineer, in outback towns and mining camps. Jill does freelance research and reviews for journals and has twice judged the Australian Christian Book of the Year Awards (in 1992 and 1993).

Peggy Jones has been a librarian at Whitley Baptist College in Melbourne, Victoria and, more recently, secretary/research assistant with Compassion, a child-development mission. She is currently doing an Arts degree, majoring in English. She and Don have four children.

Lee Kong Yee is a captain in the Salvation Army, serving in a local church in Penang, Malaysia. He has been studying part-time in the Baptist Theological Seminary, Penang, in the BTh program.

James Leong is a Malaysian Baptist pastor ministering in Sarawak. He is married with two children.

John Lewis has recently retired as Anglican Bishop of North Queensland, a position he has held since 1971. He has a special commitment to renewal and especially ministries of healing. He is also very concerned about the nurturing and developing of the total ministry concept within the church.

David Nicholas is manager of the Christian Television Association, Sydney, is a Baptist pastor and has a Master's degree in journalism and radio/television. He has written extensively for both the religious and secular press. He and his wife Judith have three adult children.

Carmen Nelson grew up in Sydney and became a Presbyterian deaconess. She teaches Religion at the Canberra Girls' Grammar School, is a lay reader and pastoral assistant in an Anglican parish in the ACT, and is active in the Movement for the Ordination of Women. She is married to Ray and they have two sons.

David Pitman, a minister in the Uniting church, is head of the Department of Ministry and Mission and director of Field Education at Trinity Theological College, Queensland. He and his wife Marcia have four adult children.

Julie Renner is a consultant specialising in interpersonal relations, team-building and cross-cultural training. After living in New Zealand, Costa Rica and Los Angeles, Julie and her husband Geoff now live in Melbourne. They have three grown children.

Doug Rowston coordinates Religious Education and teaches History at Prince Alfred College in South Australia. He is a Baptist minister, has taught in a theological college and has a PhD in New Testament. He is interested in theology, sport and music and has written religious education textbooks. He and his late wife Sue have two children. He is now married to Rosalie.

Corry Skilbeck has been a teacher/special educator until recently working as consultant in Autism with the Directorate of School Education, Eastern Metropolitan Region in Victoria. She and her husband, Peter, have shared in various ministries involving people with disabilities. They have three children.

Bette Smith is a hospital scientist and is also a Diploma of Charismatic Ministry graduate of Tabor Theological College. She is actively involved in a Pentecostal church, leading several home fellowship groups, and is currently teaching English in Asia.

Morris Stuart is on the pastoral team of Truth and Liberation Concern Community Church in Melbourne. Born in what was British Guiana and graduating from London Bible College, for the last twenty-five years he has ministered in England, New Zealand and Australia. He is the author of two books, including *Does God Need the Church?* Morris is married to Barbara and they have four children.

Kim Thoday trained for ministry at the Churches of Christ Theological College in Melbourne. At present, Kim is completing studies in New Testament and Australian culture. He is married to Heather and they have two children.

Chris Venning pastored Baptist churches in South Australia, was chaplain at Brauer College, Warrnambool, and is now chaplain at McLeod High School. He and his wife Dorothy have two adult children. He has tertiary qualifications in arts, theology and education.

Susan Warren has been ministering at Christian Life Assembly, Vancouver, BC, where she is involved in counselling, Bible studies and speaking assignments. Susan and her husband are involved with the Single Adults and Friends group at their church.

Index
to the 'Still Waters, Deep Waters' series

Abbreviations:

SW — *Still Waters, Deep Waters*
HM — *High Mountains, Deep Valleys*
RD — *Rivers in the Desert*
GD — *Gentle Darkness*
GS — *A Garden of Solitude*

Page numbers for the respective publications are given after the title abbreviation.